FAMILY LAW

TITLES IN THE SERIES

Administrative Law

Business Law

Child Law

Civil Liberties

Commercial Law

Company Law

Conflict of Laws

Constitutional & Administrative Law

Contract Law

Criminal Law

Criminal Litigation and Sentencing

Criminology

Employment Law

English Legal System

Equity & Trusts

European Community Law

Evidence

Family Law

Intellectual Property Law

International Trade Law

Jurisprudence

Land Law

Public International Law

Law of Tort

Revenue Law

Succession, Wills & Probate

'A' Level Law - Paper I

'A' Level Law - Paper II

Cavendish
Publishing
Limited

FAMILY LAW

LB Curzon
Barrister

First published in Great Britain 1995 by Cavendish Publishing Limited, The Glass House, Wharton Street, London WC1X 9PX
Telephone: 0171-278 8000 Facsimile: 0171-278 8080

© Curzon, LB 1995

All rights reserved. No part of this publication may be reproduced, stored in a retrieval system, or transmitted in any form or by any means, electronic, mechanical, photocopying, recording or otherwise, without the prior permission of the publisher and copyright owner.

The right of the author of this work has been asserted in accordance with the Copyright, Designs and Patents Act 1988.

Any person who infringes the above in relation to this publication may be liable to criminal prosecution and civil claims for damages.

British Library Cataloguing in Publication Data

Curzon LB
Family Law – (Lecture Notes Series)
I Title II Series
344.20615

ISBN 1-874241-70-8
Cover photograph by Jerome Yeats
Printed and bound in Great Britain

Preface

This text, which is intended primarily for law degree students, is built around an exposition of the main principles of contemporary English family law. The presentation takes the form of a structured series of lecture notes in which aspects of the law are stated and illustrated by reference to cases and other materials such as reports of the Law Commission. Summaries of the chapters are given. The range of topics selected for discussion is derived from the content of the family law element of a number of law degree course syllabuses; other material included should be of particular interest to students on child law courses and social workers.

The old adage that law cannot but mirror the deep concerns of society is particularly appropriate in the case of family law. The current flux of ideas within our society in relation to the concepts of marriage, cohabitation, the family, the rights of children and the legal responsibilities of parents, is evident in recent law-making by the legislature and the judiciary. The stream of amendments to older legislation dealing with, eg, adoption, financial settlements, divorce procedure, and modern statutes such as the Children Act 1989, the Child Support Act 1991, the Marriage Act 1994, are testimony to social concern with those legal principles and procedures which affect fundamental relationships within the family group.

Students using this text might wish to consider structuring their schemes of work so as to include the reading of a wide selection of the reports, journals and other literature referred to in the notes: this can be a rewarding task, not least because the literature of family law throws an unusually penetrating light on many aspects of 'the human condition' within our society.

L B Curzon
1995

Outline of Table of Contents

Preface i
Table of Cases xxxiii
Table of Statutes xliii

1   AN INTRODUCTION TO FAMILY LAW   1

1.1	Family law described	1
1.2	Sources of family law	2
1.3	Functions of family law	4
1.4	Some current data concerning contemporary family life	4
1.5	Definitions of 'the family'	5
1.6	Classification of types of family	6
1.7	The family in socio-political theory	7
1.8	The jurisdiction of the courts in the area of family law	8
1.9	Family law criticised	9
	Summary of Chapter 1	13

2   MARRIAGE: CAPACITY, FORMALITIES, NULLITY   15

2.1	Introductory matters	15
2.2	Formalities	17
2.3	The legal capacity to marry	19
2.4	Void and voidable marriages	21
2.5	Essential features of the void marriage	22
2.6	Essential features of the voidable marriage	22
2.7	Bars to relief under s 13 MCA 1973	24
2.8	Jurisdiction of English courts in a nullity suit	25
2.9	Unmarried cohabitation	25
2.10	Changes in governmental attitudes to unmarried cohabitants	26
2.11	Marriage: a redundant concept?	27
	Summary of Chapter 2	29

3   DIVORCE (1): BACKGROUND; PROCEDURES   31

3.1	Definition	31
3.2	Background	31
3.3	Development of divorce legislation	32
3.4	Jurisdiction and divorce procedure	34
3.5	The divorce petition	34
3.6	The decree	35
3.7	Following grant of decree	36
3.8	The 'special procedure' in undefended causes	36
3.9	Divorce and wills	38
3.10	Decree of presumption of death	39
3.11	Reconciliation and conciliation	40
	Summary of Chapter 3	41

4		**DIVORCE (2): THE GROUND FOR DIVORCE**	43
	4.1	The sole ground	43
	4.2	The five facts	43
	4.3	Adultery and intolerability	44
	4.4	Behaviour	45
	4.5	Desertion	47
	4.6	Living apart for two years	49
	4.7	Lived apart for five years	50
	4.8	Bars to the granting of a divorce	51
	4.9	Recognition of foreign divorces	52
	4.10	Proposals for reform: Law Commission (1990); criticisms	52
	4.11	The Law Commission's conclusions	53
	4.12	Proposals for reform: the Lord Chancellor's Green Paper (1994)	54
	4.13	Comments of the Law Society on family mediation	54
	4.14	Comments of the SFLA on family mediation	55
		Summary of Chapter 4	57
5		**JUDICIAL SEPARATION AND DOMESTIC VIOLENCE**	59
	5.1	Background	59
	5.2	Grounds for the decree	59
	5.3	Comparison with decree of divorce	59
	5.4	Jurisdiction of the court	59
	5.5	Presenting the petition	60
	5.6	Effect of the decree	60
	5.7	Orders concerning children and financial relief	60
	5.8	Discharge of decree of judicial separation	61
	5.9	Recommendations of the Law Commission	61
	5.10	Domestic violence: the essence of the problem	61
	5.11	Aspects of criminal law in relation to domestic violence	62
	5.12	Exclusion of the violent spouse	63
	5.13	Order under MHA 1983	63
	5.14	Order under DVMPA 1976	64
	5.15	Order under DPMCA 1978	65
	5.16	Injunctions granted under the inherent power of the court	66
	5.17	Accommodation for victims of violence in the home	67
	5.18	Improving protection for victims of domestic violence	68
	5.19	A footnote to the recommendations of the Law Commission	69
		Summary of Chapter 5	71
6		**RIGHTS IN FAMILY PROPERTY (1): INTERESTS; SUCCESSION**	73
	6.1	Introductory concepts	73
	6.2	Development of property law as it relates to the wife	74
	6.3	The creation of interests in personal property	75
	6.4	Some problems arising	78
	6.5	Proposals for reform	79
	6.6	Law Commission Report: Matrimonial Property (1988)	79

6.7	Property rights on the death of a spouse	79
6.8	Intestacy of a spouse	80
6.9	The Inheritance (Provision for Family and Dependants) Act 1975	81
6.10	The unmarried partner	82
	Summary of Chapter 6	85

7 RIGHTS IN FAMILY PROPERTY (2): THE MATRIMONIAL HOME — 87

7.1	Problems relating to the matrimonial home	87
7.2	Acquisition of rights in land	87
7.3	Acquisition of an interest through proprietary estoppel	87
7.4	Acquisition of an interest through a resulting trust	89
7.5	Acquisition of an interest through a constructive trust	89
7.6	The problem of rights of occupation of the matrimonial home	91
7.7	Property to which MHA 1983 applies	91
7.8	Rights of occupation of the matrimonial home	92
7.9	Orders under MHA 1983	92
7.10	Rights concerning matrimonial home where both spouses have estate, etc	93
7.11	Protection of rights of occupation against third parties	93
7.12	Registration of rights of occupation in the case of unregistered land	93
7.13	Land Registration Act 1925, s 70(1)(g)	94
7.14	Order for sale where spouses are co-owners	95
7.15	Bankruptcy of spouse in relation to matrimonial home	95
7.16	A note on the wife and charges over the matrimonial home	97
	Summary of Chapter 7	99

8 FINANCIAL PROVISION DURING MARRIAGE; STATE BENEFITS — 101

8.1	The 'duty to maintain': background	101
8.2	Obtaining financial provision during marriage	101
8.3	Order from magistrates' court under DPMCA 1978	102
8.4	Consent orders	104
8.5	Orders for periodical payments: means of payment	104
8.6	Matters to be taken into account	104
8.7	Orders under s 27 MCA 1973, as amended	105
8.8	Enforcing maintenance rights under separation or maintenance agreements	106
8.9	State benefits	107
8.10	Income support	107
8.11	The 'liable relatives'	108
8.12	The Social Fund	109
8.13	Family credit	109
8.14	Child benefit	110
8.15	One-parent benefit	111
8.16	Housing benefit	111
	Summary of Chapter 8	113

9		**FINANCIAL PROVISION ON BREAKDOWN OF THE MARRIAGE (1): COURT ORDERS**	115
	9.1	Background	115
	9.2	Initial procedure relating to an application for ancillary relief	116
	9.3	Orders available for ancillary relief	117
	9.4	Maintenance pending suit	117
	9.5	Periodical payments in favour of spouses or children	117
	9.6	Lump sum orders	118
	9.7	Property adjustment orders	118
	9.8	Orders for the sale of property	120
	9.9	The guidelines of s 25 MCA 1973	120
	9.10	First consideration	121
	9.11	Income, earning capacity, etc	121
	9.12	Needs for foreseeable future	122
	9.13	Former standard of living	122
	9.14	Parties' age, duration of marriage	122
	9.15	Parties' disabilities	123
	9.16	Contribution to family welfare	123
	9.17	Conduct of parties	123
	9.18	Loss of benefits	123
	9.19	The 'clean break' principle	123
	9.20	Financial relief following a foreign divorce	125
		Summary of Chapter 9	127
10		**FINANCIAL PROVISION ON BREAKDOWN OF THE MARRIAGE (2): CONSENT ORDERS, VARIATION, ENFORCEMENT**	129
	10.1	Problems	129
	10.2	The privately-made agreement for maintenance on divorce	129
	10.3	The consent order	131
	10.4	Variation, etc of orders	133
	10.5	A note on unmarried cohabitation in relation to applications for variation	137
	10.6	The enforcement of court orders	138
	10.7	Prevention of dispositions intended to defraud	139
	10.8	The *Mareva* injunction	140
	10.9	The *Anton Piller* injunction	141
		Summary of Chapter 10	143
11		**FINANCIAL PROVISION CONCERNING CHILDREN, AND THE CHILD SUPPORT ACT 1991**	145
	11.1	Recent legislation	145
	11.2	Orders for financial relief under s 15 and Sch 1 ChA 1989	145
	11.3	Persons who may apply for a financial order under ChA 1989	146
	11.4	Orders where no application has been made	146
	11.5	Against whom orders may be made	146
	11.6	Matters to which the court will have regard	147
	11.7	Financial orders which the court may make, and variations	147

11.8	Effect of the Child Support Act 1991 on the jurisdiction of the courts	149
11.9	The Child Support Act 1991	149
11.10	Objectives of the CSA 1991	150
11.11	Definitions	150
11.12	The duty to maintain	151
11.13	The 'welfare principle'	151
11.14	The Child Support Agency	151
11.15	A 'parent' under CSA 1991	152
11.16	Aspects of the assessment of maintenance	153
11.17	Application for assessment	153
11.18	Jurisdiction	154
11.19	Collection and enforcement	154
11.20	Review and appeal	155
11.21	Criticisms of the CSA 1991	156
11.22	The Government White Paper	157
Summary of Chapter 11		161
12	**PARENTAGE; LEGITIMACY; PARENTAL RESPONSIBILITY**	**163**
12.1	Changing concepts within English family law	163
12.2	The concept of 'parentage'	163
12.3	Who is 'a parent'?	163
12.4	Aspects of HAR	163
12.5	Surrogacy	164
12.6	The 'legal mother'	165
12.7	The 'legal father'	166
12.8	Orders under s 30 HFEA 1990	167
12.9	Proving parentage	167
12.10	Blood tests	168
12.11	DNA profiling	168
12.12	Register of births	168
12.13	Information concerning parentage kept under HFEA 1990	169
12.14	Illegitimacy: changing attitudes	169
12.15	FLRA 1987: the general principle	169
12.16	Abolition of affiliation proceedings	170
12.17	Children of void marriages	170
12.18	Children of voidable marriages	171
12.19	Legitimation	171
12.20	The effect of adoption	171
12.21	Declarations	171
12.22	Remaining discrimination against the illegitimate person	171
12.23	Parental responsibility: rights and duties	172
12.24	Who possesses parental responsibility?	173
12.25	Other matters concerning parental responsibility	174
12.26	A new look at children's rights and parental responsibilities: the *Gillick* case	174
12.27	Some post-*Gillick* cases	177
Summary of Chapter 12		179

13	**THE CHILD'S WELFARE: SECTION 8 ORDERS UNDER THE CHILDREN ACT 1989**	**181**
13.1	General background to the Children Act 1989	181
13.2	The 'welfare principle'	181
13.3	The 'no-delay principle'	182
13.4	The 'non-intervention (or 'no order') principle'	183
13.5	The 'welfare checklist'	183
13.6	Welfare reports	185
13.7	The essence of s 8 orders	185
13.8	Family proceedings	185
13.9	Who may apply for a s 8 order	186
13.10	Limitations upon the making of s 8 orders	188
13.11	Timetables and other provisions	188
13.12	The contact order	188
13.13	Prohibited steps order	189
13.14	Specific issue order	189
13.15	Residence order	190
13.16	Other orders under ChA 1989	190
	Summary of Chapter 13	193
14	**LOCAL AUTHORITY SERVICES FOR CHILDREN AND FAMILIES (1)**	**195**
14.1	Background	195
14.2	Definitions	195
14.3	Providing services for children and their families	196
14.4	Assistance in kind or cash	198
14.5	The provision of day care for pre-school and other children	198
14.6	Duty to provide accommodation for children	199
14.7	Providing accommodation for children in protection, etc	200
14.8	Duties of local authority in relation to children looked after by them	201
14.9	Possibility of serious injury to the public	201
14.10	Accommodation etc for children who are being looked after	202
14.11	Local authority foster parents	202
14.12	Regulations concerning placement with local authority foster parents	202
14.13	Other matters concerning provision of accommodation	202
14.14	Child allowed to live with parents	202
14.15	Contact between the child and his family	202
	Summary of Chapter 14	205
15	**LOCAL AUTHORITY SERVICES FOR CHILDREN AND FAMILIES (2)**	**207**
15.1	Further matters covered by ChA 1989, Part III	207
15.2	Advice and assistance for certain children	207
15.3	Financial matters involved in providing advice and assistance	208
15.4	Duties related to contact with other local authorities	208
15.5	Complaints concerning advice and assistance	208

15.6	The provision of secure accommodation	209
15.7	Removal of the child from secure accommodation	210
15.8	Restricting the liberty of children: a reminder	210
15.9	Review of progress of children	211
15.10	Inquiries into representations	211
15.11	Other procedures for dealing with complaints	212
15.12	Co-operation between authorities	213
15.13	Consultation by local authorities with local education authorities	213
15.14	Recoupment of cost of services, etc	213
15.15	Contributions towards maintenance of children looked after by local authorities	214
	Summary of Chapter 15	215

16 CARE AND SUPERVISION ORDERS — 217

16.1	Essence of ChA 1989, Part IV	217
16.2	Definitions	217
16.3	Basis of Part IV	217
16.4	Features of s 31	218
16.5	Principles which the court will keep in mind	218
16.6	The threshold criteria	219
16.7	Aspects of the criteria	219
16.8	Timetables	221
16.9	Essential features of the care order	221
16.10	Contact between children in care and their families	223
16.11	Essence of the supervision order	224
16.12	Duties of the supervisor	224
16.13	Duration of the order	224
16.14	Features of the supervision order	224
16.15	The education supervision order	225
16.16	Further matters concerning education supervision orders	226
16.17	Investigation of a child's circumstances	226
16.18	Interim orders	227
16.19	Discharge and variation of care and supervision orders	228
16.20	Orders pending appeals	228
16.21	Guardians *ad litem*	228
	Summary of Chapter 16	231

17 SHORT-TERM PROTECTION OF CHILDREN AT RISK — 233

17.1	Essence of ChA 1989, Part V	233
17.2	The Child Assessment Order	233
17.3	Purpose of the CAO: a summary	235
17.4	The Emergency Protection Order	236
17.5	No automatic making of an EPO	236
17.6	Application by 'any person'	236
17.7	Application by a local authority	237
17.8	Application by an 'authorised person'	237

	17.9	General procedure	237
	17.10	Orders taken over by a local authority	238
	17.11	Effects of the EPO	238
	17.12	Directions	238
	17.13	Return of child	239
	17.14	Duration of EPO	239
	17.15	Discharge of EPO	239
	17.16	Police protection	240
	17.17	Investigation by local authority	240
	17.18	Powers to assist in discovery of children	241
	17.19	Abducting children in care	241
	17.20	Refuges for children at risk	242
	17.21	A note on self-incrimination in relation to proceedings under Part V	242
	Summary of Chapter 17		243
18		**COMMUNITY, VOLUNTARY AND REGISTERED HOMES FOR CHILDREN**	**245**
	18.1	Residential care of children	245
	18.2	Community homes provided by local authorities	245
	18.3	Management and conduct of community homes	246
	18.4	Voluntary homes and voluntary organisations	247
	18.5	The registration and regulation of voluntary homes	247
	18.6	Duties of voluntary organisations	248
	18.7	Duties of local authorities	249
	18.8	Registered children's homes	249
	18.9	Registration of children's homes	250
	18.10	Regulations concerning children's homes	250
	18.11	Inspection of children's homes	250
	18.12	Inquiries	251
	18.13	Default power of Secretary of State	251
	18.14	A note on the welfare of children accommodated in independent schools	251
	Summary of Chapter 18		253
19		**FOSTERING CHILDREN; CHILD MINDING AND DAY CARE**	**255**
	19.1	Background	255
	19.2	Local authority foster placements	255
	19.3	Private foster parents	255
	19.4	Power of local authority to impose requirements	256
	19.5	Welfare of privately fostered children	256
	19.6	Notification of fostering	257
	19.7	Appeals	257
	19.8	Prohibition of advertisements	257
	19.9	Disqualifications	257
	19.10	Power to prohibit private fostering	257
	19.11	Offences	258
	19.12	Child minding and day care	258

19.13	Requirements imposed on child minders	260
19.14	Cancellation of registration	260
19.15	Inspection of premises	260
19.16	Enforcement notices	260
	Summary of Chapter 19	261

20 GUARDIANSHIP 263

20.1	The concept of guardianship	263
20.2	Guardianship prior to the ChA 1989	263
20.3	Changes introduced by the ChA 1989	263
20.4	Appointment of guardians by the court	264
20.5	Appointment of guardians privately	265
20.6	Appointment in writing	265
20.7	Disclaimer	265
20.8	Revocation	266
20.9	Time at which appointment becomes effective	266
20.10	General legal effect of appointment as a guardian	267
20.11	Ending guardianship	267
20.12	A note on 'the guardian's allowance'	268
	Summary of Chapter 20	269

21 WARDSHIP 271

21.1	The essential feature of wardship	271
21.2	Background	271
21.3	Wardship jurisdiction and the inherent jurisdiction of the High Court	271
21.4	Some features of the wardship jurisdiction	272
21.5	Jurisdiction to make a child a ward	273
21.6	Section 41 of the Supreme Court Act 1981	273
21.7	Exercise of the court's discretion	274
21.8	The enforcing of court orders	274
21.9	Persons who may or may not be made wards of court	274
21.10	Persons who may apply to make a child a ward of court	276
21.11	The child's welfare and the public interest	276
21.12	Effects of ChA 1989 on wardship	277
21.13	The inherent jurisdiction of the High Court	277
21.14	Local authorities and the use of wardship jurisdiction	277
	Summary of Chapter 21	279

22 ADOPTION 281

22.1	Background	281
22.2	Current trends	281
22.3	Adoption agencies	282
22.4	Who may apply for an adoption order	283
22.5	The question of adoption by relatives and step-parents	284
22.6	Who may be adopted	284
22.7	The welfare principle	285

	22.8	Private placements	286
	22.9	Agency placements	287
	22.10	Consent to the adoption order	287
	22.11	Dispensing with consent	288
	22.12	Freeing for adoption and its effect	290
	22.13	General procedures for adoption	290
	22.14	Some legal effects of the order	292
	22.15	Registration	293
	22.16	Reform proposals	293
	Summary of Chapter 22		295
23		**CHILDREN'S RIGHTS AND THEIR SIGNIFICANCE (1)**	297
	23.1	The question of children's rights	297
	23.2	The basic concept of rights	297
	23.3	The problem of the correlative	298
	23.4	The international recognition of children's rights	298
	23.5	The criminal law and the life of the child	301
	23.6	Manslaughter	301
	23.7	Child cruelty	301
	23.8	Neglect	302
	23.9	The question of corporal punishment and the child	302
	23.10	Assault, battery, wounding	303
	23.11	Sexual offences involving children	303
	23.12	Child abuse	304
	23.13	Kidnapping	306
	23.14	Child abduction	306
	23.15	A note on the literature concerning children's rights	308
	Summary of Chapter 23		311
24		**CHILDREN'S RIGHTS AND THEIR SIGNIFICANCE (2)**	313
	24.1	Protection of the child from harmful goods and activities	313
	24.2	Protecting the child from exploitation as an employee	313
	24.3	Protecting young persons	314
	24.4	A note on the criminal responsibility of minors	315
	24.5	Accountability of parents	316
	24.6	Children as witnesses in criminal proceedings	317
	24.7	Children as witnesses in civil proceedings	317
	24.8	Minors and the law of contract	318
	24.9	Minors and the law of torts	319
	24.10	The minor's capacity to sue	320
	24.11	Liability of minor to be sued	321
	24.12	Responsibility of a minor's parents for his torts	321
	Summary of Chapter 24		323

Recommended Reading List   325
Index   327

Detailed Table of Contents

Preface i
Table of Cases xxxiii
Table of Statutes xliii

1 AN INTRODUCTION TO FAMILY LAW 1
- 1.1 Family law described — 1
  - 1.1.1 Significance of social and cultural thought — 1
  - 1.1.2 Reflection of religious doctrines — 1
  - 1.1.3 The wide scope of contemporary family law — 2
- 1.2 Sources of family law — 2
  - 1.2.1 The common law — 2
  - 1.2.2 Canon law — 3
  - 1.2.3 Legislation — 3
  - 1.2.4 Conventions, etc — 4
  - 1.2.5 Myth as a source of family law? — 4
- 1.3 Functions of family law — 4
- 1.4 Some current data concerning contemporary family life — 4
- 1.5 Definitions of 'the family' — 5
  - 1.5.1 *Blackwell v Bull* (1836) — 5
  - 1.5.2 *R v Inhabitants of Darlington* (1792) — 6
  - 1.5.3 A formal religious view — 6
  - 1.5.4 Statutory definitions — 6
- 1.6 Classification of types of family — 6
  - 1.6.1 The extended family — 7
  - 1.6.2 The nuclear family — 7
  - 1.6.3 What of the one-parent family? — 7
- 1.7 The family in socio-political theory — 7
- 1.8 The jurisdiction of the courts in the area of family law — 8
  - 1.8.1 The family proceedings courts — 8
  - 1.8.2 The county courts — 8
  - 1.8.3 The Family Division — 9
  - 1.8.4 Children Act 1989, Sch 11 — 9
- 1.9 Family law criticised — 9
  - 1.9.1 Professor O'Donovan's criticisms — 9
  - 1.9.2 Professor Rifkin's objections to a 'one-sided' family law — 10
  - 1.9.3 Professor Finley's criticisms — 11
- Summary of Chapter 1 — 13

2 MARRIAGE: CAPACITY, FORMALITIES, NULLITY 15
- 2.1 Introductory matters — 15
  - 2.1.1 Definitions — 15
  - 2.1.2 Changes in the nature and consequence of marriage — 15
  - 2.1.3 The basic principle of marriage today — 16
  - 2.1.4 Marriage viewed as a contract — 16
  - 2.1.5 The engagement to marry — 16
  - 2.1.6 The 'common law spouse' — 17
- 2.2 Formalities — 17
  - 2.2.1 Consent where a party is over 16 and under 18 — 17
  - 2.2.2 Licences, registration — 18
  - 2.2.3 Ceremonies permitted by law — 18

2.3	The legal capacity to marry		19
	2.3.1	*Lex domicilii*, etc.	19
	2.3.2	Minimum age	20
	2.3.3	One male, one female	20
	2.3.4	Monogamous union	21
	2.3.5	Parties must not be within 'prohibited degrees'	21
2.4	Void and voidable marriages		21
2.5	Essential features of the void marriage		22
	2.5.1	Formal defects relating to the marriage	22
	2.5.2	Formal defects which will not invalidate a marriage	22
2.6	Essential features of the voidable marriage		22
	2.6.1	Failure to consummate the marriage owing to incapacity of either party or respondent's wilful refusal	23
	2.6.2	Lack of consent in consequence of duress, mistake, unsoundness of mind or otherwise	23
	2.6.3	At the time of the marriage, a spouse was suffering from a mental disorder so that he/she was unfitted for marriage	24
	2.6.4	At the time of marriage respondent was suffering from a venereal disease or was pregnant per alium	24
2.7	Bars to relief under s 13 MCA 1973		24
2.8	Jurisdiction of English courts in a nullity suit		25
2.9	Unmarried cohabitation		25
2.10	Changes in governmental attitudes to unmarried cohabitants		26
2.11	Marriage: a redundant concept?		27
Summary of Chapter 2			29
3	**DIVORCE (1): BACKGROUND; PROCEDURES**		31
3.1	Definition		31
3.2	Background		31
3.3	Development of divorce legislation		32
	3.3.1	The early Christian attitude	32
	3.3.2	The influence of canon law	32
	3.3.3	Basis of pre-Reformation attitudes	33
	3.3.4	Post-Reformation attitude	33
	3.3.5	19th century legislation	33
	3.3.6	20th century legislation	33
3.4	Jurisdiction and divorce procedure		34
3.5	The divorce petition		34
	3.5.1	Petition served on respondent	35
	3.5.2	Essential features of the petition	35
	3.5.3	Bar on petitions for divorce within one year of marriage	35
3.6	The decree		35
3.7	Following grant of decree		36
3.8	The 'special procedure' in undefended causes		36
3.9	Divorce and wills		38
	3.9.1	Effect of s 18A WA 1937	38
	3.9.2	*Re Sinclair* (1985)	39
	3.9.3	Law Reform (Succession) Bill	39

3.10	Decree of presumption of death		39
	3.10.1	Statutory period of absence	40
	3.10.2	The decree	40
3.11	Reconciliation and conciliation		40
Summary of Chapter 3			41

4 DIVORCE (2): THE GROUND FOR DIVORCE — 43

4.1	The sole ground		43
	4.1.1	Duty of the court	43
	4.1.2	Failure to establish a fact	43
4.2	The five facts		43
4.3	Adultery and intolerability		44
	4.3.1	Adultery defined	44
	4.3.2	Proof of adultery	44
	4.3.3	Intolerability	45
	4.3.4	Living together after knowledge of adultery	45
4.4	Behaviour		45
	4.4.1	'Behaviour' interpreted	45
	4.4.2	Behaviour connotes conduct, not merely a mental state	46
	4.4.3	*Pheasant v Pheasant* (1972)	46
	4.4.4	The 'right-thinking person' test	46
	4.4.5	Positive and negative conduct	46
	4.4.6	Defences	47
4.5	Desertion		47
	4.5.1	The essence of desertion	47
	4.5.2	The fact of separation	47
	4.5.3	*Animus deserendi*	48
	4.5.4	Desertion for two years	48
	4.5.5	'Constructive' desertion	49
	4.5.6	Lack of consent	49
	4.5.7	No 'just cause'	49
4.6	Living apart for two years		49
	4.6.1	Living apart	49
	4.6.2	Respondent's consent to grant of decree	50
4.7	Lived apart for five years		50
	4.7.1	Refusal of a decree in a five-year separation case	50
	4.7.2	Grave hardship	50
	4.7.3	Financial arrangements after pronouncement of decree nisi	51
4.8	Bars to the granting of a divorce		51
4.9	Recognition of foreign divorces		52
4.10	Proposals for reform: Law Commission (1990); criticisms		52
	4.10.1	The present law is confusing and misleading	52
	4.10.2	The present law is discriminatory and unjust	53
	4.10.3	The present law distorts the parties' bargaining positions	53
	4.10.4	The present law provokes unnecessary hostility and bitterness	53
	4.10.5	The present law does nothing to save marriages	53
	4.10.6	The present law can make things worse for the children	53
4.11	The Law Commission's conclusions		53
4.12	Proposals for reform: the Lord Chancellor's Green Paper (1994)		54
4.13	Comments of the Law Society on family mediation		54
4.14	Comments of the SFLA on family mediation		55
Summary of Chapter 4			57

5		**JUDICIAL SEPARATION AND DOMESTIC VIOLENCE**	59
	5.1	Background	59
	5.2	Grounds for the decree	59
	5.3	Comparison with decree of divorce	59
	5.4	Jurisdiction of the court	59
	5.5	Presenting the petition	60
	5.6	Effect of the decree	60
	5.7	Orders concerning children and financial relief	60
		5.7.1 Welfare of the children	60
		5.7.2 Financial relief	61
	5.8	Discharge of decree of judicial separation	61
	5.9	Recommendations of the Law Commission	61
	5.10	Domestic violence: the essence of the problem	61
		5.10.1 Involvement of the police	62
		5.10.2 Arguments against invoking the criminal law	62
	5.11	Aspects of criminal law in relation to domestic violence	62
	5.12	Exclusion of the violent spouse	63
	5.13	Order under MHA 1983	63
	5.14	Order under DVMPA 1976	64
		5.14.1 Persons to whom s 1(1) applies	64
		5.14.2 Effect of *Richards v Richards* (1984)	64
		5.14.3 Molestation	65
		5.14.4 Power of arrest under DVMPA 1976	65
		5.14.5 Emergency	65
		5.14.6 Orders under ChA 1989	65
	5.15	Order under DPMCA 1978	65
		5.15.1 Power of arrest	66
		5.15.2 *Ex parte* orders	66
	5.16	Injunctions granted under the inherent power of the court	66
	5.17	Accommodation for victims of violence in the home	67
		5.17.1 Meaning of 'homeless'	67
		5.17.2 Priority need	67
		5.17.3 Becoming homeless intentionally	67
		5.17.4 The local authority's duty	67
	5.18	Improving protection for victims of domestic violence	68
		5.18.1 Extension of the range of applicants for orders	68
		5.18.2 Non-molestation orders	68
		5.18.3 Occupation orders	69
		5.18.4 Extension of rights of unmarried cohabitants	69
		5.18.5 *Ex parte* orders	69
		5.18.6 Powers of arrest	69
	5.19	A footnote to the recommendations of the Law Commission	69
	Summary of Chapter 5		71
6		**RIGHTS IN FAMILY PROPERTY (1):** **INTERESTS; SUCCESSION**	73
	6.1	Introductory concepts	73
		6.1.1 Property and ownership in relation to spouses	73
		6.1.2 Real and personal property	73
		6.1.3 A trust	73

		6.1.4	Co-ownership	73
		6.1.5	Joint tenancy	74
		6.1.6	Tenancy in common	74
	6.2		Development of property law as it relates to the wife	74
		6.2.1	Alleviation of common law rules	74
		6.2.2	Legislation in the 19th and 20th centuries	74
	6.3		The creation of interests in personal property	75
		6.3.1	Rights arising under statute	75
		6.3.2	The implied trust	76
		6.3.3	The presumption of advancement	76
		6.3.4	Rebutting the presumption of advancement	76
		6.3.5	The constructive trust	77
		6.3.6	Common intention and the constructive trust	77
	6.4		Some problems arising	78
		6.4.1	H and W pay into a joint bank account	78
		6.4.2	Account is held in the name of one spouse only	79
		6.4.3	H alone pays into a joint account	79
		6.4.4	W alone pays into a joint banking account	79
	6.5		Proposals for reform	79
	6.6		Law Commission Report: Matrimonial Property (1988)	79
	6.7		Property rights on the death of a spouse	79
		6.7.1	Valid will made by spouse	80
		6.7.2	Wills made by testator prior to marriage, and on divorce	80
	6.8		Intestacy of a spouse	80
		6.8.1	D leaves a spouse but no issue or blood relations	80
		6.8.2	D leaves a spouse and issue	80
		6.8.3	D leaves a spouse, and blood relations, but no issue	81
		6.8.4	D leaves no surviving spouse	81
		6.8.5	D leaves no surviving spouse, no issue, and no blood relatives	81
		6.8.6	Illegitimacy and succession on intestacy	81
	6.9		The Inheritance (Provision for Family and Dependants) Act 1975	81
		6.9.1	Persons who may apply	81
		6.9.2	Reasonable financial provision	82
		6.9.3	Types of order available	82
		6.9.4	Matters to be taken into account	82
	6.10		The unmarried partner	82
	Summary of Chapter 6			85
7			**RIGHTS IN FAMILY PROPERTY (2): THE MATRIMONIAL HOME**	87
	7.1		Problems relating to the matrimonial home	87
	7.2		Acquisition of rights in land	87
	7.3		Acquisition of an interest through proprietary estoppel	87
		7.3.1	Essence of the doctrine	88
		7.3.2	*Pascoe v Turner* (1979)	88
		7.3.3	*Maharaj v Chand* (1986)	88
	7.4		Acquisition of an interest through a resulting trust	89
	7.5		Acquisition of an interest through a constructive trust	89
		7.5.1	Relevance of an express agreement	89
		7.5.2	*H v M (Property: Beneficial Interest)* (1992)	90

	7.5.3	*Thomas v Fuller-Brown* (1988)	90
	7.5.4	Quantum of interest	91
7.6	The problem of rights of occupation of the matrimonial home		91
7.7	Property to which MHA 1983 applies		91
7.8	Rights of occupation of the matrimonial home		92
7.9	Orders under MHA 1983		92
	7.9.1	Discretion of the court	92
	7.9.2	Duration of order	92
	7.9.3	Other matters under s 1	92
7.10	Rights concerning matrimonial home where both spouses have estate, etc		93
7.11	Protection of rights of occupation against third parties		93
7.12	Registration of rights of occupation in the case of unregistered land		93
7.13	Land Registration Act 1925, s 70(1)(g)		94
	7.13.1	*Williams & Glyn's Bank v Boland* (1981)	94
	7.13.2	*Kingsnorth Finance Ltd v Tizard* (1986)	94
7.14	Order for sale where spouses are co-owners		95
	7.14.1	Refusal of trustees for sale to exercise powers	95
	7.14.2	Exercise of the court's discretion to order a sale	95
7.15	Bankruptcy of spouse in relation to matrimonial home		95
	7.15.1	What the court will take into account	95
	7.15.2	The 'breathing space'	96
	7.15.3	Protection of children	96
	7.15.4	*Re Citro* (1990)	96
7.16	A note on the wife and charges over the matrimonial home		97
	Summary of Chapter 7		99
8	**FINANCIAL PROVISION DURING MARRIAGE; STATE BENEFITS**		**101**
8.1	The 'duty to maintain': background		101
8.2	Obtaining financial provision during marriage		101
8.3	Order from magistrates' court under DPMCA 1978		102
	8.3.1	Application under the 1978 Act, s 1	102
	8.3.2	Failure to provide reasonable maintenance	102
	8.3.3	Respondent's behaviour	103
	8.3.4	Respondent's desertion	103
	8.3.5	Reconciliation	103
	8.3.6	Orders under s 2	103
8.4	Consent orders		104
8.5	Orders for periodical payments: means of payment		104
8.6	Matters to be taken into account		104
8.7	Orders under s 27 MCA 1973, as amended		105
	8.7.1	Orders which can be made under s 27 MCA 1973	106
	8.7.2	Variation of orders	106
8.8	Enforcing maintenance rights under separation or maintenance agreements		106
8.9	State benefits		107
8.10	Income support		107
	8.10.1	Entitlement	107
	8.10.2	Severe hardship cases	108

		8.10.3	The 'applicable amount'	108
	8.11		The 'liable relatives'	108
	8.12		The Social Fund	109
		8.12.1	Non-discretionary payments	109
		8.12.2	Discretionary payments	109
		8.12.3	Principles of determination	109
	8.13		Family credit	109
		8.13.1	Amount of family credit	109
		8.13.2	Termination of credit	110
	8.14		Child benefit	110
		8.14.1	Meaning of 'child'	110
		8.14.2	Meaning of 'person responsible for child'	110
		8.14.3	Rate of benefit	110
		8.14.4	Exclusion from entitlement to child benefit	110
	8.15		One-parent benefit	111
	8.16		Housing benefit	111
	Summary of Chapter 8			113
9			**FINANCIAL PROVISION ON BREAKDOWN OF THE MARRIAGE (1): COURT ORDERS**	**115**
	9.1		Background	115
		9.1.1	MPPA 1970	115
		9.1.2	MFPA 1984	115
	9.2		Initial procedure relating to an application for ancillary relief	116
		9.2.1	The affidavit	116
		9.2.2	Guidelines for affidavits	116
		9.2.3	The hearing	116
	9.3		Orders available for ancillary relief	117
	9.4		Maintenance pending suit	117
	9.5		Periodical payments in favour of spouses or children	117
		9.5.1	Unsecured payments	117
		9.5.2	Secured payments	117
	9.6		Lump sum orders	118
	9.7		Property adjustment orders	118
		9.7.1	Transfer of property order	118
		9.7.2	Settlement of property order	119
		9.7.3	Variation of ante-nuptial or post-nuptial settlement	119
	9.8		Orders for the sale of property	120
		9.8.1	Death or re-marriage	120
		9.8.2	Third party interests	120
	9.9		The guidelines of s 25 MCA 1973	120
	9.10		First consideration	121
	9.11		Income, earning capacity, etc	121
		9.11.1	Assets	122
		9.11.2	Earning capacity, resources	122
	9.12		Needs for foreseeable future	122
	9.13		Former standard of living	122
	9.14		Parties' age, duration of marriage	122
	9.15		Parties' disabilities	123

	9.16	Contribution to family welfare	123
	9.17	Conduct of parties	123
	9.18	Loss of benefits	123
	9.19	The 'clean break' principle	123
		9.19.1 Essence of the 'clean break'	124
		9.19.2 The immediate and deferred 'clean break'	125
	9.20	Financial relief following a foreign divorce	125
	Summary of Chapter 9		127
10		**FINANCIAL PROVISION ON BREAKDOWN OF THE MARRIAGE (2): CONSENT ORDERS, VARIATION, ENFORCEMENT**	129
	10.1	Problems	129
	10.2	The privately-made agreement for maintenance on divorce	129
		10.2.1 Purported ouster of the court's jurisdiction	129
		10.2.2 Variation of a private maintenance agreement	129
		10.2.3 *Camm v Camm* (1983)	130
		10.2.4 *Edgar v Edgar* (1980)	130
	10.3	The consent order	131
		10.3.1 Need for the provision of adequate information	131
		10.3.2 Effect of non-disclosure	131
		10.3.3 All circumstances to be taken into account	132
		10.3.4 Effect of unforeseen change in circumstances, and appeal out of time	133
	10.4	Variation, etc of orders	133
		10.4.1 Orders which may not be varied	133
		10.4.2 Prohibited variations under s 31(5) MCA 1973	133
		10.4.3 Challenging orders	134
		10.4.4 Matters to be taken into account	134
		10.4.5 *Dinch v Dinch* (1987)	135
		10.4.6 Lump sum variation: a recent decision	136
		10.4.7 The 'clean break'	136
	10.5	A note on unmarried cohabitation in relation to applications for variation	137
	10.6	The enforcement of court orders	138
		10.6.1 Enforcing the lump sum order	138
		10.6.2 The periodical payments order	138
		10.6.3 Limitation period	138
		10.6.4 Overpayments	138
	10.7	Prevention of dispositions intended to defraud	139
		10.7.1 Section 37 MCA 1973	139
		10.7.2 Disposition to *bona fide* purchaser for value	139
	10.8	The *Mareva* injunction	140
		10.8.1 Principles of the *Mareva* injunction	140
		10.8.2 Limited nature of the *Mareva* injunction in matrimonial proceedings	141
	10.9	The *Anton Piller* injunction	141
	Summary of Chapter 10		143
11		**FINANCIAL PROVISION CONCERNING CHILDREN, AND THE CHILD SUPPORT ACT 1991**	145
	11.1	Recent legislation	145

11.2		Orders for financial relief under s 15 and Sch 1 ChA 1989	145
11.3		Persons who may apply for a financial order under ChA 1989	146
11.4		Orders where no application has been made	146
11.5		Against whom orders may be made	146
11.6		Matters to which the court will have regard	147
11.7		Financial orders which the court may make, and variations	147
	11.7.1	Orders for periodical payments	147
	11.7.2	Orders for payment of a lump sum	147
	11.7.3	Orders for the transfer or settlement of specified property	148
	11.7 4	Duration of orders for financial relief	148
	11.7.5	Variation of lump sum orders	148
	11.7.6	Variation of periodical payments order	148
	11.7.7	Interim orders	149
11.8		Effect of the Child Support Act 1991 on the jurisdiction of the courts	149
11.9		The Child Support Act 1991	149
11.10		Objectives of the CSA 1991	150
11.11		Definitions	150
11.12		The duty to maintain	151
11.13		The 'welfare principle'	151
11.14		The Child Support Agency	151
11.15		A 'parent' under CSA 1991	152
11.16		Aspects of the assessment of maintenance	153
	11.16.1	The 'maintenance requirement'	153
	11.16.2	The 'assessable income'	153
	11.16.3	The 'maintenance assessment'	153
11.17		Application for assessment	153
11.18		Jurisdiction	154
11.19		Collection and enforcement	154
	11.19.1	The liability order	154
	11.19.2	Distress procedure	154
	11.19.3	Committal to prison	155
11.20		Review and appeal	155
	11.20.1	Periodical reviews	155
	11.20.2	Reviews on change of circumstances	155
	11.20.3	Reviews of decisions of child support officers	155
	11.20.4	Reviews at instigation of child support officers	155
	11.20.5	Appeals	156
	11.20.6	Child Support Commissioners	156
11.21		Criticisms of the CSA 1991	156
11.22		The Government White Paper	157
Summary of Chapter 11			161
12		**PARENTAGE; LEGITIMACY; PARENTAL RESPONSIBILITY**	**163**
12.1		Changing concepts within English family law	163
12.2		The concept of 'parentage'	163
12.3		Who is 'a parent'?	163
12.4		Aspects of HAR	163

		12.4.1	*In vitro* fertilisation	164
		12.4.2	Egg donation	164
		12.4.3	Embryo donation and transfer	164
	12.5	Surrogacy		164
		12.5.1	Statutory definitions	164
		12.5.2	Surrogacy on a commercial basis	164
		12.5.3	Surrogacy advertisements	165
		12.5.4	Offences under the 1985 Act	165
	12.6	The 'legal mother'		165
	12.7	The 'legal father'		166
		12.7.1	The genetic father	166
		12.7.2	The non-genetic father	166
	12.8	Orders under s 30 HFEA 1990		167
	12.9	Proving parentage		167
	12.10	Blood tests		168
	12.11	DNA profiling		168
	12.12	Register of births		168
	12.13	Information concerning parentage kept under HFEA 1990		169
	12.14	Illegitimacy: changing attitudes		169
	12.15	FLRA 1987: the general principle		169
	12.16	Abolition of affiliation proceedings		170
	12.17	Children of void marriages		170
	12.18	Children of voidable marriages		171
	12.19	Legitimation		171
	12.20	The effect of adoption		171
	12.21	Declarations		171
	12.22	Remaining discrimination against the illegitimate person		171
		12.22.1	Section 50 British Nationality Act 1981	172
		12.22.2	Section 2(2) ChA 1989	172
	12.23	Parental responsibility: rights and duties		172
	12.24	Who possesses parental responsibility?		173
	12.25	Other matters concerning parental responsibility		174
	12.26	A new look at children's rights and parental responsibilities: the *Gillick* case		174
		12.26.1	At first instance	174
		12.26.2	Court of Appeal	175
		12.26.3	House of Lords	175
		12.26.4	Lord Scarman's speech in *Gillick*	176
	12.27	Some post-*Gillick* cases		177
	Summary of Chapter 12			179
13	**THE CHILD'S WELFARE: SECTION 8 ORDERS UNDER THE CHILDREN ACT 1989**			181
	13.1	General background to the Children Act 1989		181
	13.2	The 'welfare principle'		181
		13.2.1	The meaning of 'welfare'	181
		13.2.2	'Paramount'	182
		13.2.3	Restrictions on the application of the welfare principle	182
	13.3	The 'no-delay principle'		182

13.4	The 'non-intervention (or 'no order') principle'		183
	13.4.1	View of the Law Commission (1988)	183
	13.4.2	Essence of the 'non-intervention principle'	183
13.5	The 'welfare checklist'		183
	13.5.1	Wishes and feelings of the child: s 1(3)(a)	184
	13.5.2	Needs of the child: s 1(3)(b)	184
	13.5.3	Changed circumstances: s 1(3)(c)	184
	13.5.4	Relevant characteristics: s 1(3)(d)	184
	13.5.5	Harm: s 1(1)(e)	185
	13.5.6	Capability of parents and others: s 1(3)(f)	185
	13.5.7	Powers available to the court: s 1(3)(g)	185
13.6	Welfare reports		185
13.7	The essence of s 8 orders		185
13.8	Family proceedings		185
13.9	Who may apply for a s 8 order		186
	13.9.1	Persons entitled to apply without leave	186
	13.9.2	Persons entitled to apply with leave	187
	13.9.3	Criteria in relation to granting leave	187
13.10	Limitations upon the making of s 8 orders		188
13.11	Timetables and other provisions		188
13.12	The contact order		188
13.13	Prohibited steps order		189
13.14	Specific issue order		189
13.15	Residence order		190
13.16	Other orders under ChA 1989		190
	13.16.1	Family assistance orders	190
	13.16.2	Effect of the family assistance order	191
Summary of Chapter 13			193
14	**LOCAL AUTHORITY SERVICES FOR CHILDREN AND FAMILIES (1)**		195
14.1	Background		195
14.2	Definitions		195
14.3	Providing services for children and their families		196
	14.3.1	The identification of children in need	196
	14.3.2	Assessment of children's needs	197
	14.3.3	Prevention of neglect and abuse	197
	14.3.4	Provision of accommodation in order to protect a child	197
	14.3.5	Provision for disabled children	197
	14.3.6	Provision to reduce need for care proceedings, etc	197
	14.3.7	Provision for children living with their families.	197
	14.3.8	Family centres	197
	14.3.9	Maintenance of the family home	198
	14.3.10	Duty to consider racial groups	198
14.4	Assistance in kind or cash		198
14.5	The provision of day care for pre-school and other children		198
	14.5.1	The duty	198
	14.5.2	Outside school hours	198
	14.5.3	Review of provision for day care, etc	199

14.6	Duty to provide accommodation for children		199
	14.6.1	The duty of local authorities	199
	14.6.2	The child's wishes	200
	14.6.3	Restriction on the provision of accommodation	200
	14.6.4	Removal of the child from accommodation	200
14.7	Providing accommodation for children in protection, etc		200
	14.7.1	Duty under s 21(2)	201
	14.7.2	Financial matters	201
14.8	Duties of local authority in relation to children looked after by them		201
14.9	Possibility of serious injury to the public		201
14.10	Accommodation etc for children who are being looked after		202
14.11	Local authority foster parents		202
14.12	Regulations concerning placement with local authority foster parents		202
14.13	Other matters concerning provision of accommodation		202
14.14	Child allowed to live with parents		202
14.15	Contact between the child and his family		202
	14.15.1	Promotion of contact	202
	14.15.2	Visits to or by children	203
	14.15.3	Appointment of visitors	203
	14.15.4	Arrangements to assist children to live abroad	203
Summary of Chapter 14			205

15 LOCAL AUTHORITY SERVICES FOR CHILDREN AND FAMILIES (2) — 207

15.1	Further matters covered by ChA 1989, Part III		207
15.2	Advice and assistance for certain children		207
	15.2.1	Persons qualifying for care and assistance	207
	15.2.2	Conditions for the giving of advice	207
15.3	Financial matters involved in providing advice and assistance		208
	15.3.1	Payment of expenses, making of grants	208
	15.3.2	Continuation of assistance	208
15.4	Duties related to contact with other local authorities		208
15.5	Complaints concerning advice and assistance		208
15.6	The provision of secure accommodation		209
	15.6.1	Regulations under s 25	209
	15.6.2	The making of an order	209
	15.6.3	Interim order	210
	15.6.4	Directions by the court	210
15.7	Removal of the child from secure accommodation		210
15.8	Restricting the liberty of children: a reminder		210
15.9	Review of progress of children		211
	15.9.1	Review of cases	211
	15.9.2	Regulations	211
15.10	Inquiries into representations		211
	15.10.1	Persons who can complain	211
	15.10.2	Procedure concerning complaints	211
15.11	Other procedures for dealing with complaints		212
	15.11.1	Secretary of State: default powers	212
	15.11.2	Complaints to the Ombudsman	212

		15.11.3 Hearing by European Court of Human Rights	212
		15.11.4 Judicial review	213
		15.11.5 Application for private orders	213
	15.12	Co-operation between authorities	213
	15.13	Consultation by local authorities with local education authorities	213
	15.14	Recoupment of cost of services, etc	213
	15.15	Contributions towards maintenance of children looked after by local authorities	214
		15.15.1 Agreed contributions	214
		15.15.2 Contribution orders	214
	Summary of Chapter 15		215
16	**CARE AND SUPERVISION ORDERS**		217
	16.1	Essence of ChA 1989, Part IV	217
	16.2	Definitions	217
	16.3	Basis of Part IV	217
	16.4	Features of s 31	218
		16.4.1 Restrictions	218
		16.4.2 Consultation with local authority	218
		16.4.3 Residence of child	218
		16.4.4 Nature of proceedings	218
	16.5	Principles which the court will keep in mind	218
	16.6	The threshold criteria	219
	16.7	Aspects of the criteria	219
		16.7.1 'Is suffering ... or is likely to suffer ...'	219
		16.7.2 'Significant harm'	220
		16.7.3 'Attributable to'	220
		16.7.4 'Reasonable to expect a parent to give to him'	221
		16.7.5 'Beyond parental control'	221
	16.8	Timetables	221
	16.9	Essential features of the care order	221
		16.9.1 Parental responsibility	221
		16.9.2 Restrictions concerning religious upbringing	222
		16.9.3 Restrictions concerning change of name, removal from the UK	222
	16.10	Contact between children in care and their families	223
		16.10.1 Orders concerning contact	223
		16.10.2 Orders refusing to allow contact	223
		16.10.3 Where no application has been made	223
		16.10.4 Other matters	223
	16.11	Essence of the supervision order	224
	16.12	Duties of the supervisor	224
	16.13	Duration of the order	224
	16.14	Features of the supervision order	224
		16.14.1 Selection of the supervisor	224
		16.14.2 Supervisor's directions	224
		16.14.3 Psychiatric and medical examinations	225
		16.14.4 Appeals	225
	16.15	The education supervision order	225
		16.15.1 Designated local authority	225

	16.15.2	Appropriate local authority	225
16.16	Further matters concerning education supervision orders		226
	16.16.1	Effect of education supervision orders	226
	16.16.2	Duration and discharge of orders	226
	16.16.3	Offences	226
	16.16.4	Failure of child to comply	226
16.17	Investigation of a child's circumstances		226
16.18	Interim orders		227
	16.18.1	Examination of child	227
	16.18.2	Duration	227
16.19	Discharge and variation of care and supervision orders		228
16.20	Orders pending appeals		228
16.21	Guardians *ad litem*		228
	16.21.1	Appointment of solicitor	228
	16.21.2	Rules of court	229
	16.21.3	Withdrawal of proceedings	229
	16.21.4	Independence of guardians *ad litem*	229
	16.21.5	Guardian *ad litem* as co-ordinator of expert evidence	229
Summary of Chapter 16			231

17	**SHORT-TERM PROTECTION OF CHILDREN AT RISK**		**233**
17.1	Essence of ChA 1989, Part V		233
17.2	The Child Assessment Order		233
	17.2.1	Making a CAO	233
	17.2.2	The assessment	234
	17.2.3	Threshold principles	234
	17.2.4	Giving notice of application	234
	17.2.5	Duration of the order	234
	17.2.6	CAO and EPO	235
	17.2.7	Effect of the order	235
	17.2.8	Right of the child to refuse assessment	235
	17.2.9	Keeping the child away from home	235
17.3	Purpose of the CAO: a summary		235
17.4	The Emergency Protection Order		236
17.5	No automatic making of an EPO		236
17.6	Application by 'any person'		236
	17.6.1	Significant (future) harm	237
	17.6.2	'Likely'	237
17.7	Application by a local authority		237
17.8	Application by an 'authorised person'		237
17.9	General procedure		237
	17.9.1	*Ex parte* applications	238
	17.9.2	Identification of parents	238
17.10	Orders taken over by a local authority		238
17.11	Effects of the EPO		238
	17.11.1	Authorisation, etc	238
	17.11.2	Applicant's duties	238
	17.11.3	Offences	238
17.12	Directions		238
	17.12.1	Refusal by child	238

	17.12.2	Directions under subsection (6)	239
	17.12.3	Contact of child with parents, etc	239
17.13	Return of child	239
17.14	Duration of EPO	239
17.15	Discharge of EPO	239
17.16	Police protection	240
	17.16.1	Duties of the police under s 46(3)	240
	17.16.2	Application for EPO	240
	17.16.3	Release of child	240
17.17	Investigation by local authority	240
17.18	Powers to assist in discovery of children	241
17.19	Abducting children in care	241
	17.19.1	Recovery of abducted children	241
	17.19.2	Who may apply for a recovery order	241
	17.19.3	Features of the recovery order	241
17.20	Refuges for children at risk	242
17.21	A note on self-incrimination in relation to proceedings under Part V	242
	Summary of Chapter 17	243

18 COMMUNITY, VOLUNTARY AND REGISTERED HOMES FOR CHILDREN — 245

18.1	Residential care of children	245
18.2	Community homes provided by local authorities	245
	18.2.1	Nature of the community home	245
	18.2.2	Homes provided by voluntary organisations	245
18.3	Management and conduct of community homes	246
	18.3.1	Controlled and assisted community homes	246
	18.3.2	Regulations concerning community homes	246
	18.3.3	Directions concerning use of premises	246
	18.3.4	Disputes concerning controlled and assisted community homes	246
	18.3.5	Discontinuance of voluntary organisation of homes	247
	18.3.6	Closure of community home by a local authority	247
18.4	Voluntary homes and voluntary organisations	247
	18.4.1	Provision of accommodation by voluntary organisations	247
	18.4.2	Foster parents	247
18.5	The registration and regulation of voluntary homes	247
	18.5.1	Rules of registration	247
	18.5.2	Registration procedure	248
	18.5.3	Representations	248
	18.5.4	Regulations	248
18.6	Duties of voluntary organisations	248
18.7	Duties of local authorities	249
18.8	Registered children's homes	249
	18.8.1	General rules	249
	18.8.2	Persons disqualified from carrying on or being employed in children's homes	249
18.9	Registration of children's homes	250
	18.9.1	Conditions imposed on registration	250
	18.9.2	Cancellation of registration	250

	18.10	Regulations concerning children's homes	250
	18.11	Inspection of children's homes	250
	18.12	Inquiries	251
	18.13	Default power of Secretary of State	251
	18.14	A note on the welfare of children accommodated in independent schools	251
		Summary of Chapter 18	253
19		**FOSTERING CHILDREN; CHILD MINDING AND DAY CARE**	**255**
	19.1	Background	255
	19.2	Local authority foster placements	255
	19.3	Private foster parents	255
		19.3.1 Relatives	256
		19.3.2 Exclusions from the category of 'fostered child'	256
	19.4	Power of local authority to impose requirements	256
	19.5	Welfare of privately fostered children	256
	19.6	Notification of fostering	257
	19.7	Appeals	257
	19.8	Prohibition of advertisements	257
	19.9	Disqualifications	257
	19.10	Power to prohibit private fostering	257
	19.11	Offences	258
	19.12	Child minding and day care	258
		19.12.1 The register	258
		19.12.2 'Child minder', 'day care' defined	258
		19.12.3 Refusal of registration	259
		19.12.4 Disqualification from registration	259
	19.13	Requirements imposed on child minders	260
	19.14	Cancellation of registration	260
	19.15	Inspection of premises	260
	19.16	Enforcement notices	260
		Summary of Chapter 19	261
20		**GUARDIANSHIP**	**263**
	20.1	The concept of guardianship	263
	20.2	Guardianship prior to the ChA 1989	263
	20.3	Changes introduced by the ChA 1989	263
	20.4	Appointment of guardians by the court	264
		20.4.1 Appointment of an individual	264
		20.4.2 Exercise of the court's powers	264
		20.4.3 Appointment of more than one person	264
		20.4.4 'The court may appoint'	264
		20.4.5 Who may apply	264
		20.4.6 Persons in respect of whom application may be made	265
		20.4.7 Section 8 orders	265
	20.5	Appointment of guardians privately	265
	20.6	Appointment in writing	265
	20.7	Disclaimer	265

20.8	Revocation		266
	20.8.1	Basic principle	266
	20.8.2	Revocation by written instrument	266
	20.8.3	Revocation by destruction of instrument	266
20.9	Time at which appointment becomes effective		266
20.10	General legal effect of appointment as a guardian		267
20.11	Ending guardianship		267
	20.11.1	Death of the guardian	267
	20.11.2	Majority or death of child	267
	20.11.3	Removal of guardian by the court	267
20.12	A note on 'the guardian's allowance'		268
Summary of Chapter 20			269

21 WARDSHIP — 271

21.1	The essential feature of wardship		271
21.2	Background		271
21.3	Wardship jurisdiction and the inherent jurisdiction of the High Court		271
21.4	Some features of the wardship jurisdiction		272
	21.4.1	Control during wardship	272
	21.4.2	Control over ward's 'important steps'	272
	21.4.3	Wide nature of court's powers	272
	21.4.4	Detailed enquiries	273
21.5	Jurisdiction to make a child a ward		273
21.6	Section 41 of the Supreme Court Act 1981		273
21.7	Exercise of the court's discretion		274
21.8	The enforcing of court orders		274
21.9	Persons who may or may not be made wards of court		274
	21.9.1	British subjects	275
	21.9.2	Non-British subjects	275
	21.9.3	Restrictions	276
21.10	Persons who may apply to make a child a ward of court		276
21.11	The child's welfare and the public interest		276
21.12	Effects of ChA 1989 on wardship		277
21.13	The inherent jurisdiction of the High Court		277
21.14	Local authorities and the use of wardship jurisdiction		277
	21.14.1	Local authorities and the inherent jurisdiction	277
	21.14.2	Leave of the court	278
Summary of Chapter 21			279

22 ADOPTION — 281

22.1	Background		281
22.2	Current trends		281
22.3	Adoption agencies		282
	22.3.1	The Adoption Service	282
	22.3.2	Voluntary societies	282
	22.3.3	Adoption panels	282
22.4	Who may apply for an adoption order		283
	22.4.1	Married couple	283
	22.4.2	Unmarried person aged 21 or over	283

	22.4.3	Married person aged 21 or over	283
	22.4.4	Application by mother or father of the child alone	283
	22.4.5	Convention adoption orders	284
	22.4.6	Suitability of applicants	284
22.5		The question of adoption by relatives and step-parents	284
22.6		Who may be adopted	284
	22.6.1	Child to live with adopters before order is made	285
	22.6.2	Seeing the child in the home environment	285
22.7		The welfare principle	285
	22.7.1	Duty to promote welfare of child	285
	22.7.2	The child's religious upbringing	286
22.8		Private placements	286
	22.8.1	'Relative of the child'	286
	22.8.2	Prohibition on payments	286
	22.8.3	Foster placements	287
	22.8.4	Application to adopt a child placed independently	287
22.9		Agency placements	287
22.10		Consent to the adoption order	287
22.11		Dispensing with consent	288
	22.11.1	The parent or guardian cannot be found or is incapable of giving assent.	288
	22.11.2	Agreement is withheld unreasonably	288
	22.11.3	Persistent failure to discharge parental responsibility	289
	22.11.4	Abandonment or neglect of child	289
	22.11.5	Persistent ill-treatment of the child	289
	22.11.6	Serious ill-treatment of the child, and his rehabilitation is unlikely	290
22.12		Freeing for adoption and its effect	290
	22.12.1	Father lacking parental responsibility	290
	22.12.2	Effects of freeing order	290
	22.12.3	Abolition recommended	290
22.13		General procedures for adoption	290
	22.13.1	Application	291
	22.13.2	Appointment of a reporting officer or guardian ad litem	291
	22.13.3	Making the order	291
	22.13.4	Order with conditions	292
22.14		Some legal effects of the order	292
	22.14.1	The child's status	292
	22.14.2	Rights of succession	292
	22.14.3	Nationality rights	292
	22.14.4	The problem of prohibited degrees	293
	22.14.5	Revocation	293
22.15		Registration	293
22.16		Reform proposals	293
		Summary of Chapter 22	295

23		**CHILDREN'S RIGHTS AND THEIR SIGNIFICANCE (1)**	297
	23.1	The question of children's rights	297
	23.2	The basic concept of rights	297
	23.3	The problem of the correlative	298

23.4	The international recognition of children's rights		298
	23.4.1	The Geneva Declaration 1924	299
	23.4.2	The Universal Declaration of Human Rights 1948	299
	23.4.3	The European Convention on Human Rights 1950	299
	23.4.4	Declaration of the Rights of the Child 1959	299
	23.4.5	The United Nations Convention on the Rights of the Child 1989	299
23.5	The criminal law and the life of the child		301
23.6	Manslaughter		301
23.7	Child cruelty		301
23.8	Neglect		302
23.9	The question of corporal punishment and the child		302
23.10	Assault, battery, wounding		303
23.11	Sexual offences involving children		303
	23.11.1	Rape	303
	23.11.2	Incest	303
	23.11.3	Intercourse with girls under 13	303
	23.11.4	Intercourse with girls between 13-16	303
	23.11.5	Indecent assault	304
	23.11.6	Indecency with Children Act 1960	304
	23.11.7	Abduction of females	304
	23.11.8	Protection of Children Act 1978	304
23.12	Child abuse		304
	23.12.1	Standard of proof	305
	23.12.2	Interviews, investigation	305
23.13	Kidnapping		306
23.14	Child abduction		306
	23.14.1	Defences	306
	23.14.2	The Hague Convention	307
	23.14.3	The European Convention	308
	23.14.4	Abduction within the UK	308
23.15	A note on the literature concerning children's rights		308
Summary of Chapter 23			311
24	**CHILDREN'S RIGHTS AND THEIR SIGNIFICANCE (2)**		313
24.1	Protection of the child from harmful goods and activities		313
24.2	Protecting the child from exploitation as an employee		313
	24.2.1	General restriction upon the employment of children	313
	24.2.2	Specific restrictions upon the employment of children	314
24.3	Protecting young persons		314
24.4	A note on the criminal responsibility of minors		315
24.5	Accountability of parents		316
	24.5.1	Section 56 Criminal Justice Act 1991	316
	24.5.2	Section 57 Criminal Justice Act 1991	316
	24.5.3	Section 58 Criminal Justice Act 1991	316
24.6	Children as witnesses in criminal proceedings		317
	24.6.1	The determining of competence	317
	24.6.2	The child's unsworn evidence	317
24.7	Children as witnesses in civil proceedings		317
	24.7.1	Section 96 Children Act 1989	318
	24.7.2	Examination of a child in relation to proceedings	318

24.8	Minors and the law of contract		318
	24.8.1 The current situation: valid contracts		318
	24.8.2 Voidable contracts		319
	24.8.3 Void contracts		319
24.9	Minors and the law of torts		319
	24.9.1 Liability of occupiers under the Occupiers' Liability Act 1957		320
	24.9.2 Liability of occupiers under the Occupiers' Liability Act 1984		320
	24.9.3 Liability of parents, foster parents		320
24.10	The minor's capacity to sue		320
24.11	Liability of minor to be sued		321
24.12	Responsibility of a minor's parents for his torts		321
Summary of Chapter 24			323

Recommended Reading List — 325
Index — 327

Table of Cases

A (A Minor: Custody), Re [1991] 2 FLR 394 ....13.5.3
A (A Minor) (Adoption: Contact Order), Re [1993] 2 FLR 645.................................22.12.2
A (Minors) (Parental Responsibility), Re [1993] Fam Law 464 ....12.24
A (Minors) (Contact Application: Grandparent), Re (1995) The Times, 6 March 13.12
A (A Minor) (Supervision Order: Extension), Re (1994) The Times, 11 Nov....................16.13
A (A Minor) (Paternity: Refusal of Blood Test), Re [1994] 2FLR 463 ....12.10
A and W (Minors) (Residence Order: Leave to Apply), Re [1992] 2 FLR 154 .....13.2.3; 13.9.2
AB, Re (1985) FLR 470 ....21.4.3
A v DPP [1991] COD 442 ....24.4
A v J (Nullity) [1989] Fam Law 63..2.6.1
Abercrombie v Abercrombie [1943] 2 All ER 465 ....4.5.2
Adams v Adams [1984] FLR 768 ....13.5.1
Adoption Application (Surrogacy), Re [1987] 3 WLR31 ....22.7
A.-G. v London Borough of Wandsworth [1981] 1 All ER 1162 ....14.3
Aggett v Aggett [1962] 1WLR 183 ....9.5.1
Ainsbury v Millington [1986] 1 FLR 331 ....5.1.6
Alford, Re [1941] St R Qd 213..13.21
Allen v Jambo Holdings [1980] 1 WLR 1252 ....10.8.1
Ampthill Peerage Case [1977] AC 547 ....12.6
Anton Piller KG v Manufacturing Processes Ltd [1976] 1 All ER 779 ....10.9
Ash v Ash [1972] 2 WLR 347 ....4.4.1
Atkinson v Atkinson [1988] 2 FLR 353 ....10.5
Attar v Attar [1985] FLR 653...9.13

B, Re [1965] Ch 1112...21.5; 21.8
B, Re (1994) The Independent, 10 May 22.14.5
B (A Minor) (Sexual Abuse: Standard of Proof), Re (1994) The Times, 27 Dec..............23.12.1
B (Minors) (Termination of Contact: Paramount Consideration), Re [1993] 3 WLR 63.....16.5
B (A Minor) (Abduction), Re [1994] 2 FLR 2949 ....23.14.2
B, Re (1994) The Times, 27 May 15.6.2
B-M (A Minor) (Wardship: Jurisdiction), Re [1993] 1 FLR 979.................................21.9.2
B v B [1968] 1 WLR 109..10.4.4
B v B (Grandparent: Residence Order), Re [1992] 2 FLR 327....................................13.4.2
B v B (Minors) (Periodical Payments: Variation) (1994) The Times, 30 Dec 10.4
B-T v B-T (Divorce Procedure) [1990] 2 FLR 1 ....10.3.2
Banbury Peerage Case (1811) 1 Sim & St 153 ....1.2.1
Banco Exterior Internacional v Mann (1994) The Times, 19 Dec 7.16
Bannister v Bannister [1980] 10 Fam Law 240...4.4.1
Barclays Bank v O'Brien [1994] 1 AC 180..7.16
Barder v Barder [1987] 2 All ER 440..10.3.4
Bartram v Bartram [1949] 2 All ER 270...4.5.3
Baxter v Baxter [1948] 2 All ER 886 ....2.6.1
Beard v Beard [1981] 1 All ER 783...5.16
Beatty v Guggenheim Exploration Co (1919) 225 NY 380 ....6.3.5
Beaumont, Re [1979] 3 WLR 818..6.10
Bennet v Bennet (1879) 10 Ch D 474..6.3.3
Bennett v Bennett [1969] 1 WLR 430...26.3
Bennett v Bennett (1978) 9 Fam Law 19..9.18
Bergin v Bergin [1983] 1 WLR 279...4.4.1; 8.3.3
Bernard v Josephs [1982] 2 WLR 1052 ....7.14.2
Besterman, Re [1984] 2 All ER 656 ....6.9.2
Biggs v Biggs [1977] 1 All ER 20 ....4.1.2; 4.3.4
Birch v Birch [1992] 1 FLR 564..4.4.1
Birmingham CC v H (A Minor) [1994] 2 WLR 31 ....16.10.2
Bishop v Plumley [1991] 1 All ER 236...6.10
Blackwell v Bull (1836) 1 Keen 176..1.5.1

Blythe v Blythe [1966] AC 643..4.3.2
Bradley v Bradley [1973] 1 WLR 1291..4.4.6
Bradshaw v Bradshaw [1956] P 274..3.10.1
Brickell v Brickell [1973] 3 All ER 508..4.7.2
Brooks v Brooks (1994) The Times, 27 May..9.7.3
Browne v Pritchard [1975] 1 WLR 1366..9.7.2
Buchanan-Wollaston's Conveyance, Re [1939] Ch 738..7.14.2
Buckland v Buckland [1967] 2 WLR 1506..2.6.2
Buffery v Buffery [1985] 2 FLR 365...4.1.2
Bunning, Re [1984] 3 All ER 1..6.9.2
Burns v Burns [1984] FLR 216..6.3.6
Burton v Islington Health Authority [1992] 3 All ER 833...24.10
Butler v Butler [1990] Fam Law 21...3.5.3

C (An Infant), Re [1964] 3 WLR 1041..22.11.2
C (A Minor) (Custody of Child), Re [1980] 2 FLR 163..13.5.6
C, Re [1988] 1 All ER 705..22.13.4
C (Minors), Re [1992] 2 All ER 86...12.24
C (A Minor) (Adoption Application), Re [1993]1 FLR 87...22.8.2
C, Re (1994) The Times, 7 February..11.14
C (A Minor) (Adoption Notice: Local Authority), Re (1994) The Times, 28 June..............22.7
C (Minor) (Access: Attendance of Court Welfare Officer),
  Re (1994), The Times, 21 Nov..13.6
C (Children Act 1989: Expert Evidence), Re (1994) The Times, 7 Dec..............................16.21.5
CB (A Minor) (Parental Responsibility Order), Re [1993] 1 FLR 920................................12.24
C v C (Minors: Custody), Re [1988]2 FLR 291...13.5.2
C v Humberside CC (1994) The Times, 24 May...15.6.3
Cackett v Cackett [1950] 1 All ER 677..2.6.1
Cahill v Cahill [1986] Fam Law 102..3.8
Callaghan v Andrew-Hanson [1992] 1 All ER 56...3.7
Camden LBC v R (A Minor) (Blood Transfusion) [1993] 91 LGR 623..............................21.14.2
Camm v Camm (1983) 13 Fam Law 112..10.2.3
Campbell v UK (1982) 4 EHRR 293...23.4.3
Carr v Carr [1974] 1 WLR 1534...4.3
Chard v Chard [1956] P 259...3.10.1
Chaudhry v Chaudhry [1987] 1 FLR 347..7.6
Cheshire CC v M [1993] 1 FLR 463..13.9.2
CIBC Mortgages v Pitt [1993] 3 WLR 802...7.16
Citro, Re [1990] 3 All ER 952..7.15.4
City of London BS v Flegg [1987] AC 54...7.13
Cleary v Cleary [1974] 1 WLR 73..4.3
Cleveland CC v DPP (1994) The Times, 1 Dec..14.8
Cole, Re [1964] Ch 175..6.3
Cook v Cook [1988] 1 FLR 521..10.3.2
Cooke v Head [1972] 1 WLR 518..7.4
Corbett v Corbett [1970] P 110...2.3.3
Cornick v Cornick [1994] 2 FLR 530..10.3.4
Cossey v UK [1991] 2 FLR 492..1.2.4; 2.3.3
Costello-Roberts v UK (1993) The Times, 26 March...23.9
Court v Court [1982] 3 WLR 199..4.4.6
Cowcher v Cowcher [1972] 1 WLR 425...7.5
Cox v Cox [1958] 1 All ER 569...4.5.7
Crabb v Arun DC [1976] Ch 179...7.3.1
Crittenden v Crittenden [1990] 2 FLR 361..10.7.1
Cruse v Chittum (1974) 118 SJ 499...11.18
Curry v DPP [1994] 3 All ER 190..24.4

D (A Minor) (Wardship: Sterilisation)) (1976) Fam 185..21.10
D, Re (1977) Fam 158..21.1
D, Re [198) AC 317..16.7.1
D (Minors) (Adoption Reports: Confidentiality), Re (1994) The Times, 8 Dec 22.13.2
D (A Minor) (Contact: Interim Order) Re (1995) The Times 1 Feb 13.12
D v A (1845)   Rob Eccl 279...2.6.1
D v D [1979] 3 All ER 337..2.7
D v D [1994] 1 FCR 694..13.12
Dackham v Dackham [1987] 2 FLR 358...3.7
Daubney v Daubney [1976] 2 WLR 959...9.11.1
Davies v Davies [1957] P 357..8.3
Davis v Davis [1993] 1 FLR 54...6.9.2
Davis v Johnson [1979] AC 264..5.14.3
Dean v Dean [1978] 3 WLR 288...8.8
De Dampierre v De Dampierre [1988] 2 WLR 1006...3.4
Delaney v Delaney [1990] 2 FLR 457...9.12
Dennis. Re [1981] 2 All ER 140..6.9.3
Dennis v Dennis [1955] 2 WLR 187..4.3.1
De Reneville v De Reneville [1948] 1 All ER 56..2.6
Dinch v Dinch [1987] 1 WLR 252..10.4.5
DPP v Boardman [1975] AC 241..23.11
Dredge v Dredge [1947] 1 All ER 29..2.6.1
Duxbury v Duxbury [1987] 1 FLR 7..9.6; 10.33
Dyson Holdings v Fox [1975] 3 All ER 1030..2.1.6

E, Re [1984] 1 All ER 289..21.4; 21.5
E, Re [1991] 1 FLR 420...21.4; 21.4.4
E, Re [1994] Fam Law 483...22.12.2
EH and MH (Step Parent Adoption), Re [1993] Fam Law 187...22.11.2
E v E [1990] 2 FLR 233...9.7.3
Edgar v Edgar [1980] 3 All ER 887..10.2.4
Elsworth v Elsworth (1978) 9 Fam Law 21..5.13
Essex CC v F [1993] 1 FLR 847..17.15
Evans v Evans [1989] 1 FLR 351...8.7.2; 9.9.2; 9.17

F (In Utero), Re [1988] 2 All ER 193..21.9
F (Minors) (Contact), Re [1993] 1 FCR 945..13.12
F (Minors) (Contact Restraint Order) Re (1995) The Times 2 Feb..13.9.2
F, Re [1993] 2 FLR 9..16.21.3
F (A Minor) (Blood Tests: Parental Rights), Re [1993] 3 All ER 596......................................12.10
F v F [1989] 2 FLR 451..5.14.3
F v Kent CC [1993] 1 FLR 432..13.9.2
F v Leeds City Council [1994] 2 FLR 60...13.2.2
F v Suffolk CC [1981] 2 FLR 208..23.12
Fisher v Fisher [1989] 1 FLR 423..8.7.2
Foley v Foley [1981] 3 WLR 284..9.13
Ford v Ford [1987] Fam Law 232...2.6.1

G, Re [1984] 2 All ER 811..21.4.2
G, Re [1990] 3 All ER 102..21.4.2
G (Minors) (Interim Care Order), Re (1993) The Times, 2 Aug..16.18
G, Re [1993] 2 FLR 842..16.18.2
G (Minors) (Care: Leave to Place Outside Jurisdiction), Re [1994] 2 FLR 301 ....14.15.4
Garcia v Garcia [1992] 1 FLR 256...4.7.3
Gascoigne v Gascoigne [1918] 1 KB 223...6.3.4

Gaskin v UK (1990) 12 EHRR 36...15.11.3
Gateshead MBC v N [1993] 1 FLR 811..16.18.2
Ghoth v Ghoth [1992] 2 All ER 920..10.8.2
Gibson v Austin [1993] 2 FLR 437..13.2.3
Gillick v West Norfolk and Wisbech Area Health Authority [1986] AC 112.......12.26; 12.26.4
Gillies v Keogh (1989) 2 NZLR 327..7.3.1
Gissing v Gissing [1971] AC 886..6.3.6
Gojkovic v Gojkovic [1992] 2 All ER 77..9.6; 9.16
Goldsmith v Sands (1907) 4 CLR 1648...13.2.1
Gollins v Gollins [1963] 2 All ER 966..4.5.6
Goodrich v Goodrich [1971] 1 WLR 1142..4.3.3
Gorely v Codd [1967] 1 WLR 19..24.11
Gorman v Gorman [1964] 1 WLR 1440..8.8; 10.2.2

H (Infants) (Adoption: Parental Consent), Re [1977] 2 All ER 339.....................................22.11.2
H, Re [1990] 2 FLR 439..23.14.2
H (Minors) (Wardship: Sexual Abuse), Re [1991] 2 FLR 416..23.12
H, Re [1993] 3 WLR 1109...16.21
H (A Minor) (Parental Responsibility), Re [1993] 1 FLR 484..12.24
H (A Minor) (Section 37 Direction), Re [1993] 2 FLR 541...16.17
H (Minors: Prohibited Steps Order) Re (1995) TheTimes 8 Feb..13.13
H v M (Property; Beneficial Interest) [1992] 1 FLR 229..7.5.2
Haddon v Haddon (1887) 18 QBD 778...5.8
Harben v Harben [1957] 1 WLR 261..21.9.1
Hardy v Hardy [1981] 11 Fam Law 153..4.7.3
Harriman v Harriman [1909] P 123...4.5.6
Harrington v Gill [1983] 4 FLR 265..6.10
Harrogate BC v Simpson [1986] 2 FLR 91...1.5.4
Hereford and Worcester CC v S [1993] 1 FLR 360..15.6
Hereford and Worcester CC v T & S Stores (1994) The Times 4 Nov....................................24.1
Heseltine v Heseltine [1971] 1 All ER 952..6.4.3
Hewitson v Hewitson (1994) 144 NLJ 1478..9.20
Hoddinott v Hoddinott [1949] 2 KB 406..6.4.3
Holmes v Holmes [1989] 3 All ER 786..9.20
Hope v Hope (1854) 4 De G M & G..21.9.2
Hopes v Hopes [1949] P 227..4.5.2
Hopper v Hopper [1979] 1 All ER 181..5.14.4
Horton v Horton [1947] 2 All ER 871..2.6.1
Howker v Robinson [1973] 1 QB 178..24.1
Humberside CC v B [1993] 1 FLR 257..16.5; 16.7.2
Hyde v Hyde (1866) LR1 P&D 130..2.1.1.

J (A Minor) (Change of Name), Re [1993]1 FCR 74..16.9.3
JK, Re [1991] 2 FLR 340..22.2
JS, Re [1990] 3 WLR 119...21.7
J v C [1970] AC 668...13.2.2; 13.3
J v J (A Minor: Property Transfer) [1993] 2 FLR 56...11.3; 12.3
J v J [1955] 2 All ER 617..9.11.2
Jackson v Jackson [1993] 2 FLR 851...4.7.2
Jelley v Illife [1981] 2 WLR 801..6.10
Jennings v Rundall (1799) 8 TR 335..24.11
Johnson v Walton [1990] 1 FLR 350..5.14.3
Jones v Maynard [1951] Ch 572...6.4

K, Re [1953] 1 QB 117..22,10
K, Re [1987] 3 WLR 1233...21.7

K, Re [1988] 1 FLR 435 ....21.4
K (A Minor) (Adoption Order: Nationality), Re [1994]3 WLR 572..............................22.7
K (Minors) (Care Proceedings: Disclosure), Re [1994] 2 FCR 805..............................17.21
K v K [1990] 2 FLR 225..9.17
K.T. (A Minor) (Adoption), Re [1993] Fam Law 567 ....22.6.1
K, W and H (Minors) (Medical Treatment), Re [1993] 1 FLR 855..............................12.27
KVS v GGS (1992) 156 JPN 268...23.12.1
Kacmarz v Kacmarz [1967] 1 WLR 317 ....4.5.3
Katz v Katz [1972] 1 WLR 9655..4.4.2
Kemmis v Kemmis [1988] 1 WLR 1307 ....10.7.2
Kent CC v C [1992] 3 WLR 808..16.10.1
Khan v Khan [1980] 1 All ER 499 ....9.14
Kingsnorth Finance Ltd v Tizard [1986] 2 All ER 54...7.13.2
Knowles v Knowles [1962] P 161 ....12.9
Krystmann v Krystmann [1973] 1 WLR 927 ....9.14

L v L (Lump Sum: Interest) [1944] 2 FLR 324..9.6
L v L (1994) 1 FLR 156...16.21.1
Langley v Langley [1994] Fam Law 564 ....10.7.1
Lawlor v Lawlor (1994) The Times, 20 Oct..3.5.1
Layton v Martin [1986] 2 FLR 277..6.10
Leadbeater v Leadbeater [1985] FLR 789 ....9.12
Le Brocq v Le Brocq [1964] 2 All ER 464 ....4.5.2
Lee v Lee [1984] FLR 243...5.14.2
Le Marchant v Le Marchant [1977] 1 WLR 559..4.7.2
Livesey v Jenkins [1985] 1 All ER 106 ....10.3.2
Livingstone-Stallard v Livingstone-Stallard [1974] 3 WLR 302 ....4.4.4
Lloyds Bank v Rosset [1990] 2 WLR 867 ....6.3.6; 7.5.1
London Borough of Sutton v Davis (1994) The Times, 17 March...............................23.9

M (Minors) (Sexual Abuse: Evidence), Re [1993] 1 FLR 822.....................................23.12.2
M (A Minor) (Care Order: Threshold Conditions) [1994] 3 WLR 558 ....16.7.1
M (A Minor) (Secure Accommodation Order), Re (1994) The Times, 15 Nov 15.6
M and N (Wards) (Publication of Information), Re [1990] 1 All ER 205 ....21.3; 21.11
M v M (1976) 6 Fam Law 243 ....9.14
M v M [1994] 2 FCR 449...9.20
MT v MT (Financial Provision: Lump Sum) [1992] 1 FLR 362 ....9.6
Maharaj v Chand [1986] 3 WLR 440...7.3.3
Malone v Harrison [1979] 11WLR 1353...6.9.2
Manser v Manser [1940] P 224 ....3.10.2
Mareva Compania Naviera SA v International Bulk Carriers
  SA [1980] 1 All ER 213 ....10.8; 10.8.1
Marsh v Von Sternberg [1986] 1 FLR 526..7.4
Martin v Martin [1976] 2 WLR 901...9.17
Masefield v Masefield (1994) The Times, 19 Aug...10.4.6
Mason v Mason [1972] 3 All ER 315...4.6.2
McGrath, Re [1993] 1 Ch 143...20.2
McMichael v UK (1995), The Times, 2 March 15.11.13
McVeigh v Beattie [1988] 2 All ER 500...12.10
Mehta v Mehta [1945] 2 All ER 690 ....2.6.2
Mesher v Mesher [1990] 1 All ER 126 ....9.7.2
Militante v Ogunwomoju [1993] 2 FCR 355 ....2.5
Mills v Mills [1940] 2 All ER 3254...10.4.4
Minton v Minton [1979] 1 All ER 79 ....9.19.1; 10.2
Mouncer v Mouncer [1972] 1 All ER 289...4.6.1
Mummery v Mummery [1942] 1 All ER 453 ....4.5.2

N, Re [1993] 2 FLR 124...23.14.2
N v N [1992] 1 FLR 266..3.8
National Provincial Bank Ltd v Ainsworth [1965] 3 WLR 1..................................7.6; 7.11
Naylor v Naylor [1961] 2 WLR 751..4.5.2
Newham LBC v A.-G. [1993] 1 FLR 281..16.7.1
Newton v Edgerley [1959] 1 WLR 1031..24.12
Norman v Norman [1983] 1 All ER 486..10.4.1

O (A Minor) (Care Order: Education: Procedure), Re [1992] 2 FLR 7.......................16.7.2
O (A Minor) (Medical Treatment), Re [1993] 4 Med LR 272......................................21.14.2
Ogden v Ogden [1908] P 46..2.3.1
O'Neill v O'Neill [1975] 3 All ER 289..4.4.4
Oram v Oram (1923) 129 LT 159...5.8
Oxfordshire CC v M [1994] 2 WLR 393...16.4.4

P, Re [1965] Ch 568...21.9.2
P, Re (1989) The Times, 24 Aug..14.3.10
P (Minors) (Interim Order), Re [1993] 2 FLR 742...16.18
P v P (Ouster: Decree Nisi of Nullity) [1994] 2 FLR 400...2.6
P v P (Periodical Payments: Appeals) (1994) The Times, 19 Dec.............................16.14.4
Parghi v Parghi (1973) 117 SJ 582..4.7.2
Parkinson v Parkinson [1939] P 346..3.10.2
Pascoe v Turner [1979] 1 WLR 431..7.3.2
Patching v Patching (1958) The Times, 25 April...4.5.5
Paton v UK (1980) 3 EHRR 408...1.2.4
Pearson v Franklin [1994] 1 WLR 370..13.14
Penrose v Penrose [1994] 2 FLR 621..10.3.4
Perry v Perry [1964] 1 WLR 91..4.5.3
Pettit v Pettit [1962] 3 WLR 919...2.7
Pheasant v Pheasant [1972] 2 WLR 353..4.4.1; 4.4.6
Poon v Poon [1994] 2 FCR 777...1.8.3
Popat v Popat [1991] 2 FLR 163...10.4.1
Prinsep v Prinsep [1930] P 35..9.7.3
Pugh v Pugh [1951] 2 All ER 680..2.3.2
Pulford v Pulford [1923] P 18..4.5.2
Puttock v A.-G. [1979] 3 WLR 542...2.5.2

Quoraishi v Quoraishi [1985] FLR 780...4.5.7

R, Re [1966] 3 All ER 613...22.11.1
R (A Minor) (Child Abuse: Access), Re [1988] 1 FLR 206..23.12
R (A Minor) (Wardship: Criminal Proceedings), Re [1991] Fam 56...........................23.3
R (A Minor) (Wardship: Medical Treatment), Re [1992] 1 FLR 190..........................12.27
R v Central TV [1994] 3 All ER 641..21.11
R (Minor: Child Abduction), Re (1994) The Times, 5 Dec..23.13.2
R and G, Re [1994] 1 FLR 793...16.14
R v Clarence (1888) 2 QBD 23..1.2.1
R v Cornwall CC [1992] 1 WLR 427..16.21.4
R v D [1984] 3 WLR 186..23.13
R v Dunne [1929] 99 LJKB 117..24.6.1
R v Ealing LBC ex p Sidhu (1982) 3 FLR 438..5.17.4
R v Francis (1989) 88 Cr App R 127...23.11.6
R v Gyngall [1893] 2 QB 232..13.2.1
R v Hale [1974] QB 819...23.13
R v Harvey (1987) 9 Cr App R (S) 524...23.8
R v Hayes [1977] 1 WLR 234..24.7

R v Inhabitants of Darlington (1792) Nolan 124 .... 1.5.2
R v Kingswood BC ex p Smith-Morse (1994) The Times, 8 Dec 5.17.2
R v Kowalski (1988) 86 Cr App R 339 .... 23.11.5
R v Luffe (1907) 8 East 193 .... 12.9
R v Newham LBC ex p Dada (1995) The Times 3 Feb 5.17.2
R v Oakley (1990) 12 Cr App R (S) 215 .... 23.11.3
R v Oldham MBC ex p B (1993) The Times, 19 March 5.17.4
R v Pelling (1988) 10 Cr App R (S) 185 .... 23.8
R v R [1952] 1 All ER 1194 .... 2.6.1
R v R [1992] 1 AC 599 .... 1.2.1; 2.1.2
R v Rawlings (1994) 144 NLJ 1626 .... 24.6.2
R v Registrar General ex p Smith [1991] 2 WLR 782 .... 22.15
R v Reid [1973] QB 299 .... 23.13
R v Scott [1973] Crim LR 708 .... 23.5
R v Secretary of State for Health ex p Luff [1992] 1 FLR 259 .... 22.4.6
R v Sherry [1993] Crim LR 536 .... 23.14
R v Smith (1845) 9 JP 682 .... 24.4
R v Surgenor [1940] 2 All ER 249 .... 24.6.1
R v Thomas [1985] Crim LR 677 .... 23.11.5
R v Wellard [1978] 1 WLR 921 .... 23.13
R v X [1990] Crim LR 515 .... 24.6.2
R v Young (1993) 897 Cr App R 280 .... 23.7
Rance v Mid-Downs Health Authority [1991] 1 QB 587 .... 23.5
Rathwell v Rathwell (1978) 83 DLR (3d) 289 .... 7.4
Rawlings v Rawlings [1964] P 398 .... 7.14.1
Rees v UK [1987] Fam Law 157 .... 2.3.3
Richards v Richards [1984] AC 174 .... 5.14.2; 5.18; 13.2.3
Richardson v Richardson (1978) 9 Fam Law 86 .... 9.18
Rignell v Andrews [1990] STC 410 .... 2.1.6
Risch v McFee [1991] 1 FLR 105 .... 7.5.4
Roberts v Gray [1913] 1 KB 520 .... 24.8.1
Rukat v Rukat [1975] 3 WLR 201 .... 4.7.2
Russell v A-G [1949] P 391 .... 1.2.1
Rutherford v Richardson [1923] AC 1 .... 4.3.2

S, Re [1967] 1 All ER 202 .... 21.4.2
S (A Minor) (Custody), Re [1991] 2 FLR 388 .... 13.5.2
S (A Minor), Re [1993] 3 All ER 316 .... 16.21.1
S (Children: Interim Care Order), Re [1993] 2 FCR 475 .... 16.18
S (A Minor) (Medical Treatment), Re (1993) 1 FLR 377 .... 13.2.2
S (A Minor) (Independent Representation), Re [1993] 3 All ER 36 .... 13.9.2
S, Re [1994] 2 WLR 228 .... 23.14.2
S (A Minor) (Parental Responsibility), Re (1995) The Times, 22 Feb 13.16
S v S [1954] 3 All ER 736 .... 2.6.1
S v W (1980) 11 Fam Law 81 .... 13.5.3
Sakkas v Sakkas [1987] Fam Law 414 .... 9.18
Sandford v Sandford [1986] 1 FLR 412 .... 10.4.5
Santos v Santos [1972] 2 All ER 246 .... 4.6.1
Saunders v Saunders [1965] P 499 .... 4.5.5
Scallon v Scallon [1990] 1 FLR 194 .... 9.19
Schuller v Schuller [1990] 2 FLR 193 .... 9.11.2
Seaton v Seaton [1986] 2 FLR 398 .... 9.19.2
Secretary of State for the Home Office v Robb (1994) 144 NLJ 1695 .... 5.11
Sekhon v Alissa [1989] 2 FLR 94 .... 7.4
Serio v Serio [1983] 4 FLR 756 .... 4.3.2
Shaw v Fitzgerald [1992] 1 FLR 357 .... 2.1.5

Shephard v Cartwright [1955] AC 431 ....6.3.4
Sherry v Sherry [1991] 1 FLR 307 ....10.7.2
Shipman v Shipman [1991] 1 FLR 250 ....10.7.1
Simkiss v Rhondda BC (1983) 81 LGR 660 ....24.9
Sinclair, Re [1985] Ch 446 ....3.9.2; 3.9.3
Smith v Smith (1973) 118 SJ 184 ....4.4.5
Smith v Smith [1990] 1 FLR 438 ....3.6
Sottomayor v De Barros (1877) 3 PD 1 ....2.3.1
South Glamorgan CC v B [1993] 1 FCR 626 ....16.18.1
Spence, Re [1990] Ch 652 ....12.17
Springette v Defoe [1992] 2 FLR 437 ....7.4
Steinberg v Scala (Leeds) Ltd [1923] 2 Ch 452 ....24.8.2
Stevens v Stevens [1979] 1 WLR 885 ....4.4.1
Stockford v Stockford (1981) 3 FLR 58 ....9.12
Strand Securities Ltd v Caswell [1965] 1 All ER 820 ....7.13
Surtees v Kingston Upon Thames BC [1991] 2 FLR 559 ....24.9.3
Suter v Suter [1987] 2 All ER 336 ....9.10
Szechter v Szechter [1971] 2 WLR 170 ....2.6.2

T (A Minor) (Blood Tests), Re [1993] 1 FLR 901 ....12.11
T (A Minor) (Care and Order: Conditions), Re (1994), The Times 5 May 16.10.4
Talbot v Talbot (1971) 115 SJ 870 ....4.7.2
Tallack v Tallack [1927] P 211 ....9.2
Taylor v Taylor [1967] P 25 ....3.10.1
Taylor v Taylor [1970] 2 All ER 609 ....4.3.2
Taylor v Taylor [1987] 1 FLR 142 ....10.4.1
Thain, Re [1926] Ch 676 ....13.2.1
Thomas v Fuller Brown [1988] 1 FLR 237 ....7.5.3
Thurlow v Thurlow [1975] 3 WLR 161 ....4.4.5
Thwaite v Thwaite [1981] 2 All ER 789 ....10.4.3
Torok v Torok [1973] 3 All ER 101 ....3.6
TSB Bank v Camfield (1994) The Times, 7 Dec 7.16
Twiname v Twiname [1992] 1 FLR 29 ....9.2

U (A Minor), Re [1993] 2 FLR 992 ....22.12
Ungurian v Lesnoff [1989] 3 WLR 840 ....6.3.6

V v B [1991] 1 FLR 266 ....11.18
Valier v Valier (1925) 133 LT 830 ....2.6.2
Vaughan v Vaughan [1973] 3 All ER 449 ....5.14.3
Vicary v Vicary [1992] 2 FLR 271 ....9.16; 10.33

W (An Infant), Re [1971] 2 WLR 1011 ....22.11.2
W (A Minor: Custody), Re (1982) 13 Fam Law 47 ....13.5.2
W (A Minor), Re [1983] 4 FLR 492 ....13.5.4
W (Minors: Surrogacy), Re [1991] 1 FLR 385 ....12.6
W (A Minor) (Medical Treatment), Re [1992] 3 WLR 758 ....12.27
W (A Minor), Re [1994] 2 FLR 441 ....13.12
W (Minors) (Sexual Abuse: Standard of Proof), Re [1994] 1 FLR 419 ....23.12.1
W v K (Proof of Paternity) [1988] 1 FLR 86 ....12.9
W v W (1992) 142 NLJ 15 ....9.11.1
Walker v Hall [1984] FLR 126 ....7.5.4
Walker v Walker [1978] 1 WLR 533 ....5.13
Walker and Walker v Harrison [1981] NZ Law 257 ....13.2.1
Walters v Lunt [1951] 2 All ER 645 ....24.4
Watson v Nickolaisen [1955] 2 QB 286 ....22.11.4

Way v Way [1950] P 71 .... 2.6.2
West Glamorgan CC v P (No 1) (1992) 156 JPN 602 .... 6.10.2
Whiston v Whiston [1944] 2 FCR 529 .... 9.17
Whiting v Whiting [1988] 1 WLR 565 .... 10.4.7
Williams & Glyn's Bank v Boland [1981] AC 487 .... 7.13.1
Wilson v Wilson [1973] 2 All ER 17 .... 4.7.3
Winnans v Winnans [1948] 2 All ER 862 .... 4.5.5
Worlock v Worlock [1994] 2 FLR 689 .... 10.3.4
Wroth v Tylor [1974] 2 WLR 405 .... 7.6

X (A Minor) (Adoption Details: Disclosure), Re [1994]3 WLR 327 .... 22.15
X (A Minor) (Wardship: Jurisdiction), Re [1975] 1 All ER 690 .... 21.11

Y, Re [1994] Fam Law 127 .... 13.15
Y v UK (1994) 17 EHRR 238 .... 23.9

Z, Re [1990] 2 QB 355 .... 24.6.1
Z v Z (Foreign Divorce: Financial Provision) [1992] 2 FLR 291 .... 9.20

Table of Statutes

Abortion Act 1967
   s 5(1) 23.5

Administration of Estates Act 1925 .... 6.8

Administration of Justice Act 1982 .... 3.9; 9.6
   s 1(2) .... 21(2)
   s 18 .... 6.7.2

Adoption Act 1958 .... 22.4

Adoption Act 1976 .... 1.2.3; 1.8.4; 12.15; 13.8; 22.1
   s 1(1) .... 22.3(1)
   s 1(2) 22.3.1
   s 1(4) 22.3.1
   s 3(1) 22.3.2
   s 3(4) 22.3.2
   s 7 .... 22.7.2
   s 11(1) 22.8
   s 12(1) 22.4
   s 12(5) 22.6
   s 12(6) 22.13.4
   s 12(7) 22.6
   s 13(1) 22.6.1
   s 13(2) 22.6.1
   s 13(3) 22.6.2
   s 14(1) 22.4
   s 14(1B) 22.4.1; 22.5
   s 14(3) 22.5
   s 15(1) 22.4.2; 22.4.3
   s 15(3) 22.4.4
   s 16(1) 22.10; 22.11
   s 16(2) 22.12
   s 16(2)(a) 22.11.1
   s 16(2)(b) 22.11.2
   s 16(2)(c) 22.11.3
   s 16(2)(d) 22.11.4
   s 16(2)(e) 22.11.5
   s 16(2)(f) 22.11.6
   s 16(4) 22.10
   s 16(5) 22.11.6
   s 18 .... 22.10; 22.12.2
   s 18(1) 22.12
   s 18(2) 22.12
   s 18(5) 22.12.2
   s 18(7) 22.12.1
   s 20(3) 22.12.2
   s 22(1A) 22.8.3
   s 25 .... 22.13.3
   s 27(1) 22.10
   s 30(3) 22.13.3
   s 32 .... 19.3.2
   s 39(1) 22.14.1; 22.14.2
   s 39(1)(a) 12.20
   s 39(2) 22.14.1
   s 39(3) 22.14.1
   s 39(4) 22.14.1
   s 42(1) 22.14.2
   s 42(2) 22.14.2
   s 47(1) 22.14.4
   s 50(1) 22.15
   s 51A 22.15
   s 52(1) 22.14.5
   s 57 .... 22.8.2
   s 57A 22.8.2
   s 57(1) 22.8.2
   s 72(1) 22.6; 22.8.1

Adoption of Children Act 1926 .... 22.1

Affiliation Proceedings Act 1957 .... 12.16

Age of Marriage Act 1929 .... 2.3.2

Attachment of Earnings Act 1971 .... 8.5

Bettings and Loans (Infants) Act 1892
   s 5 .... 24.8.3

Births and Deaths Registration Act 1953
   s 2 .... 12.12

British Nationality Act 1981
   s 1(5) 22.14.3
   s 1(6) 22.7; 22.14.3
   s 50(9) 12.22.1

Child Abduction Act 1984 .... 12.25
   s 1 .... 23.14; 23.14.1
   s 1(4) 23.14.1
   s 1(4A) 23.14.1
   s 1(5) 23.14.1
   s 1(5A) 23.14.1

Child Abduction and
   Custody Act 1985 .... 21.9.3; 23.14.2

Child Care Act 1980 .... 14.6
   s 1 .... 14.3
   s 13(2) 14.6.4
   s 21A 15.6
   s 21A(1) 15.6
   s 27 .... 15.2
   s 29 .... 15.2
   s 69 .... 15.2
   s 74 .... 18.11
   s 75 .... 18.11

Children Act 1975 .... 11.1; 20.2
   s 37(1) 22.5
   Sch 3 .... 2.3.5
   Sch 12, para 31 .... 4.8

Children Act 1989 .... 1.2.3; 1.3; 1.8.3; 2.2.1;
                               2.9; 5.14.6; 11.1; 11.2; 12.2

s 1	15.6; 16.11; 22.16
s 1(1)	11.2; 13.2; 13.2.3; 16.5; 17.2.3; 20.11.3; 21.4.4
s 1(2)	13.3; 16.5; 16.8
s 1(3)	13.5; 16.5; 17.2.3; 20.4.4
s 1(3)(a)	13.5.1
s 1(3)(b)	13.5.2
s 1(3)(c)	13.5.3
s 1(3)(d)	13.5.4
s 1(3)(e)	13.5.5
s 1(3)(f)	13.5.6
s 1(3)(g)	13.5.7; 16.5
s 1(4)	13.5; 17.2.3
s 1(4)(b)	16.5
s 1(5)	13.4; 16.5
s 2(1)	12.24
s 2(2)	12.22.2; 12.24
s 2(3)	12.25
s 2(4)	12.25
s 2(6)	12.25
s 2(7)	12.25
s 2(9)	12.25
s 3(1)	12.23
s 3(4)(a)	8.2
s 3(5)	12.25
s 4	13.8; 13.15; 13.16
s 5	13.8; 13.16; 20.3
s 5(1)	20.4; 20.4.1; 20.4.3
s 5(1)(a)	11.3
s 5(2)	20.4; 20.4.2; 20.4.5
s 5(3)	20.5; 20.7; 20.8.1; 20.8.2; 20.8.3
s 5(4)	20.5; 20.7; 20.8.1; 20.8.2; 20.8.3; 20.11.1
s 5(5)	20.6
s 5(6)	20.3; 20.7; 20.10
s 5(7)	20.9
s 5(8)	20.9
s 5(9)	20.9
s 5(11)	20.3
s 5(12)	20.3
s 5(13)	20.4
s 6	13.8; 20.3
s 6(1)	20.8.1
s 6(2)	20.8.2
s 6(3)	20.8.3
s 6(4)	20.8.3
s 6(5)	20.7
s 6(7)	20.11.3
s 7	20.11.3
s 7(1)	13.6
s 7(3)	13.6
s 8	13.7; 13.9; 13.9.1; 13.9.2; 13.10; 13.11; 13.16; 13.16.1; 13.16.2; 15.11.5; 20.4.7; 20.11.3; 22.5; 23.2
s 8(1)	13.12; 13.13; 13.14; 13.15
s 8(3)	13.8
s 8(4)	13.8
s 9	13.14
s 9(1)	13.10
s 9(2)	13.10; 13.12
s 9(3)	13.9.2; 19.2
s 9(5)	13.13
s 9(6)	13.10; 13.12
s 9(7)	13.10; 13.12
s 10	13.7; 13.9
s 10(1)	13.8; 13.9.2; 20.4.7
s 10(2)	13.8
s 10(4)	13.9
s 10(5)	12.25; 13.9.1
s 10(8)	13.9.2
s 10(9)	13.9.3
s 11(1)	13.3; 13.11
s 11(4)	13.15
s 11(5)	13.15
s 11(6)	13.12
s 11(7)	13.7; 13.11; 13.12
s 12(1)	13.15
s 13(1)	13.15
s 14	13.15
s 15	11.2; 11.3; 11.5; 11.7; 13.16
s 15(1)	11.1
s 15(2)	11.2; 15.2
s 16	13.16.1
s 16(1)	13.16.2
s 16(2)	13.16.2
s 16(5)	13.16.1
s 16(6)	13.16.1
s 17	15.14
s 17(1)	14.3
s 17(2)	14.3
s 17(3)	14.3
s 17(6)	14.4
s 17(7)	14.4
s 17(8)	14.4
s 17(9)	14.4
s 17(10)	14.2
s 17(11)	14.2
s 18	14.5; 15.14
s 18(1)	14.5.1
s 18(2)	14.5.1
s 18(3)	14.5.1
s 18(4)	14.5
s 18(5)	14.5.2
s 18(6)	14.5.2
s 18(7)	14.5.2
s 19(1)	14.5.3
s 19(5)	14.5.3
s 19(6)	14.5.3
s 19(7)	14.5.3
s 20	14.6; 14.8
s 20(1)	14.6; 14.6.1
s 20(2)	14.6.1

Table of Statutes

s 20(3)	14.6.1
s 20(5)	14.6.1
s 20(6)	14.6.2
s 20(7)	14.6.3; 14.6.4
s 20(8)	14.6.4; 15.7
s 20(9)	14.6.4
s 20(11)	15.7
s 21	14.8
s 21(1)	14.7
s 21(2)	14.7.1
s 21(3)	14.7.2
s 22(2)	15.2
s 22(3)	14.8; 14.11
s 22(4)	14.8; 14.11
s 22(6)	14.8; 14.9
s 23	19.2
s 13(1)	14.10
s 23(2)(a)	14.12; 19.2
s 23(4)	19.2
s 23(7)	14.13
s 23(8)	14.13
s 24	15.2; 15.2; 15.5
s 24(1)	14.8; 15.2
s 24(2)	15.2.1
s 24(4)	15.2
s 24(4)	15.2.2
s 24(5)	15.2.2
s 24(6)	15.3
s 24(7)	15.3
s 24(8)	15.3.1
s 24(9)	15.3.2
s 24(11)	15.4
s 25	14.9; 15.6; 15.6.1; 15.6.4
s 25(1)	15.6
s 25(2)(a)	15.6.1
s 25(2)(b)	15.6.1
s 25(3)	15.6.2
s 25(4)	15.6.2
s 25(5)	15.6.3
s 25(6)	15.6.1
s 25(8)	15.6.4
s 25(9)	15.7
s 26	15.9
s 26(1)	15.9.1
s 26(3)	15.10.1
s 26(4)	15.10.2
s 26(7)	15.10.2
s 27	15.12
s 27(1)	15.12
s 27(3)	15.12
s 28(1)	15.13
s 29(1)	15.14
s 29(2)	15.14
s 29(3)	15.14
s 29(5)	15.14
s 31	13.8; 13.16; 16.1; 16.4
s 31(1)	16.3; 16.4.2; 16.6; 16.10.4; 16.11
s 31(b)	16.11
s 31(2)	16.5; 16.6; 16.7.1; 16.18
s 31(3)	16.4
s 31(4)	16.4
s 31(5)	16.4
s 31(6)	16.4.2
s 31(7)	16.4.1
s 31(8)	16.4.3
s 31(9)	16.2; 16.10.4
s 31(10)	13.4.4; 16.7.2; 16.10.4
s 31(11)	16.10.4
s 32(1)	13.3; 16.8
s 33	16.9
s 33(1)	16.9
s 33(2)	16.9
s 33(3)	16.9.1
s 33(4)	16.9.1
s 33(5)	16.9.1
s 33(6)(a)	16.9.2
s 33(7)	16.9.3
s 33(9)	16.9.1
s 34	13.8; 16.5; 17.2.4; 17.12.3
s 34(1)	16.10
s 34(2)	16.10.1
s 34(3)	16.10.1
s 34(4)	16.10.2
s 34(5)	16.10.3
s 35(1)	16.12
s 36	13.8; 13.16
s 36(1)	16.15
s 36(3)	16.15
s 36(4)	16.15
s 36(5)	16.15
s 36(6)	16.15
s 36(7)	16.15.1
s 36(8)	16.15.2
s 36(9)	16.15.2
s 37	16.3; 17.17
s 37(1)	16.17; 16.18
s 37(2)	16.17
s 37(6)	16.17
s 38	16.3; 16.18
s 38(2)	16.18
s 38(4)	16.18.2
s 38(5)	16.18.2
s 38(6)	16.18.1
s 39(1)	16.19
s 39(2)	16.19
s 39(3)	16.19
s 39(4)	16.19
s 40	16.20
s 40(1)	16.20
s 40(4)	16.20
s 41(1)	16.21
s 41(3)	16.21.1

Section	Reference
s 41(10)	16.21.2
s 42	16.1
s 43	13.16; 17.1; 17.3
s 43(1)	17.2; 17.2.3
s 43(3)	17.2.6
s 43(4)	17.2.6
s 43(5)	17.2.5
s 43(6)	17.2; 17.2.7
s 43(7)	17.2.7
s 43(8)	17.2.8
s 43(9)	17.2.9
s 43(10)	17.2.9
s 43(11)	17.2.4
s 44	13.16; 17.4
s 44(1)(a)	17.6
s 44(1)(b)	17.7
s 44(1)(c)	17.8
s 44(2)(a)	17.8
s 44(2)(b)	17.7
s 44(3)	17.9.2
s 44(4)	17.11.1; 17.14
s 44(5)	17.11; 17.11.2
s 44(6)	17.12; 17.12.1; 17.12.2
s 44(7)	17.12.1
s 44(9)	17.12.2
s 44(10)	17.13
s 44(13)	17.2.3
s 44(16)	17.11.3
s 45	17.4
s 45(1)	17.14
s 45(2)	17.14
s 45(9)	17.15
s 45(10)	17.15
s 46	17.16
s 46(1)	17.16
s 46(2)	17.16
s 46(5)	17.16.3
s 46(6)	17.16.3
s 46(7)	17.16.2
s 46(9)	17.16.2
s 47	17.17
s 47(1)	17.17
s 47(1)(b)	17.17
s 47(6)	17.17
s 48(1)	17.18
s 48(2)	17.18
s 48(3)	17.18
s 48(7)	17.18
s 49(1)	17.19
s 49(2)	17.19
s 50(1)	17.19.1
s 50(3)	17.19.3
s 50(4)	17.19.2
s 50(9)	17.19.3
s 51(1)	17.20
s 52	17.1
s 52(3)(c)	17.10
s 53	18.1
s 53(1)	18.2
s 53(2)	18.2
s 53(3)	18.2.1
s 53(4)	18.2.2
s 53(5)	18.2.2
s 54(1)	18.3.3
s 55(3)	18.3.4
s 56(1)	18.3.5
s 56(3)	18.3.5
s 57(1)	18.3.6
s 57(5)	18.3.6
s 58	18.1
s 59	18.1
s 59(1)	18.4.1
s 59(2)	18.4.2
s 60	18.5.1
s 60(1)	18.5
s 60(3)	18.4
s 61	18.6
s 61(1)	18.6
s 61(2)	18.6
s 61(3)	18.6
s 62	18.1
s 62(1)	18.7
s 62(3)	18.7
s 62(6)	18.7
s 63	18.1
s 63(1)	18.8.1
s 63(3)	18.8
s 63(6)	18.8
s 63(8)	18.8
s 63(10)	18.8.1
s 64(1)	18.10
s 65	18.1
s 65(1)	18.8.2
s 65(2)	18.8.2
s 65(4)	18.8.2
s 66	19.1
s 66(1)	19.3
s 66(2)	19.3.2
s 66(4)	19.3
s 67(1)	19.5
s 67(2)	19.5
s 67(3)	19.5; 19.11
s 67(5)	19.5
s 68	18.8.2
s 68(1)	19.9
s 68(2)	19.9
s 68(3)	19.9
s 68(4)	19.9
s 69(2)	19.10
s 69(3)	19.10
s 69(4)	19.10
s 70	19.1; 19.11

s 71(1)	19.2.1; 19.12.3; 19.12.4
s 71(2)	19.12.2
s 71(4)	19.12.2
s 71(5)	19.12.2
s 71(7)	19.12.3
s 71(8)	19.12.3
s 71(11)	19.12.3
s 71(13)	19.12.2
s 71(15)	19.12.1
s 72	19.14
s 72(1)	19.13
s 72(2)(a)	19.13
s 72(2)(b)	19.13
s 72(2)(c)	19.13
s 73	19.14
s 75	19.14
s 75(3)	19.14
s 76(1)	19.15
s 76(7)	19.15
s 78(4)	19.16
s 78(5)	19.16
s 78(6)	19.16
s 80	18.11
s 80(1)	18.11
s 80(6)	18.11
s 80(10)	18.11
s 81(1)	18.12
s 84	15.11; 15.11.1; 18.11
s 84(1)	15.11.1; 18.13
s 84(2)	18.13
s 84(3)	18.13
s 84(4)	15.11.1
s 87(1)	18.14
s 87(4)	18.14
s 87A	18.14
s 91(2)	13.12
s 91(4)	21.12
s 91(7)	20.11.2
s 91(8)	20.11.2
s 91(14)	13.9.2
s 92	16.3
s 92(1)	1.8.1
s 94(1)	16.14.4
s 96	24.7.1
s 96(1)	24.7.1
s 96(2)	24.7.1
s 96(3)	24.7.1
s 98(1)	17.21
s 100	21.12
s 100(1)	21.14
s 100(2)	13.13; 21.14.1
s 100(2)(c)	21.9.3; 21.12
s 100(3)	21.13; 21.14.2
s 100(4)	21.14.2
s 100(5)	21.14.2
s 105	2.3.5
s 105(1)	8.3.2; 13.5.5; 14.2; 18.4; 19.3.1; 20.4.6
Sch 1	11.1; 11.3; 11.7; 13.8
Sch 1 para 1	11.2; 11.3; 11.4.1; 11.7.2; 11.7.3; 11.4.4
Sch 2 para 2	11.3; 11.7.1
Sch 1 para 2(3)	11.3
Sch 1 para 2(4)	11.3
Sch 1 para 3	11.7.4
Sch 1 para 4(1)	11.6
Sch 1 para 4(2)	11.6
Sch 1 para 4(3)	11.3
Sch 1 para 4(4)	11.3
Sch 1 para 5(1)	11.7.2
Sch 1 para 5(6)	11.7.5
Sch 1 para 6	11.7.6
Sch 1 para 7	11.7.6
Sch 1 para 9	11.7.7
Sch 2 para 3	14.3.2
Sch 2 para 4	14.3.3
Sch 2 para 5	14.3.4
Sch 2 para 6	14.3.5
Sch 2 para 7	14.3.6
Sch 2 para 8	14.3.7
Sch 2 para 9	14.3.8
Sch 2 para 10	14.3.8
Sch 2 para 12	14.12
Sch 2 para 14	14.14
Sch 2 para 15	14.15
Sch 2 para 15(3)	14.15.1
Sch 2 para 15(4)	14.15.1
Sch 2 para 16(2)	14.15.2
Sch 2 para 17(1)	14.15.3
Sch 2 para 17(5)	14.15.3
Sch 2 para 19(1)	14.15.4
Sch 2 para 21	15.15
Sch 2 para 21(3)	15.15
Sch 2 para 22(5)	15.15.1
Sch 2 para 23(1)	15.15.2
Sch 2 para 24(1)	15.15.2
Sch 3 para 1	16.14
Sch 3 para 3(1)	16.14.2
Sch 3 para 5(1)	16.14.3
Sch 3 para 5(5)	16.14.3
Sch 3 para 9(1)	16.14.1
Sch 3 para 12(1)	16.16.1
Sch 3 para 12(2)	16.16.1
Sch 3 para 15(1)	16.16.2
Sch 3 para 15(2)	16.16.2
Sch 3 para 15(4)	16.16.2
Sch 3 para 15(6)	16.16.2
Sch 3 para 17	16.16.2
Sch 3 para 18(1)	16.16.3
Sch 3 para 18(2)	16.16.3
Sch 3 para 19	16.16.4
Sch 4 para 1(1)	18.3
Sch 4 para 1(8)	18.3
Sch 4 para 2(3)	18.3

Sch 4 para 3(1)	18.3.1
Sch 4 para 3(4)	18.3.1
Sch 4 para 3(15)	18.3.1
Sch 4 para 4(2)	18.3.2
Sch 5 para 1(1)	18.5.1
Sch 5 para 1(4)	18.5.1
Sch 5 para 1(5)	18.5.1
Sch 5 para 2(1)	18.5.2
Sch 5 para 2(3)	18.5.2
Sch 5 para 3(1)	18.5.3
Sch 5 para 3(4)	18.5.3
Sch 5 para 7(2)	18.5.4
Sch 5 para 7(3)	18.5.4
Sch 6 para 1(1)	18.9
Sch 6 para 2(2)	18.9.1
Sch 6 para 2(3)	18.9.1
Sch 6 para 3(2)	18.9.1
Sch 6 para 4(1)	18.9.2
Sch 6 para 4(4)	18.9.2
Sch 6 para 8	18.9.2
Sch 6 para 10	18.10
Sch 8 para 1	19.3.2
Sch 8 para 2(1)	19.3.2
Sch 8 para 6	19.4
Sch 8 para 7(1)	19.6
Sch 8 para 7(2)(e)	19.6
Sch 8 para 8(1)	19.7
Sch 8 para 8(2)	19.7
Sch 8 para 8(4)	19.7
Sch 8 para 10	19.8
Sch 9	19.1
Sch 9 para 2	19.12.4
Sch 9 para 2(4)	19.12.4
Sch 10	22.4.1; 22.11; 23.11.7
Sch 10 para 4	22.4; 22.5
Sch 10 para 5(2)	22.11.3
Sch 10 para 6	22.12
Sch 10 para 6(2)	22.12.2
Sch 10 para 3	22.12.1
Sch 10 para 8(2)	22.12.2
Sch 10 para 10(1)	22.8.3
Sch 10 para 17	22.13.3
Sch 10 para 18(4)	22.8.3
Sch 10 para 21	22.15
Sch 10 para 24(1)	22.8.2
Sch 10 para 25	22.8.2
Sch 11	1.8.4; 16.3
Sch 12 Para 6	12.12
Sch 13 para 45(2)	21.12
Sch 15	13.7; 22.5

Children and Young Persons Act 1933 ..... 22.2; 24.2.2
s 12	2.11.4
s 1(1)	23.7
s 1(2)	23.8
s 18	24.2.1
s 21	24.2.1
s 34A	24.5.1
s 39	24.2.2
s 49	24.6
s 53(2)	24.4
s 55	24.5
s 55(1)	24.5; 24.5.2
s 55(1B)	24.5.2

Children and Young Persons Act 1963
s 3	16.7.5
s 16	24.4
s 28	17.4

Children and Young Persons Act 1969 ..... 24.2.2; 24.4
s 1(2)	23.12
s 7(7)(b)	16.4
s 28(2)	17.16

Children and Young Persons (Protection from Tobacco) Act 1991 ..... 24.1

Child Support Act 1991 ..... 1.2.3; 2.9; 9.10; 11.1; 11.8; 11.10; 12.2
s 1	11.12
s 1(1)	11.12
s 1(2)	11.12
s 1(3)	11.12
s 2	11.13
s 3(1)	11.11
s 3(2)	11.11
s 3(3)	11.11
s 3(5)	11.11
s 3(6)	11.11
s 6(1)	11.17
s 8	11.8
s 8(6)	11.8
s 8(7)	11.8
s 8(8)	11.8
s 8(10)	11.8
s 9(1)	11.17
s 9(2)	11.17
s 9(4)	11.17
s 13	11.14
s 16(1)	11.20.1
s 16(3)	11.20.1
s 17(1)	11.20.2
s 17(2)	11.20.2
s 18(1)	11.20.3
s 18(2)	11.20.3
s 18(7)	11.20.3
s 19(1)	11.20.4
s 20(1)	11.20.5
s 22(1)	11.20.6
s 24(1)	11.20.6
s 24(2)	11.20.6

s 25(1)	11.20.6
s 25(2)	11.20.6
s 26	11.15
s 27	11.15
s 29	11.19
s 31	11.19.1
s 35	11.19.2
s 40	11.19; 11.19.3
s 40(7)	11.19.3
s 50	11.14
s 54	11.11; 12.3
s 55	11.8
s 55(1)	11.11
s 55(2)	11.11
Sch 1	11.16
Sch 3	11.20.5

Chronically Sick and Disabled Persons Act 1970 .... 14.3.2

Civil Evidence Act 1968
s 11	4.3.2
s 12	11.15; 12.9
s 12(1)	4.3.2

Congenital Disabilities (Civil Liability) Act 1976 .... 24.10

County Courts Act 1984
s 38	10.7
s 38(1)	5.16

Courts and Legal Services Act 1990
s 13	5.16
s 20	18.3
Sch 16 para 13	15.5
Sch 16 para 19	17.15
Sch 16 para 23	16.14.4

Criminal Justice Act 1988
s 32A	24.6.2
s 33A	24.6
s 34(2)	24.6.2

Criminal Justice Act 1991
s 52(2)	24.6
s 54(7)	24.6.2
s 56	24.5.1
s 57	24.5.2
s 58	24.5.3
Sch 13	24.4

Criminal Justice and Public Order Act 1994
s 1	24.4
s.16	24.4
s 19	18.5.1
s 24	14.7.1

s 32(2)	24.6.2
s 49	24.6
s 50	24.6.2
s 84	23.11.8
s 142	23.11.1

Deregulation and Contracting Out Act 1994
s 38	18.14

Divorce Reform Act 1969 .... 3.2; 3.3.6; 3.8

Domestic Proceedings and Magistrates' Courts Act 1978 .... 5.12; 5.14.6; 5.15; 8.2; 8.3; 8.6; 11.2; 13.8
s 1	8.3.1; 8.3.6; 8.7
s 2	8.3.6
s 2(1)	8.3.6
s 2(3)	8.3.6
s 4(1)	8.3.6
s 5	8.3.6
s 6	8.4; 8.7
s 6(2)	8.4
s 6(9)	8.4
s 16(2)	5.15
s 16(3)	5.15
s 16(7)	5.15.2
s 18(1)	5.15.1
s 26	8.3.5
s 27	8.3
s 30(1)	8.3
s 30(3)	8.3
s 63	8.7
s 75	8.3.6

Domestic Violence and Matrimonial Proceedings Act 1976 .... 1.3; 1.8.3; 2.10; 5.12; 5.14; 5.14.3; 5.14.6; 13.8
s 1 (1)	5.14
s 1(2)	5.14.1
s 2(1)	5.14.4
s 2(3)	5.14.4

Domicile and Matrimonial Proceedings Act 1973 .... 5.4
s 5(2)	3.4; 5.4
s 5(3)	2.8
s 5(4)	3.10.2
s 6(3)	3.4
s 5(5)	5.4

Education (No 2) Act 1968
s 47	23.9

Education Act 1993
s 292	18.8

s 293	23.9
Employment Act 1989	**24.2; 24.3**
s 9	24.2.2; 24.2.3
Sch 3	24.2.1
Factories Act 1961	
s 167	24.2.1
Family Law Act 1986	**1.8.3; 21.7; 23.14.4**
s 1(1)(d)	21.9.3
s 2	21.9.3
s 3	21.9.3
s 33	23.14.4
s 35	23.14.4
s 37	23.14.4
s 46	4.9
s 51	4.9
s 56	11.15; 12.21
Family Law Reform Act 1969	
s 7	22.14
s 20(1)	12.10
s 20(2)	12.10
s 21(1)	12.10
s 26	12.9
Family Law Reform Act 1987	**12.14; 12.21**
s 1	12.15
s 1(1)	12.15
s 1(2)	12.15
s 1(3)	12.15
s 1(4)	12.15
s 2(1)	20.10
s 2(3)	20.10
s 12	12.9
s 15	11.1
s 17	11.1
s 18	6.8.6
s 24	12.12
Fatal Accidents Act 1976	2.10
Guardianship Act 1975	20.2
Guardianship of Minors Act 1971	10.4; 20.2
Housing Act 1985	
s 17	5.17.1
s 58(1)	5.17.1
s 58(3)	5.17.1
s 59(1)	5.17.2
s 60(1)	5.17.3
s 62	5.17.4
s 65	5.17.2
s 70	5.17.4
s 75	5.17.2
s 113(1)	1.5.4

Human Fertilisation and Embryology Act 1988	**12.2; 12.3; 22.4.4**
s 2(3)	12.6
s 5	12.13
s 27(1)	12.6
s 28	11.11; 12.7.2
s 28(2)	12.7.2
s 28(3)	12.7.2
s 28(4)	12.7.2
s 28(6)	12.7.1
s 29	11.11
s 30	11.15; 12.8
s 30(1)	12.8
s 30(2)	12.8
s 30(3)	12.8
s 30(4)	12.8
s 30(7)	12.8
s 31(1)	12.13
s 31(2)	12.13
s 31(7)	12.13
s 36	12.5.2
s 37	23.5
Sch 3 para 5	12.7.1
Sch 4 para 4	24.4
Indecency with Children Act 1960	23.11.6
Infanticide Act 1938	23.5
Infant Life (Preservation) Act 1929	**23.8; 24.8.3**
s 1(1)	23.5
Infants Relief Act 1874	24.8; 24.8.3
Inheritance (Provision for Family and Dependants) Act 1975	**3.9; 6.7; 6.9**
s 1(1)	6.9
s 1(1)(a)	6.9.1; 6.9.2
s 1(1)(b)	6.9.1
s 1(1)(c)	6.9.1
s 1(1)(d)	6.9.1
s 1(1)(e)	2.10; 6.9.1; 6.10
s 1(2)(a)	6.9.2
s 1(2)(b)	6.9.1
s 1(3)	2.10; 6.9.1
s 2	6.9; 6.9.3; 6.9.4
s 3(1)	6.9.4
s 4	6.9.3
s 9	6.7.1
s 18	6.7.2
s 25(1)	6.9
Insolvency Act 1986	
s 336	7.15
s 336(2)	7.15
s 336(4)	7.15.1

Table of Statutes

s 336(5) 7.15.2
s 337 ....7.15.3
s 337(1) 7.15.3
s 337(2) 7.15.3

Interpretation Act 1978
s 5 ....9.20
s 6(c) 20.4.3
s 16 ....10.4
Sch 1 ....9.20

Intoxicating Substances (Supply) Act 1985
s 1(1) 24.1

Land Charges Act 1972
s 2(7) 7.12
s 4(8) 7.12

Land Registration Act 1925
s 70 ....7.13
s 70(1)(g) 7.13; 7.13.1

Law of Property Act 1925
s 1(6) 6.1.5
s 25 ....7.14
s 30 ....7.14.1; 10.4.1
s 52 ....7.2
s 52(2) 7.2
s 53(1)(a) 7.2
s 53(l)(b) 7.2
s 53(3) 7.2
s 205(1)(xx) 6.1.1

Law of Property (Miscellaneous Provisions) Act 1989 ....7.2

Law of Property (Miscellaneous Provisions) Act 1994 ....6.8

Law Reform (Married Women and Tortfeasors) Act 1935 ....6.2.2

Law Reform (Miscellaneous Provisions) Act 1970
s 1 ....2.1.5
s 3(1) 2.1.5

Law Reform (Parent and Child) (Scotland) Act 1986 ....11.15

Legal Aid Act 1988 ....3.8

Legitimacy Act 1976
s 1 ....12.15
s 1(1) 12.17
s 1(3) 12.17

s 1(4) 12.17
s 2 ....12.19
s 8 ....12.19
s 10 ....12.15

Licensing Act 1964
s 169 ....24.1

Local Government Act 1978 ....15.11.2

Magistrates' Courts Act 1980 ....11.2
s 24(1) 24.4
s 29 ....24.4
s 59 ....8.5
s 75 ....8.3.6
s 127(1) 8.3
s 150(1) 15.15.2

Maintenance Enforcement Act 1991 ....10.6; 10.6.2
s 2 ....8.5

Marriage Act 1949 ....2.5.1
s 1 ....2.3.5
s 1(1)(bb) 2.2.3
s 2 ....2.3.2
s 3 ....2.2.1
s 15 ....2.2.2
s 26 ....2.2.3
s 28 ....2.2.2
s 33 ....2.2.2
s 45 (2) 2.2.3
s 46 ....2.2.3
s 46B 2.2.3
Sch 1 ....2.3.5; 22.14.4

Marriage Act 1965 ....2.2.3

Marriage Act 1994 ....2.2.3

Marriage (Prohibited Degrees of Relationship) Act 1986 ....2.3.5

Marriage (Registrar General's Licence) Act 1970 ....2.2.2

Married Women (Restraint Upon Anticipation) Act 1949 ....6.2.2

Married Women's Property Act 1870 ....6.2.2

Married Women's Property Act 1882 ....6.2.2

Married Women's Property Act 1964 ....6.3.1

Matrimonial and Family Proceedings Act 1984 ....3.3.6; 9.20; 13.8
s 1 ....3.5.3
s 3 ....9.9; 9.19

Section	References
s 6(3)	10.4.4
s 7	10.3.1
s 9	8.6
s 12(1)	9.20
s 12(2)	9.20
s 13(1)	9.20
s 13(2)	9.20
s 18(2)	9.20
s 27	9.20
s 38	21.5
s 38(2)(b)	21.2

Matrimonial Causes Act 1857 ..... 1.1.2; 2.1.1; 3.3.5; 5.1; 6.2.2

Matrimonial Causes Act 1973 ..... 1.2.3; 1.3; 3.2; 3.3.6; 11.2; 13.8

Section	References
s 1(1)	3.5.2; 4.1
s 1(2)	3.5.2; 4.1; 4.7; 4.8
s 1(2)(a)	4.3; 4.3.3; 4.3.4
s 1(2)(b)	4.4; 4.4.1; 4.4.5; 4.4.6
s 1(2)(c)	4.5
s 1(2)(d)	4.6; 4.6.1; 4.8
s 1(2)(e)	4.6.1; 4.7
s 1(3)	4.1.1
s 1(5)	3.6
s 2(1)	4.3.4; 4.8
s 2(1)(b)	4.1.2
s 2(3)	4.4.6
s 2(5)	4.5.4; 4.6
s 3	3.5.3
s 5	4.7.1; 4.8
s 8	4.8
s 8(1)(b)	3.7
s 9(1)	3.7
s 10	4.8
s 10(1)	4.8
s 10(2)	4.7.3
s 10(3)	4.7.3
s 11	2.5
s 11(b)	2.3.4
s 11(c)	2.3.3
s 12	2.6
s 12(a)	2.6
s 12(b)	2.6
s 12(c)	2.6.2
s 12(d)	2.6.2
s 12(e)	2.6.4
s 12(f)	2.6.4
s 13	2.7
s 13(1)	2.7
s 13(2)	2.7
s 16	2.6; 12.18
s 17	5.1; 5.2
s 17(2)	5.3
s 18(1)	5.6
s 18(2)	5.6
s 19	2.3.4
s 19(3)	3.10.1
s 22	5.7.2; 8.3; 9.2.3; 9.4; 9.10
s 23(1)(a)	9.5; 9.11; 9.19
s 23(1)(b)	9.11; 9.19
s 23(1)(c)	9.6; 9.11
s 23(3)(c)	9.6
s 23(6)	9.6
s 24	9.3; 9.7; 9.10; 9.11; 10.3.1; 10.4.5
s 24(1)(a)	9.7.1
s 24(1)(b)	9.7.2
s 24(1)(c)	9.7.3
s 24(1)(d)	9.7.3
s 24A	5.7.2; 9.3; 9.11; 10.3.1; 10.6
s 24A(1)	9.8; 9.8.1
s 24A(2)	9.8
s 24A(3)	9.8
s 24A(5)	9.8; 9.8.1
s 24A(6)	9.8.2
s 25	9.1.1; 9.1.2; 9.9; 9.11.2; 10.3.3; 10.4.4
s 25(1)	9.1.2; 9.8.2; 9.10; 10.3.2
s 25(2)(a)	9.11; 9.11.1; 10.5
s 25(2)(b)	9.12; 10.5
s 25(2)(c)	9.13
s 25(2)(d)	9.14
s 25(2)(e)	9.15
s 25(2)(f)	9.16
s 25(2)(g)	9.17
s 25(2)(h)	9.18
s 25A	9.19
s 25A(1)	9.19
s 25A(2)	9.19
s 25A(3)	9.19
s 27	8.2; 8.7; 8.7.1; 10.3.1
s 27(2)	8.7
s 27(5)	8.7.1
s 27(7)	8.7.1
s 28(1)	9.5.1
s 28(1A)	10.4.2
s 31	8.7.2; 10.4; 10.4.5; 10.4.6
s 31(5)	10.4.2
s 31(7)	10.4.4; 10.4.7
s 31(7)(a)	10.4.7
s 32	10.6.3
s 33	10.6.4
s 33A	10.3.1
s 34	10.2.1
s 34(1)	8.8; 10.2.1
s 35	8.8; 10.2.2
s 35(2)	8.8; 10.2.2
s 37	9.2.1; 10.7; 10.7.1
s 37(2)(a)	10.7.1
s 37(2)(b)	10.7.1
s 37(5)	10.7.1
s 41	4.8; 5.7.1

Statute	Reference
Matrimonial Homes Act 1967	7.6
Matrimonial Homes Act 1983	5.12; 5.13; 5.14.2; 5.18; 7.6; 7.15
s 1	5.13; 7.9.1; 7.9.2; 7.15; 7.15.1; 7.15.3
s 1(1)	5.13; 7.12
s 1(2)	7.9
s 1(3)	5.14.2; 7.9.1
s 1(4)	5.13; 7.9.2
s 1(5)	7.9.3
s 1(10)	5.13; 7.7
s 2(4)	5.13
s 9(1)	7.10
s 10(1)	7.7
Matrimonial Homes and Property Act 1981	
s 7	5.7.2; 9.8
Matrimonial Proceedings (Magistrates' Courts) Act 1960	8.3
Matrimonial Proceedings and Property Act 1970	3.3.6; 9.1
s 37	6.3.1
s 41	8.1
Mental Health Act 1983	2.6.2
s 1	13.8
s 4	2.6.3
s 9	13.8
Mines and Quarries Act 1954	24.2.2
Minors' Contracts Act 1987	24.8.3
s 2	24.8.3
s 3	24.8.3
National Assistance Act 1948	14.1
National Health Service Act 1977	14.1
Nurseries and Child Minders Regulation Act 1948	19.1
Occupiers' Liability Act 1957	24.9.1
Occupiers' Liability Act 1984	
s 1(3)	24.9.2
Offences Against the Person Act 1861	
s 18	5.11
s 20	5.11
s 57	2.3.4
Police and Criminal Evidence Act 1984	
s 38	14.7.2
Protection of Children Act 1978	23.11.8
Protection of Children (Tobacco) Act 1986	24.1
Registered Homes (Amendment) Act 1991	
s 1	18.14
s 2(6)	18.5
Sale of Goods Act 1979	
s 3(3)	24.8.1
Settled Land Act 1925	
s 36(6)	6.1.5
Sexual Offences Act 1956	
s 1	23.11.1
s 5	23.11.3
s 6(1)	23.11.4
s 6(2)	23.11.4
s 6(3)	23.11.4
s 10(1)	23.11.2
s 14	23.11.5
s 15	23.11.5
s 19(1)	23.11.7
s 20(1)	23.11.7
s 28	12.26.3
Sexual Offences Act 1993	
s 1	23.1.1
Social Security Act 1986	
s 26	20.10
s 26(3)	8.2
Social Security Administration Act 1992	
s 78(6)	8.2
s 106(1)	8.11
s 106(2)	8.11
s 167	8.12
s 169	8.12
Social Security Contributions and Benefits Act 1992	
s 77	20.12
s 77(2)(a)	20.12
s 124	8.10.1
s 124(1)	8.10.1
s 124(2)	8.10.1
s 125(1)	8.10.1; 8.10.2
s 125(3)	8.10.2
s 125(4)	8.10.2
s 128(1)	8.13
s 128(2)	8.13.1
s 128(3)	8.13.1
s 128(4)	8.13.2
s 130(1)	8.16
s 130(3)	8.16
s 134(1)	8.16

s 137(1) 1.3.4; 8.10.1
s 138 ....8.12
s 138(1) 8.12.1
s 138(2) 8.12.1
s 141 ....8.14
s 142(1) 8.14.1
s 143(1) 8.14.2
s 145(1) 8.14.3
s 145(2) 8.14.3
Sch 9 para 1 ....8.14.4
Sch 9 para 3 ....8.14.4

Supreme Court Act 1981
s 29 ....15.11.1
s 31 ....15.11.1
s 37(1) 5.16; 10.7
s 37(2) 5.16
s 41(1) 21.6
s 41(2) 21.6
s 41(2)A 21.12
s 41(3) 21.6

Surrogacy Arrangements Act 1985 ....12.5
s 1(2) 12.5.1
s 1(3) 12.5.1
s 1A 12.5.2
s 2(1) 12.5.2
s 2(2) 12.5.2
s 2(3) 12.5.2
s 3 ....12.5.3
s 3(1) 12.5.3
s 3(2) 12.5.3
s 3(3) 12.5.3
s 4 ....12.5.4
s 4(3) 12.5.4

Taxation of Chargeable Gains Act 1992
Sch 6 para 1(2) 1.5.4

Wills Act 1837 ....3.9; 6.7.1
s 9 ....20.6
s 18A 3.9; 3.9.1

Young Persons (Employment) Act 1938 ....24.3

Young Persons (Employment) Act 1964 ....24.3

Abbreviations of Statutes in Text

AA	Adoption Act
ChA	Children Act
CJPOA	Criminal Justice and Public Order Act
C&YPA	Children and Young Persons Act
CSA	Child Support Act
DMPA	Domicile and Matrimonial Proceedings Act
DPMCA	Domestic Proceedings and Magistrates' Courts Act
DVMPA	Domestic Violence and Matrimonial Proceedings Act
FLRA	Family Law Reform Act
HA	Housing Act
HFEA	Human Fertilisation and Embryology Act
I(PFD)A	Inheritance (Provision for Family and Dependants) Act
LPA	Law of Property Act
MA	Marriage Act
MCA	Matrimonial Causes Act
MFPA	Matrimonial and Family Proceedings Act
MHA	Matrimonial Homes Act
MHPA	Matrimonial Homes and Property Act
MPPA	Matrimonial Proceedings and Property Act
MWPA	Married Women's Property Act
SSAA	Social Security Administration Act
SSCBA	Social Security Contributions and Benefits Act
WA	Wills Act

Chapter 1

An Introduction to Family Law

1.1 Family law described

Family law is the body of statutes, rules, regulations and practices related essentially to the development and organisation of the fundamental social unit known as 'the family' and the legal relationships existing among its members. It has developed as a distinct branch of English law and is now differentiated from the general law of property and succession under which it was formerly subsumed. The class of problem with which it now deals may have originated in the early phenomenon of 'linkage' among families resulting from the transfer of a woman from her family to the power of her husband and his family. 'The husband was head of the household, and, in virtue of his position as such, he might choose the place of abode, reasonably correct his wife, and demand from her such domestic duties as were consonant with her social position' (*The Legacy of the Middle Ages* (1926), ed Crump and Jacob). Social, political and legal doctrines reflected these circumstances; the law relating to the power structures and economic interests of the family burgeoned as the importance of the function of *social cohesion*, to which the family contributed, was recognised.

1.1.1 Significance of social and cultural thought

Family law reflects, in singular fashion, not only aspects of economic and political reality, but also contemporary changes in social attitudes and fundamental thought relating to topics such as rights and duties of family members and the responsibilities of the State towards families. In recent legislation such as the Children Act 1989, the rights of the child, parental responsibility, duties of local authorities have been re-defined in the light of changes in family patterns and cultural concepts concerning the significance of the welfare of the child. Changes in family law are no longer made in isolation from a wider social and cultural context.

1.1.2 Reflection of religious doctrines

Much of the earlier law concerning the family and its problems fell within the jurisdiction of the ecclesiastical courts. Marriage and its legal consequences came within the scope of church doctrine such as canon law (see 1.2.2 below) and its interpretation. Until 1857 the ecclesiastical courts possessed an exclusive jurisdiction over matrimonial disputes; the Matrimonial Causes Act 1857 created the Divorce Court which was given the powers formerly exercised by the ecclesiastical courts (and, additionally, it was empowered to dissolve marriage in some few, restricted circumstances). Doctrinal attitudes towards marriage as a sacrament, divorce and the role of the family promulgated today by the Church of England and the Roman Catholic Church have contributed in considerable measure to the formulation of widely-held views on aspects of the role and content of family law.

1.1.3 The wide scope of contemporary family law

The recent growth of the welfare state and a framework of social benefits, the development of secular attitudes to the concept of marriage and, in particular, the marriage ceremony, an increased concern for the welfare of children, have resulted in an extension of the area of family law. Within its province may be discerned the following vital areas:

- The formalities of marriage. How is it defined? How may it be legally celebrated and registered?
- Nullity, divorce, separation. When and how may the rights and duties associated with marriage be legally suspended or terminated?
- Family property rights. What proprietorial rights accrue to family members and how may they be varied?
- Children's rights. How does the law view the status of the child? What is 'parental responsibility'? What does the law expect from parents in relation to the welfare of their children?
- Adoption. How may a child be legally transferred from one family to another?
- Care and supervision of children. What is expected from local authorities in relation to the problems of the child?

1.2 Sources of family law

The following may be discerned as being among the most important of the sources of contemporary family law: the common law; canon law (and its basic principles derived from religious thought); legislation; the influence of recent international Conventions and movements towards a recognition of children's rights. These are noted briefly below.

1.2.1 The common law

The common law has been described as 'the common sense of the community, crystallised and formulated by our forefathers'. Blackstone spoke of it as: 'The chief cornerstone of the laws of England ... from time to time declared in the decisions of the courts ... preserved among our records, explained in our reports'. Common law doctrine in family law may be exemplified by: the presumption of marriage validity ('Where there is evidence of a ceremony of marriage having been followed by cohabitation of the parties, the validity of the marriage will be presumed, in the absence of decisive evidence to the contrary': *Russell v A-G* (1949)); the presumption of legitimacy (a child born during lawful wedlock is presumed to be legitimate: *Banbury Peerage Case* (1811)).

- Note that under the common law, husband and wife 'are one person: that is, the very being or legal existence of the woman is suspended during the marriage, or at least is incorporated and consolidated into that of the husband, under whose wing, protection and cover she performs every act': Blackstone (*Commentaries* (1765)).

- In *R v Clarence* (1888), Hawkins J enunciated the essence of an old common law doctrine concerning sexual relations within marriage: 'The wife submits to her husband's embraces because at the time of the marriage she gave him an irrevocable right to her person. The intercourse which takes place between them after marriage is not by virtue of any special consent on her part, but is mere submission to an obligation imposed upon her by law. Consent is immaterial'. (See now *R v R* (1992) in which the court rejected the supposed 'marital exemption in rape'.)

1.2.2 Canon law

Canon law is a body of ecclesiastical jurisprudence compiled originally in the 12th century, based upon the decrees and opinions of the Roman Catholic Church. The principles of canon law are held to be derived from the authority of Scripture. Consider, for example, the influence of the many exegeses of texts such as: 'What therefore God hath joined together, let not man put asunder' (*Matthew*, 19:6) and 'Wives ... submit yourselves unto your husbands ... for the husband is the head of the wife, even as Christ is the head of the church' (*Ephesians*, 5:23-24). Berman, in *Law and Revolution: the Formation of the Western Legal Tradition* (1983), suggests that canon law introduced concepts of formality into the marriage ceremony, insisted upon evidence of a physical union (*copula carnalis*) before the sacrament of marriage could be considered complete, stressed the element of free consent to that union, formulated conditions relating to the validity of a marriage, simplified and relaxed rules concerning consanguinity as a bar to marriage and offered some protection to the wife. The marriage sacrament took on the character of a *legal transaction* within the legal system of the church.

1.2.3 Legislation

Acts of Parliament have been responsible for most of the significant changes in family law. Today they constitute the sole source of changes to that law. Examples are landmark statutes such as the Matrimonial Causes Act 1973, Adoption Act 1976, Children Act 1989, Child Support Act 1991. Note also sets of regulations such as the Family Proceedings Rules 1991.

1.2.4	Conventions, etc	The European Convention on Human Rights (1950), which is outlined at 23.4.3, is an example of international agreements on matters affecting the individual which have affected our thinking on family law: see, eg, *Paton v UK* (1980) – reference to the Court of Human Rights of a husband's attempt to prevent his wife from having an abortion; *Cossey v UK* (1991) – reference to the Court concerning rights of transsexuals.
1.2.5	Myth as a source of family law?	Professor Katherine O'Donovan (see *Family Law Matters* (1991)), a trenchant critic of the conventions underlying the theory and practice of family law, criticises the ideology of 'the family' for a variety of reasons including the failure of jurists to note that myths 'inform the discourse' concerning relationships of men and women. Certain universal themes of human existence which have mythical overtones, such as birth and childhood are woven into the fabric of family law, but this is rarely acknowledged or understood. The process of 'theorising the family' so as to provide an appropriate rationale for an examination of institutional explanations for current family law has become essential: see, further, 1.9.1 below.
1.3	**Functions of family law**	The functions of family law in the 1990s have been enunciated by some jurists as arising from certain objectives which reflect current social concerns. They include:

- the provision of a basis of certainty for the adjudication by the courts of disputes concerning status arising from marriage (example: the Matrimonial Causes Act 1973);
- the construction of a pattern of principles for the analysis and resolution of dispute-situations arising from tensions within the family unit (example: the Domestic Violence and Matrimonial Proceedings Act 1976);
- the granting of a measure of protection to individuals and their economic interests arising from their membership, past or present, of a family unit (example: the Child Support Act 1991);
- the provision of a legal basis for the personal development of members of the family unit (example: the Children Act 1989).

1.4	**Some current data concerning contemporary family life**	Data extracted from current surveys (including *Social Trends* 1995 (HMSO)) point to important changes in the pattern of family life in the UK.

- More than one-quarter of households in 1993 consisted of one person living alone: almost double the proportion in 1961.
- Lone-parent families accounted for some 19% of families with dependent children in 1993.
- 10% of divorces in the UK now occur within the first two years of marriage. Over one-quarter of divorces in 1993 occurred after 5-9 years of marriage; one-fifth occurred after 20 or more years of marriage.
- The UK had the highest divorce rate in 1993 in the group of countries now comprising the European Union. The UK rate was 3.0 divorces per 1,000 population, as compared with the average rate of 1.6 for other countries in the EU.
- The 25-29 age group currently accounts for the highest rate of divorce amongst both men and women in the UK.
- Almost 18% of non-married persons in the UK, aged 16-59, cohabit, ie, live in partnerships as husband and wife without having legally married.
- Over the past decade within the UK, the proportion of births outside marriage has doubled and is now one in every three births.

It may be that we are witnessing a qualitative transformation of some important aspects of family life in the UK. Given that the basis of much current family law was designed with a relatively stable 'traditional' family unit in mind, has the time for a radical transformation of that law now arrived? Are we witnessing more than a temporary shift in attitudes and should legislators and others recognise that former 'standard' views on unmarried cohabitation, divorce, have changed fundamentally?

1.5 Definitions of 'the family'

A typical dictionary definition of 'family' reads: 'The members of a household, especially parents and their children (*familia* = household, *famulus* = servant)'. This literal meaning of the word should be kept in mind when the following definitions and descriptions are considered.

1.5.1 *Blackwell v Bull* (1836)

In *Blackwell v Bull* (1836), Lord Langdale MR stated: 'It is evident that the word 'family' is capable of so many applications that if any one particular construction were attributed to it in wills, the intention of testators would be more frequently defeated than carried into effect. Under different circumstances it means a man's household, consisting of himself, his wife, children and servants; it may mean his wife and children, or his children excluding his wife; in the absence of wife and children, it may mean his brother and sisters or his next of kin, or it may mean the genealogical stock from which he may have sprung. All these applications of the word and some others are found in common parlance'.

1.5.2 *R v Inhabitants of Darlington* (1792)

Per Lord Kenyon CJ: 'In common parlance the family consists of those who live under the same roof with the *pater familias*: those who form ... his fireside'. It is of interest to note at this point a comment by the legal historian, Maine, in *Ancient Law* (1861): 'The persons theoretically amalgamated into a family by their common descent are practically held together by common obedience to their highest living ascendant, the father, grandfather, or great-grandfather ... The peculiarities of law in its most ancient state lead us irresistibly to the conclusion that it took precisely the same view of the family group which is taken of individual men by the system of rights and duties now prevalent throughout Europe'.

1.5.3 A formal religious view

The *Catholic Encyclopaedia* states that the family is 'a group of persons who are related by marriage or blood and who typically include a father, mother and children. A family is a natural society whose right to existence and support is provided by the divine law. According to the Second Vatican Council, the family is the foundation of society'.

1.5.4 Statutory definitions

The following definitions from statutes are of interest:

- Section 113(1) Housing Act 1985: 'A person is a member of another's family ... if (a) he is the spouse of that person, or if he and that person live together as husband or wife, or (b) he is that person's parent, grandparent, child, grandchild, brother, sister, uncle, aunt, nephew or niece'. A homosexual relationship is not included in the expression 'live together as husband or wife': *Harrogate BC v Simpson* (1986).

- Taxation of Chargeable Gains Act 1992, Sch 6, para 1(2). '"Family" means, in relation to an individual, the husband or wife of the individual and a relative of the individual or of the individual's husband or wife and, for this purpose, "relative" means brother, sister, ancestor or lineal descendant.'

See also s 137(1) Social Security Contributions and Benefits Act 1992.

1.6 Classification of types of family

Social scientists, jurists and others accept that there is no single, universal method of classifying households in which people live together. Two types of family feature in current social and legal research: the 'extended' and the 'nuclear' family. Much of the content of current English family law seems to have in mind the 'nuclear family' and its problems.

1.6.1	**The extended family**

The extended family unit is often found in agricultural societies and involves two or more generations living under the same roof. It may include parents, unwed children, married children and their spouses and offspring.

1.6.2	**The nuclear family**

The nuclear family comprises immediate kin, usually monogamous parents and their children. It is found almost universally and is probably among the oldest type of family. Families of this type characterise societies with relatively advanced levels of culture and seem to have developed as industrialisation and geographical mobility were intensified.

1.6.3	**What of the one-parent family?**

In past times the one-parent family was often regarded as an aberration; hence it rarely featured in the jurisprudential thought behind English family law. Given a change in social attitudes, however, it may be that this type of family unit ought to be considered as an integral feature of the community, and that the content of family law ought to be modified accordingly: see, further, the question of unmarried cohabitation noted at 2.9.

1.7	**The family in socio-political theory**

Changes in the legal status of parent and child and modifications of the legal basis of the nuclear family unit have reflected shifts in social and political theory often as a prelude to an evolution within jurisprudential theory. The following examples illustrate some notable theories concerning the 'family as institution'.

In his treatise *On Power: the Natural History of its Growth* (1945), De Jouvenel explores the classical concept of political and legal authority as the child of paternal authority. The first authority to enter our lives is the paternal. The family is 'the first society – the primary cell from which the social structure afterwards grew', and political authority is 'the first command and stay of all the others ... Families, like men, reproduce themselves, until there is reached a family of families, over which the natural ruler is a sort of "father of fathers"'.

Aristotle, in his *Politics* (c 355 BC) argued in favour of marriage, the family and an organised household. Institutions of this nature were essential to the stability of a society.

Hegel (1770-1831) taught that the family was a necessary part of the process and context of individual development, and that the bond provided by the institution of the family constituted a good model for the citizen's political allegiance.

Engels, in his *Origin of the Family* (1884), emphasised the inter-connections of State, family and private property. Family relationships had developed in response to property relationships. The transformation of society necessitated the total, simultaneous abolition of private property and the formal family. That was an objective of political endeavour for all revolutionary workers.

Susan Okin, a precursor of contemporary 'feminist jurisprudence', maintains, in *Women in Western Political Thought* (1979), that the transformation of the family into a more egalitarian group is essential for the health of the political community as a whole. The family must lose the last vestiges of its 'patriarchal character' and become a democratically-run unit 'in which the only differential in terms of authority is the temporary one of age'. A democratic, egalitarian family structure would play a decisive role in preparing future citizens for 'a life of political participation and equality'.

Note Article 16 of the *Universal Declaration of Human Rights*, adopted in 1948 by the General Assembly of the United Nations: '(3) The family is the natural and fundamental group unit of society and is entitled to protection by society and the State.'

1.8 The jurisdiction of the courts in the area of family law

The system of courts responsible for the exercise of family law jurisdiction has been described as 'a patchwork with little evidence of a single design'. Some critics call for a total overhaul of the existing system of courts and the building of one comprehensive system involving a 'Family Court' which will embrace the requirements of family law as a whole. Aspects of the existing system are noted below.

1.8.1 The family proceedings courts

The 'family proceedings courts' are the former 'domestic courts'. See s 92(1) Children Act 1989. Justices from a special panel consider applications for orders relating to financial provision, etc. Appeals from orders go to the Family Division where they are heard by a divisional court.

1.8.2 The county courts

Almost all types of family matters are dealt with by the county courts. Those designated as 'divorce county courts' may grant decrees of divorce, nullity and judicial separation: see the Family Proceedings Rules 1991, r 2.2. Proceedings may be transferred from one county court to another, and between a county court and the High Court: see also the 'special procedure', concerning divorce at 3.8.

The Family Division of the High Court was known formerly as the Probate, Divorce and Admiralty Division. It comprises a President and fifteen puisne judges nominated by the Lord Chancellor. The Supreme Court Act 1981 Sch 1, assigns the following work to the Family Division:

- All High Court matrimonial causes and matters (whether at first instance or on appeal).
- All causes and matters relating to legitimacy, the exercise of the inherent jurisdiction of the High Court concerning minors, maintenance of minors and proceedings under the Children Act 1989, except proceedings related to the appointment of the guardian of a minor's estate.
- Matters concerning adoption.
- Applications for consent to a minor's marriage; appeals from an order to enforce orders of a magistrates' court made in matrimonial proceedings or in relation to the guardianship of a minor; proceedings under various statutory provisions, eg, Domestic Violence and Matrimonial Proceedings Act 1976, Family Law Act 1986, Children Act 1989. See *Poon v Poon* (1994).

1.8.3 The Family Division

Under the Children Act 1989, Sch 11, the Lord Chancellor may by order specify proceedings under the 1989 Act (or the Adoption Act 1976) which may only be commenced in a specified level of court. He may by order provide for the transfer of proceedings and may specify that the jurisdiction of a magistrates' court to make an emergency protection order (see 17.4) be exercised by a single justice.

1.8.4 Children Act 1989, Sch 11

The prevailing general legal philosophy perceived as underpinning the body of current family law and its institutions has attracted much criticism. It is said by some to reflect an outdated view of the family's significance as a social unit, to be based upon a set of assumptions 'deeply mired in an ecclesiastical past', and to be derived from exclusively masculine preconceptions. Proponents of feminist jurisprudence in particular tend to reject the pretensions of a family law which they perceive as being based upon a continuing concern of male jurists with a sexual polarity in which the 'male principle' is held to be superior. Some typical criticisms are noted below.

1.9 Family law criticised

Professor O'Donovan suggests that family law as taught and practised in our society has had adverse effects, resulting in 'the institutionalisation of discrimination and injustice'. See

1.9.1 Professor O'Donovan's criticisms

1.2.5 above. She argues that there has been a failure to examine the reality of the theory surrounding the concept of the family, which has resulted in a myopic vision of the family as a natural unit. The persons responsible are almost always male jurists and political writers whose vision is weakened by a lack of involvement in, and understanding of, the actual functioning of the household. Discrimination against certain sections of society is bolstered by reasoning processes which, consciously or unconsciously, 'reinforce the viewpoint of power'. Much in the organisation and development of family power has been excluded from analysis or marginalised.

1.9.2 Professor Rifkin's objections to a 'one-sided' family law

In *Toward a Theory of Law and Patriarchy* (1980) (3 Harvard WLJ 83) Professor Janet Rifkin, an American jurist, advances arguments against what she interprets as the one-sided nature of the basis of principles of American family law. Support has been given to her arguments by jurists in the UK who believe that her analysis has fundamental application to the principles of Anglo-American jurisprudence, with particular reference to the ideological basis of English family law.

Rifkin argues that the power of law as both a symbol and vehicle of the authority of the male reflects an ideology of law and an ideology of women. As an example, she cites an extract from the American court's much-criticised decision in *Bradwell v State* 83 US (16 Wall) 130: 'Civil law, as well as nature herself, has always recognised a wide difference in the respective spheres and destinies of man and woman. Man is, or should be, woman's protector and defender. The natural and proper timidity and delicacy which belongs to the female sex evidently unfits it for many of the occupations of civil life.'

Comments of this nature, according to Rifkin's interpretation, encapsulate the lack of reality which is at the basis of much family law. Law's function in general, is as a form of 'hegemonic ideology'. 'Ideology becomes hegemonic when it is widely accepted as describing "the way things are", inducing people to consent to their society and its way of life as natural, good, and just': Kellner (1978). Law – and family law in particular – is based on a mythological vision which cannot produce an accurate view of society, its functioning and its problems.

The paradigm of law noted above remains, according to many critics, male-dominated and virtually unchallenged in its essentials. Unless and until the thinking inherent in a legal ideology of this nature is understood, analysed, challenged and defeated, family law will remain incapable of comprehending the fundamental and everyday problems which emerge from family stress and conflict – this is the essence of Rifkin's thesis. (The reader is invited, on completion of his study of this text, to venture an opinion as to the validity of Professor Rifkin's thesis. Is the thesis merely unwarranted hyperbole, or does it point to errors in the formulation of principles of family law resulting from the 'patriarchal gender bias' of a majority of jurists and legal practitioners?)

1.9.3 Professor Finley's criticisms

Professor Lucinda Finley, in *Breaking Women's Silence in Law: The Dilemma of the Gendered Nature of Legal Reasoning* (1989), argues that the male-gendered language of Anglo-American jurisprudence has emanated largely from white, educated, economically-privileged men who have given that language distorted meanings consistent with their understanding of the world. The voices of others have been excluded or marginalised, a process evident in the meanings attached in jurisprudence to 'family' and 'family law'. The term 'family' seems to be based on a norm derived from the concept of 'a household headed by a man with a wife who is wholly or somewhat dependent on him'. Any other type of family – especially that without a man – is regarded as of an abnormal character. The discipline of family law has as its purpose the sanctioning of the formation of 'ideal families' and the control and limitation of the formation and existence of 'non-ideal families'. Family law may be perceived, therefore, as an attempt 'to control the status and lives of women'.

(Titles of texts which are critical of Anglo-American legal thought as it relates to many of the concepts now embedded in family law are included in the extensive bibliographies given in Professor Katherine O'Donovan's *Family Law Matters* (1991), and Professor Patricia Smith's *Feminist Jurisprudence* (1993).)

Summary of Chapter 1

An Introduction to Family Law

What is family law?

Family law is the body of legislation, rules, regulations and practice concerning the development and organisation of the family. It is a distinct branch of English law and reflects the growing significance of social cohesion as an aim of community policy. Social and cultural thought and religious doctrine are mirrored in its general concepts.

The wide scope of contemporary family law

The area of family law is now very wide, reflecting increased social concern for problems involving the welfare of children. Specifically, it embraces legal doctrine relating to the formalities of marriage, the growing importance of nullity, divorce and separation, the complexities of family property rights, adoption, the care and supervision of children and – of burgeoning significance – the question of children's rights generally, and specifically in relation to parental rights and duties.

Sources of family law

Contemporary family law has emerged from the common law, canon law (and its principles derived from religious thought), legislation, international Conventions and movements working towards a recognition of the rights of the child. Legislation is now the most important source. Parliamentary concern for the rights of children, reflecting wider social acceptance of communal responsibilities, has resulted in landmark legislation such as the Children Act 1989, which promised to effect a revolution in the attitude of the law towards family and State duties in relation to children. The growing importance of international agreements involving personal rights has affected some doctrines of family law, eg, child abduction.

Functions of family law

The functions of contemporary family law include the provision of a basis of certainty in adjudications relating to status, the building of a foundation of principles upon which family disputes may be analysed and resolved, the extension of protection to individuals and their economic interests, and the provision of a legal basis upon which the family unit may flourish.

Defining the family	Definitions of 'the family' must take into account changing objectives, attitudes and practices. There is no standard definition. Some statutory definitions, eg s 113(1) Housing Act 1985, concentrate on 'spouses', 'persons living together as husband or wife', relationships as parent, child, etc. Essentially, today, the family is seen in terms of *relationships* and *responsibilities*.
Types of family	Social scientists, jurists and other investigators differentiate the 'extended family' from the 'nuclear family'. The former involves two or more generations living under the same roof; the latter comprises immediate kin (usually monogamous parents and their children). The growth of the 'one-parent family' is of significance; it has been suggested that family law must embrace the problems of this type of social unit.
Jurisdiction of the courts	The exercise of family law jurisdiction falls to the family proceedings courts, the county courts, and the Family Division of the High Court. The Supreme Court Act 1981, Sch 1, assigns particular work to the Family Division. Note the Children Act 1989, Sch 11, concerning the transfer of hearings from one level of court to another.
Criticisms of family law	Family law has come under intensive and fundamental criticism. It is said to be built on an inadequate theory of the family which fails to recognise the significance of 'power' in the family unit. Other criticisms rest on a perception of the principles of family law as reflecting, consciously or unconsciously, a male-dominated society within which legal doctrine is predicated on male superiority. A re-thinking of the basis of family law in the light of contemporary attitudes towards equality of the sexes has been demanded by a number of jurists.

Chapter 2

Marriage: Capacity, Formalities, Nullity

2.1 Introductory matters

The term 'marriage' is used in family law in three specific senses: to indicate an institution within society as a whole; to name a ceremony resulting in a change in the legal status of the parties; and to refer to the joint status of husband and wife. The precise meaning to be attached to the term will appear from its context. In general terms, 'marriage' is viewed in this text as *a culturally approved and legally binding set of formal relationships of one man and one woman*. It involves, in our society, a fusion of social, political, sexual and legal principles, although within our time a number of these principles appear to have been found increasingly unacceptable, giving rise to questions as to their relevance for contemporary life and law. To a significant extent, family law reflects changes in attitudes towards the principle of marriage and its legal effects.

2.1.1 Definitions

A general dictionary defines 'marriage' as 'the legal union of a man and a woman in order to live together'.

- A much-cited definition is provided by Lord Penzance in *Hyde v Hyde* (1866): 'I conceive that marriage, as understood in Christendom, may be defined as the voluntary union for life of one man and one woman to the exclusion of all others' (see Matrimonial Causes Act (MCA) 1857). Four basic conditions of marriage are apparent within this definition: the union is generally intended for life; the marriage reflects real consent; the union is intended to be monogamous; it is heterosexual.

- 'Marriage, as distinguished from the agreement to marry and from the act of becoming married, is the legal status, condition, or relation of one man and one woman united in law for life, or until divorced, for the discharge to each other and the community of the duties legally incumbent on those whose association is founded on the distinction of sex': Black.

2.1.2 Changes in the nature and consequence of marriage

Informal marriages were recognised in England prior to the mid-16th century, provided that parties demonstrated their free consent to a permanent social union. From 1753-1836 a valid marriage required a ceremony in accordance with the rites of the Church of England. After 1836 civil marriages were allowed to take place. Almost invariably, the consequence of marriage involved the establishing of a legal relationship of dominance by the male partner. The situation has now changed: 'Marriage is in modern times regarded as *a partnership of equals*, and no longer one in which the wife must be the subservient chattel of the husband': *per* Lord Keith in *R v R* (1992).

2.1.3 The basic principle of marriage today

A marriage can be created between any male and female who possess the appropriate legal capacity to marry and who comply fully with the appropriate formal requirements: see 2.2 below.

2.1.4 Marriage viewed as a contract

For many persons, marriage is to be considered, in its full sense, as little more than a voluntary agreement partaking of the nature of a contract – 'this we do so that certain binding consequences shall ensue'. Mutual rights and duties are created and the resulting contract may be valid, void or voidable: see 2.4 below. It should be noted, however, that capacity to marry is not to be equated with general capacity to make a contract, and that unique formalities are required in the case of marriage. Further, the conditions of discharge of a contract by agreement or breach have no application to the marriage agreement. In strict terms, therefore, it is doubtful whether one may equate the *principles* of a general contract with those of the marriage agreement.

In *Contract Obligation and the Human Will* (1943), reprinted in *The Nature and Process of Law*, ed P Smith (1993), Professor Radin noted that while it was true that the marital relationship retained 'the vestiges of an undoubted status', in a number of respects it had become 'much more nearly a contract relationship than ever before'. *Status* involves 'a complex of legal relations, obligations, rights, privileges and powers', just as in the case of many other legal transactions and situations. Obligations are of great importance in status and cannot be seriously modified by a mere act of will. Persons become husband and wife *by contract*; anything that vitiates the contract, such as fraud, duress, incompetence, may be made to annul the marriage. But, following a marriage, the complex of rights and duties which constitute status is fixed by the very fact of the status, and no contractual arrangement between parties to the marriage can effectively withdraw them from that status.

2.1.5 The engagement to marry

Under common law, the engagement to marry was considered to be in the nature of a contract, the breach of which might lead to an action for breach of promise. The action was abolished under s 1 Law Reform (Miscellaneous Provisions) Act 1970. Under s 3(1), a party to an agreement to marry who makes a gift of property to the other party on the condition, express or implied, that it is to be returned if the agreement is ended is not to be prevented from recovering the property by reason only of his having terminated the agreement: see *Shaw v Fitzgerald* (1992). Note that the engagement ring is presumed to be an absolute gift, except where it can be shown that it was given conditionally on the marriage taking place. In the case of other gifts between the parties, each case will turn upon its own facts. Engagement presents from third parties are considered as having been given conditionally on the marriage taking place; they ought to be returned if the engagement is brought to an end.

The expression 'common law wife/husband' is a colloquialism and a misnomer, generally referring to one person who lives with another in an extra-marital relationship. The phrase 'common law marriage' was described by Bridge LJ in *Dyson Holdings v Fox* (1975) as 'inaccurate but expressive'. See also *Rignall v Andrews* (1990) – the term 'wife', for the purposes of the Taxes Act, is confined to a woman who has entered into marriage with a man. 'Marriage' does not cover mere cohabitation: either a person is legally married or he is not.	2.1.6 The 'common law spouse'
Given the unique nature of marriage, the formalities attached to it are of particular importance, so that a failure to comply with some requirements may render a marriage void: see 2.5 below. We note here the question of parental consent to a marriage, licences relating to the ceremony, and the four types of ceremony permitted by law.	**2.2** **Formalities**
In general, where a party to a proposed marriage is over 16 but under 18, the parents' consent may be required. Where consent is withheld or is impossible to obtain, the consent of a family proceedings court may be obtained. Where the minor is a widow/widower no consent is required: s 3(1) Marriage Act 1949, as amended. A person who has parental responsibility for the minor may give consent. Under the Children Act 1989, where a residence order is in force (see 13.15), consent is required from the person(s) with whom the minor is living or is to live under the terms of the order. Should a care order be in force (see 16.9), local authority consent is required, as well as that of parents, guardians: see s 3 MA 1949, as amended.	2.2.1 Consent where a party is over 16 and under 18

    Lack of consent will not, in general, render a marriage void, except where the parent has made a public objection to the marriage banns.

2.2.2 Licences, registration

Marriages which take place in the UK require appropriate licences and must be registered.

One in two of all religious ceremonies in the UK are conducted in the Church of England. Banns, declaring the names of the couple intending to marry, are read aloud ('published') on three occasions in a church in the parish in which the couple reside. Seven days' notice is required by the priest before publication. Objections must be voiced publicly. A common licence, granted by a diocesan bishop, dispenses with banns and takes immediate effect: see s 15 MA 1949. A special licence, issued in the name of the Archbishop of Canterbury, authorises a marriage to be celebrated at any place or time. It is used where, for example, one of the parties is very ill.

Where a non-Anglican religious ceremony or a civil ceremony is to be celebrated, a Superintendent Registrar's Certificate allows for marriage within three months after the display of notice in the marriage notice book: see s 33 MA 1949. A person who has an objection to the proposed marriage can enter a caveat at the office of the Superintendent Registrar. The parties must provide a solemn declaration that they know of no lawful impediments to the marriage, that appropriate consents have been obtained. An offence is committed where false information is given wilfully: s 28 MA 1949.

A Registrar General's licence (see Marriage (Registrar General's Licence) Act 1970 allows the solemnisation of a marriage in any named premises.

2.2.3 Ceremonies permitted by law

Four types of ceremony are allowed by law:

In the case of a *Church of England ceremony*, a clergyman must celebrate the marriage in the presence of two or more witnesses. The wedding should take place in an open church between 8 am and 6 pm. The wedding rites as expressed in the Book of Common Prayer (or in accordance with some other authorised form) are used. Solemnisation of a marriage is required within three months of the publication of the banns. A clergyman has a right to refuse to marry a party whose former marriage has been dissolved and whose former spouse is alive. (The Church is currently reviewing its attitude.) See MCA 1965.

Jewish and Quaker weddings are permitted to take place anywhere and at any time and according to the usages and doctrinal demands of the faith involved. Appropriate preliminaries are required and registration is essential: see s 26 MA 1949.

Non-Anglican marriages, such as those celebrated by the Roman Catholic Church, may take place in any building registered by the Registrar General and classified as a place of meeting for religious purposes. The ceremony must include an appropriate declaration in the presence of witnesses that one party takes the other to be his/her lawful wedded wife/husband.

Marriage in a register office is a secular ceremony. Two witnesses are required. The ceremony, which must be open to the public, takes place in the presence of the Superintendent Registrar and the Registrar, after which the register is signed. Where the civil ceremony is followed by a religious ceremony, it is the former which is legally binding: see ss 45(2), 46 MA 1949.

Note the White Paper (1990, Cm 939), *Registration: Proposals for Change*, which rejected uniformity in civil ceremony preliminaries.

(MA 1994 amends s 26 MA 1949, so as to enable civil marriages (in which no religious service is to be used) to be solemnised on premises approved for the purposes by local authorities: see s 1(1)(bb) MA 1949; s 46B, inserted by s 1 MA 1994.)

Assume that John and Joan wish to marry. May they do so validly? Suppose that Joan will be aged 15 years and 11 months at the date of the proposed ceremony; or that she is John's niece. Suppose that John is married already to Jane, but believes her to be dead. Suppose that Joan is a transsexual, born as 'Jack'. In some of these circumstances the parties will lack the legal capacity to marry, and the resulting irregularities in any marriage ceremony in which they are involved may render the marriage void (ie, invalid).	2.3	**The legal capacity to marry**
The legal capacity to marry will be governed in general by the law of the country in which parties are domiciled at the date of their marriage – *lex domicilii*. Where one party is domiciled *in England*, the marriage will be considered by the English courts to be valid if both parties had capacity according to English law. Where both parties are domiciled *outside UK* and do not possess capacity to marry according to the law of their domicile, their marriage will be considered as void even though they possessed capacity according to English law: see *Sottomayor v De Barros* (1877). See also *Ogden v Ogden* (1908).	2.3.1	*Lex domicilii*, etc.

2.3.2 Minimum age

Both parties must be over 16, even though parental consent may have been given in the case of one or both parties under this age: see Age of Marriage Act 1929; s 2 MA 1949. Where both parties are domiciled abroad and the law of the country of domicile recognises a marriage of parties, one of whom is under 16, the marriage may be recognised in the UK as valid (see *Pugh v Pugh* (1951)).

2.3.3 One male, one female

Legal problems have arisen in cases where advances in surgical techniques have made possible so-called sex-change operations: see s 11(c) MCA 1973. The following cases should be noted.

- *Corbett v Corbett* (1970). X and Y were parties to a marriage ceremony in 1963, three years after Y, a male, had undergone sex-change surgery, involving the construction of an artificial vagina, following which he had lived as a woman and had married X. In subsequent hearings concerning a decree of nullity, the question of Y's sex was considered. *Per* Ormrod J:

    'Since marriage is essentially a relationship between man and woman, the validity of the marriage in this case depends, in my judgment, on whether the respondent (Y) is or is not a woman. The question then becomes what is meant by the word 'woman' in the context of a marriage, for I am not concerned to determine the 'legal sex' of the respondent at large. Having regard to the essentially heterosexual character of the relationship which is called marriage, the criteria must, in my judgment, be biological, for even the most extreme degree of transsexualism in a male or the most severe hormonal imbalance which can exist in a person with male chromosomes, male gonads and male genitalia cannot produce a person who is naturally capable of performing the essential role of a woman in marriage ... My conclusion is that the respondent is not a woman for the purposes of marriage, but is a biological male and has been so since birth. It follows that the so-called marriage (of X and Y) is *void*.'

- *Cossey v UK* (1991). A and B had married following sex-change surgery undergone by B, who appeared to be psychologically a female. The marriage was declared *void*. B alleged that rights to family life and to marriage under Articles 8 and 12 of the European Convention for the Protection of Human Rights had been violated. The European Court of Human Rights held that the right to marry, guaranteed under Article 12, referred to the traditional form of marriage between persons of the opposite biological sex. B's rights had not been violated.

(Note that the Court referred to the need to keep appropriate legal measures under review in the context of changing circumstances.) See also *Rees v UK* (1987).

2.3.4 Monogamous union

A valid marriage is not possible while a party is already married to some other person: see s 11(b) MCA 1973. A reasonable belief by a person that his previous marriage had ended on the death of the spouse may be a defence to a charge of bigamy: see Offences against the Person Act 1861, s 57; but it will not suffice to prevent a marriage being declared void: see also s 19 MCA 1973.

2.3.5 Parties must not be within 'prohibited degrees'

See Sch 1 MA 1949, amended by Sch 3 ChA 1975, and Marriage (Prohibited Degrees of Relationship) Act 1986. In general, the law excludes from marriage persons within certain degrees of *consanguinity* (blood relationships) and *affinity* (relationships through marriage).

- In the case of *blood relationship*, a man may not marry his mother, daughter, grandmother, granddaughter, sister, niece or aunt. Similarly, a woman 'may not marry equivalent male relations'. See s 1 MA 1949.

- In the case of relationships based on affinity, a man or woman may not marry an ex-spouse of certain blood relations, nor may he/she marry certain relations through marriage of the opposite sex. Note, however, that following s 1 MA 1949, as amended by the 1986 Act, except in the case of marriage between a man and his former mother-in-law, or daughter-in-law, a marriage will not be held to be void merely on grounds of affinity where both parties are at least 21 *and* the younger party to the marriage has not been a 'child of the family' before the age of 18. ('Child of the family' is defined under s 105 ChA 1989 in relation to the parties to a marriage, as '(a) a child of both of those parties; (b) any other child, not being a child who is placed with those parties as foster parents by a local authority or voluntary organisation, who has been treated by both of those parties as a child of their family'.)

2.4 Void and voidable marriages

A 'void' marriage 'never was'; it is void *ab initio* and, therefore, no decree is needed for its formal termination. A 'voidable' marriage remains valid until the date of a nullity decree. Void marriages are based on grounds which differ from those of voidable marriages. There are statutory bars to a decree of nullity in the case of a voidable marriage which have no application to the case of a void marriage. For a consideration of the rationale of the void and voidable marriage and for retaining the process of nullity in relation to a voidable marriage, see Law Commission Report (1970), *Nullity of Marriage*.

2.5 Essential features of the void marriage

A void marriage is *invalid from its inception*; the status of husband and wife has, therefore, never been acquired validly by the parties: see s 11 MCA 1973.

Such a marriage may result from lack of capacity in either party or from a failure to comply with certain formal requirements concerning the ceremony. Lack of capacity is outlined at 2.3 above; the question of formal defects is considered below: see, eg, *Militante v Ogunwomoju* (1993) (misrepresentation of identity by husband – marriage declared void).

2.5.1 Formal defects relating to the marriage

On the question of formal defects in relation to a marriage, see the Law Commission Report (1973), *Solemnisation of Marriage*. MA 1949 provides that where the parties knowingly and wilfully disregard certain requirements, the marriage shall be void. Formal defects which will invalidate a marriage *ab initio* include (where parties were aware of them): failure to publish banns; where more than three months had passed from publication of the banns; failure to obtain an appropriate licence or certificate; marriage service conducted improperly (eg, in the case of an Anglican ceremony, by some person who was not a clergyman).

2.5.2 Formal defects which will not invalidate a marriage

A marriage will not necessarily be declared void where, for example, there has been a failure to fulfil a statutory residence requirement, or a failure to obtain necessary consents for a minor's marriage. A marriage will not necessarily be void if the ceremony takes place in an unregistered building: see *Puttick v A-G* (1979) in which a marriage was not held void merely because a party had misdescribed herself in documents relating to the ceremony.

2.6 Essential features of the voidable marriage

'A voidable marriage is one that will be regarded by every court as a valid and subsisting marriage until a decree annulling it has been pronounced by a court of competent jurisdiction': *per* Lord Greene MR in *De Reneville v De Reneville* (1948). (Note that a decree of nullity requires two stages: *decree nisi*, which is followed by *decree absolute*. Final annulment of the marriage is made according to the date upon which the decree is made absolute. Until that date a party to a voidable marriage must not remarry.) See MCA 1973, ss 12, 16. The grounds upon which a marriage is voidable are considered at 2.6.1-2.6.4 below: see *P v P (Ouster: Decree Nisi of Nullity)* (1994).

2.6.1 Failure to consummate the marriage owing to incapacity of either party or respondent's wilful refusal

Failure to consummate the marriage because of incapacity or respondent's wilful refusal will be a ground for holding a marriage to be voidable: see s 12(a), (b) MCA 1973. 'Consummation' refers to ordinary, complete sexual intercourse, involving full penetration, and 'not partial and imperfect intercourse': *per* Dr Lushington in *D v A* (1845). The fact of sexual intercourse *before* marriage will not prevent a party petitioning; the petition relates to intercourse *after* the marriage: *Dredge v Dredge* (1947).

- *Incapacity*. The incapacity must be of a permanent nature and must be proved by the petitioner. Either party may petition. It may be derived from a physical abnormality or from some psychological cause: see *Cackett v Cackett* (1950); *Baxter v Baxter* (1948), in which the House of Lords held that the use of contraceptives did not prevent consummation. The incapacity must be incurable. Note that an inability to ejaculate does not prevent consummation: *R v R* (1952).

- *Wilful refusal*. Respondent's refusal may be shown by, eg, a wilful refusal to undergo reasonable and appropriate treatment: see *S v S* (1954). *Per* Lord Jowitt LC in *Horton v Horton* (1947): 'I do not think it desirable to attempt any definition of the phrase 'wilful refusal to consummate the marriage'. The words connote, I think, a settled and definite decision come to without just excuse, and in determining whether there has been such a refusal, the judges should have regard to the whole history of the marriage'. See also *Ford v Ford* (1987); *A v J (Nullity)* (1989). See *Wilful Refusal to Consummate*, by A Berkowski (1994) Fam Law 684.

2.6.2 Lack of consent in consequence of duress, mistake, unsoundness of mind or otherwise

It must be shown that there was an *absence of real consent* by either party: see s 12(c) MCA 1973. Validity of consent is vitiated if it can be shown that a spouse, at the time of the ceremony, was under threats which effectively destroyed the reality of that consent (even if the threats had been made justly). See *Szechter v Szechter* (1971). Mistake may negate consent, as where a spouse was in error as to the identity of the person he/she was marrying, or the nature of the ceremony (see *Mehta v Mehta* (1945)); but not where the mistake relates to the legal consequences of the marriage: see *Valier v Valier* (1925).

- *Way v Way* (1950). The petitioner failed where he was under a misapprehension that, following marriage, his wife would have been allowed to leave the USSR in order to live with him.

- *Buckland v Buckland* (1967). Petitioner claimed that, while in Malta, he had been threatened with imprisonment for corrupting a young girl. He married her later so as to avoid imprisonment. 'I have come to the conclusion that the petitioner agreed to his marriage because of his fears, and that his fears, which were reasonably entertained, arose from external circumstances for which he was in no way responsible. Accordingly, in my judgment, he is entitled to a declaration that the marriage ceremony was null and void' *per* Scarman J.

'Unsoundness of mind' refers to an inability to understand the nature, significance of marriage and its attendant responsibilities.

2.6.3 At the time of the marriage, a spouse was suffering from a mental disorder so that he/she was unfitted for marriage

A person will be unfitted for marriage if he is suffering from a mental disorder within the Mental Health Act 1983: see s 12(d) MCA 1973. *Per* Ormrod J in *Bennett v Bennett* (1969): 'Concerning the definition of mental disorder in s 4 Mental Health Act 1959, the question is, what did Parliament mean by the use of the phrase "unfitted for marriage and the procreation of children" because they are not disjunctive but conjunctive. "Unfitted" is a word which is not easy to construe. It might be given a very wide interpretation on the one hand, or a very narrow one on the other. It is quite plain, to my mind, having regard to the context in which this amendment was made, with the background of mental deficiency in mind, that Parliament cannot possibly have intended to use the word "unfitted" in an extended sense at all. This must really mean something very much like the test of unsoundness of mind although perhaps not quite the same; it really must mean something in the nature of: "Is this person capable of living in a married state, and of carrying out the ordinary duties and obligations of marriage?" I do not think it could possibly be given any wider meaning than that.'

2.6.4 At the time of marriage respondent was suffering from a venereal disease or was pregnant *per alium*

Where, at the time of the marriage, the respondent was suffering from a venereal disease in a communicable form or was pregnant by some person other than the petitioner, the marriage may be held voidable: see s 12(e)(f) MCA 1973. 'Venereal disease' is not defined in the Act. (Some commentators have expressed doubts concerning the relevance of AIDS to s 12.)

2.7 Bars to relief under s 13 MCA 1973

There are *three bars* which will prevent the court granting a decree of nullity on the ground that the marriage is voidable

- Where the petitioner, with knowledge that it was open to him to have the marriage avoided, so conducted himself in relation to the respondent as to lead the respondent to believe reasonably that he would not seek to do so; and that it would be unjust to the respondent to grant the decree: s 13(1). Note that considerations of public policy do *not* constitute a bar: *D v D* (1979). *Per* Willmer LJ in *Pettit v Pettit* (1962): '(The wife) has given up her whole life to the husband, has served him faithfully as a wife and mother to his child ... To pronounce a decree of nullity against her now would be a matter of serious prejudice to her ... I can see no ground on which it could possibly be held that it was fair and equitable to grant relief to this husband.'

- Where the petitioner had knowledge of the defect alleged. A petitioner who alleges that the respondent was suffering from venereal disease or was pregnant *per alium* must show the court that the fact was not known to him at the time of the marriage. Failure to show this will act as a bar to the grant of a decree.

- Unless proceedings have been instituted *within three years* of the date of the marriage (or, if later, with the leave of the court), a petitioner may be barred from proceeding on the ground of lack of consent or allegation of venereal disease, pregnancy *per alium*: see s 13(2) MCA 1973.

2.8 Jurisdiction of English courts in a nullity suit

Under s 5(3) DMPA 1973, an English court may exercise jurisdiction in a nullity suit only if: either party to the marriage is domiciled in England and Wales on the date proceedings are started; either party was habitually resident there for one year ending on that date; either party died prior to that date and the deceased was domiciled at his/her death in England and Wales or had been habitually resident there for one year ending at the date of his/her death.

2.9 Unmarried cohabitation

Cohabitation generally means in the context of family law 'living together as husband and wife without having legally married'. It has a long history in our society, has attracted considerable opprobrium on religious grounds, but in recent years appears to have become acceptable to many persons within the community: see the data presented at 1.4. Legislators and jurists must now take into account a state of affairs in which, for growing numbers, marriage is being replaced by informal, extra-marital relationships. Writing in 1981, in *Consortium Rights for the Unmarried,* Meade suggests that the move away from traditional marriage may be the result of a growing belief that formal marriage involves the uncritical acceptance of sex-stereotyped roles, that, where children are not involved, a marriage ceremony might appear unnecessary and irrelevant, that a test-period prior to entering a long-term relationship is advantageous to both parties.

Cohabitation differs from formal marriage in a variety of ways. There are, in general, no restrictions as to those who may cohabit, but the selection of marriage partners may be restricted by law (see 2.3.5). Cohabitants are not under any legal obligation to support each other during their relationship or following its termination (but note the provisions of the Child Support Act 1991); but husband and wife have mutual obligations of support. Procedures intended to resolve family disputes concerning money are not generally available to unmarried cohabitants. A married couple have parental responsibility for children (see Ch A 1989 at 12.23), whereas responsibility for the child of an unmarried mother tends to devolve on her.

The advantages of unmarried cohabitation are said to include the economic benefits which may accrue within the context of taxation, the chance to terminate swiftly, decisively and without recourse to the machinery of the State and its legal institutions, a relationship which has foundered and is destined for disaster. Disadvantages are claimed to include the adverse effect of lack of stability within the family unit, the emergence of problems concerning finance and provision for children of cohabitants, and the ever-present possibility of exploitation of a partner under the guise of remaining unmarried so as to 'keep one's options open'.

2.10 Changes in governmental attitudes to unmarried cohabitants

There are growing signs of interest by some governments in regulating the legal situation created by cohabitants. Note, for example, the significant Australian (New South Wales) De Facto Relationships Act 1984, intended to regulate property rights and claims of a contractual nature between unmarried cohabitants. Under s 14(1) a *de facto* partner may apply to the court for an order for the adjustment of interests with respect to the property of the *de facto* partners or either of them or for the granting of maintenance, or both. Parties to the application are expected to have lived together for not less than two years: s 17(1). Note, also, that in Canada, the Victoria Property Law (Amendment) Act 1988 allows a court engaged in settling disputes concerning cohabitants' property to have regard to contributions by each of them to the welfare of the family.

Consider the Fatal Accidents Act 1976, allowing a claim to be made by a dependant of the deceased person against the tortfeasor. A 'dependant' is defined so as to include 'any person who had been living with the deceased in the same household ...'. See also DVMPA 1976, allowing the making of orders designed to prevent violence in the home: the orders are available to cohabitants who are 'living together as husband and wife', and the I(PFD)A 1975, ss 1(1)(e), 1(3) (see 6.9).

In *Marriage and Cohabitation in Contemporary Societies* (1980) ed Eekelaar and Katz, Professor Clive argues that there is no logic in the view that marriage is legally necessary. In 'Is marriage redundant?' (1992) (*Student Law Review Yearbook*) John Dewar suggests that it is unlikely that marriage will retain for long its privileged position, or, perhaps, any legal significance. The focus of State regulation appears to be shifting in the direction of the concept of 'parenthood'; it is possible to bypass the institution of marriage and endow parents with duties resulting in financial obligations to children. Dewar doubts whether, in particular, there is any point to the law's regulation of childless marriages. His answer to the question as to whether marriage is needed at all for purposes connected with legislation is a cautious, but firm negative: see also 'Marriage – Sacred Union or Determinable Contract' by K O'Donovan, in *Family Law Matters* (1993); *The Marriage Contract* by L Weitzman (1981); *Legal Regulation of Marriage: Tradition and Change*, by L Weitzman (1974); *A Short History of Cohabitation and Marriage* by V Chaveau and A Hutchinson (1995) 145 NLJ 304. For a considered reply to those who proclaim the virtues of unmarried cohabitation over the advantages of the married state, see *Marriage* (1990) by H Oppenheimer.	**2.11 Marriage: a redundant concept?**

Summary of Chapter 2

Marriage: Capacity, Formalities, Nullity

'I conceive that marriage, as understood in Christendom, may be defined as the voluntary union for life of one man and one woman to the exclusion of all others': Lord Penzance in *Hyde v Hyde* (1866). Some jurists seek to define marriage in terms of a contract, but the capacity to marry may not be equated with the capacity to make a contract, the formalities of marriage are unique and the principles of breach of contract have no application in the case of marriage.

Definition of marriage

Consent is generally required where a party is over 16 and under 18. Appropriate licences are required and the marriage must be registered. Church of England marriages are to be conducted in accordance with prescribed rites. Four types of ceremony are allowed by law: the Church of England ceremony, celebrated in an open church; Jewish, and Quaker weddings, according to appropriate doctrinal ritual; non-Anglican marriages (eg, those celebrated by the Roman Catholic Church); marriage (with a secular ceremony) in a register office and approved premises.

Formalities

Both parties must be over 16; one partner must be male and the other female (English law does not recognise the surgical 'sex-change'); neither party must be already married to some other person; parties must not be within the 'prohibited degree'.

Legal capacity to marry

The void marriage 'never was'; it is void *ab initio*; no decree is needed for its formal termination and the parties have never acquired the status of husband and wife. A marriage may be void as a result of lack of legal capacity in either party or a failure to comply with certain formalities.

Void marriages

The voidable marriage is one that is regarded by the courts as valid until a decree annulling it has been pronounced. The grounds upon which a marriage is voidable are as follows (see s 12 MCA 1973).

Voidable marriages

- Failure to consummate the marriage owing to incapacity of either party or respondent's wilful refusal.

- Lack of consent in consequence of duress, mistake, unsoundness of mind or otherwise.
- At the time of the marriage a spouse was suffering from a mental disorder within the Mental Health Act 1983.
- At the time of the marriage respondent was suffering from a venereal disease or was pregnant *per alium*.

Bars to relief under s 13 MCA 1973

The court will *not* grant a decree of nullity on the ground of a marriage being voidable where: the petitioner, knowing that he could have the marriage avoided, so conducted himself as to lead the respondent to believe that he would not seek to do so; the petitioner had knowledge of the defect alleged; proceedings have been delayed.

Unmarried cohabitation

Some jurists and social scientists claim to discern a trend away from formal marriage to an informal partnership; this is said to reflect a rejection of sex-stereotyped roles, the questioning of a ceremony seen as irrelevant, and growing doubts as to the significance of the advantages said to flow from the married state. Family law, if it is to be relevant to the needs of society as a whole, must show awareness of the new thinking on topics of this nature.

Chapter 3

Divorce (1): Background; Procedures

3.1 Definition

The general meaning of 'divorce' suggests the breaking of a unity by separation of its constituent elements. In family law the term refers to *a mode of dissolution of the marriage contract*, a formal termination of the status derived from marriage, so that, following the grant of a decree, both spouses have neither the duties nor the rights of husband and wife.

In this text the word 'divorce' is used to indicate the formal, voluntary ending of a marriage by the granting of a decree of dissolution of that marriage on the petition of either party thereto, in a manner which allows the parties to remarry. Assume that Peter married Rebecca in 1990 and that in 1993 he petitioned the court to grant a decree which would dissolve the marriage on the ground of Rebecca's admitted adultery; Peter is the *petitioner*, Rebecca is the *respondent*.

Note the uses of the term 'divorce' by the ecclesiastical courts in earlier times. A divorce *a mensa et thoro* ('from table and bed', or 'bed and board') was granted where a spouse was shown to have been guilty of conduct rendering ordinary married life impossible (because of, eg, cruelty or adultery). The parties were allowed to separate. A divorce *a vinculo matrimonii* ('from the bond of marriage') was granted where a marriage was held to be void or voidable, as where a spouse was within the prohibited degrees (see 2.3.5). The marriage tie was broken and the parties released from all their marriage obligations.

3.2 Background

The rate of divorce in the western world has grown rapidly in the last half-century: views of marriage have changed so that it is now seen by many as a partnership rather than a relation which should not be broken. The growth of women's independence, an intensification of secular attitudes to an institution formerly held to be in the nature of a sacrament, a modification of views concerning individual liberty and freedom, have resulted in an acceptance of divorce, not as 'a threat to the family and to the conception of marriage as a lifelong obligation', but as a recognition of the fact that matrimonial obligations can and do collapse and that it is in neither the interests of the parties nor of society to maintain the legal form of a relationship which lacks a foundation. Goode, in *Women in Divorce* (1956) noted that all family systems 'have some kinds of escape mechanisms built into them, to permit individuals to survive the pressures of the system'; divorce is one of these mechanisms.

The situation in the UK is epitomised by the statistics presented in 1.4.

- Problems concerning divorce are now embedded firmly in the ambit of our family law; the aftermath of divorce in relation to the children of divorced parties is viewed as a matter of concern for family law.

- The most important legislative sources of today's divorce law include the Divorce Reform Act 1969, the Matrimonial Causes Act 1973 (re-enacting the 1969 Act).

- Note, in particular, Law Commission Discussion Paper, No 1070, *Facing the Future: a discussion paper on the Ground for Divorce* (1988); Law Commission Report, No 102, *Family law: the Ground for Divorce* (1990). See also *Regulating Divorce* (1991) by J Eekelaar.

3.3 Development of divorce legislation

For centuries, matters concerning marriage – the form of celebration, attendant rights and duties, dissolution – were dominated in strict, unyielding fashion by the church. It is only in recent times that non-religious attitudes to marriage and its termination have been given legal recognition and expression.

3.3.1 The early Christian attitude

In the early church, marriage was considered as a sacrament, imparting spiritual benefit to participants. The attitude to dissolution of marriage was based upon teachings derived from the Gospel according to *Mark* (10:11, 12): 'Whosoever shall put away his wife and marry another committeth adultery against her. And if a woman shall put away her husband and be married to another, she committeth adultery.' The sacrament of marriage involved the creation of an indissoluble union, provided that it had been made in the presence of a priest, blessed by him, and consummated.

3.3.2 The influence of canon law

Canon law embodied rules and regulations ('canons') fashioned by Roman Catholic ecclesiastical jurists and commentators in the 12th-14th centuries. A few of the more restrictive interpretations of scriptural doctrine relating to dissolution of marriage were questioned and modified. Thus, impotence which existed at the time of the marriage (the so-called 'canonical disability') was recognised as a justification for nullity; a marriage between a Christian and a heathen (who could not participate in a sacrament) could be declared void; judicial separation (*divortium*, resulting in a divorce *a mensa et thoro*) could follow on allegations of serious cruelty, apostasy or fornication. In general, however, the sacramental bond of marriage was held to be indissoluble until the death of a spouse.

3.3.3 Basis of pre-Reformation attitudes

Pre-Reformation attitudes were based upon the enunciation and interpretation of canon law. A divorce *a vinculo matrimonii* was rarely granted and the 'everlasting marriage' was proclaimed widely. Where it could be shown that some impediment to the validity of a marriage had existed at the time of its celebration, ecclesiastical law maintained that no true marriage had taken place.

3.3.4 Post-Reformation attitude

Following the Reformation in the 16th century, the canon law as it affected marriage was revised and a number of its rigours modified or rejected. (It will be remembered that the Reformation was inspired in part by dissatisfaction with the refusal of the Pope to allow Henry VIII to divorce Catherine of Aragon.) Marriage was seen more as a rite than a sacrament; some reformers were bold enough to argue in favour of marriage as a State-regulated contract. But the newly-founded Church of England affirmed many of the generalities of the doctrine of 'the lasting marriage', to be tempered only by the availability, in restricted measure, of the divorce *a mensa et thoro*. 'Parliamentary divorce' through the use of a procedure based on private Acts of divorce became possible. Rules promulgated in 1798 made it necessary for a petitioner to have obtained a decree of divorce *a mensa et thoro* and an award for 'criminal conversation' against his wife's seducer. The system of Parliamentary divorces was ended in 1857.

3.3.5 19th century legislation

The important MCA 1857 transformed the situation in relation to divorce. The ecclesiastical courts lost their matrimonial jurisdiction; a new court, the Court for Divorce and Matrimonial Causes, was created. The divorce *a mensa et thoro* was transformed into a decree of judicial separation (see 5.2). A husband was allowed to petition for divorce on the ground of adultery; a wife could petition on the same ground, aggravated by other conduct, such as cruelty or desertion for two years or more.

3.3.6 20th century legislation

The following 20th century statutes are of much significance in relation to divorce.

- MCA 1937. By virtue of this legislation a petition could now be based on the additional grounds of cruelty, desertion for three years, and, in certain circumstances, incurable insanity (the first appearance in divorce legislation of a 'no-fault' ground).

- Divorce Reform Act 1969. This followed on a report in 1966 of a committee set up by the Archbishop of Canterbury (*Putting Asunder*). The Law Commission, in its report, *Reform of the Grounds of Divorce – the Field of Choice* (1966), suggested that the objectives of a good divorce law should include the support of marriages which have a chance of survival and 'the decent burial with the minimum of embarrassment, humiliation and bitterness of those that are indubitably dead. The 1969 Act abolished the former grounds for divorce, replacing them with one ground only – that *the marriage in question has broken down irretrievably*.
- MPPA 1970. This statute reformed the law relating to the powers of the High Court and county courts to grant financial relief for spouses and children of the family following divorce.
- MCA 1973. This was a consolidating statute. As amended by the MFPA 1984 (concerning, eg, the time within which proceedings for divorce or nullity of marriage may be instituted: see Part I), the 1973 Act is the basis of much of today's divorce law.

3.4 Jurisdiction and divorce procedure

Under s 5(2) DMPA 1973, a court has jurisdiction in the following circumstances: where either of the parties is domiciled in England and Wales at the time when the proceedings are commenced, or was habitually resident in England and Wales throughout the period of one year ending with that date.

The word 'domiciled' refers to a party's domicile of origin or domicile of choice. DMPA 1973 allows (see s 6(3)) the discretionary staying of proceedings by the court where it appears that proceedings in relation to the marriage in question, or capable of affecting its validity, have commenced in some country outside England and Wales: see De *Dampierre v De Dampierre* (1988), in which the House of Lords held that, in determining whether proceedings should be stayed, the court should not be deterred from granting a stay merely because plaintiff in this country would be deprived of a legitimate personal or judicial advantage, provided that the court was satisfied that substantial justice would be done in the overseas forum.

3.5 The divorce petition

A suit for divorce necessitates initially the presentation of a petition to an appropriate court (see s 33 MFPA 1984). Information must be given in the petition in accordance with the requirements of the Family Proceedings Rules 1991. The petition should be accompanied by a document setting out the proposed arrangements concerning children of the family under the age of 16, or those receiving education and training.

3.5.1 Petition served on respondent

The petition served on the respondent is accompanied by a statement of the steps he/she is obliged to take, and information concerning the results of the granting of a decree of divorce. Additionally, he/she must acknowledge service. Respondent is asked whether he/she wishes to raise a defence. An answer must be returned within 29 days of receiving notice: see Family Proceedings Rules 1991, r 2.12 (for undefended causes, see 3.8 below). See *Lawlor v Lawlor* (1994).

3.5.2 Essential features of the petition

The petition will allege that the marriage has broken down irretrievably: see s 1(1) MCA 1973. The petitioner has to satisfy the court of one or more of the 'facts' stated in s 1(2) (see 4.2) from which the alleged breakdown may be inferred. If the relevant 'fact' is proved by the petitioner, a decree of divorce will be granted, unless respondent is able to show that the marriage has not broken down irretrievably, or that if the marriage were to be dissolved respondent would suffer grave financial or other hardship.

3.5.3 Bar on petitions for divorce within one year of marriage

The bar on the presentation of divorce petitions within *one year* of marriage is stated in s 3 MCA 1973, substituted by s 1 MFPA 1984.

> '(1) No petition for divorce shall be presented to the court before the expiration of the period of one year from the date of the marriage. (2) Nothing in this section shall prohibit the presentation of a petition based on matters which occurred before the expiration of the period.'

This is an *absolute bar*; the exceptions to the previous three-year bar (exceptional hardship or depravity) now have no application: see *Butler v Butler* (1990) (petition for judicial separation, which was subsequently amended to one seeking divorce and presented less than one year after marriage, was held null and void).

3.6 The decree

Initially, the court will grant a *decree nisi*. The petitioner may apply for a *decree absolute* after the expiration of a period of 6 weeks from the date of grant of the decree nisi: see s 1(5) MCA 1973. Grant of the decree absolute rests within the discretion of the court: see *Smith v Smith* (1990) (registrar is not compelled to make a decree absolute where all the requirements of the Matrimonial Causes Rules 1977 were satisfied but ancillary relief proceedings were pending). Where the petitioner does not apply for a decree absolute, respondent may apply at any time after the expiration of three months from the earliest date upon which the petitioner could have made application: see Matrimonial Causes (Decree Absolute) General Order 1972. Note *Torok v Torok* (1973), in which the court expedited the decree absolute, since to do otherwise would have been to produce injustice.

3.7 Following grant of decree

The marriage status is dissolved only when the decree is made absolute. Either spouse may then remarry. A marriage which takes place after the *decree nisi* but before the decree absolute is *void*.

- In *Dackham v Dackham* (1987), the registrar granted a decree absolute; in the event he lacked jurisdiction to do so. In subsequent proceedings following the death of the petitioner, it was held that the marriage had not been dissolved, so that the couple were to be considered as still married at the date of the petitioner's death.

- In *Callaghan v Andrew-Hanson* (1992), the court held that, following the pronouncing of a decree absolute by a court of competent jurisdiction, and after all procedural requirements had been complied with, it was in the public interest that the decree should be recognised as unimpeachable. A decree absolute may not be challenged subsequently by a party alleging, as in this case, that the decree has been obtained fraudulently.

- After *decree nisi* but before the grant of decree absolute, the court may adjourn proceedings should a chance of reconciliation emerge (see 3.11). There can be an intervention by the Queen's Proctor requiring further argument: see s 8(1)(h) MCA 1973. A third party may intervene in order to raise material facts which have not been drawn to the attention of the court: s 9(1) MCA 1973.

3.8 The 'special procedure' in undefended causes

Over 90% of proceedings for divorce in the UK are uncontested and are dealt with according to the rules of the 'special procedure' introduced in 1973. Before 1973, the petitioner was obliged to give oral evidence in open court in support of his allegations. This was often distressing for the parties and, additionally, involved considerable expense for them and for the Legal Aid Fund. Further, because of the increase in the number of divorces following the Divorce Reform Act 1969, the courts experienced an overload of work. In 1973 a 'special procedure' was announced which made the giving of evidence in court unnecessary where the case was not contested; it was available originally for childless couples only, but in 1977 it was extended so as to govern *all undefended divorce cases*: see Practice Direction (1977) 1 All ER 845: see also Family Proceedings Rules 1991. (Note that legal aid is *not* available for the employment of a solicitor in relation to the 'special procedure'; it may be available, however, in relation to ancillary proceedings. Legal advice may be made available in relation to drawing up the petition, under the 'green form scheme': see Legal Aid Act 1988.)

In *N v N* (1992), the court held that an agreement not to defend a divorce petition was *not* contrary to public policy; it was a proper agreement, and a spouse who had agreed that in the event of a failure of reconciliation attempts he would not defend, was debarred from defending.

The 'special procedure', which is intended to be simple, swift and economical, involves the following steps. (P is the petitioner, R is the respondent.)

- P sends the divorce petition and fee (or a certificate of exemption) to the county court. P must send, additionally, a statement of arrangements concerning the children, the marriage certificate and a statement relating to P's consideration of reconciliation.

- Copies of the petition, other statements and notice of proceedings are then sent to R.

- R may (within eight days of the service of the petition) acknowledge service, admit the allegations, and state that the case will not be defended. A copy of the acknowledgement is sent to P who may then apply to a district judge for directions. P should also file an affidavit of evidence and lodge any supporting evidence on which he intends to rely.

- R may return acknowledgement of service to the court, deny P's allegations and (within eight days of receipt of notice) decide to defend. R should file answer to the petition. The petition is then sent to the High Court as a 'defended petition'. If, however, no answer is filed, a request is made to the district judge for directions, the petition being considered as 'undefended'.

- R may take no action; in this case P should attempt personal service of copies of the documents on R. If there is no reply following service, P may file notice of application for leave to proceed in the absence of an acknowledgement of service. Following the granting of leave by the district judge, P may apply for directions.

- The district judge will consider, without the presence of either party, the petition, affidavit in support, etc, and will decide whether P has proved his case, based on an irretrievable breakdown of the marriage. Where the judge decides that P's case is proved and that he is entitled to a decree, he will certify this. P and R will be notified of the date on which a *decree nisi* is to be announced. Neither party is required to be present at the announcement.

- Following the *decree nisi*, P is entitled to apply for a decree absolute which will terminate the marriage.

The judge's certification of P having proved his case *must* be followed by the pronouncement of a *decree nisi unless* R is given special leave to have it set aside. R's request may be granted if he can show that he did not know about the proceedings because of some deception or error for which he was not responsible, or that the award of a decree would be unjust in the circumstances. In *Cahill v Cahill* (1986), P had filed a petition based on R's unreasonable behaviour (see 4.4). R was misinformed as to the date of a hearing; a decree nisi was pronounced. The Court of Appeal allowed R's appeal: it was not enough for P to allege irretrievable breakdown, even if admitted by R. P had to prove one of the relevant 'facts' (see 4.2). R was entitled to contest the case and had been debarred from doing so by a mistake which arose through no fault of his.

3.9 Divorce and wills

Under WA 1837, divorce did not affect the wills of parties to the marriage. This was discussed by the Law Reform Committee in 1980; the result of the discussions was evident in AJA 1982, which substituted a new section in WA 1837.

Under s 18A WA 1837 where, after a testator has made a will, a court dissolves his marriage or declares it void, the will takes effect as if any appointment of the former spouse as an executor or as the executor and trustee of the will were omitted, and any devise or bequest to the former spouse shall lapse, except insofar as a contrary intention appears by the will. This does not affect the right of a former spouse to apply for financial provision under I(PFD)A 1975. Further, where by the terms of a will an interest in remainder is subject to a life interest and the life interest lapses, 'the interest in remainder shall be treated as if it had not been subject to the life interest and, if it was contingent upon the termination of the life interest, as if it had not been so contingent'.

3.9.1 Effect of s 18A WA 1937

Where a marriage is ended by decree of the court, the effects of s 18A are (except where a contrary intention appears in the will) as follows:

- The appointment of a former spouse as executor or executor/trustee is rendered *ineffective*.

- Any devise or bequest to a former spouse will be considered as having *lapsed*. The relevant property will fall into residue or (where there is no residue) it will pass as on an intestacy (except where it is a life interest).

- Any interest in remainder, vested or contingent, which is considered to be dependent on the termination of the life interest of a spouse will be *accelerated*. In a case of this type, a former spouse may make an appropriate claim for reasonable provision under the I(PFD)A 1975, as amended.

In *Re Sinclair* (1985), the Court of Appeal held that where a bequest lapsed by virtue of s 18A WA 1837, it merely failed, no more and no less. It was not possible to read into the section from the word 'lapse' any deeming provision that a bequest should fail with the same consequences as if a spouse had died in the testator's lifetime.

3.9.2 *Re Sinclair* (1985)

The Law Commission published in 1993 *The Effect of Divorce on Wills* (Law Com No 217). Some of the Commission's proposals appear in the Law Reform (Succession) Bill, which received its Second Reading in the House of Lords in February, 1995. The Bill provides for changes to the law, including the following:

3.9.3 Law Reform (Succession) Bill

- Property which would otherwise have passed to a former spouse will pass as if that former spouse had died on the date on which the marriage had legally ended. (The situation which occured in *Re Sinclair* (1985) would be avoided.)

- Subject to any expressed intention to the contrary, any appointment of a former spouse as guardian will be revoked on the termination of the marriage.

The death of a spouse terminates a marriage. A decree of presumption of death and of dissolution of marriage may be made by the court where it is satisfied that *reasonable grounds* exist for presuming that the spouse of the petitioner is dead. The appropriate proceedings commence in a divorce county court; they may be transferred to the High Court: see s 33(3) MFPA 1984; Practice Direction (Family Division; Distribution of Business) (1992) 3 All ER 151.

3.10 Decree of presumption of death

3.10.1	Statutory period of absence	Under s 19(3) MCA 1973, the fact that for a period of *seven years or more* the other party to the marriage has been continually absent from the petitioner *and* the petitioner has no reason to believe that the other party has been living within that time shall be evidence that the other party is dead, until the contrary is proved. For a case involving the *common law presumption*, see *Chard v Chard* (1956). See *Bradshaw v Bradshaw* (1956); *Taylor v Taylor* (1967).
3.10.2	The decree	Prior to pronouncement of the decree, the petitioner is expected to give evidence to the court: *Parkinson v Parkinson* (1939). A decree will not be pronounced where the court accepts the *probability* that the missing spouse may be alive. A decree nisi may be rescinded if the missing spouse is found to be alive. But a decree absolute terminates the marriage; this applies even where the missing spouse eventually reappears: see *Manser v Manser* (1940). Note that the jurisdiction of the court is exercisable where the petitioner is domiciled in England at the commencement of the proceedings or he/she has been resident here for one year only ending with that date: see s 5(4) DMPA 1973.
3.11	**Reconciliation and conciliation**	The Divorce Reform Act 1969 was intended as a measure 'to facilitate reconciliation in matrimonial causes'. 'Reconciliation' as encouraged by the legislature, involved the provision of support and counselling services so that estranged spouses might be brought back together: see s 6(1) MCA 1973, under which a solicitor acting for a petitioner is obliged to file with the petition a certificate stating whether or not he has discussed with the client the possibility of reconciliation, or has given the client names and addresses of persons qualified to assist in this task.

There appears to have been a significant move in recent years away from 'reconciliation' to 'conciliation'. The Finer Report (1974), *One-Parent Families*, states: 'By "reconciliation" we mean the reuniting of the spouses. By "conciliation" we mean assisting the parties to deal with the consequences of the established breakdown of their marriage, whether resulting in a divorce or a separation, by reaching agreements or giving consents or reducing the area of conflict upon custody, support, access to and education of the children, financial provision ... and every other matter arising from the breakdown which calls for a decision on future arrangements.'

Summary of Chapter 3

Divorce (1): Background; Procedures

Divorce means the formal, voluntary ending of a marriage by the granting of a decree of dissolution of that marriage on the petition of either party thereto, in a manner which allows the parties to remarry.	**Divorce defined**
The concept of a dissolution of marriage was viewed for many centuries as an unacceptable interference with the 'indissoluble union for life' proclaimed by the Christian church. Canon law allowed for a marriage to be declared void under very few circumstances. It was not until the 19th century that the ecclesiastical courts lost their matrimonial jurisdiction. In the 20th century the secular approach to marriage became widespread and the concept of the 'indissoluble union' lost its predominance. The Matrimonial Causes Act 1973 was a consolidating statute which is the basis of today's divorce procedures.	**Background**
Section 5(2) DMPA 1973, allows a court jurisdiction in divorce proceedings where either of the parties is domiciled in England and Wales at the time when the proceedings are commenced, or was habitually resident in England and Wales throughout the period of one year ending with that date. 'Domiciled' refers to a party's domicile of origin or domicile of choice.	**Jurisdiction**
A suit for divorce involves the presentation of a petition to the court. It should be accompanied by a statement of proposed arrangements for any children under 16. Respondent must acknowledge service of the petition. The petition alleges that the marriage has broken down irretrievably, a state of affairs to be inferred from one of the 'five facts' stated in s 1 MCA 1973.	**The divorce petition**
No petition for divorce shall be presented to the court before the expiration of the period of one year from the date of the marriage: s 3 MCA 1973, substituted by s 1 MFPA 1984. This is an *absolute bar*.	**Bar on petition**
Initially, the court will grant a decree nisi. Petitioner may apply for a decree absolute after the expiration of six weeks from the grant of the decree nisi. Grant of the decree absolute	**The decree**

is within the discretion of the court. The marriage status is dissolved only when the decree is made absolute; only then may either spouse remarry.

The 'special procedure'

Few proceedings for divorce are now defended. A special procedure, introduced in 1973, is utilised in the case of an undefended petition. The district judge examines, in the absence of the parties, the petition, affidavits, etc. Where he certifies that the petitioner's case is proved, a decree nisi will be pronounced. Neither party need attend court. Decree absolute is pronounced at a later date, terminating the marriage.

Divorce and wills

The effect of s 18A WA 1837 is that where a marriage ends in divorce, and no contrary intention appears in the will, the appointment of a former spouse as executor or executor/trustee is rendered ineffective, any devise to a former spouse is considered to have lapsed, and any interest in remainder which is considered dependent on the termination of a spouse's life interest is accelerated.

Decree of presumption of death

A decree of presumption of death and termination of marriage may be granted by the court. The statutory period of continuous absence from which death may be presumed is seven years: s 19(3) MCA 1973.

Reconciliation and conciliation

There appears to have been a policy move from 'reconciliation' to 'conciliation' as objectives. *Reconciliation* involves the reuniting of the spouses. *Conciliation* refers to assisting the parties to deal with the consequences of the breakdown of the marriage.

Chapter 4

Divorce (2): The Ground for Divorce

A petition for divorce may be presented to the court by either party to a marriage on the ground that *the marriage has broken down irretrievably*: s 1(1) MCA 1973. No other ground will suffice. But s 1(1) must be read in conjunction with s 1(2) which states that the court hearing the petition for divorce shall not hold the marriage to have broken down irretrievably *unless* the petitioner satisfies the court of one or more of certain facts (set out at 4.2 below).	4.1	**The sole ground**
On the presentation of a petition for divorce it is the duty of the court to inquire, so far as it reasonably can, into the facts alleged by the petitioner, and into any facts alleged by the respondent: s 1(3). If the court is satisfied on the evidence of any such fact (mentioned in s 1(2)) then, unless it is satisfied on all the evidence that the marriage has not broken down irretrievably, it will grant a decree of divorce.	4.1.1	Duty of the court
Failure to establish a fact, as set out in 4.2 below, results invariably in the refusal of a decree. Thus, in *Buffery v Buffery* (1985), the Court of Appeal agreed that a marriage had broken down, but that the husband's incompetence in dealing with family finances, and the wife's assertion that they had nothing in common, did not constitute the kind of behaviour contemplated in s 1(2)(b). The fact in question remained unproved, so that a decree would not be granted. In *Biggs v Biggs* (1977), the court accepted proof of adultery but was not convinced that the marriage had broken down irretrievably. The petition was dismissed: see 4.3.4.	4.1.2	Failure to establish a fact

- Proof of a fact raises a *presumption* of irretrievable breakdown.
- The breakdown need not be consequent on the specific fact relied on by the petitioner.

The five facts are set out in s 1(2) MCA 1973. They are as follows.	4.2	**The five facts**

'(a) that the respondent has committed adultery *and* the petitioner finds it intolerable to live with the respondent;

(b) that the respondent has behaved in such a way that the petitioner cannot reasonably be expected to live with the respondent;

(c) that the respondent has deserted the petitioner for a continuous period of at least two years immediately preceding the presentation of the petition;

(d) that the parties to the marriage have lived apart for a continuous period of at least two years immediately preceding the presentation of the petition (hereafter in this Act referred to as "two years' separation") *and* the respondent consents to a decree being granted;

(e) that the parties to the marriage have lived apart for a continuous period of at least five years immediately preceding the presentation of the petition (hereafter in this Act referred to as "five years' separation").'

4.3 Adultery and intolerability

Adultery *plus* intolerability constitute the second most widely-used fact in petitions. It should be noted carefully (see s 1(2)(a) MCA 1973) that adultery, as such, will not suffice: the petitioner must show, *additionally*, that he finds it intolerable to live with the respondent. The section does not state that the intolerability must be a result of the respondent's adultery; it would seem, therefore, that the requirements of s 1(2)(a) are to be read disjunctively. Note *Cleary v Cleary* (1974), in which the Court of Appeal held that the section required that the fact that the petitioner found it 'intolerable' to live with the respondent could be proved by evidence other than that related to the alleged adultery: see also *Carr v Carr* (1974).

4.3.1 Adultery defined

'Adultery cannot be proved unless there be some penetration. It is not necessary that the complete act of sexual intercourse should take place. If there is penetration by the man of the woman, adultery may be found, but if there is not more than an attempt, I do not think that a finding of adultery would be right': *per* Singleton LJ in *Dennis v Dennis* (1955). Essentially, adultery is an act involving consensual sexual intercourse between a married person and a person of the opposite sex who is not that married person's spouse, during the period of subsistence of the marriage.

- Because the act must be voluntary, a married woman has not committed adultery if she has been raped: see *Clarkson v Clarkson* (1930).

- Under the Family Proceedings Rules 1991, r 27(1), it is not necessary to state in the petition the name of the other party involved in the adultery.

4.3.2 Proof of adultery

Adultery may be proved in a variety of ways: by confession (see *Rutherford v Richardson* (1923)); by reference to respondent's previous convictions for rape, incest (see *Taylor v*

Taylor (1970) and s 11 Civil Evidence Act 1968); by a finding of adultery in previous civil proceedings (see s 12(1) Civil Evidence Act 1968; by tests (eg DNA prints) which establish that a husband is not the father of his wife's child. The standard of proof would seem to be on a balance of probabilities: see *Blythe v Blythe* (1966); *Serio v Serio* (1983).

4.3.3 Intolerability

The general test of intolerability within the context of s 1(2)(a) is apparently *subjective*. The question to be determined is not what a 'reasonable petitioner' would find intolerable, but what the petitioner in the case finds intolerable: see *Goodrich v Goodrich* (1971).

4.3.4 Living together after knowledge of adultery

A party to a marriage may not rely for purposes of s 1(2)(a) on adultery committed by the other if, after it became known to that party that the other had committed adultery, the parties had lived with each other for a period exceeding, or periods together exceeding, six months: s 2(1) MCA 1973: see *Biggs v Biggs* (1977), in which a wife had obtained a decree nisi based upon the fact of her husband's adultery but had lived with him for over six months after that decree. She was refused a decree absolute.

4.4 Behaviour

'Behaviour' (see s 1(2)(b)) is the most widely-used fact in petitions for divorce. It is necessary for the petitioner to show that the respondent's behaviour has been of a particular type *and* that because of that behaviour it would be unreasonable to expect the petitioner to live with the respondent.

4.4.1 'Behaviour' interpreted

Note *Bannister v Bannister* (1980), *per* Ormrod LJ:

'The learned judge, I am afraid, fell into the linguistic trap which is waiting for all of us when we speak of "unreasonable behaviour" in relation to s 1(2)(b) cases. The basis of this subsection is not "unreasonable behaviour" but behaving in such a way that the petitioner "cannot reasonably be expected to live with the respondent", a significantly different concept. It is difficult to find an alternative shorthand expression for this subsection, so we all talk, inaccurately, of "unreasonable behaviour". It seems to me that the wife here has made out a clear case of behaviour such that she could reasonably be expected to live with the husband, and that she therefore proved irretrievable breakdown of the marriage.'

- The respondent's conduct must be considered by the court within the context of all the circumstances. 'I have to consider not only the behaviour of the respondent ... but the character, personality, disposition and behaviour of the petitioner. The general question may be expanded thus:

can this petitioner, with his or her character and personality, with his or her faults and other attributes, good and bad, and having regard to his or her behaviour during the marriage, reasonably be expected to live with this respondent': *per* Bagnall J in *Ash v Ash* (1972).

- See also *Bergin v Bergin* (1983) (physical violence); *Stevens v Stevens* (1979) (invasion of privacy, continuous insults); *Birch v Birch* (1992) (dogmatic and chauvinistic attitudes towards a sensitive wife).

4.4.2 Behaviour connotes conduct, not merely a mental state

'Behaviour is something more than a mere state of affairs or a state of mind, such as, for example, a repugnance to sexual intercourse, or a feeling that the wife is not reciprocating the husband's love, or not being as demonstrative as he thinks she should be. Behaviour in this context is action or conduct by one which affects the other. Such conduct may either take the form of acts or omissions or may be a course of conduct, and, in my view, it must have some reference to the marriage': *per* Baker P in *Katz v Katz* (1972).

4.4.3 *Pheasant v Pheasant* (1972)

In *Pheasant v Pheasant* (1972), the husband alleged that his wife was unable to give him 'the spontaneous demonstrative affection' which he expected, and, as a consequence, he could not reasonably be expected to live with her. He did not attempt to provide evidence which might have been interpreted as a serious criticism of her behaviour. The wife stated that she would welcome his return to her. *Per* Ormrod J: 'I have no hesitation in holding that there is nothing in the wife's behaviour which could be regarded as a breach on her part of any of the obligations of the married state or as effectively contributing to the break-up of the marriage. This, in my opinion, has been caused, if his evidence be true, by a change in the personality of the husband and the development in him of some psychoneurotic condition which has made him totally egocentric and obsessed with grievances.' The petition was dismissed.

4.4.4 The 'right-thinking person' test

Note the comments of Roskill LJ in *O'Neill v O'Neill* (1975): 'Would any right-thinking person come to the conclusion that this husband has behaved in such a way that this wife cannot reasonably be expected to live with him, taking into account the whole of the circumstances and the characters and personalities of the parties?' See also *Livingstone-Stallard v Livingstone-Stallard* (1974).

4.4.5 Positive and negative conduct

Behaviour in relation to s 1(2)(b) can include not only positive, but negative, conduct which might be of an involuntary nature, such as that associated with mental illness. In *Thurlow v*

Thurlow (1975), the wife suffered from epilepsy and was frequently bedridden. She damaged the house as the result of fits of aggression and needed institution care. It was held that her involuntary 'negative' behaviour amounted to 'behaviour' within s 1(2)(b), and, taking into account the strain imposed on the husband, he was entitled to a decree. See also *Smith v Smith* (1973).

	4.4.6 Defences

A respondent may deny petitioner's allegations. Additionally, under s 2(3): 'Where in any proceedings for divorce the petitioner alleges that the respondent has behaved in such a way that the petitioner cannot reasonably be expected to live with him, but the parties to the marriage have lived with each other for a period or periods after the date of the occurrence of the final incident relied on by the petitioner and held by the court to support his allegation, that fact shall be disregarded in determining for the purposes of s 1(2)(b) whether the petitioner cannot reasonably be expected to live with the respondent if the length of that period or of those periods together was six months or less'. See *Bradley v Bradley* (1973); *Court v Court* (1982).

4.5 Desertion

Desertion is now one of the least-used grounds for a petition: see s 1(2)(c) above. The petitioner is obliged to prove the fact of desertion by the respondent, that the desertion has lasted for a continuous period of two years immediately preceding the presentation of the petition.

4.5.1 The essence of desertion

Desertion involves the unjustifiable withdrawal from the state of cohabitation without the consent of the spouse and with the intention of effecting a permanent separation. It necessitates a *de facto* separation of the spouses, the *animus deserendi* (intention to remain separated) and the absence of reasonable cause for ending cohabitation.

4.5.2 The fact of separation

The fact of separation involves withdrawal of the deserting spouse not necessarily from a place, but from 'a state of things': see *Pulford v Pulford* (1923) (no need for leaving a matrimonial home). Separation may take place even though the parties live under the same roof, if it can be shown that they have ceased to constitute one household: see *Naylor v Naylor* (1961) (spouses living within the same dwelling but sharing no communal life).

- In *Hopes v Hopes* (1949), the parties had withdrawn to separate bedrooms, but the husband's meals were cooked by the wife and he joined his wife and children for meals in the dining room. It was held that there was no *de facto* separation and, therefore, no desertion. 'It is most important to draw a clear line between desertion, which is a ground for divorce, and gross neglect or chronic discord, which is not. That line is drawn at the point where the parties are living separately and apart. In cases where they are living under the same roof, that point is reached when they cease to be one household and become two households, or, in other words, when they are no longer residing with one another or cohabiting with one another': *per* Denning LJ.

- In *Le Brocq v Le Brocq* (1964) the wife had placed a bolt on the door of the bedroom so as to exclude the husband. There was no communication between them but the husband paid the wife for housekeeping and she cooked his meals. It was held that there was one household and, therefore, no desertion.

- Where there is a resumption of cohabitation which reflects the intention of both spouses, desertion will be considered as terminated: see *Mummery v Mummery* (1942). See also *Abercrombie v Abercrombie* (1943): resumption of cohabitation need not take place in the matrimonial home; *Bartram v Bartram* (1949): after wife's return husband was treated as a lodger, and it was held that cohabitation had not resumed.

4.5.3 *Animus deserendi*

The appropriate intention by one spouse, H, to desert the other, W, may be inferred from H's words and conduct. H's prolonged absence on holiday, or his imprisonment, will not, in themselves, constitute evidence of *animus deserendi*. Note *Perry v Perry* (1964) in which the wife left her husband because of an insane delusion that he was attempting to kill her. It was held that her conduct had to be judged as though her belief were true; there was no *animus* and, therefore, no desertion: see also *Kacmarz v Kacmarz* (1967).

4.5.4 Desertion for two years

Periods of desertion may *not* be added together so as to produce the required period of two years: the desertion must be of a continuous nature. The desertion should be continuing when the proceedings in relation to the petition commence. Section 2(5) MCA 1973 provides an exception: 'No account shall be taken of any one period (not exceeding six months) or of any two or more periods (not exceeding six months in all) during which the parties resumed living with each other, but no period during which the parties lived with each other shall count as part of the period of desertion or of the period for which the parties to the marriage lived apart, as the case may be.'

The term 'constructive desertion' is used where H's behaviour results in driving out W; in that case H is said to have constructively deserted W. Note *Saunders v Saunders* (1965) in which the test appeared to be whether the respondent had been guilty of 'such grave and weighty misconduct' that the sole inference to be drawn was that he knew that the petitioner would withdraw permanently from cohabitation had she acted as would any reasonable person in her position: see, eg, *Patching v Patching* (1958): H's religious beliefs, to which he had been converted, resulted in his disregarding his wife who was left alone for almost the whole of every week. H was held to be in constructive desertion of his wife: see also *Winnans v Winnans* (1948); *Gollins v Gollins* (1963).	4.5.5 'Constructive' desertion
The deserted spouse, W, should not have been a willing party to H's departure: see *Harriman v Harriman* (1909). An express separation agreement, or W's assisting H to leave, would constitute a bar to constructive desertion.	4.5.6 Lack of consent
Where the deserting spouse is able to establish a just (ie, reasonable) cause for his leaving, there is no desertion: see *Quoraishi v Quoraishi* (1985), in which W left H who (on the basis of Muslim law) took a second wife. H was unable to establish desertion because W had 'just cause' to live apart from H. An honest and reasonable belief in a just cause might suffice even though based upon error: see *Cox v Cox* (1958).	4.5.7 No 'just cause'
Section 1(2)(d) MCA 1973 requires that parties shall have lived apart for a continuous period of two years immediately preceding the petition. It must be shown, *additionally*, that the respondent agrees to the granting of a decree. Note *Pheasant v Pheasant* (1972) in which it was said that separation was the best evidence of the breakdown of a marriage. The requirement of two years' separation is to be read in conjunction with s 2(5) (see 4.5.4 above).	**4.6** **Living apart for two years**
For the purposes of s 1(2)(d),(e), a husband and wife are treated as living apart unless they are living with each other in the same household: see s 2(6). See *Mouncer v Mouncer* (1972): it was held that H and W were not living apart where they shared meals with the children, and each performed household tasks. Note *Santos v Santos* (1972) in which the Court of Appeal stated that 'living apart' is a 'state of affairs to establish which it is in the vast generality of cases arising under ((d) and (e)) necessary to prove something more than that the husband and wife are physically separated. For the purposes of that vast generality, it is sufficient to say that the relevant state of affairs does not exist while both parties recognise the marriage as subsisting': *per* Sachs LJ.	4.6.1 Living apart

4.6.2 Respondent's consent to grant of decree

The respondent must indicate his consent to the granting of a decree in some positive manner: see Matrimonial Causes Rules 1977, r 16. Under r 16(2) a consent may be withdrawn at any time *before* the granting of a decree nisi: see *Mason v Mason* (1972) (respondent must have the capacity to give consent).

4.7 Lived apart for five years

The five-year separation period is the least-used ground for the presentation of petitions: see s 1(2)(e) MCA 1973. The basis of this ground is similar to that of the two-year separation. It is important to note that the consent of the respondent is *not* needed in s 1(2)(e).

4.7.1 Refusal of a decree in a five-year separation case

Section 5 MCA 1973 sets out the circumstances in which a decree might be refused in a five-year separation case. The respondent may oppose the grant of a decree on the ground that dissolution of the marriage will result in grave financial or other hardship to him and that 'it would in all the circumstances be wrong to dissolve the marriage'. Where a grant of a decree is opposed, the court will consider all the circumstances, including the conduct of the parties to the marriage and the interests of those parties and of any children or other persons concerned, and if the court is of the opinion that the dissolution of the marriage would cause grave financial or other hardship, etc, the petition will be dismissed.

4.7.2 Grave hardship

The question of grave hardship in a particular case should be considered by the court 'subjectively in relation to the particular marriage and the circumstances in which the parties lived while it subsisted': *per* Dunn J in *Talbot v Talbot* (1971). (In *Jackson v Jackson* (1993), the court urged caution in comparing the facts of one reported case with another.) The term 'grave' carries its ordinary meaning and qualifies 'financial hardship' and 'other hardship': *Rukat v Rukat* (1975). 'Hardship' will include any loss of acquiring a benefit which the respondent might acquire were the marriage not dissolved, eg, a pension: see *Le Marchant v Le Marchant* (1977). In that case, H was a post office worker who, when he was about to retire, petitioned for divorce on the ground of a five-year separation. His wife, W, argued that the possible loss of an index-linked widow's pension would cause her grave financial hardship and she appealed against the grant of a decree nisi. The Court of Appeal held that W had to show not that she would lose something by a divorce, but that she would suffer grave financial hardship 'which is quite another matter altogether'. H offered a transfer of the matrimonial home, and the taking out of an insurance policy on his life to provide a lump sum for W on his death. The Court found his offer 'reasonable' and allowed the decree nisi to stand: see *Brickell v Brickell* (1973); *Parghi v Parghi* (1973).

Respondent may apply to the court after a *decree nisi* has been granted on the basis of a two-year or five-year separation for consideration of his/her financial position on divorce: s 10(2) MCA 1973. The court will consider all the relevant circumstances concerning the parties, eg, age, earning ability, financial resources: see *Hardy v Hardy* (1981). A decree absolute must not be pronounced unless the court is satisfied that the petitioner ought not to be obliged to make financial provision for the respondent, or that financial provision made by the petitioner for the respondent is reasonable, fair, or the best in all the circumstances: s 10(3). See *Wilson v Wilson* (1973). In *Garcia v Garcia* (1992) the Court of Appeal held that a court may delay making a decree absolute under s 10 pending the making of financial provision by the remedying of past financial injustice, and that s 10(3) covered 'any financial provision'.

The failure of a petitioner to show that the marriage has broken down irretrievably is a bar to the granting of a decree, as is the failure to prove one of the facts in s 1(2): see 4.2 above. Note also: s 2(1) at 4.3.4 (living together for six months after adultery); s 5 (at 4.7.1 above); s 10 (at 4.7.3).

In relation to s 1(2)(d) (see 4.6 above), where a respondent is misled intentionally or unintentionally into giving his consent to the granting of a decree, he may apply to the court for the exercise of its discretion in rescinding the decree before it is made absolute: see s 10(1).

The Law Commission, in its 1990 report (*Family Law: A Ground for Divorce*) has argued for the retention and extension of the s 5 bar. 'It provides an important protection for a small group of people who may still face serious hardship which the law is unable at present to redress in other ways. If it retains substantially the same form as the present bar, it is unlikely to be invoked, and even less likely to succeed, in any but a tiny minority of cases ... We recommend that it should be possible to resist the grant of a divorce, on the ground that the dissolution of the marriage would result in grave financial or other grave hardship to the person concerned, and that it would be wrong, in all the circumstances for the marriage to be dissolved.'

Under s 41 MCA 1973, as substituted by Sch 12, para 31 ChA 1989, the court may direct that a decree of divorce or nullity is not to be made absolute if the court, having considered proposed arrangements for children of the marriage, considers it necessary to exercise any of its powers under the 1989 legislation, or where there are exceptional

4.7.3 Financial arrangements after pronouncement of *decree nisi*

4.8 **Bars to the granting of a divorce**

circumstances which make it desirable in the interests of a child that the court should give a direction.

Note the rarely-used powers of the *Queen's Proctor*, a solicitor usually appointed by the Treasury Solicitor. He may instruct counsel to argue any question in relation to that case and may show cause why a decree nisi ought not to be made absolute: see s 8 MCA 1973; *Ebrahim v Ali* (1983).

4.9 Recognition of foreign divorces

Section 46 of the Family Law Act 1986 sets out the grounds for the recognition of the validity of an overseas divorce, annulment or legal separation.

- Recognition is given if the divorce, etc, is effective under the law of the country in which it was obtained and at the relevant date either party to the marriage was habitually resident in the country in which it was obtained, *or* was domiciled in that country, *or* was a national of the country.

- The validity of an overseas divorce, etc, obtained otherwise than by means of proceedings is recognised if the divorce, etc, was effective under the law of the country in which it was obtained, and at the relevant date each party to the marriage was domiciled in that country *or* either party was domiciled in that country and the other was domiciled in a country under whose law the divorce, etc, is recognised as valid, and neither party was habitually resident in the UK throughout the period of one year immediately preceding that date.

For refusal of recognition see s 51: see *International Aspects of Divorce* by S Beck (1994) Fam Law 570.

4.10 Proposals for reform: Law Commission (1990); criticisms

The Law Commission Report (1990), *The Ground for Divorce*, was in no doubt that the present law is 'confusing and unjust'. It now fulfils neither of its earlier objectives which were, first, the support of marriages, and, secondly, the decent burial of marriages which are dead. There is overwhelming support, the Report claimed, for the view that the irretrievable breakdown of marriage should remain the sole ground for divorce. Six criticisms of the law were stated.

4.10.1 The present law is confusing and misleading

The Report suggested that confusion in the law relating to divorce leads to a lack of respect for it. It tells couples that the only ground for divorce is irretrievable breakdown of the marriage, which apparently involves no fault, then states that this can be demonstrated only by one of five so-called 'facts', which do involve fault. 'The bogus adultery cases of the past have all but disappeared, but their modern equivalents are the flimsy behaviour petition or the pretence that the parties have been living apart for two full years.'

The fault-based facts can be intrinsically unjust. There are practical problems of defending or bringing a cross-petition. It is not easy to resist or counter allegations of behaviour. Further, it is very difficult to attempt to live apart, for purposes of meeting the appropriate requirements of the 'fact' without either substantial reserves of one's own, or the full co-operation of the other spouse, or an ouster order (see 5.14).

The Report notes that negotiations can be distorted by 'whichever of the parties is in a stronger position in relating to the divorce itself'.

The Report notes that an arbitrary, unjust law exacerbates feelings of bitterness and distress. 'The more we expect of marriage, the greater the anger and grief when the marriage ends.' The present law, concerned as it is with the most complex of human relations, adds needlessly to the attendant misery of a marriage breakdown.

The existing law may make a reconciliation very difficult. Attention must centre on how the petitioner is to prove the existence of the ground for divorce. The reality of what it would be like to live apart is rarely contemplated in detail until the *decree nisi* is pronounced.

A divorce, it is claimed, may result in children suffering where parents remain in conflict. Children's needs are often not comprehended fully by parents wrapped up in problems related to the divorce.

The Report of the Law Commission argues that the courts should keep to their proper sphere of adjudicating upon practical disputes, ensuring that appropriate steps are properly taken, and enforcing orders made. 'They should not be pretending to adjudicate upon matters they cannot decide or in disputes which need never arise.' Divorce ought to be recognised as part of a process: it should be granted only after a defined period has been used for consideration of the situation, and of alternatives and their specific consequences. The Report suggested that, following a sworn statement by both parties that they believe the marriage to have broken down, each party would be given an 'information pack' explaining the purpose of a period of consideration and reflection, the powers of the court, etc. After 11 months, either or both parties could apply for an order for divorce or

4.10.2 The present law is discriminatory and unjust

4.10.3 The present law distorts the parties' bargaining positions

4.10.4 The present law provokes unnecessary hostility and bitterness

4.10.5 The present law does nothing to save marriages

4.10.6 The present law can make things worse for the children

4.11 The Law Commission's conclusions

separation, following a declaration that the party, or parties, believe(s) that the marriage has broken down irreparably. An order for divorce or separation would be made one month after the application (ie, 12 months from the date of lodging of the initial statement).

4.12 Proposals for reform: the Lord Chancellor's Green Paper (1994)

The Lord Chancellor commented that the 1990 Report (see 4.11 above) had not recognised sufficiently the need for the law to strengthen the institution of marriage. In the Green Paper 1994 he expressed his belief that marriage 'is a divinely appointed arrangement fundamental to the well-being of the community'.

The existing system allows divorce to be obtained quickly and easily without the parties being required to have regard to the consequences; it does nothing to save the marriage.

- The Green Paper urges adoption of 'Family Mediation'. If parties cannot save their marriage they need to resolve questions about the consequences of its dissolution. These must be faced. 'Family mediation' refers to the various ways in which a couple can negotiate agreements directly 'with the help of a neutral third party, about their children, their finances and their property.' Mediation will remove the need for adjudication by the courts.

- 'We should look to see what we can do through mediation and other ways to keep the costs of divorce down.'

- A good law would support the institution of marriage. Where it is not possible to prevent the dissolution of the marriage, the law should seek to eliminate unnecessary conflict for the parties, but particularly for their children.

4.13 Comments of the Law Society on family mediation

In its response to the Green Paper, the Law Society (see [1944] Fam Law 340) recommends the establishment of a regulatory framework for mediation services to ensure a high standard. Any expansion in mediation should be gradual and should not lead to restrictions on the ability of a person to seek legal advice. Mediation should not be made compulsory: it is inappropriate where there has been domestic violence or 'other power imbalances in the relationship'.

4.14 Comments of the SFLA on family mediation

The Solicitors Family Law Association responded to that section of the Green Paper dealing with family mediation by noting (see [1994] Fam Law 179) that although the process had a part to play in a reformed divorce system, it was not suited to all of the divorcing population. It was wrong to extrapolate the present success of mediation and build an entire new system upon it. Mediation does not automatically resolve the emotional difficulties attendant upon divorce proceedings. In particular, solicitors have a key role to play in buttressing the mediation process by offering information and advice when required.

Summary of Chapter 4

Divorce (2): The Ground for Divorce

The only ground for divorce is irretrievable breakdown of the marriage: see s 1(1) MCA 1973. Further, the court will not accept that the marriage has broken down irretrievably unless satisfied of one or more of five facts set out in s 1(2) MCA 1973.

The sole ground for divorce

Fact 1: Respondent's adultery and petitioner finds it intolerable to live with respondent.

Adultery *plus* intolerability constitute the fact; adultery on its own will not suffice. Adultery involves consensual sexual intercourse between a married person and a person of the opposite sex who is not that married person's spouse, during the period of the marriage. The standard of proof of adultery seems to be on a balance of probabilities. The test of intolerability is subjective.

Fact 2: Respondent has behaved in such a way that the petitioner cannot reasonably be expected to live with respondent.

'Unreasonable behaviour' is not the issue: rather it must be shown that respondent has behaved in a particular manner so that petitioner cannot be expected to live with respondent. All the circumstances must be taken into account.

Note the 'right-thinking person' test in *O'Neill v O'Neill* (1975).

Fact 3: Respondent has deserted petitioner for a continuous period of at least two years immediately preceding the presentation of the petition.

It must be shown that the deserting spouse has withdrawn not necessarily from a place, but rather from a state of things, eg, a communal existence. *Animus deserendi* must be shown. 'Constructive desertion' involves one spouse's behaviour driving out the other. (But an express separation agreement would constitute a bar to constructive desertion.)

Fact 4: Parties have lived apart for a continuous period of two years immediately preceding presentation of petition, and repondent consents to decree being granted.

In relation to this fact, husband and wife are treated as living apart unless they are living together in the same household. Respondent must indicate in a positive manner that he consents to grant of decree.

Fact 5: Parties to the marriage have lived apart continuously for five years immediately preceding presentation of petition.

The basis of this fact is similar to that of the two year separation; but respondent's consent is *not* needed. Respondent may oppose grant of decree on the ground that it would result in grave financial or other hardship to him.

Bars to grant of divorce

Bars to grant of divorce include: failure of petitioner to show irretrievable breakdown of marriage, to prove one of the five facts, or, eg, where petitioner seeking to rely on adultery committed by respondent has, after the fact of adultery became known, lived with respondent for a period, or periods together exceeding six months.

A decree may not be made absolute where the court is not satisfied that appropriate arrangements have been made for the children.

Recognition of foreign divorces obtained by proceedings

Recognition is given if the foreign divorce is effective under the law of the country in which it was obtained and either party was habitually resident in that country or was a national of that country or domiciled there.

Proposals for reform: the 1994 Green Paper

The Green Paper urges adoption of 'family mediation' to allow the resolution of questions arising from the possible consequences of dissolution of the marriage. The law should aim at supporting the institution of marriage. Where dissolution cannot be prevented, the elimination of conflict, particularly where it might involve children, ought to be pursued.

Chapter 5

Judicial Separation and Domestic Violence

Judicial separation is based upon a decree as a result of which it becomes no longer necessary for the petitioner to cohabit with the respondent: see s 17 MCA 1973. The decree replaced the divorce *a mensa et thoro* (see 3.1) which was abolished by MCA 1857. Its popularity appears to be diminishing: in 1992 there were some 2,500 petitions, as compared with almost 190,000 petitions for divorce. The decline in its use has been attributed to the speed with which decrees of divorce may now be obtained, the growth in the modes of provision of maintenance, and the increasing availability and use of injunctions. The remedy of judicial separation remains in use, however, for the following reasons:	5.1	Background

- It is available where less than one year has elapsed since the date of the marriage.

- It is preferable where spouses have a religious or other objection to the principle of divorce.

- It is useful where spouses wish to obtain financial orders but neither wishes to remarry. It should be noted that the decree has no application to unmarried cohabitants.

Any one of the five facts upon which a petitioner relies to establish irretrievable breakdown of marriage (see 4.2) can constitute the grounds for judicial separation (see s 17 MCA 1973). Where one of those facts is proved, a decree of judicial separation will generally be granted.	5.2	Grounds for the decree
The parties to a decree of judicial separation may not remarry, since the decree does not bring their marriage to an end; this differs from the effect of a decree of divorce. Further, the petition for a decree of judicial separation may be presented within one year of the date of the marriage; this has no application to the date of presentation of a petition for a decree of divorce. Further, unlike the decree of divorce, the granting of a decree of judicial separation does not demand proof of the irretrievable breakdown of the marriage (see s 17(2) MCA 1973).	5.3	Comparison with decree of divorce
Under DMPA 1973, the court has jurisdiction to hear a petition for judicial separation only if the following conditions exist:	5.4	Jurisdiction of the court

- either of the parties was domiciled in England or Wales when proceedings commenced or has been resident there throughout the period of one year ending with that date; or

- proceedings for divorce, nullity, judicial separation, over which the court exercises jurisdiction, have begun already: see s 5(2), (5).

The court's discretion to impose stays in separation proceedings is the same as in divorce proceedings (see 3.4).

5.5 Presenting the petition

The petition is presented to a divorce county court; proceedings may be transferred to the High Court. But where no defence to the petition is offered, it is possible to obtain a decree in the county court under the terms of the 'special procedure' (see 3.8).

5.6 Effect of the decree

The decree of judicial separation becomes effective immediately upon its pronouncement by the court. It is not necessary, as in the case of a decree of divorce, to await a second stage. Because the decree removes from the petitioner his duty to cohabit with the respondent (see s 18(1) MCA 1973) during the period in which it is in existence, neither petitioner nor respondent can be held to be in desertion. But because the marriage has not been dissolved, *neither party is free to remarry*. A decree of judicial separation does not act as a bar to a subsequent petition for divorce; indeed, the very fact of a judicial separation may be considered by the court hearing the petition as constituting proof of one or more of the facts necessary to establish irretrievable breakdown of the marriage.

The decree of judicial separation has an effect on the succession rights of the parties. Under s 18(2) MCA 1973, should either of the spouses die wholly or partly intestate during a period in which a decree of judicial separation is in force and should it be shown that the separation is continuing in effect, then the property of the deceased spouse will devolve as though the other spouse were dead.

5.7 Orders concerning children and financial relief

The court is empowered to make orders relating to the financial affairs of the spouses and the future of their children.

5.7.1 Welfare of the children

Under s 41 MCA 1973, as substituted by Sch 12, para 31 ChA 1989, the court, in granting a decree of judicial separation, must consider whether to exercise its powers in relation to a child of the family who has not reached the age of 16, and any other child to whom the court directs that the section shall apply. A decree of judicial separation will not be granted, until the court orders otherwise, where there are exceptional circumstances in relation to the children and directions by the court are considered to be necessary.

The following orders are among those available in relation to a decree of judicial separation:

- *Maintenance pending suit.* On a petition for judicial separation, a spouse may be ordered by the court to make whatever periodical payments to the other are considered reasonable (see s 22 MCA 1973). The order may impose retrospective payment from presentation of the petition until the decree or dismissal of the petition.

- *Periodical payments.* On grant of the decree, the court may order a spouse to make unsecured or secured periodical payments (see s 22 MCA 1973).

- *Lump sum payments.* The court may order a party to pay a lump sum (or sums) to the other. The sums may be paid in instalments (see s 23 MCA 1973).

- *Orders for the sale of property.* Where the court makes a secured periodical payment order or a lump sum order, it may make, additionally, an order for the sale of such property as may be specified, being property in which or in the proceeds of sale of which either or both of the parties to the marriage has/have a beneficial interest either in possession or reversion: s 24A MCA 1973, added by s 7 MHPA 1981 (see 9.8).

5.7.2 Financial relief

Either party may apply for the discharge of the decree when cohabitation has been resumed. *Haddon v Haddon* (1887) appeared to suggest that the discharge would be automatic in these circumstances: see also *Oram v Oram* (1923).

5.8 **Discharge of decree of judicial separation**

In *The Ground for Divorce* (1990), the Law Commission recommended that judicial separation be retained and renamed 'a separation order', to be utilised by persons who have objections, eg, of a religious nature, to divorce, and those who are unable to obtain a decree of divorce because of the time restriction. A separation order would not be made available until at least one year after the date of the marriage. Either spouse would be able to convert the decree into a divorce. Irretrievable breakdown of the marriage should become the sole ground for judicial separation.

5.9 **Recommendations of the Law Commission**

The phrase 'domestic violence' remains undefined specifically by statute. The Home Office Order (60/1990) (*Domestic Violence*) states that the phrase encompasses all aspects of

5.10 **Domestic violence: the essence of the problem**

physical, sexual and emotional abuse, ranging from threatening behaviour and minor assaults which lead to cuts and bruises, to serious injury, and sometimes even death. The common characteristics of cases of domestic violence are that they are rarely isolated occurrences, they are repeated over varying periods of time, are common during pregnancy, and tend to involve children living in the home. (It should be noted that, in the case of children, a measure of protection is afforded under C&YPA 1933 and ChA 1989.) In recent years some 50,000 cases have been reported annually.

5.10.1 Involvement of the police

Arguments in favour of involving the police in a case of domestic violence rest on their ability to react swiftly to provide protection for victims and to prevent any escalation of violence. Invoking the criminal law is, in the words of the Home Office Order, 'making at the outset the strongest statement that society can make denouncing the act'.

The Home Secretary has recommended that chief police officers should consider issuing a force policy statement concerning their likely response to domestic violence. Such a statement would be based upon an overriding duty to protect victims and children from further attack, the need to treat domestic violence as seriously as any other form of violence, the use and value of powers of arrest, the importance of record-keeping so as to allow monitoring of the value of the policy in practice.

5.10.2 Arguments against invoking the criminal law

It has been suggested that invoking the criminal law in cases of domestic violence is a 'blunt tool': it tends to place emphasis on the offender rather than the victim, it cannot deal with the treatment required by the offender, it is often counter-productive for the ill-treated wife in that she may suffer financial disadvantage and her children may experience traumas. The Home Office Circular concludes, nevertheless, that there are cases where the criminal law *must* be used. Such cases ought to be restricted to those occasions where there is a need present 'for coercive prevention of violence in view of serious physical or emotional danger to the wife'. The choice of remedy must be 'a professional principled decision'.

5.11 Aspects of criminal law in relation to domestic violence

The circumstances of domestic violence often involve offences such as assault, battery and wounding. They carry penalties of fines, imprisonment, or both. (Note the general principle that 'every person's body is inviolate and proof against any form of physical molestation': *per* Thorpe J in *Secretary of State for the Home Office v Robb* (1994).)

- *Assault* is constituted by the creation in the mind of a person the belief that unlawful force is to be used immediately against him/her. Words in themselves do not constitute an assault and there is no assault when it is obvious to the wife who is threatened by her husband that he is unable to carry out his threat.

- *Battery* is the actual, intended use of unlawful force on a person without his consent. 'Violence' includes the slightest force; no actual harm need result.

- *Wounding* is covered by the Offences against the Person Act 1861. It is an offence under s 18 to unlawfully and maliciously wound or cause grievous harm: see also s 20.

Note that, in addition to police prosecution in relation to offences involving violence, a private prosecution can be brought by a spouse laying a complaint before the magistrates.

5.12 Exclusion of the violent spouse

There may be circumstances in which one spouse commits or threatens to commit violence against the other spouse and/or children within the matrimonial home. The following remedies exist:

- An order under the Matrimonial Homes Act 1983.
- An order under the DVMPA 1976.
- An order under the DPMCA 1978.
- An order involving the inherent jurisdiction of the court.

Each of these remedies is discussed below.

5.13 Order under MHA 1983

If one spouse has rights of occupation (see s 1(1) MHA 1983), then either spouse may apply for an order to be made by the High Court or a county court enforcing or terminating those rights, suspending or prohibiting the right to occupy the home, or requiring a spouse to allow the other spouse to exercise the rights. Before the court makes an order ousting a spouse, it will take into account the conduct of the parties and will seek to consider the reasonableness of the wish to exclude, the needs and resources of the spouse, the needs of the children and the possibility of a reconciliation being effected. An application will be refused where there is no evidence of conduct which would justify an order for ouster (see s 1 at 7.9).

In *Elsworth v Elsworth* (1978), the wife left the matrimonial home and refused to return while her husband was there; but she was unable to produce a satisfactory reason for not returning. The court refused an order to oust the husband. In *Walker v Walker* (1978), an order was granted where the wife suffered from acute depression, making it impossible for the parties to live together. The court held that all the circumstances of the case had to be regarded – the husband's behaviour, the wife's behaviour, the effect on the children if the husband stays or if he does not, the husband's personal circumstances, the likelihood of injury to either spouse, their physical and mental health.

Any order made by the court under MHA 1983 endures as long as the marriage continues; it ends on divorce, unless continued by the court: see ss 1(10) and 2(4). An ouster order generally lasts for three months, but can be granted indefinitely: see s 1(4).

5.14 Order under DVMPA 1976

Under s 1(1) DVMPA 1976 the court has jurisdiction to grant an injunction containing one or more of the following provisions: a provision restraining the other party to the marriage from molesting the applicant; a provision restraining the other party from molesting a child living with the applicant; a provision excluding the other party from the matrimonial home or a part of it or a specified area in which it is situated; a provision requiring the other party to allow the applicant to enter and remain in the matrimonial home or part of it: s 1(1). The injunction may be granted whether or not any other relief is sought in the proceedings.

5.14.1 Persons to whom s 1(1) applies

Section 1(1) of the 1976 Act applies to a man and woman who are living with each other in the same household as husband and wife as it applies to the parties to a marriage, and any reference to the matrimonial home is to be construed accordingly: s 1(2).

5.14.2 Effect of *Richards v Richards* (1984)

In *Richards v Richards* (1984), the House of Lords decided that applications for ouster injunctions in proceedings involving husband and wife ought to be made under MHA 1983. This means that when the court is deciding upon an ouster application it must take into account the principles set out under s 1(3) MHA 1983 (ie, conduct of spouses in relation to each other, respective needs and financial resources, needs of children and all circumstances of the case). It will be noted that the needs of the children are *not* considered paramount in this context. (In *Richards v Richards*, the judge had found that the wife, who had made an application for ouster of the husband, had no reasonable ground for refusing to live in the same house; the application was granted, however in the interests of the children. The House of Lords held that the judge was *wrong:* the order was neither just nor reasonable.)

Note *Lee v Lee* (1984) in which the Court of Appeal held that the s 1(3) criteria were to be applied if proceedings were brought in disputes between unmarried cohabitants.

5.14.3 Molestation

'Molestation' in the context of the DVMPA 1976 has not been defined by statute; it seems to be wider than mere 'violence'. 'Violence is a form of molestation but molestation may take place without the threat or use of violence and still be serious and inimical to mental and physical health': *Davis v Johnson* (1979). In *Vaughan v Vaughan* (1973), Stephenson LJ spoke of "molest" as a 'wide plain word which ... if I had to find one synonym for it, I should select "pester".' The word has been interpreted by some commentators as involving acts intended to injure or annoy a complainant, creating such a degree of harassment as to call for the intervention of the court: see *F v F* (1989); *Johnson v Walton* (1990).

5.14.4 Power of arrest under DVMPA 1976

Under s 2(1), where, on an application by a party to a marriage, a judge grants an injunction containing a provision restraining the other party from using violence against the applicant or a child living with the applicant, or excluding the other party from the matrimonial home or from a specified area in which the home is included, the judge may, if he is satisfied that the other party has caused actual bodily harm to the applicant or child and considers it likely that he will do so again, attach a power of arrest to the injunction.

- A power of arrest is granted for a limited period, usually of three months: see *Hopper v Hopper* (1979).
- Under s 2(3), where a power of arrest is attached to an injunction, a constable may arrest without warrant a person whom he has reasonable cause for suspecting of being in breach of the injunction by reason of that person's use of violence or his entry into any premises or area.

5.14.5 Emergency

Application for an injunction may be heard swiftly after notice has been given to: the respondent: see Order 13, r 6(3). Interim orders may be obtained *ex parte* where there is real, immediate danger of serious injury or incurable damage.

5.14.6 Orders under ChA 1989

For purposes of the ChA 1989, proceedings under MHA 1983, DVMPA 1976, DPMCA 1978, are classified as 'family proceedings'. The court may, in hearings under this legislation, issue orders (residence orders, prohibition orders, etc (see 13.1.)) concerning the future upbringing of the children.

5.15 Order under DPMCA 1978

Under DPMCA 1978, on the application of a spouse – the Act is not available where the parties are unmarried – magistrates may issue *personal protection* and *exclusion orders*.

Under s 16(2), where the court is satisfied that the respondent has used, or threatened to use, violence against the applicant or a child of the family and that it is necessary for the protection of either of them that an order should be made, it will make one or both of the following orders: an order that the respondent shall not use or threaten to use violence against the applicant; an order that the respondent shall not use or threaten to use violence against a child of the family.

Under s 16(3), where the court is satisfied that the respondent has used violence against the applicant or a child of the family, or has threatened to use violence against either of them, *and* has used violence against some other person, or respondent has, in contravention of an order made under s 16(2), threatened to use violence against the applicant or a child of the family, and that either of them is in danger of being physically harmed by the respondent (or would be in such danger if either were to enter the matrimonial home), the court may make one or both of the following orders: an order requiring the respondent to leave the matrimonial home; an order prohibiting the respondent from entering the matrimonial home.

Where appropriate, the court may make an order requiring the respondent to allow the applicant to enter and remain in the matrimonial home.

5.15.1 Power of arrest

Where the court is satisfied that the respondent has physically harmed the applicant or child *and* that this is likely to be repeated, a power of arrest may be attached to the order: s 18(1).

A power of arrest may be made for a limited period or indefinitely. The usual period is three months.

5.15.2 *Ex parte* orders

Where danger of physical harm to the applicant or a child is believed to be imminent, an *ex parte* order may be made. It continues for 28 days: see s 16(7).

5.16 Injunctions granted under the inherent power of the court

Injunctions may be granted under the inherent jurisdiction of the court by the High Court and county court where it appears just and convenient to do so: see Supreme Court Act 1981, s 37(1), (2) and County Courts Act 1984, s 38(1), as amended by Courts and Legal Services Act 1990, s 3. The injunction sought must be ancillary to other proceedings; it will be granted only in support of some existing right (legal or equitable). An application may be made by married or unmarried persons: see *Ainsbury v Millington* (1986); *Beard v Beard* (1981).

5.17 Accommodation for victims of violence in the home

There are circumstances in which victims of domestic violence may be made homeless or may be threatened with being made homeless. In cases of this nature the victim can make application for appropriate assistance from the housing authority. HA 1985, Part III, imposes duties upon housing authorities to assist such persons.

5.17.1 Meaning of 'homeless'

For purposes of HA 1985, a person is homeless if he has no accommodation in England, Wales or Scotland: s 58(1). By virtue of s 58(3) a person is also homeless if he cannot secure entry to the home, or it is probable that occupation of it will lead to violence from some other person residing in it or to threats of violence from some other person residing in it and likely to carry out the threats. A person is threatened with homelessness if it is likely that he will become homeless within 28 days: s 58(3).

5.17.2 Priority need

Persons with a 'priority need' for accommodation include: a pregnant woman or a person with whom a pregnant woman resides or might be expected to reside; a person with whom dependent children reside or might reasonably be expected to reside; a person who is vulnerable because of old age, mental illness or handicap or physical disability or other special reason: s 59(1). See *R v Kingswood BC ex p Smith-Morse* (1994).

Under s 75, 'accommodation shall be regarded as available for a person's occupation only if it is available for occupation both by him and by any other person who might be reasonably be expected to reside with him ...'. In *R v Newham LBC ex p Dada* (1995), the Court of Appeal held that a child *en ventre sa mère* was not a 'person who might reasonably be expected to live with' the mother, for purposes of s 75. A housing authority, therefore, carrying out its duty under the Act to secure that accommodation became available for a homeless pregnant woman was *not* required to take account of the unborn child when considering the suitability of accommodation offered (see s 65).

5.17.3 Becoming homeless intentionally

A person becomes homeless intentionally if he deliberately does or fails to do anything in consequence of which he ceases to occupy accommodation which is available for his occupation and which it would have been reasonable for him to continue to occupy: s 60(1).

5.17.4 The local authority's duty

The duty of the local authority is determined by whether or not they consider the person concerned to have become intentionally homeless. Where a victim of violence is homeless unintentionally (or threatened with homelessness) and has a priority need, the local authority are obliged to find accommodation for that person. Where a person is homeless intentionally and has a priority need, the local authority have the duty to find temporary accommodation for that person. Where a person is intentionally homeless and has no priority need, the local authority need give advice and assistance only: see ss 62-70: see *R v Ealing LBC ex p Sidhu* (1982); *R v Oldham MBC ex p B* (1993).

5.18 Improving protection for victims of domestic violence

Existing law concerning domestic violence has been criticised as 'a hotchpotch of enactments of limited scope': *per* Lord Scarman in *Richards v Richards* (1984). Others have commented upon the law's failure to grant appropriate protection to family members such as grandparents in situations characterised by sudden violence. The criteria in MHA 1983 (see 5.1 above) have been criticised because they omit any reference to the absolute priority of the child's welfare. In 1992, the Law Commission published a Report, *Family Law (Domestic Violence and Occupation of the Family Home)* (Law Com No 207): existing family law concerning domestic violence was criticised as complex and confusing, and an integrated range of remedies available to courts with appropriate jurisdiction was suggested. Some of the principal reforms proposed are noted below.

5.18.1 Extension of the range of applicants for orders

The range of persons who can apply for a non-molestation order and an occupation order (see 5.18.3) should be extended so as to include persons 'associated' with the respondent through a family or similar relationship. Persons entitled to apply would include spouses, former spouses, cohabitants and former cohabitants, other persons living in the same household, certain specified relations, engaged and former engaged couples, parents and other persons who have or have had parental responsibility for a child. Protection should be made available for a 'relevant child', ie, one who is living with, or might reasonably be expected to live with either of the parties, or any child whose interests are considered by the court to be relevant.

5.18.2 Non-molestation orders

The Law Commission recommends that orders related to molestation should be flexible so that they can fit the facts of particular cases. To define 'molestation' would be unduly restrictive. The relevant law ought to be cast in broad terms so as to allow the court to act with speed and to issue orders whenever it is just and reasonable to do so, and particularly where it is essential that the health, safety and well-being of the applicant or child be secured. Orders should be made for a fixed term or 'until further notice'.

5.18.3 Occupation orders

Where an applicant is entitled to occupy property as the result of some statutory or contractual right or a beneficial interest, he/she should be able to obtain an 'occupation order' where the property has served as the home of the parties. An applicant who has no right to occupy the property ought to be able to make application for an order against a former spouse, a cohabitant or former cohabitant. Further, the court ought to be able to make an order/concerning property which was intended to, but did not, become the home.

5.18.4 Extension of rights of unmarried cohabitants

The power of the court to transfer a tenancy from one spouse to the other (which can be exercised on divorce, judicial separation, nullity) should be enlarged so as to allow the transfer of a tenancy from one unmarried cohabitant to the other in the event of a breakdown of the relationship.

5.18.5 *Ex parte* orders

Courts should retain their discretion to grant *ex parte* orders whenever it appears just and convenient to do so. Matters to be considered should include the risk of significant harm to the applicant or child should there be no immediate order, and the likelihood that the applicant may be deterred if an order were not issued without delay.

5.18.6 Powers of arrest

The court should be obliged to attach a power of arrest to an order where there has been violence or the threat of violence, unless it can be shown that the applicant or child is protected adequately. (Additionally, the police ought to be given a right to apply for civil proceedings on behalf of the victim in cases where he/she is unwilling to take this step.)

5.19 A footnote to the recommendations of the Law Commission

In 1994 the Lord Chancellor announced that the Government intended to implement most of the recommendations of the Law Commission. But the Government had not accepted some of the proposals concerning persons who should be allowed to apply for orders, nor could it accept the suggestion of empowering the police to take civil action on behalf of victims of domestic violence.

In 1994 the Lord Chancellor announced that the Government intended to implement most of the recommedations of the Law Commission. But the Government had not accepted some of the proposals concerning persons who should be allowed to apply for orders, nor could it accept the suggestion of empowering the police to take civil action on behalf f of victims of domestic violence.

On 9 February 1995, the Family Homes and Domestic Violence Bill received its first reading on the House of Lords. Among its proposals are the following.

- There shall be a unified code for the protection of 'associated persons', ie, close relatives, family household members, individuals having parental responsibility.
- Non-molestation orders will be available to all 'associated persons'.
- Orders available will include: prohibition of molestation, exclusion from the matrimonial home, occupation orders, declaratory orders concerning legal rights, eg, occupation rights.
- Enforcement orders will include power of arrest, order for arrest, remand following arrest, remand for medical reports.

Summary of Chapter 5

Judicial Separation and Domestic Violence

Judicial separation is based upon a decree as a result of which the petitioner need no longer cohabit with respondent. The decree is available (unlike a decree of divorce) even where less than one year has elapsed since the date of the marriage. Grounds for the decree are constituted by any one of the five facts upon which a petitioner would rely in order to establish an irretrievable breakdown of marriage: see s 17 MCA 1973. A decree is generally granted, therefore, upon proof of any of the five facts. The decree becomes effective immediately on its pronouncement. Neither party is free to remarry; but the decree may be considered as constituting proof of one of the five facts necessary in any subsequent proceedings for divorce.

The decree of judicial separation

The court has jurisdiction to hear a petition for judicial separation only where either of the parties was domiciled in England or Wales when proceedings commenced or had been resident there throughout the year ending on that date; or where proceedings for divorce, nullity have already begun.

Jurisdiction of the court

The following orders are available in relation to a decree of judicial separation: maintenance pending suit; periodical payments (secured or unsecured); lump sum payments (which may be paid in instalments); sale of property.

Financial relief

When cohabitation is resumed, either party may apply for the discharge of a decree of judicial separation.

Discharge of the decree

The phrase is used to encompass all aspects of abuse – physical, sexual, emotional. The criminal law may, of course, be invoked, but there has been a marked reluctance on the part of individuals involved to pursue this course of action.

Domestic violence

The following remedies exist in circumstances where one spouse commits or threatens to commit violence against the other spouse and/or children within the matrimonial home.

Exclusion of the violent spouse

- *Order under MHA 1983*. The High Court or county court may make an order where one spouse has rights of occupation, terminating, suspending, or prohibiting the right to occupy the home, or requiring a spouse to allow the other to exercise the right.

- *Order under DVMPA 1976.* The court may grant an injunction restraining one party from molesting another, or from molesting a child living with the applicant, or excluding a party from the matrimonial home, or requiring a party to allow applicant to enter and remain in the matrimonial home.
- *Order under DPMCA 1978.* On the application of a spouse, magistrates may issue personal protection and exclusion orders. A power of arrest may be attached to the order. Ex parte orders, continuing for 28 days, may be made where the danger of physical harm to the child is believed to be imminent.
- *Injunctions granted under court's inherent jurisdiction.* Injunctions may be granted under the court's inherent jurisdiction where it appears just and convenient to do so. Application may be made by married or unmarried persons.

Accommodation for victims of violence in the home

HA 1985, Part III, imposes duties on housing authorities to assist victims of domestic violence who may be made homeless, or are threatened with being made homeless: see, eg, *R v Oldham MBC ex p B* (1993).

Proposals for reform

Suggestions have been made for an extension in the range of applicants for orders, for greater flexibility in the granting of non-molestation orders, for an extension of the rights of unmarried cohabitants in this area of legislation, and for the obligatory attachment of powers of arrest to orders where violence has been used or is threatened.

Chapter 6

Rights in Family Property (1): Interests; Succession

6.1 Introductory concepts

The 'property' of a family comprises the matrimonial home, financial assets, etc. The 'ownership', transfer and division of family property may give rise to a variety of problems, for example, the precise nature of the ownership of the family home which has been given 'in trust' for husband and wife, or the ownership of a joint account into which the husband alone pays money, or the remedy, if any, possessed by a widow for whom the deceased husband has failed to make appropriate financial provision. Problems of this nature constitute an important area of the province of family law.

6.1.1 Property and ownership in relation to spouses

For the purposes of this text, 'property' is understood in a relatively narrow sense as that which is the subject of ownership; it may be tangible or intangible, corporeal or incorporeal, real or personal: see, eg, s 205(1)(xx) LPA 1925: 'Property includes any thing in action, and any interests in real or personal property.'

'Ownership' is to be understood as a bundle of rights '... the entirety of the powers of use and disposal allowed by law' (Pollock). Hence, the ownership of the matrimonial home gives rights (eg, of use, disposal) to the spouses in occupation.

6.1.2 Real and personal property

'Real property' is generally constituted by freehold interests in land. A married couple's real property is the freehold interest it possesses in the matrimonial home. 'Personal property' comprises leasehold interests, and property other than land, such as the goods possessed by a family.

6.1.3 A trust

A trust is, in essence, an equitable obligation which imposes upon a trustee certain duties of dealing with property held and controlled by him for the benefit of persons described as beneficiaries. Thus, A, the owner of land, conveys it to B in fee simple, directing B to hold it in trust for C: A is the settlor, B is the trustee, C is the beneficiary, the land in question is the trust property.

6.1.4 Co-ownership

Where two (or more) persons, say husband and wife, have simultaneous and not consecutive interests in the same land at any one time, those persons are said to be entitled to concurrent interests and the land is said to be subject to co-ownership, as where there is a grant 'to John and his wife, Mary, in fee simple', or 'to John and his wife Mary, equally'. Examples are the joint tenancy and tenancy in common.

6.1.5 Joint tenancy

A *joint tenancy* exists where an entire estate or interest in land is vested simultaneously in the co-owners, John and his wife, Mary. Each co-owner is possessed of the entire joint property 'by every part and by the whole', that is, neither John nor Mary holds a specific share in the land. The total interest in the land is vested in each and both. As between themselves, the husband and wife possess separate rights, but as against others they are a single, composite owner.

The principal feature of the joint tenancy is the 'right of survivorship', ie, on the death of one joint tenant, say, Mary, her interest will pass to the surviving tenant, ie, John. Where the land in its entirety (ie, all the legal and beneficial interests) vests in a sole tenant, the joint tenancy is determined.

6.1.6 Tenancy in common

A *tenancy in common* exists where land is limited to two (or more) tenants and appropriate words of severance are used, as where land is granted 'to John and Mary equally'. The tenancy in common exists only in equity: s 1(6) LPA 1925. It cannot be created except behind a trust for sale: s 36(6) Settled Land Act 1925.

The right of survivorship does not have application to the tenancy in common. Thus, where John and Mary are tenants in common, and Mary dies, her share passes in accordance with her will or the rules of intestacy.

6.2 Development of property law as it relates to the wife

Substantial changes in the concept of 'a wife's property' have characterised the development of English family law. Today, a wife acquires and deals with property as if she were, in the eyes of the law, a single person. This is in total contrast to principle and practice in earlier eras during which rigid common law rules removed from the wife many of her personal proprietary rights; in practice, her property and earnings were vested absolutely in her husband. So-called 'matrimonial property' was under the total control of the husband.

6.2.1 Alleviation of common law rules

Doctrines formulated by the Court of Chancery resulted in the growth of a new concept – the wife's 'separate equitable estate' – allowing the settlement of property to the wife's 'sole and separate use'. The growth of the trust enabled the wife to ensure that, in considerable measure, property in trust might be dealt with according to her wishes.

6.2.2 Legislation in the 19th and 20th centuries

The legislation which is noted briefly below is of particular significance in the development of the wife's separate estate.

- MCA 1857. During a period of judicial separation, a wife was considered a *feme sole* in relation to property she acquired and, on the resumption of cohabitation, property thus acquired was deemed to be for her separate use. Further, on desertion, a protection order would protect her property and earnings from seizure by her husband by vesting them in her.

- MWPA 1870. In some cases, as where the wife acquired property such as earnings, the money was deemed to be held 'for her use'.
- MWPA 1882. A woman who married after 1882 was allowed to retain the property which she owned at the time of the marriage as her separate property. Additionally, she was to be considered capable of acquiring, holding, and disposing by will or otherwise, of any real or personal property as her separate property, in the same manner as if she were a *feme sole*, without the intervention of any trustee.
- Law Reform (Married Women and Tortfeasors) Act 1935. The principle of 'the separate estate' was abolished and the wife could henceforth hold and dispose of any property in all respects as if she were a *feme sole*.
- Married Women (Restraint upon Anticipation) Act 1949. This statute removed the restraints which prevented a wife exercising full powers of alienation of property.

6.3 The creation of interests in personal property

The property interests of husband or wife may emerge, for example, from the creation of a valid contract, or, in the case of a gift, from an intention to transfer, followed by delivery.

Note the significance of an appropriate mode of transfer in the creation of property rights. Thus, in *Re Cole* (1964), a husband bought a house in London and furnished it for his family, the members of which were living elsewhere at the time. When his wife subsequently came to London, he showed her over the house and said, 'It's all yours.' When the husband was later declared bankrupt, the wife claimed that the articles of furniture in the house belonged to her. The court held that a gift of chattels cannot be perfected by merely showing them to an intended donee and speaking words of gift. It must be shown that there was an unequivocal act of delivery or change in possession; the wife was not able to do so.

6.3.1 Rights arising under statute

The following statutes are of significance in interpreting the precise nature of the rights of a spouse:

- MWPA 1964. In the absence of any agreement to the contrary, where savings are made by a wife from a housekeeping allowance, they are considered as belonging to husband and wife in equal shares.

- Matrimonial Proceedings and Property Act 1970, s 37. Where a spouse makes a contribution of a substantial nature in money or money's worth to the improvement of property, then, in the absence of any agreement to the contrary, he/she is considered as having acquired a share, or an enlarged share, in the property.

6.3.2 The implied trust

Interests may arise from an implied trust, ie, one which will be enforced by the court as the result of surrounding circumstances or the language of the parties so that effect can be given to their implied, though unexpressed, intentions. An appropriate intention may be inferred by the court from, eg, payment of a deposit as part of the purchase price of the matrimonial home, or payment of mortgage instalments.

6.3.3 The presumption of advancement

The general principle in relation to advancement is that where a voluntary conveyance has been made to the wife of a donor, there will arise a presumption that a gift was intended. *Per* Jessel MR in *Bennet v Bennet* (1879): 'The doctrine of equity as regards presumption of gifts is this, that where one person stands in such a relation to another that there is an obligation on that person to make a provision for the other, and we find either a purchase or investment in the name of the other, or in the joint names of the person and the other, of an amount which would constitute a provision for the other, the presumption arises of an intention on the part of the person to discharge the obligation to the other, and therefore, in the absence of evidence to the contrary, that purchase or investment is held to be in itself evidence of a gift. In other words, the presumption of gift arises from the moral obligation to give.'

If we assume, therefore, that a husband buys property and that he has it conveyed to his wife, or that it is conveyed to husband and wife jointly (see 6.1.5 above), it will be considered in the first of these cases *prima facie* as a gift to the wife, and in the second case, both husband and wife will hold jointly as beneficial joint tenants. But should an intending husband buy property in the name of his intended wife, the presumption of a gift will arise if the marriage later takes place: *Wirth v Wirth* (1956).

6.3.4 Rebutting the presumption of advancement

The presumption of advancement may be rebutted by appropriate evidence of actual intention. *Per* Viscount Simonds in *Shephard v Cartwright* (1955): 'It must then be asked by what evidence can the presumption be rebutted, and it would, I think, be very unfortunate if any doubt were cast ... upon the well-settled law on the subject. It is, I think, correctly stated in substantially the same terms in every textbook that I have consulted and supported by authority extending over a long period of time. I will take as an example, a passage from *Snell's Equity* (24th edition): "The acts and declarations of the parties before or at the time of purchase, or so immediately after it as to constitute a part of the transaction, are admissible in evidence either for or against the party who did the act or made the declaration ... But subsequent declarations are admissible as evidence only against the party who made them, and not in his favour." The burden of authority in favour of the broad proposition I have cited is overwhelming and should not be disturbed.'

Note that the presumption of advancement may not be rebutted by evidence that a transfer of property was made for a fraudulent or illegal purpose: see *Gascoigne v Gascoigne* (1918) – attempt by husband to rebut presumption of advancement by evidence of a scheme designed deliberately with the intention of defrauding his creditors.

A spouse's rights in property may emerge through a constructive trust. In this context, 'constructive' is used to mean inferred, presumed from circumstances. *Per* Cardozo J in *Beatty v Guggenheim Exploration Co* (1919): 'A constructive trust is the formula through which the conscience of equity finds expression. When property has been acquired in such circumstances that the holder of the legal title may not in good conscience retain the beneficial interest, equity converts him into a trustee.'	6.3.5 The constructive trust
In recent years the courts have stressed the significance of the existence of a common intention of the parties that where a party has legal title to, say, the family home, the other party should have a beneficial interest in it. It must be shown, additionally, that the other party has acted to his/her detriment on the basis of the *common intention*.	6.3.6 Common intention and the constructive trust

In *Burns v Burns* (1984), X and Y lived together but did not marry. In 1963 X bought a house which was conveyed into his name. Y did not make a direct contribution to the purchase price or mortgage payments, but she looked after the house and children and paid the rates. The relationship ended in 1980 and Y claimed a beneficial interest in the house. *Per* Fox LJ: 'If the plaintiff is to establish that she has a beneficial interest in the property, she must establish that the defendant holds the legal estate upon trust to give effect to that interest. That follows from *Gissing v Gissing* (1971). For present purposes I think that such a trust can only arise (a) by express declaration or agreement or (b) by way of a trust where the claimant has directly provided part of the purchase price, or (c) from the common intention of the parties.' The court held that points (a) and (b) did not apply, and that Y's case rested upon her being able to show a common intention that she should have a beneficial interest in the property. Nothing had occurred between the parties at the time of acquisition of the house and thereafter to raise an equity which would act to prevent X denying Y's claim. Y was not able, therefore, to show any trust in her favour.

In *Lloyds Bank v Rosset* (1990), H bought a semi-derelict property for himself and his wife, W, which was intended to be used as their matrimonial home. H provided the purchase money and the house was conveyed into his name. W carried out considerable restoration work on the house. Later they separated and W claimed a beneficial interest under a constructive trust. The House of Lords held that W had no beneficial interest, There was no evidence of any express agreement as to how a beneficial interest was to be held. The work done by W was insufficient to establish any common intention that H and W were to hold jointly: see 7.5.1.

In *Ungurian v Lesnoff* (1989), X, a Polish citizen gave up her career, nationality and property in Poland to live with Y who purchased a London house in his name. X and Y lived in the house as man and wife, and X carried out important repairs to the property. After the relationship ended, she remained in the London house and claimed a beneficial interest in it. The court held that there was evidence of a common intention that X would have the right to reside in the London house for life. The house was to be considered as settled land and X was to be regarded as a tenant for life in accordance with the Settled Land Act 1925. She was entitled, therefore, to call for a vesting deed, appoint trustees and sell the house, reinvesting the proceeds in another property.

6.4 Some problems arising

Property rights on the death of a spouse are considered at 6.7 below. Problems relating to a bank account held by spouses are noted at 6.4.1-6.4.4 below.

6.4.1 H and W pay into a joint bank account

In *Jones v Maynard* (1951), husband and wife had paid into and withdrawn from a joint banking account. They were later divorced. It was held that the balance in the account belonged to them jointly, being considered by the court as 'a joint purse'. *Per* Vaisey J: 'I think that the principle which applies here is Plato's definition of equality as a "sort of justice". If you cannot find any other, equality is the proper basis.'

Money held in an account which is in the name of one spouse only belongs to the named spouse unless there is clear proof of an intention to the contrary.

Where the husband alone makes payments into a joint account, there is a rebuttable presumption of advancement (see 6.3.3 above) which operates in favour of the wife: see *Hoddinott v Hoddinott* (1949).

Generally, in a case where W alone makes payments into a joint banking account, the court will order the money to be held on trust for the wife: see *Heseltine v Heseltine* (1971).

The following proposal was advanced in the Law Commission Working Paper (1985), *Transfer of Money between Spouses*. 'Property acquired with the money should be co-owned in the same way as the money itself is co-owned. Property acquired with the money in effect represents the money and it would be illogical not to extend co-ownership so far. The effect would therefore be to impose co-ownership on some household goods of married couples, and in some cases on the matrimonial home ... Where chattels are concerned we provisionally recommend that, if acquired with money made available to buy the chattel itself if it is a joint one, they should be jointly owned at law, and not merely in equity. There are no special formalities required to create legal interests in chattels and we do not think there is any difficulty in creating legal co-ownership by statute ...'.

The Law Commission Report (1988) stated: 'Where money is paid by either spouse to the other or to buy property and the payment or purchase is for common purposes, the money or property will be jointly owned, subject to a contrary intention on the part of the purchasing spouse known to the other spouse ... We would retain the idea of making money paid by one spouse to the other for common purposes into jointly owned money.'

The mode of devolution of property owned by a spouse will be determined by whether he has died testate or intestate. In the case of testacy, the testator has relative freedom of alienation. There are some few restrictions on his freedom.

- Failure to make reasonable provision for certain family members and dependants may result in applications by such persons under the I(PFD)A 1975, discussed at 6.9 below.

6.4.2 Account is held in the name of one spouse only

6.4.3 H alone pays into a joint account

6.4.4 W alone pays into a joint banking account

6.5 Proposals for reform

6.6 Law Commission Report: Matrimonial Property (1988)

6.7 Property rights on the death of a spouse

- Where property is owned by spouses as joint tenants (see 6.1.3) it devolves to the surviving spouse; where it is owned by spouses as tenants in common (see 6.1.3), the share of the deceased spouse may pass in accordance with his wishes as indicated in the will.

6.7.1 Valid will made by spouse

Under WA 1837, there is no capacity to make a valid will in the case of a person under 18 or a person of unsound mind. A will made by any person is not valid unless it is in writing, and signed by the testator, or by some other person in his presence and by his direction, and it appears that the testator intended by his signature to give effect to the will. Further, the signature must be made and acknowledged by the testator in the presence of two or more witnesses present at the same time, and each witness must either attest and sign the will or acknowledge his signature in the presence of the testator, but no other form of attestation is necessary: s 9.

6.7.2 Wills made by testator prior to marriage, and on divorce

A will made by a person is revoked by his/her marriage: see s 18 WA 1837; s 18 Administration of Justice Act 1982. This provision has application to individuals domiciled in England and Wales at the time of the marriage. But where the will gives an indication that at the time of its having been made the testator intends to marry X, and that he intended also that the will was not to be revoked as a result, the marriage to X does not revoke the will.

For the effect of divorce on wills, see 3.9 above.

6.8 Intestacy of a spouse

Where a deceased spouse (D) has failed to make a will, the distribution of his estate, after payment of expenses and debts, is made by the personal representatives on the basis of the rules contained in the Administration of Estates Act 1925. (Note that where a person dies intestate, property vests in the Public Trustee – not, as formerly, in the President of the Family Division – until there is a grant of administration: s 14 LP (Miscellaneous Provisions) A 1994.) (See the Law Reform (Succession) Bill.)

6.8.1 D leaves a spouse but no issue or blood relations

Where D leaves a spouse and there are no children or blood relations, the residuary estate goes to the surviving spouse absolutely.

6.8.2 D leaves a spouse and issue

Where D leaves a spouse and issue, the spouse receives the personal chattels absolutely, a net sum (currently £125,000: see Family Provision Intestate Succession Order 1993, No 2906) and a life interest in half of the residuary estate. The other half is held on statutory trusts for the issue of the intestate.

Where D leaves a spouse and no issue, but blood relatives (parent, brother or sister of the whole blood or issue of such brother or sister), the spouse takes the personal chattels, a net sum of (currently) £200,000 and half the residue absolutely. The other half is held on the statutory trusts for the blood relatives.

6.8.3 D leaves a spouse, and blood relations, but no issue

Where D leaves no surviving spouse, the estate will be held on the statutory trusts for any issue. If there is no issue, the blood relatives take according to the following priority: parents, brothers and sisters, grandparents, uncles and aunts.

6.8.4 D leaves no surviving spouse

Where D leaves no surviving spouse, no issue and no blood relations, the entire estate passes as *bona vacantia* to the Crown. In such a case the Crown can exercise a discretion so as to provide for those dependants for whom D might have been expected to make provision.

6.8.5 D leaves no surviving spouse, no issue, and no blood relatives

Under s 18 FLRA 1987, illegitimacy is not taken into consideration in determining the rights of succession of an illegitimate person, the rights of succession to the estate of an illegitimate person, and the rights of succession which are traced through any illegitimate relationship.

6.8.6 Illegitimacy and succession on intestacy

Where, after the commencement of I(PFD)A 1975, an individual dies domiciled in England and Wales and is survived by any of the persons enumerated below, such persons may apply for an order under s 2 on the ground that the disposition of the estate of the deceased (D) effected by his will or the law relating to intestacy, or the combination of his will and that law, is not such as to make reasonable financial provision for the applicant: ss 1(1), 25(1).

6.9 **The Inheritance (Provision for Family and Dependants) Act 1975**

The following persons may apply under the Act:

6.9.1 Persons who may apply

- D's wife or husband: s 1(1)(a).

- A former wife or former husband of D who has not remarried: s 1(1)(b).

- A child of D: s 1(1)(c). 'Child' includes an illegitimate child and a child *en ventre sa mère* at D's death.

- Any person (not being D's child) who in the case of any marriage to which D was at any time a party, was treated by D as a child of the family in relation to that marriage: s 1(1)(d).

- Any person (not being a person mentioned above) who immediately before D's death was being maintained either wholly or partly by D: s 1(1)(e). A person is treated as being maintained by D, either wholly or partly, if D, otherwise than for full valuable consideration, was making a substantial contribution in money or money's worth towards the reasonable needs of that person: s 1(3).

6.9.2 Reasonable financial provision

'Reasonable financial provision', in relation to s 1(1)(a) means such provision as it would be reasonable in all the circumstances of the case for a husband or wife to receive, whether or not that provision is required for his/her maintenance: s 1(2)(a). In the case of any other application made under s 1(1) the phrase means such financial provision as it would be reasonable in all the circumstances of the case for the applicant to receive for his maintenance: s 1(2)(b). See *Malone v Harrison* (1979).

See also *Re Besterman* (1984); *Re Bunning* (1984); *Davis v Davis* (1993).

6.9.3 Types of order available

Except with the court's special permission, an application for an order under s 2 must be made within six months from the date on which representation with respect to D's estate is first taken out: s 4: see *Re Dennis* (1981). Where the court is satisfied that D failed to make reasonable financial provision for an applicant, one of the following orders may be made under s 2:

- order for periodical payments out of D's net estate;
- order for lump sum payment out of D's net estate;
- order for transfer of property comprised in D's net estate;
- order for the acquisition of property comprised in D's estate and its transfer to the applicant for his benefit;
- order for the variation of any ante-nuptial or post-nuptial settlement made on the parties to a marriage to which D was one of the parties.

6.9.4 Matters to be taken into account

In exercising its powers under the 1975 Act, s 2, the court will consider: the financial resources and needs which the applicant is likely to have in the foreseeable future, D's obligations and responsibilities towards an applicant, the size and nature of D's estate, any disability of the applicant, any other matter, including the applicant's conduct, considered as relevant by the court: s 3(1).

6.10 The unmarried partner

An unmarried partner may, if he/she wishes, make a will in which property is devised to the other partner. But a surviving unmarried cohabitant is *not* covered by the ordinary rules of intestacy. (See the Law Reform (Succession) Bill.)

In considering responsibility for maintenance under the 1975 Act, the fact of unmarried cohabitation does not in itself give rise to that responsibility. In *Jelley v Illiffe* (1981), the plaintiff, J, had cohabited for eight years before her death, with I, a widow. J had applied for reasonable financial provision out of I's estate. The question was whether J had given full and valuable consideration in return for I having contributed substantially to his reasonable needs. *Per* Stephenson LJ: '[The object of I(PFD)A 1985] is surely to remedy, wherever reasonably possible, the injustice of one, who has been put by a deceased person in a position of dependency upon him, being deprived of any financial support, either by accident or by design of the deceased, after his death. To leave a dependant, to whom no legal or moral obligation is owed, unprovided for after death may not entitle the dependant to much, or, indeed, any financial provision in all the circumstances, but he is not disentitled from applying for such provision if he can prove that the deceased by his conduct made him dependent upon the deceased for maintenance, whether intentionally or not.' The Court of Appeal held that a reasonable cause of action existed and allowed the trial to proceed.

In *Bishop v Plumley* (1991), the Court of Appeal considered the question of whether a person had been 'maintained'. C and the deceased, D, cohabited for 10 years. D became extremely ill and received 'exceptionally devoted care and attention' from C. In D's will he made no provision for C, who continued to live on social security benefit in D's house. C applied for provision from D's estate, under s 1(1)(e), on the ground that she was being maintained by D, because D otherwise than for full valuable consideration was making a substantial contribution in money or money's worth towards C's reasonable needs.

The Court of Appeal held that where D had provided a secure home for his partner, C, and she had provided him with connubial services, that would demonstrate that D had made a substantial contribution towards C's needs for the purposes of s 1(3) of the 1975 Act.

See also *Re Beaumont* (1979); *Harrington v Gill* (1983); *Layton v Martin* (1986).

Summary of Chapter 6

Rights in Family Property (1): Interests; Succession

Ownership is to be understood, in relation to family law, as 'a bundle of rights', eg, rights to own, use, dispose of the matrimonial home. Formerly-existing restrictions on the ownership rights of a wife have been removed.

The *trust* is an equitable obligation which imposes upon a trustee duties in relation to property held and controlled by him: for the benefit of persons described as 'beneficiaries'.

Spouses may have simultaneous interests in the same land at any one time *concurrent ownership*. A *joint tenancy* involves an interest in land vested simultaneously in spouses as co-owners. A *tenancy in common* arises where land is limited to spouses and words of severance ('to Joe and Jane equally') are used. In the case of a joint tenancy, the *right of survivorship* applies.

Aspects of ownership in relation to family property

An implied trust is enforced by the court to give effect to the parties' implied, but unexpressed, intentions, eg, payment of a deposit as part of the purchase price of the matrimonial home.

In the case of a voluntary conveyance made to the wife of the donor, there is a presumption that a gift was intended (presumption of advancement). A presumption of gift may arise from a moral obligation to give. It may be rebutted by appropriate evidence of actual intention: see *Shephard v Cartwright* (1955).

Implied trust; presumption of advancement

'Constructive' means, in this context, 'inferred, presumed through circumstances'. The courts seek evidence of *common intention* of the parties and consider whether one party has acted to his/her detriment on the basis of that common intention: see *Burns v Burns* (1984); *Lloyds Bank v Rosset* (1990); *Ungurian v Lesnoff* (1989).

Constructive trust

Money held in account in name of one spouse only belongs to the named spouse (in absence of an intention to the contrary). Husband alone pays into joint account: rebuttable presumption of advancement which operates in wife's favour. Wife alone pays into joint banking account money to be held on trust for wife.

Spouses' banking account

Will made by spouse	Spouse-testator must be at least 18 and of sound mind: see WA 1837. Will made by a person is revoked by his/her marriage, in the absence of clear indications that the testator intends to marry a particular individual.
Intestacy of spouse	Where a deceased spouse has failed to make a will, his/her estate is distributed, after payment of expenses and debts, in accordance with rules under the Administration of Estates Act 1925, eg, the residuary estate goes to a surviving spouse absolutely where there are no children or blood relations. Where there is no surviving spouse, the estate is held on the statutory trusts for any issue.
Inheritance (Provision for Family and Dependants) Act 1975	In some cases, a surviving spouse, former spouse who has not remarried, child of the deceased, etc, may apply under the 1975 Act on the ground that the disposition of the estate of the deceased as effected by his will, or resulting from his intestacy, or the combination of both, is not such as to make 'reasonable financial provision' for the applicant. The court may make an order for periodical payments out of the net estate, or payment of a lump sum, or an order for the transfer or acquisition of property in the net estate.
The unmarried partner	An unmarried partner may devise property to the other partner, but a surviving unmarried cohabitant is *not* covered by the ordinary rules of intestacy.

Chapter 7

Rights in Family Property (2): The Matrimonial Home

The matrimonial home is 'the domicile where persons live together, actually or constructively, as man and wife': Black. How may interests in the matrimonial home be acquired? What is the relevance of the doctrine of proprietary estoppel to the acquisition of such interests? What are 'rights of occupation' in the matrimonial home and under what circumstances may a spouse ask for their restriction? How may rights of occupation be protected against third parties? What is the effect of the bankruptcy of a spouse upon the occupation rights of the other spouse? Matters of this nature are considered in this chapter in relation to the general problem of rights concerning the matrimonial home.

The acquisition of rights in the matrimonial home is discussed specifically in relation to proprietary estoppel, trusts and statute.

7.1 Problems relating to the matrimonial home

Rights in land may be acquired only on the basis of strict compliance with the formalities set out in LPA 1925, as subsequently amended. A legal estate in land may be created and conveyed *solely by deed*: s 52 LPA 1925. It is not possible to create or dispose of an interest in land except by a signed written document: s 53(1)(a) LPA 1925. A declaration of trust concerning land or an interest in it must be manifested and proved by writing: s 53(1)(b) LPA 1925. Note that s 53 does not affect the creation or operation of resulting, implied or constructive trusts: s 53(3) LPA 1925. (Hence a spouse may claim within s 52(2) an interest in the matrimonial home under a trust although there is neither deed nor conveyance.) See also Law of Property (Miscellaneous Provisions) Act 1989, stating that contracts for the sale or other disposition of interests in land can be made only in writing.

7.2 Acquisition of rights in land

Proprietary estoppel allows the creation of new rights. As applied to the matrimonial home, it means that where the owner of a title in land has given an assurance in express or implied terms concerning present or future rights in that land, he cannot in conscience withdraw that assurance if the person to whom it was given has relied on it to her detriment. (Such a principle is not confined to spouses; it relates also to unmarried cohabitants.)

7.3 Acquisition of an interest through proprietary estoppel

7.3.1 Essence of the doctrine

Proprietary estoppel has been described as rooted in the first principle upon which all courts of equity proceed, namely: 'to prevent a person from insisting on his strict legal rights – whether arising under a contract, or on his title deeds, or by statute – when it would be inequitable for him to do so having regard to the dealings which have taken place between the parties': *per* Lord Denning MR in *Crabb v Arun DC* (1976). The doctrine has been said to encapsulate a general principle 'asserting the unfairness or injustice or resiling from underlying assumptions that have been acted upon': *per* Cooke P in *Gillies v Keogh* (1989).

In relation to interests in the matrimonial home, the estoppel consists of: an assurance; a reliance; detriment.

7.3.2 *Pascoe v Turner* (1979)

X lived in Y's house, first as Y's housekeeper, later as his wife. They moved to another house for which Y paid the full purchase price; he also paid for its contents. Y later moved from the house, telling X that the house and contents were hers. She then renovated the house. Y knew of this and later gave X two months' notice to leave. It was held, in an action for possession that *Y was estopped* from denying X's right to occupy as a licensee.

Per Cumming-Bruce LJ:

'We take the view that the equity cannot here be satisfied without granting a remedy which assures to the defendant [X] security of tenure, quiet enjoyment, and freedom of action in respect of repairs and improvements: without interference from the plaintiff ... The court must grant a remedy effective to protect her [X] against the future manifestations of his [Y's] ruthlessness ... The equity to which the facts in this case give rise can only be satisfied by compelling the plaintiff [Y] to give effect to his promise and her [X's] expectations. He has so acted that he must perfect the gift.'

The fee simple in the house would be conveyed by Y to X.

7.3.3 *Maharaj v Chand* (1986)

A and B were unmarried cohabitants. A gave up her flat so as to live with B, following his representation that the flat would be a permanent home for her and her children. *B was estopped* from denying that A could remain permanently in the flat; he was not entitled to an order for vacant possession against her.

Per Cooke P: 'In the absence of evidence to the contrary, the right inference is that she acted in the belief that she would have an interest in the house, and not merely love and affection.' The Privy Council added the *caveat* that they were far from saying that whenever a union between an unmarried couple comes to an end, one who is the sole owner in law and equity of the property hitherto their home should not be able to obtain an order for possession against the other. It was the particular combination of facts which had led to estoppel in this case.

7.4 Acquisition of an interest through a resulting trust

'Resulting trusts are as firmly grounded in the settlor's interest as are express trusts, but with this difference – that the intent is inferred, or is presumed as a matter of law from the circumstances of the case': *per* Dickson J in *Rathwell v Rathwell* (1978). Thus, in *Sekhon v Alissa* (1989), mother and daughter contributed to the purchase of property conveyed into the (sole) name of the daughter. There was a presumption of a resulting trust in favour of the mother unless evidence could be produced to show that the mother had intended to make a personal loan to her daughter without acquiring an interest in the property. There was insufficient evidence and it was held that *the mother did have a beneficial interest* in the house; her share would correspond to the monetary value of her contribution. (The principle involved here has application also to spouses and unmarried cohabitants.)

- The mere expenditure of money will not in itself establish the existence of an interest. There must be proof of a shared intention in relation to beneficial interests in a property: see *Springette v Defoe* (1992).
- See also *Cooke v Head* (1972); *Marsh v Von Sternberg* (1986).

7.5 Acquisition of an interest through a constructive trust

For reference to constructive trusts in relation to a spouse's rights in property, see 6.3.5; 6.3.6. 'Strictly, constructive trusts arise where one who is already a trustee or otherwise clothed with fiduciary character seeks to retain an advantage from his trust': *Cowcher v Cowcher* (1972). The doctrine of constructive trusts in relation to the home has been used extensively where the question of beneficial interests has arisen on the breakdown of a marriage or the termination of a relationship involving an unmarried couple.

The significance of the existence of a common intention that a claimant shall have a beneficial interest in the home was discussed in 6.3.6.

7.5.1 Relevance of an express agreement

Note the speech of Lord Bridge in *Lloyds Bank v Rosset* (see 6.3.6). 'The first and fundamental question which must always be resolved is whether, independently of any inference to be drawn from the conduct of the parties in the course of sharing the house as their home and managing their joint affairs, there has been at any time prior to acquisition, or exceptionally at some later date, been any agreement, arrangement or understanding reached between them that the property is to be shared beneficially. The finding of an agreement or arrangement to share in this sense can only, I think, be based on evidence of express discussions between the partners, however imperfectly remembered, and however imprecise their terms may have been. Once a finding to this effect is made it will only be necessary for the partner asserting a claim to a beneficial interest against the partner entitled to the legal estate to show that he or she has acted to his or her detriment or significantly altered his or her position in reliance on the agreement in order to give rise to a constructive trust or proprietary estoppel.'

Lord Bridge continued thus: 'In sharp contrast with this situation is the very different one where there is no evidence to support a finding of an agreement or arrangement to share, however reasonable it might have been for the parties to reach such an agreement if they had applied their minds to the question, and where the court must rely entirely on the conduct of the parties both as the basis from which to infer a common intention to share the property beneficially and as the conduct relied on to give rise to a constructive trust. In this situation direct contributions to the purchase price by the partner who is not the legal owner, whether initially or by payment of mortgage instalments, will readily justify the inference necessary to the creation of a constructive trust. But, as I read the authorities, it is at least extremely doubtful whether anything less will do.'

7.5.2 H v M (Property: Beneficial Interest) (1992)

In *H v M* (1992), P and D were unmarried cohabitants who had two children. P purchased a property in his sole name and informed D that, when they married, she would have half the property. Purchase of the property was financed by a bank loan on P's overdraft; the charge was signed by P as purchaser and D as occupier. On the breakdown of the relationship, P began proceedings for the return of chattels removed from the property. D claimed an interest in the property. It was held that there was an agreement reached after joint discussion, that the property would be shared beneficially, as a result of which D had acted to her detriment in reliance on the agreement. *D was held to have a beneficial interest in the property.*

7.5.3 Thomas v Fuller-Brown (1988)

In *Thomas v Fuller-Brown* (1988), X and Y were unmarried cohabitants living in X's house. Y had not made any financial contribution to the purchase. Y performed substantial work on the house, which increased its value. When the relationship ended, Y claimed that his work had given him a beneficial interest in the house. The Court of Appeal held that *Y had no beneficial interest*; there was neither express agreement nor common intention, and Y was merely a licensee who had worked in return for board and lodging.

Where a claimant succeeds in establishing a beneficial interest in the matrimonial home, the amount of that interest, in monetary terms, is determined by the court on the basis of the original intention of the parties. Household expenses, expenditure involved in the upbringing of children will be considered.

In *Walker v Hall* (1984) X and Y lived together in a house owned by Y. The mortgage was paid from pooled income. The relationship ended, and the court held that the interests of X and Y were to be calculated in proportion to their contributions to the purchase price of the property; it was not open to the court, in the absence of a contrary specific intention, to hold that the house belonged to X and Y in equal shares, notwithstanding their unequal contributions, merely because it was bought as a family home at a time when X and Y intended their relationship to be permanent.

In *Risch v McFee* (1991), the evidence showed a common intention that a cohabitant should acquire a beneficial interest, and a loan by her could be taken into account by the court in assessing the quantum of her contribution to the acquisition of the property.

7.5.4 Quantum of interest

At common law a wife possesses a right to occupy the matrimonial home; the right binds the other spouse, but it cannot be enforced against a third party: see *National Provincial Bank Ltd v Ainsworth* (1963). Note *Chaudhry v Chaudhry* (1987) in which it was held that the wife's common law right could not be enforced where the home was owned jointly by the husband and a third party (his father).

The common law right of occupation is available to spouses, but *not* to other family members (eg, a parent) and, obviously, not to unmarried cohabitants. The common law right has been reinforced by statutory rights of occupation arising from the MHA 1967 and the MHA 1983. The statutory rights are purely personal and non-assignable (see *Wroth v Taylor* (1974)); they affect third parties only when registered in the appropriate form (see 7.13 below).

7.6 The problem of rights of occupation of the matrimonial home

Rights of occupation arise from MHA 1983 only in relation to a dwelling house: s 1(10). A 'dwelling house' is defined under s 10(1) as including 'any building or part thereof which is occupied as a dwelling, and any yard, garden, garage or

7.7 Property to which MHA 1983 applies

outhouse belonging to the dwelling house and occupied therewith'. The dwelling must have served as a matrimonial home of the spouses in question: s 1(10). It is of no consequence whether the home be held by freehold or leasehold.

7.8 Rights of occupation of the matrimonial home

'Where one spouse is entitled to occupy a dwelling house by virtue of a beneficial estate or interest or contract or by virtue of any enactment giving him or her the right to remain in occupation, and the other spouse is not so entitled, then, subject to the provisions of this Act, the spouse not so entitled shall have the following rights (in this Act referred to as 'rights of occupation') – (a) if in occupation, a right not to be evicted or excluded from the dwelling house or any part thereof by the other spouse except with the leave of the court given by an order under this section; (b) if not in occupation, a right with the leave of the court so given to enter into and occupy the dwelling house': s 1(1). Note that 'spouse' means a legally married spouse; the 1983 Act does not apply to unmarried cohabitants: see 5.13.

7.9 Orders under MHA 1983

So long as one spouse has rights of occupation, either of the spouses may apply to the court for an order declaring, enforcing, restricting or terminating those rights, or prohibiting suspending or restricting the exercise by either spouse of the right to occupy the dwelling house, or requiring either spouse to permit the exercise by the other of that right: s 1(2).

7.9.1 Discretion of the court

On application for an order under s 1, the court may make such order as it thinks just and reasonable, having regard to the conduct of the spouses in relation to each other and otherwise, to their respective needs and financial resources, to the needs of any children and to all the circumstances of the case. They may except part of the dwelling house from a spouse's rights of occupation, may order a spouse in occupation to make periodical payments to the other in respect of the occupation, may impose on either spouse obligations concerning repair and maintenance of the matrimonial home: see s 1(3).

7.9.2 Duration of order

Orders under s 1 may be limited for a period specified in the order or until further order: s 1(4).

7.9.3 Other matters under s 1

Under s 1(5) where a spouse is entitled under s 1 to occupy a dwelling house or part of it, any payment or tender made by that spouse towards satisfaction of any liability of the other spouse (eg rent, mortgages) shall be as good as if made by the other spouse. A landlord cannot refuse, therefore, to accept payments from a deserted wife and use the husband's non-payment as a ground for bringing possession proceedings.

No rights of occupation are conferred by the 1983 Act on spouses who have a legal interest in the property (since there is no need to do so), but s 9 gives a means of settling disputes relating to the occupation of property of this nature. Where each of two spouses is entitled by virtue of a legal estate vested in them jointly, to occupy a dwelling house in which they have or at any time have had a matrimonial home, either of them may apply to the court, with respect to the exercise during the subsistence of the marriage of the right to occupy the dwelling house, for an order prohibiting, suspending or restricting its exercise by the other or requiring the other to permit its exercise by the applicant: s 9(1).

7.10 Rights concerning matrimonial home where both spouses have estate, etc

A problem may arise in relation to, say, a wife whose husband decides on a course of action which may result in the matrimonial home being sold, without her knowledge, or against her wishes, so that her right to remain in the home is threatened. Problems of this nature were exacerbated by the ruling of the House of Lords in *National Provincial Bank v Ainsworth* (1965) which emphasised that a wife who did not have a legal or equitable interest in the matrimonial home was without any protection against a third party, so that she could *not* remain in the home merely by virtue of her status as a wife. But processes of registration of statutory rights of occupation have now, in effect, modified rights *in personam* to rights *in rem*, affording a measure of protection to the wife.

7.11 Protection of rights of occupation against third parties

(A system of compulsory registration of land now covers the entire country as from December 1990. But, because unregistered land need not be registered until the first sale, cases involving unregistered land remain of importance.)

7.12 Registration of rights of occupation in the case of unregistered land

Where a spouse enjoys statutory rights of occupation under s 1(1) MHA 1983, (see 7.8 above), such rights constitute *a registrable charge which binds a third party*.

The right is registrable as a *Class F charge* under s 2(7) Land Charges Act 1972. It is valid against the other spouse, however, whether registered or not. It is void against a purchaser of the land charged, or of any interest in such land, unless registered before completion of the purchase: s 4(8) Land Charges Act 1972. The term 'purchaser' refers in this context to a purchaser for value of a legal or equitable interest in the land.

7.13 Land Registration Act 1925, s 70(1)(g)

Section 70 of the Land Registration Act 1925 refers to interests which *override* the buyer's interests at the time of registration of a transfer of land. The category of rights under s 70(1)(g) consists of 'the rights of every person in actual occupation of the land or in receipt of the rents and profits thereof, save where enquiry is made of such person and the rights are not disclosed'. The object of this provision is 'to protect a person in actual occupation of land from having his rights lost in the welter of registration. He can stay there and do nothing. Yet he will be protected. No one can buy the land over his head and thereby take away or diminish his rights. It is up to every purchaser before he buys to make enquiry on the premises. If he fails to do so it is at his own risk': *per* Lord Denning in *Strand Securities Ltd v Caswell* (1965).

- What is protected is not the occupation of land, but the rights of those persons *in occupation*.
- 'Actual occupation is not an interest in itself': *per* Lord Templeman in *City of London BS v Flegg* (1987). 'Actual occupation' in the sense of s 70(1)(g) is a matter of fact, not a matter of law: *Hodgson v Marks* (1971).

7.13.1 Williams & Glyn's Bank v Boland (1981)

In *Williams & Glyn's Bank v Boland* (1981), the House of Lords held that where title to land is registered, the equitable right of a spouse in actual occupation of the matrimonial home legally owned by the other spouse was an overriding interest, having priority over a legal charge created by the legal owner. The wife's interest had been based on her contribution to the purchase price, but was not registered. After she had acquired the interest, the husband had mortgaged the house by way of legal mortgage to the bank, but they had made no enquiry concerning the wife's status. The husband defaulted, the bank foreclosed and obtained a possession order which was reversed on appeal. The bank's appeal was *dismissed*; the wife was a person 'in actual occupation' within s 70(1)(g), and the bank's charge was subject to the wife's overriding interest.

7.13.2 Kingsnorth Finance Ltd v Tizard (1986)

In *Kingsnorth Finance Ltd v Tizard* (1986), the court held that a wife who is separated from her husband but spends some part of almost every day in the matrimonial home (to look after the children) is to be considered as remaining 'in occupation'. A purchaser or mortgagee was obliged to carry out a full inspection of the property so as to discover who, other than the husband, is in occupation, and has to look behind the husband's attempted concealment of his wife's occupation.

7.14 Order for sale where spouses are co-owners

If the spouses are co-owners of the matrimonial home, ie, where they are joint tenants or tenants in common (see 6.1.5; 6.1.6), the property will be held on a *statutory trust for sale*. Note that a power to postpone the sale is, in the case of every trust for the sale of land, to be implied unless a contrary intention appears: s 25 LPA 1925.

7.14.1 Refusal of trustees for sale to exercise powers

If the trustees for sale refuse to sell or exercise powers, or requisite consents cannot be obtained, any person interested may apply to the court for a vesting or other order giving effect to the proposed transaction or for an order directing the trustees for sale to give effect thereto, and the court may make such order as it thinks fit: s 30 LPA 1925. Where a marriage has ended, a sale may be ordered: *Rawlings v Rawlings* (1964).

7.14.2 Exercise of the court's discretion to order a sale

The power of the court's discretion to enforce a trust for sale must be exercised 'according to well-known and ordinary principles': *per* Lord Greene in R*e Buchanan-Wollaston's Conveyance* (1939). All the circumstances of the case should be examined so as to ascertain whether it is 'right and proper that such an order shall be made'.

The same legal principles will be applied in ascertaining the beneficial interests of the parties, in the case of a proposed order for sale, whether the parties are married or not. But in the case of an unmarried couple the nature of the relationship must be considered carefully: *Bernard v Josephs* (1982).

7.15 Bankruptcy of spouse in relation to matrimonial home

Under the Insolvency Act 1986, the occupation rights of the spouse of a bankrupt will be protected: see s 336. Under s 336(2), where a spouse's rights of occupation under the MHA 1983 are a charge on the estate or interest of the other spouse, or of trustees for the other spouse, and the other spouse is adjudged bankrupt, the charge continues to subsist notwithstanding and binds the trustee of the bankrupt's estate and persons deriving title under the trustee, and any application for an order under the 1983 Act, s 1, shall be made to the court having jurisdiction in relation to the bankruptcy.

7.15.1 What the court will take into account

In making an order, eg, under the 1983 Act, s 1, the court will take into account: the interests of the bankrupt's creditors; the conduct of the spouse or former spouse, so far as contributing to the bankruptcy; the needs and financial resources of the spouse or former spouse; the needs of any children; all the circumstances of the case other than the needs of the bankrupt: s 336(4).

7.15.2 The 'breathing space'

The bankrupt's family has a 'breathing space' of one year before the sale of the property, but, after the end of that period, a sale of property, eg, the matrimonial home, will be ordered unless there are exceptional circumstances: s 336(5).

7.15.3 Protection of children

Section 337 of the Insolvency Act 1986 applies where a person who is entitled to occupy a dwelling house by virtue of a beneficial estate or interest is adjudged bankrupt, and any persons under 18 with whom that person had at some time occupied the dwelling house had their home with that person at the time when the bankruptcy petition was presented and at the commencement of the bankruptcy: s 337(1).

Whether or not the bankrupt's spouse has rights of occupation under MHA 1983, the bankrupt has the following rights as against the trustee of his estate:

- if in occupation, a right not to be evicted or excluded from the dwelling house or any part of it, except with the leave of the court; and

- if not in occupation, a right with the leave of the court to enter into and occupy the dwelling house.

The bankrupt's rights are a charge, having the like priority as an equitable interest created immediately before the commencement of the bankruptcy, on so much of his estate as vests in the trustee: s 337(2).

7.15.4 *Re Citro* (1990)

The general rule is that the rights of creditors ought usually to prevail over the interests of the wife and children. *Per* Nourse LJ in *Re Citro* (1990): 'The broad effect of [the] authorities can be summarised as follows. Where a spouse who has a beneficial interest in the matrimonial home has become bankrupt under debts which cannot be paid without the realisation of that interest, the voice of the creditors will usually prevail over the voice of the other spouse and a sale of the property ordered within a short period. The voice of the other spouse will only prevail in exceptional circumstances. No distinction is to be made between a case where the property is still being enjoyed as the matrimonial home and one where it is not....

What then are "exceptional circumstances"? As the cases show, it is not uncommon for a wife with young children to be faced with eviction in circumstances where the realisation of her beneficial interest will not produce enough to buy a comparable house in the same neighbourhood, or indeed elsewhere; and if she has to move elsewhere there may be problems ... Such circumstances, while engendering a natural sympathy in all who hear of them, cannot be described as exceptional. They are the melancholy consequences of debt and improvidence with which every civilised society has been familiar.'

The following recent decisions of the House of Lords and Court of Appeal in relation to *the wife and charges over the matrimonial home* should be noted.

In *CIBC Mortgages v Pitt* (1993) the matrimonial home owned by H and W was valued at £270,000; there was a small outstanding mortgage. H intended to obtain a loan for the purchase of shares and 'pressured' W into agreeing with his course of action. P made a loan of £150,000 secured on the matrimonial home, and H and W executed a legal charge in P's favour; W did not read the relevant documents. H purchased shares but was unable to keep up repayments on the loan following the stock market decline in 1987. P began proceedings for possession of the home and W raised a defence based on undue influence. The claim was dismissed by the judge and Court of Appeal.

The House of Lords *dismissed W's appeal*. W had succeeded in establishing undue influence against H, but this did not affect P since *H was not acting as its agent*. P had no notice of the undue influence and it could not be said that P had constructive notice by having been put on inquiry. P was entitled to enforce the charge on the matrimonial home.

In *Barclays Bank v O'Brien* (1994) the defendants, H and W, had agreed to execute a second mortgage on the matrimonial home as security for an overdraft given by P, a bank, to a company in which H alone had an interest. P instructed its branch to ensure that H and W were aware of the content and nature of documents and that they had taken legal advice. In the event, this was not done and W signed without reading the documents, relying on misrepresentations made by H. P later obtained an order for possession of the matrimonial home. W's appeal was dismissed by the judge who held that the mortgage was enforceable against her. Her appeal was allowed by the Court of Appeal. P appealed.

The House of Lords *dismissed P's appeal*, holding that a wife, induced by misrepresentation to stand as surety for a husband's debts, *possessed an equity against him* to set the transaction aside. A right of this nature was enforceable against a third party who had actual or constructive notice of those circumstances from which the equity arose. P (the bank) was fixed with constructive notice of the misrepresentation and, in the circumstances, W was entitled as against P to set aside the legal charge on the matrimonial home.

7.16 A note on the wife and charges over the matrimonial home

In *TSB Bank v Camfield* (1994) W had been induced to stand surety for a mortgage by H's innocent misrepresentations concerning the extent of their maximum liability for a loan for his business. Judgment was given for the TSB Bank ordering possession of the matrimonial home.

The Court of Appeal held that a legal charge over a matrimonial home to secure loan facilities that W, induced by H's misrepresentations, had agreed on was *wholly unenforceable* by the bank against the wife. TSB Bank, fixed with constructive notice of the misrepresentations, was *not entitled* to an order that the charge be partially enforceable against W. *Per* Nourse LJ: While the House of Lords in *O'Brien* might have extended the application of the doctrine of constructive notice to transactions to which it has not previously been held to apply, the consequences of that application had to be the same as those which followed in any other case where a third party was affected by notice, actual, constructive or imputed, of another's right. In the absence of anything to the contrary, there was no basis in principle for saying that a mortgagee in this kind of case was in any better a position than any other third party who took subject to rights of which he had notice.

In *Banco Exterior Internacional v Mann* (1994) the Court of Appeal held that a bank *had taken reasonable steps* in granting a loan to H's company secured partly by a charge created by W on the matrimonial home when it had required W to sign a form of declaration in the presence of a solicitor and required also that the form of declaration be signed by a witness certifying that, prior to its execution, its nature and effect had been explained to W.

Summary of Chapter 7

Rights in Family Property (2): The Matrimonial Home

The 'matrimonial home' is the domicile where persons live together, actually or constructively, as man and wife. Problems arise concerning: the acquisition of rights in the matrimonial home; the question of proprietary estoppel; rights of occupation and their protection; effect of bankruptcy of one spouse on the occupation rights of another.

Problems related to the matrimonial home

The acquisition of rights in land by purchase involves compliance with the formalities set out in LPA 1925. *Proprietary estoppel* operates where a spouse has received an assurance, has relied upon it, and acted, as a result, to her detriment: see *Pascoe v Turner* (1979); *Maharaj v Chand* (1986). Interests may be acquired through a *resulting trust*, in which intent is inferred or is presumed as a matter of law from the circumstances of the case: see *Rathwell v Rathwell* (1978). A *constructive trust*, which will give rise to interests, emerges where it is shown that a trustee is seeking to retain an advantage from his trust. (The existence of a common intention that a claimant shall have a beneficial interest in the matrimonial home is of significance in the circumstances of a resulting trust.)

Acquisition of rights in land

At common law, a wife (not an unmarried partner) possesses a right to occupation of the matrimonial home. MHA 1967 and 1983 provide statutory rights of occupation. These include the right not to be excluded or evicted from the matrimonial home and the right, if not in occupation, to enter into and occupy the dwelling-house which constitutes the matrimonial home. Orders under MHA 1983 may be limited for a period specified in the order or until further order.

Rights of occupation of the matrimonial home

In the case of *unregistered land*, where a spouse enjoys statutory rights of occupation under MHA 1983, such rights constitute a registrable (Class F) charge under s 2(7) Land Charges Act 1972, which binds a third party. In the case of *registered land*, s 70(1)(g) Land Registration Act 1925 provides for a category of right of every person *in actual occupation of the land* or in receipt of rents and profits, *except where enquiry is made of such person and the rights are not disclosed*. What is protected is not the occupation of land, but the rights of those in occupation: see *Williams & Glyn's Bank v Boland* (1981).

Protection of rights of occupation against a third party

Orders for sale where spouses are co-owners

Where spouses are co-owners of the matrimonial home, the property is held on statutory trust for sale which includes *power to postpone sale*: see s 25 LPA 1955. The court has a discretion to order a sale, eg, where a marriage has ended: see s 30 LPA 1925.

Bankruptcy of spouse in relation to matrimonial home

The occupation rights of a bankrupt's spouse are protected: see s 336 Insolvency Act 1986. The needs of the bankrupt's spouse and children will be taken into account by the court in making an order under the 1981 Act. A 'breathing space' of one year before sale of the matrimonial home is allowed: see *Re Citro* (1990).

Chapter 8

Financial Provision During Marriage; State Benefits

8.1 The 'duty to maintain': background

The fundamental obligation at common law for a husband to protect and care for his wife and legitimate children, which broadened into a range of formal duties, including financial provision for the family, is at the basis of this chapter. Some of the legal effects of failure to make appropriate financial provision are considered in the first part; the second part outlines a number of welfare benefits made available by the State in order to prevent poverty affecting the family.

The old doctrine of 'unity of legal personality' between man and wife meant in practice that the wife, who lacked capacity to own property and to make contractual agreements, was often unable to purchase necessities, so that an obligation was created whereby the husband was responsible for purchases and debts. A wife's inability to sue her husband when that obligation was ignored led in time to the doctrine of 'agency of necessity', allowing the wife to pledge her husband's credit so as to purchase necessities. (The doctrine was abolished by s 41 MPPA 1970.) The very fact of the marriage engendered a presumption at common law that the husband had a duty to maintain his wife – a duty which was considered to end if, for example, the wife committed adultery. Today, the common law doctrine is of little importance: a mutual duty of spouses to maintain each other and their children is imposed by statute (see 8.2 below), and statute controls many other aspects of financial provision for the family.

8.2 Obtaining financial provision during marriage

The following methods of obtaining financial provision during marriage should be noted.

- The common law duty of maintenance. This is now of very limited significance (see 8.1 above).

- The statutory mutual duty to maintain. Under s 26(3) Social Security Act 1986 (see now s 78(6) SSAA 1992; s 3(4)(a) ChA 1989), 'a man shall be liable to maintain his wife and any children of whom he is the father; a woman shall be liable to maintain her husband and any children of whom she is the mother'.

- An order for financial provision from a magistrates' court under DPMCA 1978 (see 8.3 below).

- An order for financial provision on the ground of the failure by a spouse to provide reasonable maintenance, under s 27 MCA 1973 (see 8.7 below).
- The enforcing of the right to maintenance under a separation or maintenance agreement (see 8.8 below).
- Order for maintenance pending suit (see s 22 MCA 1973 at 9.4).
- Order for financial provision on judicial separation (see 5.7).

8.3 Order from magistrates' court under DPMCA 1978

DPMCA 1978 replaced Matrimonial Proceedings (Magistrates' Courts) Act 1960. Under s 30(1) of the 1978 Act, jurisdiction is conferred upon a magistrates' court if the applicant or respondent ordinarily resides within the court's commission area.

The court may exercise its jurisdiction where the respondent resides in Northern Ireland or Scotland if the applicant resides in England and Wales where both parties ordinarily resided last as husband and wife, and where the applicant resides in Northern Ireland or Scotland, if the respondent resides in England and Wales: s 30(3).

A complaint should be made within six months of the act complained of: s 127(1) Magistrates' Courts Act 1980. Where a magistrates' court is of the opinion that the case would be dealt with more conveniently by the High Court, it may refuse to hear an application: s 27 DPMCA 1978. Transfer of a case to the High Court necessitates possession by the High Court of the appropriate jurisdiction: see *Davies v Davies* (1957). Parties may not appeal against refusal of the magistrates to effect a transfer.

8.3.1 Application under the 1978 Act, s 1

Under s 1 DPMCA 1978, either spouse may make application to a magistrates' court for an order on the ground that the other has failed to provide reasonable maintenance for the applicant, has failed to provide, or make a proper contribution towards reasonable maintenance for a child of the family, has behaved in such a way that the applicant cannot reasonably be expected to live with the respondent, or the respondent has deserted the applicant.

The ground for an order must exist at the time of the application *and* the hearing: see Family Proceedings Courts (Matrimonial Proceedings) Rules 1991.

8.3.2 Failure to provide reasonable maintenance

The question of 'reasonable maintenance' is essentially one of fact: the phrase is not defined in the 1978 Act. 'Failure' involves consideration of respondent's means, which must be examined before an order is made. The phrase 'child of the family' has the meaning attached to it by s 105(1) ChA 1989 (see 2.3.5).

8.3.3	Respondent's behaviour

'Behaviour' carries the same meaning as the 'behaviour fact' in relation to divorce (see 4.4). There is no need to show irretrievable breakdown of the marriage: see *Bergin v Bergin* (1983).

8.3.4	Respondent's desertion

'Desertion' has the meaning attached to it in relation to divorce (see 4.5), but no minimum period of desertion needs to be shown. The desertion must be continuing at the time of the application *and* subsequent proceedings.

8.3.5	Reconciliation

The court will consider, in hearing an application under s 1, whether the possibility of a reconciliation between the parties exists (see 3.11). Proceedings may be adjourned where there is a reasonable possibility of reconciliation: see s 26 DPMCA 1978.

8.3.6	Orders under s 2

Where the court is satisfied of the existence of a ground under the 1978 Act, s 1, one or more of the following orders may be made under s 2(1).

- Order that the respondent shall make to the applicant such periodical payments and for such term as may be specified.
- Order that the respondent shall pay to the applicant such a lump sum as may be specified.
- Order that the respondent shall make to the applicant for the benefit of a child of the family to whom the application relates, or to such a child, such periodical payments, and for such term, as may be specified.
- Order that the respondent shall pay to the applicant for the benefit of a child of the family to whom the application relates, or to such a child, such a lump sum as may be specified.

It should be noted that in the case of periodical payments, the term is at the discretion of the court, but it may not extend beyond the death of a party: s 4(1) DPMCA 1978. There is a statutory limit (see s 2(3)) on the amount of the lump sum award. It may be paid by instalments: see s 75 Magistrates' Courts Act 1980. Where an order is made for periodical payments for the benefit of a child, it should not extend beyond the date of the child's birthday following its attaining the upper limit of the age of compulsory school attendance: s 5 DPMCA 1978.

8.4 Consent orders

Under s 6 DPMCA 1978, as amended, either party may apply to a magistrates' court for an order under s 6 on the ground that either the applicant or the other party to the marriage has agreed to make the financial provision specified in the application. If the court is satisfied that the applicant or the respondent has agreed to make that provision and it has no reason to think that it would be contrary to the interests of justice to exercise its powers in relation to the application, an order will be made for the applicant or respondent to make the financial provision specified in the application.

Where the respondent is not present at the hearing, or where he is not legally represented, the court cannot make the order: s 6(9). The time for which periodical payments is to endure will be that stated in the agreement. A lump sum payment ordered will be limited only by the terms of the agreement: s 6(2).

8.5 Orders for periodical payments: means of payment

Under s 59 Magistrates' Courts Act 1980, substituted by s 2 Maintenance Enforcement Act 1991, the powers of the court, in relation to an order for periodical payments, are:

- to order that payments under the order be made directly by the debtor to the creditor;

- to order that payments under the order be made to the clerk of the court or to the clerk of any other magistrates' court;

- to order that payments under the order be made by the debtor to the creditor by such method of payment falling within subsection 6 (standing order, transfer from one order to another] as may be specified;

- to make an order under the Attachment of Earnings Act 1971.

8.6 Matters to be taken into account

When making an order, a magistrates' court must take into account certain specified matters under the DPMCA 1978, as amended by s 9 MFPA 1984. The court is to have regard to all the circumstances of the case, 'first consideration being given to the welfare while a minor of any child of the family who has not attained the age of 18': s 3(1) DPMCA 1978.

In determining whether the respondent is to be ordered to pay a lump sum or make periodical payments, the court will have regard, in particular, to the income, earning capacity, property and other financial resources which each party to the marriage has or is likely to have in the foreseeable future, including any increase in earning capacity which, in the opinion of the court, it would be reasonable to expect a party to the marriage to take steps to acquire; financial needs, obligations and responsibilities which each of the parties to the marriage has or is likely to have in the foreseeable future; the parties' standard of living; age of parties and duration of the marriage; physical or mental disabilities of parties; contributions which each of the parties has made or is likely to make to the family's welfare; the parties' conduct.

In deciding what orders should be made in favour of a child of the family, the following additional matters must be considered: the child's financial needs; the child's income, earning capacity, property and other resources; any physical or mental disability; the family's standard of living; the manner in which the child was being – and in which the parties to the marriage expected him to be – educated or trained.

Where the court considers whether to make an order against a party to a marriage in favour of a child who is not that party's natural or adopted child, regard must be had to: whether the party has assumed responsibility for the child's maintenance; whether in assuming and discharging that responsibility he did so knowing that the child was not his own child; the liability of any other person to maintain the child.

8.7 Orders under s 27 MCA 1973, as amended

Under s 27 MCA 1973, as amended by s 63 DPMCA 1978, either spouse may make application to the High Court or county court for an order under s 27 MCA 1973, where the respondent has failed to provide reasonable maintenance for the applicant, or has failed to make a proper contribution towards reasonable maintenance for any child of the family. These grounds are the same as those stated in s 1 DPMCA 1978 (see 8.3.1 above); application may be made, therefore, in the magistrates' court and in the High Court and county court for an order. Procedure in the magistrates' court is usually quicker and cheaper than in the High Court, and the jurisdictional requirements of the High Court and county court differ from those of the magistrates' court: in the case of the High Court and county court, jurisdiction exists where the applicant or respondent is domiciled in England or Wales at the date of the application, or the applicant must have been habitually resident there throughout a period of one year ending with the date of the application, or the respondent must be resident there on that date: see s 27(2) MCA 1973 and s 6 DPMCA 1978 Note the jurisdiction of the magistrates' courts at 8.3 above.

8.7.1 Orders which can be made under s 27 MCA 1973

Orders may be made under s 27 MCA 1973, for secured or unsecured periodical payments made to the applicant, to the child concerning whom the application was made, or for that child's benefit. Under s 27(5) an interim order for periodical payments may be made where immediate financial assistance is required by the applicant or child of the family (to whom the application relates), but no final order has been made.

The award of a lump sum is subject to s 27(7), which states that such an order may be made for the purpose of enabling any liabilities or expenses reasonably incurred in maintaining the applicant or any child of the family to whom the application relates before the making of the application to be met. Further, the order may provide for payment of the sum by instalments to be secured to the satisfaction of the court.

8.7.2 Variation of orders

Under s 31 MCA 1973, the High Court or county court is empowered to vary orders for periodical payments and lump sums payable in instalments: see *Evans v Evans* (1989); *Fisher v Fisher* (1989). See 10.4.

8.8 Enforcing maintenance rights under separation or maintenance agreements

During the subsistence of the marriage the spouses may make separation agreements and maintenance agreements. The *separation agreement* allows spouses to live apart; the agreement may contain provisions relating to maintenance. The maintenance agreement involves provisions relating to the financial liability of one spouse for another and the children; it does not include an agreement to live apart.

Agreements of this nature are essentially contracts: to be enforceable the parties must have intended to create legal relations, the agreements must have been made freely (ie, without any element of duress), etc.

A term in a maintenance agreement which purports to limit the right to apply to the court for an order involving financial arrangements is void: see s 34(1) MCA 1973. Note *Dean v Dean* (1978).

Section 35 MCA 1973 allows for the variation of a written maintenance agreement by the court where one of the following conditions obtains:

- There has been a change in the circumstances which were taken into account when the financial arrangements contained in the agreement were made.

- The agreement does not contain proper financial arrangements concerning a child of the family.

Variation, revocation, etc, must appear to the court to be just, taking into account all the circumstances: s 35(2) MCA 1973: see *Gorman v Gorman* (1964).

8.9 State benefits

The interventionist welfare State is guided in its attitude to the provision of financial benefits by a central principle: the welfare of families, in particular those in the lower-income group, is a matter of concern to the State, and financial support will be made available and offered to those who might otherwise have to endure poverty. In this century, following the Second World War, public concern with the social effects of poverty, and the emergence of new principles relating to its alleviation, resulted in a system of family allowances in 1945, the abolition of the Poor Law in 1948, and the creation of a system of supplementary benefits, enabling persons over 16, in certain categories, whose resources were inadequate, to receive supplementary allowances.

The following State benefits are outlined below: Income Support, payments from the Social Fund, Family Credit, Child Benefit, Housing Benefit.

8.10 Income support

Income support, known previously as 'supplementary benefit', is of much importance in the scheme of State benefits, and is particularly advantageous in the case of single parents. It is an income-related, non-contributory benefit which is available for those who are actively seeking employment and whose income is below an applicable amount, or who have no income.

8.10.1 Entitlement

The framework for entitlement is set out in ss 124-127 SSCBA 1992, and the Income Support (General) Regulations 1987 (SI 1987/1967) as amended.

Under s 124(1), a person in Great Britain is entitled to income support if: he is over the age of 18 or, in prescribed circumstances and for a prescribed period, of or over the age of 16 or he is a person to whom s 125(1) below (see 8.10.2) applies; he has no income or his income does not exceed the applicable amount; he is not engaged in remunerative work, and, if he is a member of a married or unmarried couple, the other is not so engaged; and, except in such circumstances as may be prescribed, he is available for, and actively seeking, employment; he is not receiving relevant education.

Under s 124(4), where a person is entitled to income support, then, if he has no income, the amount shall be the applicable amount; and if he has income, the amount shall be the difference between his income and the applicable amount.

Note that only one member of a family may claim income support. 'Remunerative work' refers to 16 hours or more per week.

- 'Married couple' means a man and woman who are married to each other and are members of the same household: s 137(1).

- 'Unmarried couple' means a man and a women who are not married to each other but are living together as husband and wife otherwise than in prescribed circumstances: s 137(1).

8.10.2 Severe hardship cases

Under s 125(1), if it appears to the Secretary of State that a person over the age of 16 but under the age of 18 is not entitled to income support, and that severe hardship will result to that person unless income support is paid to him, the Secretary of State may make an award at his discretion. The award may be revoked if there is a change in circumstances: s 125(3), (4).

8.10.3 The 'applicable amount'

For purposes of determining entitlement, it is important to note that the capital of couples, married or unmarried, is aggregated. The level of income support is the amount by which a claimant's income falls short of his needs. Where a claimant or partner possesses capital above an amount stated in regulations, there is no entitlement to income support.

Income support is designed to bring a claimant's income up to the 'applicable amount'; that is calculated by aggregating the claimant's personal allowance, premiums, housing costs. The personal allowance depends on the claimant's age, whether or not he is a lone parent, children in the family, etc. 'Premiums' include sums payable where, eg, there is a disabled child. 'Housing costs' include mortgage interest payments where the loan is used to acquire an interest in the dwelling occupied as the home.

The earnings of the claimant and of other family members are calculated on a weekly basis. The final figure is used so as to reduce the amount of entitlement to benefit. The figure expresses net earnings, so that account is taken of income tax liability.

8.11 The 'liable relatives'

Under s 106(1) SSAA 1992, if income support is claimed by or in respect of a person whom another person is liable to maintain or paid to or in respect of such a person, the Secretary of State may make a complaint against the liable person to a magistrates' court for an order under this section. On hearing the complaint, the court shall have regard to all the circumstances and, in particular, to the income of the liable person, who may be ordered to pay a sum, weekly or otherwise, as the court considers appropriate: s 106(2).

8.12 The Social Fund

Payments may be made out of the Social Fund which exists so as to provide loans and grants to those who are not able to finance certain purchases or costs out of the ordinary weekly rate of benefit: see s 138 SSCBA 1992. For details of the Social Fund, see ss 167-169 SSAA 1992.

8.12.1 Non-discretionary payments

Payments may be made out of the Social Fund of prescribed amounts, whether in respect of prescribed items or otherwise, to meet, in prescribed circumstances, maternity and funeral expenses, cold-weather expenses: see s 138(1), (2) SSCBA 1992.

8.12.2 Discretionary payments

Payments may be made, under s 138(1)(b) to meet other needs, eg, loans to meet a crisis, budgeting loans, in accordance with directions given or guidance issued by the Secretary of State.

8.12.3 Principles of determination

A social fund officer will take into account, in determining whether to make an award, all the circumstances of the case, and in particular, the nature, extent and urgency of the need, the existence of resources from which the need may be met, the possibility that some other person or body may wholly or partly meet it, where the payment is repayable, the likelihood of repayment and the time within which repayment is likely: s 140(1).

8.13 Family credit

A person in Great Britain is entitled to family credit if, when the claim for it is made or is treated as made: '(a) his income (i) does not exceed the amount which is the applicable amount at such date as may be prescribed; or (ii) exceeds it, but only by such an amount that there is an amount remaining if the deduction for which subsection (2)(b) below (see 8.13.1) provides is made; (b) he or, if he is a member of a married or unmarried couple, is engaged and normally engaged in remunerative work; (c) except in such circumstances as may be prescribed, neither he nor any member of his family is entitled to a disability working allowance; and (d) he or, if he is a member of a married or unmarried couple, he or the other member, is responsible for a member of the same household who is a child or a person of a prescribed description': s 128(1).

8.13.1 Amount of family credit

Where a person is entitled to family credit, then: '(a) if his income does not exceed the amount which is the applicable amount at the date prescribed under subsection (1)(a)(i) (see 8.13 above), the amount of the family credit shall be the amount which is the appropriate family credit in his case; and (b) if his income exceeds the amount which is the applicable amount at that date, the amount of the family credit shall be what remains after the deduction from the appropriate maximum family credit of a prescribed percentage of the excess of his income over the applicable amount': s 128(2).

Family credit is payable for 26 weeks or other such period as may be prescribed: s 128(3).

8.13.2 Termination of credit

An award of family credit terminates if a person who was a member of the family at the date of the claim becomes a member of another family and some other member of that family is entitled to family credit, or if Income Support or a disability working allowance becomes payable in respect of a person who was a member of the family at the date of the claim for family credit: see s 128(4) SSCBA 1992.

8.14 Child benefit

The non-income related benefit, known as 'child benefit', which has partly replaced family allowances, is based upon s 141 SSCBA 1992. 'A person who is responsible for one or more children in any week shall be entitled, subject to the provisions of (Part IX] of this Act, to a benefit (to be known as 'child benefit') for that week in respect of the child or each of the children for whom he is responsible.'

8.14.1 Meaning of 'child'

For the purpose of Part IX of the 1992 Act, a person shall be treated as 'a child' for any week in which he is under the age of 16, or he is under the age of 18 and not receiving full-time education and prescribed conditions are satisfied in relation to him, or he is under the age of 19 and receiving full-time education either by attendance at a recognised educational establishment or, if the education is recognised by the Secretary of State, elsewhere: s 142(1).

8.14.2 Meaning of 'person responsible for child'

For the purposes of Part IX of the 1992 Act, a person shall be treated as 'responsible for a child' in any week if he has that child living with him in that week, or he is contributing to the cost of providing for the child at a weekly rate which is not less than the weekly rate of child benefit payable in respect of the child for that week: s 143(1).

8.14.3 Rate of benefit

Child benefit is payable at such a weekly rate as may be prescribed. Different rates may be prescribed in relation to different cases, whether by reference to the age of the child in respect of whom the benefit is payable or otherwise: see s 145 (1), (2).

8.14.4 Exclusion from entitlement to child benefit

No person is entitled to child benefit if the child is undergoing imprisonment or detention in legal custody, or in the care of a local authority, or in respect of a married child: Sch 9, paras 1, 3 SSCBA 1992.

8.15 One-parent benefit

One-parent benefit is available to a person who qualifies for child benefit and is bringing up a child on his/her own. A person who is single, divorced, permanently separated, a widow/widower may claim, but not one who is living with another person as husband or wife. The benefit does not affect family credit; it does affect the amount of income support received.

8.16 Housing benefit

Under s 130(1) SSCBA 1992, a person is entitled to housing benefit if '(a) he is liable to make payments in respect of a dwelling in Great Britain which he occupies as his home; (b) there is an appropriate maximum housing benefit in his case; and (c) either – (i) he has no income or his income does not exceed the applicable amount; or (ii) his income exceeds that amount but only by so much that there is an amount remaining if the deduction for which subsection 3(b) below provides is made.'

Under s 130(3), where a person is entitled to housing benefit, then '(a) if he has no income or his income does not exceed the applicable amount, the amount of the housing benefit shall be the amount which is the appropriate maximum housing benefit in his case; and (b) if his income exceeds the applicable amount, the amount of the housing benefit shall be what remains after the deduction from the appropriate maximum housing benefit of prescribed percentages of the excess of his income over the applicable amount.'

No housing benefit is payable if the applicant has capital (eg, savings) of over (currently) £16,000: see s 134(1). Capital of £3,000 or less is ignored. If a claimant's capital is between £3,000 and £16,000 (current figures), he is assumed to obtain a weekly income ('tariff income') from it, which reduces the amount of housing benefit. Example: £1 is counted for every £250 capital over £3,000. If, therefore, a claimant has cash, savings (eg, money in banks, building societies), then £3,000 is disregarded, leaving £7,000. Claimant is assessed, therefore, as having an 'extra income' of £28 per week (ie, £7,000/250).

Summary of Chapter 8

Financial Provision During Marriage; State Benefits

The duty to maintain

The common law duty to maintain involves a husband in protecting and caring for his wife and children. Today the doctrine is of little consequence in view of the statutory mutual duties imposed on husband and wife. Thus, under s 26(3) SSA 1986, a man is liable to maintain his wife and children; a woman is liable to maintain her husband and children.

Methods of obtaining financial provision

Other methods of obtaining financial provision during marriage arise as follows.

- *Order for financial provision under DPMCA 1978.* Either spouse may make application to *a magistrates' court* for an order where the other has failed to provide reasonable maintenance for the applicant, has failed to provide, or make a proper contribution towards reasonable maintenance for a child of the family, has behaved in such a way that the applicant cannot reasonably be expected to live with respondent, or respondent has deserted applicant: s 1. Where the court is satisfied that a ground under s 1 exists, it may make one or more of the following orders: periodical payments to applicant; lump sum to applicant; periodical payment or lump sum to applicant for benefit of a child of the family.

- *Order under MCA 1973, as amended.* A spouse may apply to *the High Court or county court* for an order under s 27 of the 1973 Act, where the respondent has failed to provide reasonable maintenance or to make a proper contribution towards reasonable maintenance for any child of the family. (Note that 'child of the family' is defined under s 105(1) ChA 1989, as 'a child of the parties to a marriage; or any other child, not being a child who is placed with those parties as foster parents by a local authority or voluntary organisation, who has been treated by both of those parties as a child of the family.') The order may be made for periodical payments or a lump sum.

- *Enforcing of maintenance rights under separation or maintenance agreements.* Spouses may have made separation and maintenance agreements, the latter involving provisions relating to financial liability of one spouse for the other and the children. Contractual agreements of this nature may be enforced or varied by the courts: see s 35 MCA 1973.

State benefits

A characteristic of the 'Welfare State' is its acceptance of the principle that the welfare or persons and families in the lower-income groups must be ensured by the provision of a variety of types of financial support in the form of 'benefits'. Among such benefits are the following.

- *Income support*. Known previously as 'supplementary benefit', it is available for persons over 18 (or, in some cases, 16 or over) who are seeking work, are not in receipt of income or whose income does not exceed a statutorily-fixed level: see ss 124-127 SSCBA 1992.

- *Payments from the Social Fund*. Loans and grants may be made to those who are unable to finance certain types of purchase or costs: see ss 167-169 SSAA 1992.

- *Family credit*. Payments may be made for 26 weeks or other such period as may be specified, to a person who is, or whose partner is, engaged in full-time work, whose income does not exceed a specified amount and where there is a child of the same household of which the applicant is a member: see s 128(1) SSCBA 1992.

- *Child benefit*. A person who is responsible for one or more children in any week is entitled to a benefit for that week in respect of the child or each of the children for whom he is responsible: see s 141 SSCBA 1992.

- *One-parent benefit*. A person who qualifies for child benefit and is bringing up a child on his/her own may claim one-parent benefit.

- *Housing benefit*. Under s 130(1) SSCBA 1992, a person is entitled to housing benefit where he has no income, or his income is below a specified amount and he is liable to make payments in respect of a dwelling which he occupies as his home.

Chapter 9

Financial Provision on Breakdown of the Marriage (1): Court Orders

9.1 Background

Under what type of circumstance will the court order periodical payments for maintenance pending suit? In making an order for financial provision will the court take into account the age of the parties? What is the concept of 'the clean break' in relation to the procedure of terminating spouses' financial obligations on divorce? These questions and others of a similar nature are considered in this chapter which outlines the ways in which the courts can order a distribution of spouses' resources of finance and property on the grant of a decree of divorce or annulment. The basis of orders of this nature is to be found in MPPA 1970, which was embodied in MCA 1973, and the MFPA 1984.

9.1.1 MPPA 1970

MPPA 1970 was consolidated in MCA 1973. Under the 1973 Act, s 25, the court was obliged to exercise its powers so as 'to place the parties, so far as is practicable and, having regard to their conduct, just to do so, in the financial position in which they would have been if the marriage had not broken down and each had properly discharged his or her financial obligations and responsibilities towards the other' – the so-called 'principle of minimal loss'.

The Law Commission, in *The Financial Consequences of Divorce*: the basic policy (Law Com No 103 (1980)), criticised the law concerning financial provision in relation to the breakdown of marriage: it was inconsistent with the prevailing law of divorce and made it difficult for parties to look to the future; it created hardship for ex-husbands, their second families, and divorced wives.

9.1.2 MFPA 1984

MFPA 1984 amended MCA 1973. Part II of the 1984 Act was intended specifically to amend s 25 MCA 1973: the 'principle of minimal loss' (see 9.1.1 above) would no longer apply; the guidelines of s 25(1) MCA 1973 would be revised so as to give greater emphasis to the recognition of the significance of adequate financial provision for children as a priority, and to the formulation of a principle recognising the importance of parties doing everything possible to become self-sufficient on termination of a marriage. Today the courts have extensive powers: limitations of those powers and statutory guidelines as to their interpretation exist, but the courts' wide powers of discretion ensure that they are able to take into account, in arriving at a decision, all the circumstances relating to an application for ancillary relief.

9.2 Initial procedure relating to an application for ancillary relief

'Ancillary relief' means, within the context of termination of marriage, 'incidental relief', growing out of, or auxiliary to, another action or suit (in this case, divorce). The petitioner claims ancillary relief in the divorce petition; the respondent applies in the answer which he files. Where the divorce is to be undefended, the respondent may submit a separate application at any time in the future, without leave: see Family Proceedings Rules 1991, r 2.53(3). The principle of limitation has no general application to matrimonial proceedings: see *Twiname v Twiname* (1992).

9.2.1 The affidavit

An affidavit which gives details of the applicant's financial situation should accompany the application for relief. Details concerning income, assets, etc, are required. The other spouse files a similar affidavit: see Family Proceedings Rules 1991, r 2.58(3). Either party may require further information; the court may direct discovery of documents and may order a 'production appointment' at which specified documents are to be produced. Injunctions may be issued at this point so as to preserve assets: see s 37 MCA 1973: see 10.8.

9.2.2 Guidelines for affidavits

In *Evans v Evans* (1990) (a case in which the spouses' costs were out of all proportion to the value of available assets), the court issued general guidelines for the preparation of 'substantial ancillary relief cases', which included the following. Affidavit evidence ought to be confined to relevant facts and parties should file one substantive affidavit each. Inquiries under the Matrimonial Causes Rules 1977 should be based on one comprehensive questionnaire. Evocative issues not relevant to the case ought to be avoided. A chronology of material facts should be agreed. A pre-trial review may be desirable in some cases, and the desirability of a settlement should be borne in mind throughout: see Practice Direction [1990] 1 WLR 575.

9.2.3 The hearing

The hearing takes place before a district judge (formerly known as a 'registrar'); the application may be referred to a judge, under Family Proceedings Rules 1991, r 2.65. Proceedings can be transferred to the High Court (see s 39 MFPA 1984) in a case of difficulty or unusual complexity. Under Practice Direction [1992] 3 All ER 151, where issues concerning property, periodical payments, or a lump sum are under discussion, the court should have regard to the following matters when considering transfer of proceedings to the High Court: the capital value of the assets involved and the extent to which they are available for, or susceptible to, distribution or adjustment; any substantial allegation of fraud or deception or non-disclosure; any substantial contested allegations concerning conduct.

9.3 Orders available for ancillary relief

The following orders are available in favour of a party to the marriage and/or, a child of the family, under ss 22, 23, 24, 24A MCA 1973:

- maintenance pending suit;
- financial provision orders;
- property adjustment orders;
- orders for the sale of property.

These are outlined below.

9.4 Maintenance pending suit

An order for maintenance pending suit was known formerly as 'alimony *pendente lite*'. Under s 22 MCA 1973, the court can order either spouse to make to the other such unsecured periodical payments for maintenance pending suit as it considers reasonable. The order is effective from presentation of the petition and may continue until determination of the suit, or some shorter period. It can be continued, however, if there is an appeal and if this is fair and reasonable in the circumstances. In making the order, the court will consider the interests of husband and wife.

9.5 Periodical payments in favour of spouses or children

Under s 23(1)(a),(b),(d) MCA 1973, the court can make an order on granting a decree of divorce, nullity, judicial separation: that either party to the marriage shall make to the other such periodical payments, for such term as may be specified in the order; an order that either party shall secure to the other such payments; an order that either party shall make periodical payments to a specified person for the benefit of a child of the family, or to such a child.

9.5.1 Unsecured payments

Payments may be made from unsecured income; they cannot extend beyond the parties' joint lives. The marriage of the payee terminates an order, secured or unsecured: see s 28(1) MCA 1973. Such payments, which may be ordered over a specified period (see s 23), if made in favour of a child of the family are generally made up to the age at which the child is allowed to leave school (but will not extend beyond the age of 18).

9.5.2 Secured payments

Where the payer has appropriate assets or a secured income, or where the court believes that he might default on payment, a secured order may be made. This can involve the charging of capital assets (eg company shares) which can be vested in trustees. Orders can last for the payee's life. At the end of the period of the order, property charged will revert to the payer or his estate and the charge is then cancelled: see *Aggett v Aggett* (1962).

9.6 Lump sum orders

The court may order, on granting a decree of divorce, nullity or judicial separation, that either party to the marriage shall pay to the other such lump sum or sums as may be so specified: s 23(l)(c) MCA 1973. It may be paid by instalments and can be used so as to enable a spouse to meet liabilities or expenses incurred before the making of the application. The instalments may be secured to the satisfaction of the court and may carry interest at a rate specified by the order: see MCA 1973, s 23(3)(c), s 23(6), added by the Administration of Justice Act 1982.

Regard should be had to the means of the payer and the 'reasonable needs' of the payee and child. Recognition should be given to any extraordinary contribution of the payee to the creation of assets during the marriage: see *Gojkovic v Gojkovic* (1992). Proceedings may be adjourned at the discretion of the court where the court is of the opinion that substantial capital may become available in the future: see *MT v MT (Financial Provision: Lump Sum)* (1992). Note the 'Duxbury calculations' (see *Duxbury v Duxbury* (1987)) which can be used to calculate the lump sum required to meet appropriate future living expenses: see *L v L (Lump Sum: Interest)* (1994).

9.7 Property adjustment orders

Section 24 MCA 1973 allows property adjustment orders to be made in favour of a spouse or child of the family, or any person for the benefit of such child, on the grant of a *decree nisi* or at any time following. The property must be within the jurisdiction; an order may be refused where the property is beyond the effective control of the court: see *Tallack v Tallack* (1927) (property in Holland).

9.7.1 Transfer of property order

The court may order, under s 24(1)(a), on granting a decree of divorce, nullity, judicial separation, that a party to the marriage shall transfer to the other party, to any child of the family or to such person as may be specified in the order for the benefit of such child, such property as may be specified, being property to which the first-mentioned party is entitled either in possession or reversion. The order may be used for the transfer of the matrimonial home from one spouse to another. It may be used in relation to 'the clean break' (see 9.19 below) and take the form of, eg, transfer of company shares from one spouse to another, enabling that other to live on income derived from investments.

9.7.2 Settlement of property order

The court may order, under s 24(1)(b), that a settlement of such property as may be specified, being property to which a party to the marriage is entitled, be made to the satisfaction of the court for the benefit of the other party to the marriage and of the children of the family or either or any of them. The essence of a 'settlement' is an arrangement whereby property is held in trust for beneficiaries: see 6.1.3. The order may be used in relation, eg, to shares or the matrimonial home.

- Note the 'Mesher order' (see *Mesher v Mesher* (1980)): where the matrimonial home is in joint names, the wife remains there with a child of the family, the family incomes are equally balanced, and the wife's need is primarily for a home rather than a lump sum, the proper order could involve holding the home on trust for sale with the proceeds to be divided eventually into equal parts: see *Browne v Pritchard* (1975).

- Note also the 'Martin order' (see *Martin v Martin* (1978)): the court ordered that the matrimonial home (which belonged to husband and wife beneficially in equal shares) should be held on trust for the wife for the duration of her life, or until her re-marriage or earlier date (in the event of her ceasing to live there), and thereafter on trust for both in equal shares.

9.7.3 Variation of ante-nuptial or post-nuptial settlement

The court may make an order under s 24(1)(c), (d) varying for the benefit of parties to the marriage and of the children of the family or either of them, any ante-nuptial or post-nuptial settlement (including a settlement made by will or codicil) made on the parties to the marriage, or an order extinguishing or reducing the interest of either of the parties to the marriage under any such settlement.

The settlement should be in existence at the date on which the final decree is granted. The term 'settlement' is construed widely so as to cover, eg, an insurance policy made by the husband for the benefit of his wife; but the settlement must provide for the benefit of spouses in relation to their married state: *Prinsep v Prinsep* (1930). See *E v E* (1990). Note *Brooks v Brooks* (1994) in which the Court of Appeal held that a pension scheme amounted to a post-nuptial settlement which could be varied by the court under s 24(1)(c) in order to make limited pension provision for the wife. (The House of Lords is to hear an appeal.)

9.8 Orders for the sale of property

Under s 24A(1) MCA 1973, inserted by s 7 MHPA 1981, where the court makes a secured periodical payments order, a lump sum order, or a property adjustment order, then, 'on making that order or at any time thereafter, the court may make a further order for the sale of such property as may be specified in the order, being property in which or in the proceeds of sale of which either or both of the parties to the marriage has or have a beneficial interest, either in possession or reversion.' An order made under s 24A(1) may contain supplementary provisions concerning the making of payments out of the proceeds of the sale of property to which the order relates and the offering of such property for sale to a person or class of persons specified in the order: s 24A(2).

- Where an order is made under s 24A(1) on or after the grant of a decree of divorce or nullity of marriage, the order shall not take effect unless the decree has been made absolute: s 24A(3).

- Where an order is made under s 24A(1), the court may direct that the order shall not take effect until after the occurrence of an event specified by the court or the expiration of a period so specified: s 24A(5).

9.8.1 Death or re-marriage

Where an order under s 24A(1) contains a provision requiring the proceeds of sale of the property to which the order relates to be used to secure periodical payments to a party to the marriage, the order ceases to have effect on the death or re-marriage of that person: s 24A(5).

9.8.2 Third party interests

Where a party to a marriage has a beneficial interest in property or in the proceeds of its sale, and some other person who is not a party to the marriage also has a beneficial interest in the property or proceeds of sale, then, before deciding whether to make an order under s 24A in relation to that property, it shall be the duty of the court to give that other person an opportunity to make representations with respect to the order: s 24A(6). 'Any representations by that other person shall be included among the circumstances to which the court is required to have regard under s 25(1)': s 24(6). See s 25(1) at 9.10 below.

9.9 The guidelines of s 25 MCA 1973

The principles according to which the court exercises its discretion on the award of orders on the breakdown of marriage are based generally upon s 25 MCA 1973,, substituted by s 3 MFPA 1984. (Note their similarity to the principles set out in 8.6.)

The words of Lord Hailsham LC are significant in relation to the court's discretion: 'It recognises that the circumstances of each case vary so infinitely that it is impossible to do more in the Act than to enumerate the factors which the court should take into account in making provision, and it cannot put the court in any form of simplified straitjacket compelling it to come to a conclusion contrary to justice and common sense.' (*Hansard HL*, Vol 445, col 34).

9.10 First consideration

In deciding how to exercise its powers under ss 23, 24, 24A, the courts shall have regard to all the circumstances of the case, 'first consideration being given to the welfare while a minor of any child of the family who has not attained the age of 18': s 25(1). (Note also 9.8.2 above.)

It should be noted that the welfare of the child is *not* to be regarded as 'paramount'. See *Suter v Suter* (1987), *per* Cumming-Bruce LJ: 'Having regard to the prominence which the consideration of the welfare of children is given in s 25(1), being selected as the first consideration among all the circumstances of the case, I collect an intention that this consideration is to be regarded as of first importance, to be borne in mind throughout consideration of all the circumstances, including the particular circumstances specified in s 22. But if it had been intended to be paramount, overriding all other considerations pointing to a just result, Parliament would have said so. It has not. So I construe the section in requiring the court to consider all the circumstances, including those set out in sub-section (2), always bearing in mind the important consideration of the welfare of the children, and then try to attain a financial result which is just as between husband and wife.'

Note also the provisions of the Child Support Act 1991 (see 11.9).

The provisions of s 25(2) are noted below.

9.11 Income, earning capacity, etc

The court is to have regard to the following matters in exercising its powers under s 23(1)(a), (b) or (c), s 24 and s 24A: the income, earning capacity, property, and other financial resources which each of the parties to the marriage has or is likely to have in the foreseeable future, including in the case of earning capacity any increase in that capacity which it would in the opinion of the court be reasonable to expect a party to the marriage to take steps to acquire: s 25(2)(a).

9.11.1	Assets	All the assets of the parties should be considered: see, eg, *Daubney v Daubney* (1976) (personal injury damages awarded to a spouse were taken into account). Note *W v W* (1992) in which the Court of Appeal held that damages awarded to a spouse as compensation for loss of amenity and pain and suffering are part of that spouse's financial resources for the purpose of determining an application by the other spouse for ancillary relief under s 25(2)(a), but the circumstances in which capital by way of damages came into the hands of a spouse and the size of the award are relevant factors which affect the extent of, and may, in some cases, act so as to exclude, the sharing of that capital with the other spouse.
9.11.2	Earning capacity, resources	'Earning capacity' refers to what a spouse might reasonably earn: see *Schuller v Schuller* (1990), in which the Court of Appeal held that the term 'resources' in s 25 was unqualified and, therefore, was not to be limited in any way: see *J v J* (1955) (true income was considered in relation to lifestyle, not to declaration of income).
9.12	**Needs for foreseeable future**	The court will have regard to 'the financial needs, obligations and responsibilities which each of the parties to the marriage has or is likely to have in the foreseeable future': s 25(2)(b). The term 'needs' appears to have been construed in a relative sense as 'reasonable needs' of parties: see *Stockford v Stockford* (1981). Note also *Leadbeater v Leadbeater* (1985); *Delaney v Delaney* (1990), in which the court referred to a husband's entitlement 'to order his life in such a way as will hold in reasonable balance responsibilities to his existing family which he carries into his new life, as well as aspirations for that new future.'
9.13	**Former standard of living**	The court will have regard to 'the standard of living enjoyed by the family before the breakdown of the marriage': s 25(2)(c). In *Attar v Attar* (1985), a divorced wife's pre-marital income was taken into account in establishing the value of a lump sum which would enable her to adjust (over a two-year period) to the termination of the marriage: see *Foley v Foley* (1981).
9.14	**Parties' age, duration of marriage**	The court will have regard to 'the age of each party to the marriage and the duration of the marriage': s 25(2)(d). The consideration of age may have particular relevance to the potential earning capacity of the spouse: see *Khan v Khan* (1980); *M v M* (1976). For the matter of duration of marriage, see, eg, *Krystmann v Krystmann* (1973), in which H and W lived together for only a fortnight before a separation period of 26 years, and it was held that W was not entitled to financial provision from H.

9.15 Parties' disabilities

The court should consider 'any physical or mental disability of either of the parties to the marriage': s 25(2)(e). See *Sakkas v Sakkas* (1987).

9.16 Contribution to family welfare

The court should have regard to 'the contributions which each of the parties has made or is likely in the foreseeable future to make to the welfare of the family, including any contribution by looking after the home or caring for the family': s 25(2)(f). Financial and other contributions will be considered, eg, loans from one spouse to another for use in business, unpaid assistance in the family business: see, eg, *Gojkovic v Gojkovic* (1990) – wife made extraordinary contribution to success of family business; *Vicary v Vicary* (1992).

9.17 Conduct of parties

The court should have regard to the conduct of each of the parties, if that conduct is such that it would in the opinion of the court be inequitable to disregard it: s 25(2)(g). Note *Martin v Martin* (1976), in which Cairns LJ stated that a spouse cannot be allowed 'to fritter away assets by extravagant living or reckless speculation' and then make claim to as great a share of what was left as he would have been entitled to if he had behaved reasonably: see *Evans v Evans* (1989) (Court of Appeal upheld discharge of order for periodical payments made in favour of a wife who was later convicted of incitement to murder her husband, who had made the payments); *K v K* (1990) (applicant's drinking habits had resulted in forced sale of the matrimonial home); *Whiston v Whiston* (1994) (bigamy).

9.18 Loss of benefits

The court should have regard to '... the value to each of the parties to the marriage of any benefit (for example, a pension) which, by reason of the dissolution or annulment of the marriage, that party will lose the chance of acquiring': s 25(2)(h). This provision refers to, eg, the value of a retirement lump sum (see *Richardson v Richardson* (1978)), future pension rights, surrender of a policy of insurance (*Bennett v Bennett* (1978)). See the Report of the Law Society (1991): *Maintenance and Capital Provision on Divorce*.

9.19 The 'clean break' principle

In *Scallon v Scallon* (1990), Purchas LJ referred to the 'clean break' principle as follows: 'I wish to say a word about the 'clean break' which is a phrase which arises since the amendments to the 1973 Act were introduced to ensure that, where there were short-term marriages, one party should not get what is described as "a meal ticket for life" upon the dissolution of such a marriage. Furthermore, it was to encourage spouses who hitherto had not earned their living to face up to the fact that after the dissolution they should earn their living.'

Section 25A MCA 1973, inserted by s 3 MFPA 1984, seeks to affect the use of orders for long-term periodical payments, so as to encourage the 'clean break'. It is the duty of the court to consider whether it would be appropriate so to exercise its powers that the financial obligations of each party towards the other will be terminated as soon after the grant of the decree of divorce or nullity of marriage as the court considers just and reasonable: see s 25A(1). In the case of a periodical payments or secured periodical payments order in favour of a party to the marriage, the court should consider in particular whether it would be appropriate to require those payments to be made or secured only for such term as would in the court's opinion be sufficient to enable a party in whose favour the order is made to adjust without undue hardship to the termination of his/her financial dependence on the other party: s 25A(2). On application for a periodical payments or secured periodical payments order, if the court considers that no continuing obligation should be imposed on either party, the court may dismiss the application with a direction that the applicant shall not be entitled to make any further application in relation to that marriage for an order under s 23(1)(a) or (b): s 25A(3).

9.19.1 Essence of the 'clean break'

'There are two principles which inform the modern legislation. One is the public interest that spouses, to the extent that their means permit, should provide for themselves and their children. But the other – of equal importance – is the principle of the "clean break". The law now encourages spouses to avoid bitterness after family breakdown and to settle their money and property problems. An object of the modern law is to encourage each to put the past behind them and to begin a new life which is not overshadowed by the relationship which has broken down. It would be inconsistent with this principle if the court could not make, as between the spouses, a genuinely final order unless it was prepared to dismiss the application. The present case is a good illustration. The court having made an order giving effect to a comprehensive settlement of all financial and property issues as between spouses, it would be a strange application of the principle of the "clean break" if, notwithstanding the order, the court could make a future order on a subsequent application made by the wife after the husband had complied with all his obligations': *per* Lord Scarman in *Minton v Minton* (1979).

9.19.2 The immediate and deferred 'clean break'

The court may decide upon an *immediate* termination of the parties' financial obligations, as where parties are forbidden to make further application for periodical payments: see, eg, *Seaton v Seaton* (1986), in which, because of the husband's physical disabilities, the court felt that any further financial assistance from the wife would have little material effect upon the enhancement of his life; it would be unjust, therefore, to impose a continuing obligation on the wife and it was not possible to foresee a situation which would justify such an imposition in the future. The husband was disentitled, therefore, from making any further application. A *deferred* 'clean break' emerges when, eg, the court decides that the applicant be debarred from asking for any extension of an order for a specified term.

9.20 Financial relief following a foreign divorce

The situation following a foreign divorce is covered by the MFPA 1984, Part III. In general, where a marriage has been dissolved or annulled by means of judicial proceedings overseas, and that divorce or annulment is recognised as valid in England and Wales, either party to the marriage may apply to the court for an order for financial relief: s 12(1) 1984 Act. But if after divorce or annulment overseas one of the parties to the marriage re-marries, that party shall not be entitled to make an application in relation to the original marriage: s 12(2). Leave of the court is required for an application for an order; leave will not be granted unless the court considers that there is 'substantial ground' for the making of an application: s 13(1), (2). The court will give consideration to all the circumstances of the case, first consideration being given to the welfare of a child of the family who has not attained the age of 18: s 18(2).

'Overseas country' means, for purposes of the 1984 Act, Part III, 'a country or territory outside the British Islands' (ie, the UK, the Channel Islands and the Isle of Man): see s 27 1984 Act, and s 5 and Sch 1 Interpretation Act 1978.

For refusal of the court to grant financial relief under Part III, see: *Holmes v Holmes* (1989) (no substantial ground for granting relief); *Z v Z* (1992) (a failure to discharge onus of proving, under s 16(2), that it would be appropriate to make an order). (Section 16 states that the courts shall have regard, *inter alia*, to 'the connection which parties have with the country in which the marriage was dissolved or annulled'.)

In *Hewitson v Hewitson* (1994), the Court of Appeal held that the fact that a former wife had resumed cohabitation with her former husband following a foreign 'clean break' divorce and had as a direct consequence acted to her detriment financially, was *not* a ground for the granting of leave under s 13 MFPA 1984 to apply for financial relief under s 12. *Per* Butler-Sloss LJ:

> 'There has to be finality and an end to litigation. In my view the umbrella of the dissolved marriage which covers the post-divorce period cannot remain open for ever. Upon the making and implementing of a "clean break" order between spouses with no children, that umbrella has to be closed.'

See also *M v M* (1994).

Summary of Chapter 9

Financial Provision on Breakdown of the Marriage (1): Court Orders

Recognition is to be given to the significance of adequate provision for children as a priority and to the importance of parties doing everything possible to become self-sufficient on termination of the marriage.

General principle

'Ancillary relief' means, in the context of dissolution of marriage, relief auxiliary to some other action or suit (eg divorce). An affidavit must accompany the application for relief and must state details of the party's income, assets, etc. A district judge (formerly 'registrar') hears the application which, in cases of unusual complexity, may be transferred to the High Court.

Ancillary relief

The following orders are available in favour of a party to the marriage and/or a child of the marriage, under MCA 1973.

Orders available for ancillary relief

- *Maintenance pending*: see s 22 MCA 1973. The order continues until determination of the suit, but may be made for some shorter period.

- *Financial provision orders*. Orders may be made for periodical payments, secured or unsecured. Lump sum payments may be ordered; they can be paid by instalments which may be secured: see s 23(1)(c) MCA 1973.

- *Property adjustment orders*. Under s 24 MCA 1973 property adjustment orders may be made, allowing the transfer of property, or a settlement of property whereby property is held in trust for beneficiaries; this may be used in relation to the matrimonial home.

- *Orders for the sale of property*. Under s 24A(1) MCA 1973, the court may order the sale of specified property in which either or both of the parties has or have a beneficial interest. Third party interests must be taken into account.

The principles according to which the court exercises its discretion in relation to the award of orders on the breakdown of marriage are based upon s 25 MCA 1973. Essentially, the court must have regard to all circumstances of the case, but first (not 'paramount') consideration is to be given to the welfare of minors involved.

Guidelines of s 25 MCA 1973

Other factors to be taken into account are as follows:
- Income, earning capacity of the parties.
- All the assets of the parties.
- Needs of the parties for the foreseeable future.
- The parties' former standard of living.
- The parties' age, duration of marriage.
- Any disabilities of the parties.
- Contribution of parties to family welfare.
- Conduct of the parties.
- Loss of benefits.

The 'clean break' principle

An object of the modern law (see *Minton v Minton* (1979)) is to encourage parties to put the past behind them and to begin a new life which is not overshadowed by the relationship which has broken down. The 'clean break' order may take the form of prohibition on parties making further application for periodical payments.

Financial relief following a foreign divorce

The situation concerning a foreign divorce is covered by MFPA 1984, Part III. Where an overseas divorce is recognised as valid in the UK, either party to the marriage may apply to the court for an order for financial relief: see *Hewitson v Hewitson* (1994).

Chapter 10

Financial Provision on breakdown of the Marriage (2): Consent Orders, Variation, Enforcement

10.1 Problems

Husband (H) and wife (W) have consulted their legal advisers and made *a private agreement* concerning maintenance in the event of a divorce. Would the court, in its consideration of financial provision on the divorce of H and W, at a later date, regard the private agreement as relevant? Is a court able to extend time for payment by H to W of a lump sum as contained in a court order? Could an *Anton Piller* order be used to enable W to inspect documents concerning H's capital assets at a time when H's financial provision for W is under discussion by the court? May a consent order be set aside by the court on the basis of later evidence of H's non-disclosure of important information?

In this chapter we note, in particular: the essential features of the consent order, which rests upon the private ordering by H and W of their financial affairs; the circumstances under which court orders involving financial provision may be varied; the problems involved in the enforcement of court orders; and matters which may emerge from attempts by H to defeat W's valid claim for financial relief, as when, for example, H seeks to transfer his property out of the jurisdiction prior to W's application to the court for an order for periodical payments on their divorce.

10.2 The privately-made agreement for maintenance on divorce

Parties may have made a *private financial agreement* at the time of their separation prior to the grant of a decree of divorce in an attempt to resolve financial problems for themselves. Official policy could be interpreted as encouraging private agreements of this nature. 'The law now encourages spouses to avoid bitterness after family breakdown and to settle their money and property problems': *per* Lord Scarman in *Minton v Minton* (1979).

10.2.1 Purported ouster of the court's jurisdiction

Where a term in a maintenance agreement seeks to restrict a right to apply to the court for an order containing a financial agreement, it is *void*: s 34 MCA 1973. But any other financial arrangement embodied in the private agreement is not thereby rendered void; it remains binding unless void or unenforceable for some other reason: s 34(1).

10.2.2 Variation of a private maintenance agreement

Under s 35 MCA 1973, a maintenance agreement may be varied by the court on application of a party to that agreement.

The court must be satisfied (see s 35(2)) that the circumstances under which the agreement was made have changed *or* that the agreement does not contain appropriate financial arrangements relating to any child of the family. The High Court or a divorce county court may vary or revoke a financial arrangement in a maintenance agreement or insert a financial arrangement intended to benefit a party, or a child of the family. A magistrates' court (which has power, in this context, only in matters concerning periodical payments) may insert a provision for such payments, or may vary or terminate them. The High Court or any county court may consider variation of a maintenance agreement which provides for the continuation of payments after the death of a party: see *Gorman v Gorman* (1964).

10.2.3 *Camm v Camm* (1983)

In *Camm v Camm* (1983), H and W married in 1962 and divorced in 1975. The three children were aged 19, 17 and 15. Solicitors had assisted H and W in reaching an agreement whereby a new home would be purchased, to be held by H and W in joint names and divided half to W and half to H; H undertook to pay maintenance and school fees. Later, the house was put in W's sole name. H re-married and prospered financially. W's application for periodical payments resulted in an order of £900 per annum for herself and £3,500 per annum for the children.

W's appeal was *allowed*. It was clear from the evidence that W had acquiesced in an agreement which was not satisfactory; she ought not to be bound by it. Agreements of this nature made in the context of a divorce were unreliable and ought not to be considered as contractual bargains. The arrangement was unfair: there was a huge disparity between the families' living standards. The order for W would be increased to £4,000 pa.

10.2.4 *Edgar v Edgar* (1980)

H, a multi-millionaire, had agreed a deed of separation with W in which, *inter alia*, W had agreed not to apply after divorce for additional capital provision beyond that provided in the deed. W broke the agreement by applying for financial relief on commencement of divorce proceedings. In her affidavit she asserted that she had entered the agreement because of her fear of losing the children of the marriage and because she felt overpowered by H's wealth.

The Court of Appeal allowed H's appeal. H had not exploited his bargaining power so as to induce W to act to her disadvantage. There were no grounds for holding that justice required the court to relieve W from the effects of the covenant into which she had entered.

10.3 The consent order

Where H and W have come to terms, the resulting agreement may be incorporated into a court order – a 'consent order'. Orders of this nature, relating to financial provision and property adjustment on divorce, have received support from commentators who perceive them as encouraging friendliness between parties to settlements on divorce, and as reducing expenditure because they are much cheaper than lengthy litigation which is often the only alternative.

The agreement between H and W derives its authority, when it becomes the basis of a consent order, from the order itself, so that the court cannot make an order outside the terms of the 1973 Act.

10.3.1 Need for the provision of adequate information

Note s 33A MCA 1973, inserted by s 7 MFPA 1984, concerning prescribed information. 'On an application for a consent order for financial relief the court may, unless it has reason to think that there are other circumstances into which it ought to inquire, make an order in the terms agreed on the basis only of the prescribed information furnished with the application: s 33A(1). ('Consent order', in relation to an application for an order, means an order in the terms applied for, to which the respondent agrees; 'order for financial relief' means an order under any of ss 23, 24, 24A or 27; 'prescribed' means prescribed by rules of court: s 33A(3).) Subsection (1) applies to an application for a consent order varying or discharging an order for financial relief as it applies to an application for an order for financial relief: s 33A(2).

- 'Unless [the court] has reason to think'. Where, for example, one party is not represented in proceedings, the court may wish to examine papers very carefully. Similarly, where an agreement has been drawn up in which H, who is very rich, is to pay W and the children a relatively low sum, extremely careful examination will be in order.

- 'Prescribed information'. The information required will include (see Family Proceedings Rules 1991, r 2.61): age of the parties and children of the family; duration of the marriage; parties' capital resources and estimated net income; proposed arrangements for accommodation of parties and children; details of any re-marriage (actual or intended) or cohabitation of either party; and 'any other especially significant matters'.

10.3.2 Effect of non-disclosure

Where there has been a disclosure of relevant facts which is less than full and frank, the court may set aside a consent order: see *B-T v B-T (Divorce Procedure)* (1990).

In *Livesey v Jenkins* (1985), W was granted a decree nisi on 1 March 1982; it was made absolute on 14 April. On 12 August 1982, the parties' solicitors reached agreement about a proposed consent order for financial provision and property adjustment. On 18 August 1982, W became engaged to X, but did not disclose this. On 2 September 1982, the registrar made the consent order and on 24 September 1982, W married X. H learned of the re-marriage in 1983 and his appeal against the registrar's order was dismissed, The House of Lords allowed H's appeal. It was held that the court could not properly exercise its discretion under s 25(1) MCA 1973, unless it was provided with correct, complete, and up-to-date information and each party was under a duty to make full and frank disclosure to the other party and to the court. This principle applied also to exchanges of information leading to consent orders.

In *Cook v Cook* (1988), H and W became friendly with Mr and Mrs X; eventually there was an exchange of partners. W remained in the matrimonial home, and her relationship with Mr X cooled but later revived. Solicitors advising H and W had reached agreement concerning a consent order whereby H would transfer his share of the matrimonial home to W in settlement of her financial claims. W failed to disclose her relationship with Mr X when submitting the required document (Form 91). H discovered this and appealed against the consent order, but the judge rejected the appeal and held that there had been a failure by W to disclose changed circumstances but that it would have made no difference to the registrar's order.

The Court of Appeal dismissed H's appeal, holding that W's failure to disclose the relationship had been considered fully by the judge. This was not a case of a complete change of circumstances but of the development of an existing situation. The court would not interfere with the judge's exercise of his discretion.

10.3.3 All circumstances to be taken into account

The court has the duty to enquire into, and take into account, *all* the circumstances concerning the making of the consent order, including, specifically, those stated in s 25 MCA 1973, as amended (see 9.9).

See *Vicary v Vicary* (1992), in which it was held that considerations of calculations under *Duxbury v Duxbury* (1987) (see 9.6) should not be allowed to derogate from the exercise of judicial discretion to take into account *all the circumstances* of the case under s 25.

The question of what should happen in the case of a consent order, where circumstances alter in a manner which could not have been foreseen by the parties, was considered by the House of Lords in *Barder v Barder* (1987). It was held that where, following a consent order for financial provision on divorce, a basic assumption, such as that a wife and children would need a home for a considerable period of time, has been invalidated by a supervening event (the wife killed the children and committed suicide), the other party might be allowed by the court to appeal out of time. An order giving leave to appeal out of time should be made only where the appeal, if heard, would be likely to succeed if the supervening event had happened within a short period of time after the making of an order, and, if the application was made promptly, it should not be made if to do so would prejudice an innocent third party: see *Worlock v Worlock* (1994); *Penrose v Penrose* (1994); *Cornick v Cornick* (1994).

10.3.4 Effect of unforeseen change in circumstances, and appeal out of time

Under s 31 MCA 1973, the court has power to vary or discharge orders, to suspend temporarily any provision in an order, and to revive any suspended provision. Powers under s 31 concern, in proceedings for divorce and nullity, maintenance pending suit, interim maintenance orders, secured or unsecured periodical payments, lump sum payments payable by instalments, whether secured or unsecured.

10.4 Variation, etc of orders

(The courts have power to grant an application to vary or discharge a financial provision order made under the Guardianship of Minors Act 1971, despite the repeal of that Act by ChA 1989; *B v B (Minors) (Periodical Payments)* (1994): s 16 Interpretation Act 1978.)

Some orders may not be varied. These include: lump sum orders not payable by instalments (but see 10.4.6 below); property transfer orders; orders for property settlements; variation of marriage settlements. The courts may not vary a *Mesher* order (see 9.7.2): see *Norman v Norman* (1983), in which a husband sought to invoke the court's powers of sale so as to accelerate a sale consequent on a *Mesher* order, but this was unacceptable since an order of this nature would be a mere variation of the *Mesher* order; in such a case the correct procedure would involve a sale under s 30 LPA 1925: see also *Taylor v Taylor* (1987); *Popat v Popat* (1991).

10.4.1 Orders which may not be varied

Section 31(5) MCA 1973 prohibits the court from making certain types of variation.

10.4.2 Prohibited variations under s 31(5) MCA 1973

- Orders for periodical payments, secured or unsecured, made in favour of a spouse may not be varied by making a lump sum order. (But note that a variation of this nature is possible when the order is for a child of the family.)

- Orders for periodical payments, whether secured or unsecured, made in favour of a spouse or a child of the family may not be varied by a property adjustment order.

- Orders for periodical payments made in favour of a spouse on or after the granting of a decree of divorce or nullity may not be varied where the court has directed under s 28(1A) MCA 1973 that a party is not entitled to apply for any extension of a term specified in an order for periodical payments.

10.4.3 Challenging orders

In general, orders – including consent orders – may be challenged on grounds of mistake, fraud, material non-disclosure, fresh evidence which shows, eg, that a party did not intend to carry out an agreement upon which the order had been based. In *Thwaite v Thwaite* (1981), H and W had jointly purchased a house in England, and had separated later while living in Bombay. W moved to Australia and lived there with the children. H petitioned for divorce and a consent order was made on the basis that W would use the house in England as a permanent home for the children; the house would be conveyed to her. Fresh evidence showed that W did not intend to remain in England. H applied for a variation of the order. The Court of Appeal held that a court has jurisdiction to hear an appeal against a consent order and may set it aside where fresh evidence shows that the very basis of that order is misplaced or invalid.

10.4.4 Matters to be taken into account

Under s 31(7) MCA 1973 the court, on considering an application for variation of an order, must have regard to all the circumstances of the case, with first consideration being given to the welfare of any minor child of the family. The 'circumstances of the case' include any change in the matters to which the court was required to have regard when making the original order. In effect, s 25 MCA 1973 (see 9.9), must be taken into account and the situation reviewed afresh. Where an application for variation follows the death of the person against whom the order was first made, any changed circumstances resulting from that death must be considered: see s 31(7) MCA 1973, and s 6(3) MFPA 1984. Note that where one party to an order has caused the other to act to her detriment, on the basis that the order will continue to be honoured, he may not then apply for a variation: see *B v B* (1968) – H had induced W to consent to his discharge in bankruptcy by giving an undertaking that he would maintain her; he was not permitted to argue later that he was under no liability to maintain.

Where an application is made on the basis of a change of circumstances, but that change is unlikely to be permanent, as where, for example, a husband is unemployed temporarily, the order ought to be suspended, but not discharged: see *Mills v Mills* (1940).

In *Dinch v Dinch* (1987), H and W were divorced in 1979. In 1980 a consent order was made, based upon periodical payments to be made by H to W and the child, and for the sale of the matrimonial home, proceeds to be divided equally when the child reached 17 or ceased full-time education, whichever was the later. H ceased working, fell into arrears and W was granted a charging order concerning the arrears. H applied for variation of the order; W applied for a transfer of property order and an order postponing sale of the home. H's application was granted, but the judge held that he had no jurisdiction to make the orders sought by W. The decision was reversed by the Court of Appeal.

10.4.5 *Dinch v Dinch* (1987)

The House of Lords held that the consent order had determined the rights of the parties in the matrimonial home in a final and conclusive manner; the judge was correct in concluding that he had no jurisdiction to make any further order. Once the court has made an order under ss 23, 24 MCA 1973, concerning particular property; it may not make a further order save in the limited circumstances set out in s 31.

Lord Oliver referred to the duties of professional advisers in circumstances of this nature. 'The appeal is yet another example of the unhappy results flowing from the failure to which I ventured to draw attention in *Sandford v Sandford* (1986) to take sufficient care in the drafting of consent orders in matrimonial proceedings to define with precision exactly what the parties were intending to do in relation to the disposal of the petitioner's claims for ancillary relief so as to avoid any future misunderstanding as to whether those claims, or any of them, were or were not to be kept alive. The hardship and injustice that such failure inevitably causes, particularly in cases where one or both parties are legally aided and the only substantial family asset consists of the matrimonial home, are so glaring in the instant case that I feel impelled once again to stress in the most emphatic terms that it is in all cases the imperative professional duty of those invested with the task of advising the parties to these unfortunate disputes to consider with due care the impact which any terms that they agree on behalf of their clients have or are intended to have on any outstanding application for ancillary relief and to ensure that such appropriate provision is inserted in any consent order made as will leave no room for any future doubt or misunderstanding or saddle the parties with the wasteful burden of wholly unnecessary costs.'

10.4.6 Lump sum variation: a recent decision

In *Masefield v Masefield* (1994), a consent order required H to pay W £100,000 by 1 January 1994, so that W could buy a house. The order provided that in default of payment for the sale of the former matrimonial home, the parties were to take stated shares of the proceeds. H, through no fault of his own, found that he was unable to meet the deadline. The district judge decided that the court had no jurisdiction to extend time for payment of the lump sum and dismissed H's application to discharge the default order. H was directed to execute a contract for sale. Leave to appeal was refused in the High Court and H appealed.

The problem was whether time was a part of the order. Did the court have power to extend the time for payment of the lump sum?

In the Court of Appeal, Butler-Sloss LJ noted that H's failure to pay the sum had not changed the position. H was not blameworthy for the failure to meet the deadline, nor was W prejudiced thereby. Time was not of the essence of the order and variation of the time did not go to the substance of the order. The purpose of the omission from s 31 MCA 1973 of the power to vary lump sum orders was to favour certainty and prevent the beneficiary of such an order 'having two bites of the cherry'. If the provisions of the order were implemented, H would lose the house and W would get a substantially greater sum: there was no reason for that if H was not blameworthy.

The result of the judge's approach was not fair, said Butler-Sloss LJ, and there was no reason to indulge W's vindictiveness by requiring a sale, come what may. The Court of Appeal *had jurisdiction* to extend time for payment by H of the lump sum.

10.4.7 The 'clean break'

Where the court is considering an application for variation of an order for periodical payments, it should take into account whether the facts suggest the suitability of an application of the 'clean break' doctrine (through a limited term order) which 'will in the opinion of the court be sufficient to enable the party in whose favour the order was made to adjust without undue hardship to the termination of those payments': see s 31(7)(a) MCA 1973. Note *Whiting v Whiting* (1988), in which the Court of Appeal held that s 31(7) of the 1973 Act did not prescribe any conditions, on the satisfaction of which termination of a periodical payments order would be ordered as of right. The obligation placed on the court was simply to see whether, in the light of changed circumstances, a termination of the order was appropriate. (*Per* Balcombe LJ, dissenting: to keep alive nominal periodical payments orders just in case something should happen is to frustrate completely the idea of the 'clean break'.) See 9.19 ('clean break').

The fact that a divorced spouse may be living with an unmarried partner following the grant of a decree absolute may be taken into account by the court in estimating the financial resources and needs of the parties to the marriage (see s 25(2)(a), (b) MCA 1973). Re-marriage, *but not unmarried cohabitation*, will terminate an order for periodical payments.

In *Atkinson v Atkinson* (1988), the Court of Appeal considered a submission by H that his former wife, W, was now 'in long-term cohabitation' with another person, and that her settled state of cohabitation should be 'equated to marriage', making possible a termination of H's periodical payments to W. *Per* Waterhouse J:

> 'For my part, I am unable to derive from [the cases examined] or from the amended legislation itself any binding authority or persuasive support for the basic proposition on which the husband in the instant case relies, namely that settled cohabitation by an ex-wife with a man should be equated to remarriage, at least while it lasts, and should disentitle the ex-wife to anything more than nominal maintenance whatever the particular financial and other circumstances of the parties may be ...
> I can find no warrant for equating in this context remarriage with cohabitation, a word which itself presents problems of definition ... I do not consider that it is open to the courts to add a gloss to those existing provisions by equating cohabitation, however defined, with remarriage, without legislative sanction.'

The Law Commission proposes to examine whether on the breakdown of non-marital cohabitation some method might be found of making an adjustment between the cohabitants because of any economic advantage derived by one cohabitant from the relationship or any economic disadvantage suffered by the other, and whether simpler rules might be provided concerning the proprietary rights of unmarried cohabitants against third parties: see [1994] Fam Law 406. The Scottish Law Commission has examined the Scottish law on cohabitation – see Report on Family Law (1992) Scot Law Com No 135) and has noted that cohabitation gives rise to legal difficulties and injustices which should be dealt with; but the law 'should

10.5 **A note on unmarried cohabitation in relation to applications for variation**

neither undermine marriage, nor undermine the freedom of those who have deliberately opted out of marriage'. The Report recommends that on the breakdown of non-marital cohabitation, a former cohabitant ought to be able to apply to the court for a financial order designed to redress certain unfair economic advantages or disadvantages.

10.6 The enforcement of court orders

It is essential that the terms of a court order shall be complied with. In recent years the Maintenance Enforcement Act 1991 (see 8.5), which was designed to improve arrangements for the enforcement of maintenance obligations, has supplemented the measures available to the courts in the task of ensuring that default is prevented or dealt with effectively.

10.6.1 Enforcing the lump sum order

Orders for the payment of lump sums can be enforced in the following ways:

- judgment summons, under which payment must be made by a stated date;
- charging orders, by which capital assets may be charged with the sum due;
- garnishee proceedings ordering payment by a third party, such as a bank in which the payer maintains an account;
- writ of execution, under which the payer's goods may be seized by a sheriff or bailiff;
- order for the sale of property, specified in the original order, under s 24A MCA 1973.

10.6.2 The periodical payments order

The methods of enforcement noted at 10.6.1 above are available where there is non-compliance with an order for periodical payments. Additionally, the court can make an attachment of earnings order. Payment to the clerk of the court, enforced by power of committal in the event of default, may be made through the process of registration of the order in the magistrates' court. Note the power to order payment by standing order under the Maintenance Enforcement Act 1991.

10.6.3 Limitation period

In the cases of lump sum payments, or parts thereof, payable by instalments, and periodical payments, a person may not enforce through a county court or the High Court, arrears which have accrued for a period exceeding 12 months, without the leave of the court: s 32 MCA 1973.

10.6.4 Overpayments

There may be cases in which W, the payee, has omitted to inform H, the payer, that she has experienced a significant improvement in her financial circumstances. The court may, in its discretion, order a repayment to H of a sum as it considers just: s 33 MCA 1973 (which applies to orders for maintenance pending suit and periodical payments). Repayment may also be ordered, under s 38, where an order for periodical repayments no longer has effect because the payee has re-married.

10.7 Prevention of dispositions intended to defraud

Assume that H intends to attempt to defeat an application by W for financial relief, and that he plans to do so by removing a substantial part of his property from this country. In such a case s 37 MCA 1973 allows for intervention by the court. Injunctions, issued at the discretion of the court, may be granted under s 37 or under the inherent jurisdiction of the court. The High Court is empowered to grant an injunction in all cases in which it appears to the court just and convenient to do so: s 37(1) Supreme Court Act 1981: see also s 38 County Courts Act 1984. Breach of an injunction may constitute contempt of court.

10.7.1 Section 37 MCA 1973

The court may make an order under s 37 MCA 1973, when it is satisfied that H (see 10.7 above) is acting with the intention of defeating a claim by W. The order is intended to restrain H and to protect W's claim: see s 37(2)(a); *Shipman v Shipman* (1991); *Langley v Langley* (1994).

- Where H has disposed of property, intending to defeat W's claim, that disposition may be set aside: see s 37(2)(b). An intention to defeat W's claim may be presumed when the disposition has occurred within a period of three years before submission of an application by W for financial relief: s 37(5).
- 'Property' in s 37(2) refers only to property in which one or other of the parties has, or had, a beneficial interest, in possession or reversion: see *Crittenden v Crittenden* (1990).
- An order will not be made after H's death in relation to a disposition made by him in a will or codicil.

10.7.2 Disposition to *bona fide* purchaser for value

A disposition made by H to a *bona fide* purchaser for value without notice of H's intention to defeat W's claim for financial relief will not be set aside under s 37. 'Notice' in this context may be actual or constructive: see *Kemmis v Kemmis* (1988).

In *Sherry v Sherry* (1991), W had obtained an injunction restraining H from disposing of six properties in which he had financial interests. W registered inhibitions relating to the properties on registered land and a class F charge [see 7.12] relating to property on unregistered land. At a later date four properties were deleted from the order, and in June 1988, by consent, an order was made which apparently discharged the other two. H and X made a written agreement to buy and sell four properties and X agreed to make a loan of £50,000 to H. A search revealed the inhibitions; H disclosed the 1988 order and X's solicitor advised him to ignore the inhibitions registered by W. W applied later for the dispositions to be set aside. The court found that H's transaction with X was intended to defeat W's claim and that X had constructive notice of H's intention in relation to two properties. Those dispositions were set aside. H's production of the 1988 order satisfied X's duty to make sufficient enquiries; the remaining four dispositions would not be set aside.

The Court of Appeal allowed W's appeal. The production of the June 1988 order did not suffice to discharge X's duty to make enquiries. Questions to the legal advisers acting for H and W in their matrimonial dispute would have clarified the circumstances for X. (X was quite aware of the bitter matrimonial dispute between H and W.) The dispositions in question were reviewable by the court in its discretion under the terms of s 37 and they would be set aside.

10.8 The *Mareva* injunction

The *Mareva* injunction, based upon *Mareva Compania Naviera SA v International Bulk Carriers SA* (1980), granted under the inherent jurisdiction of the court, will be of relevance where there are indications that H may move assets out of the country so as to avoid the effects of W's claim for financial relief.

Essentially, the *Mareva* injunction comprises an order which would be made against H *in personam* to ensure that assets would be available to satisfy any judgment against him.

10.8.1 Principles of the *Mareva* injunction

The following principles apply to the issue of a *Mareva* injunction.

- The plaintiff must have a good, arguable case and must demonstrate the existence of a right requiring protection: *Allen v Jambo Holdings* (1980). He must provide grounds for his belief that the defendant has assets in the UK, and for his view that there is a real risk of the assets being removed from the jurisdiction.

- An interlocutory injunction may be granted on an *ex parte* application so that the defendant is prevented from removing his assets until the pending action has been heard.

- Contempt proceedings will follow the defendant's failure to obey the order.

In *Ghoth v Ghoth* (1992), the Court of Appeal held that the purpose of a *Mareva* injunction is to prevent a party making himself 'judgment-proof'. A world-wide *Mareva* injunction is probably inappropriate in matrimonial proceedings; hence a 'court should consider inserting provisions in a worldwide *Mareva* injunction to protect third parties who would *prima facie* be guilty of contempt for assisting in its breach. In matrimonial proceedings, the *Mareva* injunction ought to be limited to the maximum amount which, taking everything in the petitioner's favour, could be achieved in divorce proceedings in England.

10.8.2 Limited nature of the *Mareva* injunction in matrimonial proceedings

Where W suspects that H might destroy essential evidence, such as bank statements indicating the extent of his assets, the court may grant, under its inherent jurisdiction, an injunction, known as an *Anton Piller order*: see *Anton Piller KG v Manufacturing Processes Ltd* (1976). The order is an interlocutory, mandatory injunction, obtained *ex parte*, designed so as to prevent a defendant from concealing, removing or destroying vital evidence, eg, documents in his possession.

10.9 **The *Anton Piller* injunction**

An order of this nature requires the defendant to allow the plaintiff to enter the defendant's premises in order to inspect and make copies of relevant documents. Failure to comply with the order is treated as contempt.

New standard forms for *Mareva* and *Anton Piller* orders were published in August 1994. It is intended that papers to be used in applications for orders shall be lodged with the judge at least two hours before the hearing. Applications must be listed before a judge in such a manner as to ensure that he has sufficient time to read and consider the papers in advance: see Practice Direction by the Lord Chief Justice [1994] 1 WLR 1233.

Summary of Chapter 10

Financial Provision on Breakdown of the Marriage (2): Consent Orders, Variation, Enforcement

Private agreements may be made relating to maintenance on divorce. Terms in such agreements seeking to oust the jurisdiction of the courts are void: s 34 MCA 1973. On application by a party to such an agreement, the court may vary its terms: see *Camm v Camm* (1983).

Private agreements for maintenance on divorce

Where husband and wife have come to terms, the resulting agreement may be incorporated into a court order – a 'consent order'. Where there has been a disclosure of relevant facts which is less than full and frank, the court may set aside a consent order: see *Livesey v Jenkins* (1985).

The consent order

Section 31 MCA 1973 empowers the court to vary or discharge orders, to suspend temporarily a provision in an order or to revive any suspended provision. Some types of variation are prohibited: thus, orders for periodical payments made in favour of a spouse may not be varied by making a lump sum order. Orders may be challenged on grounds of mistake, fraud, material non-disclosure. In considering applications for variation, first consideration will be given to the welfare of any minor child of the family: see *Masefield v Masefield* (1994).

Variation of orders

Lump sum orders may be enforced by judgment summons, charging orders, garnishee proceedings, writ of execution, order for sale of property. In the case of periodical payments, in addition to these methods of enforcement, an attachment order can be made. Note Maintenance Enforcement Act 1991.

The enforcement of court orders

The court may intervene (see s 37 MCA 1973) by granting an injunction where one spouse is acting with the intention of defeating another's claim: see *Kemmis v Kemmis* (1968); *Sherry v Sherry* (1991).

Dispositions intended to defraud

The *Mareva* injunction, granted under the inherent jurisdiction of the court, is of relevance where a party wishes to move assets out of the country so as to avoid the effects of the other party's claim for financial relief. Contempt proceedings may follow on defendant's failure to obey the order. An interlocutory injunction may be granted on an *ex parte* application to prevent the removal of assets until a pending action has been heard: see *Ghoth v Ghoth* (1992).

Mareva and Anton Piller orders

The *Anton Piller* injunction seeks to prevent a person destroying essential evidence, such as bank statements, indicating the exact extent of his assets. The order takes the form of a mandatory injunction preventing defendant from concealing, removing or destroying documents in his possession. Failure to comply with the order is treated as a contempt.

Chapter 11

Financial Provision Concerning Children, and the Child Support Act 1991

This chapter outlines aspects of recent legislation relating to financial provision for children: the Children Act 1989, and the Child Support Act 1991.

ChA 1989 gives the courts powers to make financial provision solely for the child's benefit. The legislation was based on the recommendations of the Report of the Law Commission (1988), *Review of Child Law: Guardianship and Custody* (Law Com No 172). It seeks to simplify the law by introducing measures of rationalisation. Section 15 (1) states: 'Schedule 1 (which consists primarily of the re-enactment, with consequential amendments and minor modifications, of provisions of the Guardianship of Minors Acts 1971 and 1973, the Children Act 1975 and of S5. 15, 16 of the Family Law Reform Act 1987) makes provision in relation to financial relief for children.'

CSA 1991 followed the Government Report, *Children Come First* (1990). It allows for a system of financial support to be administered through statutory procedures, and gives wide powers of collection and enforcement of payments related to maintenance agreements, and imposes a formula for the calculation of maintenance assessments which are the basis of payments to be made by liable persons. The Act is outlined at 11.10 below.

ChA 1989 was intended, in the words of Lord Mackay LC, to be 'the most comprehensive and far-reaching reform of child law which has come before Parliament in living memory'. The object of the Act, in relation to orders for financial relief, was to replace the former confusing, often inconsistent provisions with one set of internally-consistent rules. Essentially, the new provisions are to be seen within the overall context of the child's welfare, which is to be viewed as the court's *paramount consideration*: s 1(1).

Orders for financial relief with respect to children are dealt with under s 15, which must be read with Sch 1. It should be noted that the provisions of this part of the Act do not replace those in MCA 1973 and DPMCA 1978. Note that under s 15(2), the powers of a magistrates' court under the Magistrates' Courts Act 1980 to revoke, revive or vary an order for the periodical payment of money do *not* apply to an order made under the 1989 Act, Sch 1.

11.1 **Recent legislation**

11.2 **Orders for financial relief under s 15 and Sch 1 ChA 1989**

11.3 Persons who may apply for a financial order under ChA 1989

Section 15 and Sch 1 ChA 1989 allow application for orders for financial relief to be made by certain categories of persons as set out in Sch 1, paras 1, 2.

- *A parent.* This term has application to, eg, divorced and adoptive parents, and any party to a marriage (whether or not subsisting) in relation to whom the child concerned is a child of the family: see Sch 1, para 16. An unmarried party, even though he had treated a child as a child of the family, was not a parent within the meaning of Sch 1 ChA 1989: *J v J (A Minor: Property Transfer)* (1993).

- *A guardian of the child.* For guardianship, see 20.1. A guardian may be appointed if a child has no parent with parental responsibility for him: s 5(1)(a) ChA 1989.

- *Any person in whose favour a residence order is in force with respect to a child.* For 'residence orders' (which concern arrangements as to where a child is to live), see 13.15. Effectively, any person who has been given by court order the right to 'care for a child' may ask for an appropriate financial order for the support of that child.

- *A person who has reached the age of 18.* A person who has reached 18 and is or will be or (if an order is made) would be receiving instruction at an educational establishment or undergoing training for a trade, profession or vocation, whether or not while in gainful employment, or where there are special circumstances, may make application: para 2(a). But an order may not be made in relation to such an application where the parents are living together in the same household: para 2(4). In such cases, only periodical payments or a lump sum may be ordered. No application may be made under para 2 by a person if, immediately before he has reached the age of 18, a periodical payments order was in force with respect to him: para 2(3).

11.4 Orders where no application has been made

The court may make a financial order in some cases where no application has been made under Sch 1, as where it makes, varies or discharges a residence order (see 13.15): para 1(6).

11.5 Against whom orders may be made

Financial orders may be made under s 15 and Sch 1 against either or both of the parents of the child, using the term 'parents' so as to include unmarried fathers and step-parents of a child of the family. Orders may not be made against the child's guardian and persons (other than parents) who have a residence order made in their favour.

Exercise of the court's discretionary powers in making orders for financial relief is considered in Sch 1, para 4.

Para 4(1). In deciding whether to exercise its powers under para 1 or 2, and, if so in what manner, the court shall have regard to all the circumstances, including: the income, earning capacity and other finances which each person mentioned in sub-para (4) has or is likely to have in the foreseeable future; the financial needs, obligations and responsibilities which each of those persons has or is likely to have in the foreseeable future; the child's financial needs, earning capacity, property, financial resources; any physical or mental disability of the child; the manner in which the child was being, or was expected to be, educated or trained.

Para 4(2). In deciding whether to exercise its powers under para 1 against a person who is not the mother or father of the child, and if so in what manner, the court will, additionally, have regard to: whether that parent had assumed responsibility for the child's maintenance, and, if so, the extent to which and basis on which he assumed that responsibility and the length of the period during which he met that responsibility; whether he did so knowing that the child was not his child; the liability of any other person to maintain the child.

Para 4(3). Where the court makes an order under para 1 against a person who is not the child's father, this will be recorded in the court order.

Para 4(4). The persons mentioned in sub-para (1) are: in relation to a decision whether to exercise its powers under para 1, any parents of the child; in relation to whether to exercise its powers under para 2, the child's father or mother; the applicant for the order; any other person in whose favour the court proposes to make the order.

11.6 Matters to which the court will have regard

The financial orders in relation to children which the court may make under s 15 and Sch 1 ChA 1989 include periodical payments, lump sums, transfers or settlements of property.

Periodical payments may be secured or unsecured, and are made to the child himself or to the applicant for the child's benefit: see para 1(2)(a), (b). The order will be made for a term which will be specified.

Payment of a lump sum, which may be paid in instalments (see para 5(5)), may be ordered to be made to the child himself or to the applicant for the child's benefit: see para 5(1). It may be made for the purpose of enabling expenses to be met in

11.7 Financial orders which the court may make, and variations

11.7.1 Orders for periodical payments

11.7.2 Orders for payment of a lump sum

connection with the birth of the child or in relation to maintaining the child, and reasonably incurred before the making of the order. (Note that magistrates' orders concerning periodical payments or a lump sum may not exceed a sum specifically stated in paras 1(1)(b) and 5(c).)

11.7.3	Orders for the transfer or settlement of specified property	Under para 1(2)(d), (e), orders may be made for the settlement of property to which a parent is entitled in possession or reversion, for the benefit of the child, and for the transfer of that property to the child himself or an applicant for the child's benefit.
11.7 4	Duration of orders for financial relief	The term to be specified in an order made under para 1 for periodical payments in favour of a child may begin with the date of the application or a later date, but it must not, in the first instance, extend beyond the child's seventeenth birthday, unless the court thinks it right in the circumstances to specify a later date. In any event, it must not extend beyond the child's eighteenth birthday: para 3(1). (This latter statement concerning the 18th birthday does not apply if it appears to the court that the child is or would be receiving instruction (if an order were made) at an educational establishment or undergoing training for a trade, profession or vocation, whether or not while in gainful employment: see para 3(2)(a).)
11.7.5	Variation of lump sum orders	In the case of a lump sum order to be paid by instalments, the court, on application made either by the person liable to pay or the person entitled to receive that sum, has the power to vary the order by varying the number of instalments payable, the amount of any instalment payable, and the date on which an instalment becomes payable: para 5(6).
11.7.6	Variation of periodical payments order	In the case of an application for variation of a periodical payments order, the court must take into account all the circumstances of the case, including any change in any of the matters to which the court was required to have regard when making the order. The court's power to vary includes the power to suspend temporarily any provision of the order and to revive any provision suspended: para 6(2). An application for variation can be made by the child himself if he has reached the age of 16: para 6(4). Where the parent liable to make payments under a secured periodical payments order has died, the persons who may apply for variation (or discharge) of the order will include the representatives of the deceased parent: para 7(1). No application for variation shall, except with permission of the court, be made after the end of six months from the date on which representation in regard to the deceased parent's estate was first taken out: para 7(2).

Financial Provision Concerning Children, and the Child Support Act 1991

The court may make an interim order (see para 9) requiring either or both parents to make such periodical payments at such time and for such term as the court thinks fit. The order ceases to have effect when the application is disposed of, or, if earlier, on the date specified in the interim order.	11.7.7 Interim orders
It is very important to note that the situation concerning the role of the courts with respect to maintenance for children will be transformed following the transition period which is planned to end in April 1997. The court will exercise jurisdiction during the transition period, which has commenced, and, to a limited extent, afterwards.	11.8 Effect of the Child Support Act 1991 on the jurisdiction of the courts

After the transition period ends, the court will have jurisdiction in the following circumstances:

- the making of maintenance orders for step-children who are children of the family, and for children outside the definition in s 55 CSA 1991 (see 11.11 below), ie, married or formerly-married children, children aged over 16, or between 16-19 and not in education;

- maintenance in excess of the assessment level (see 11.16 below): 1981 Act, s 8(6);

- orders intended solely to meet the expenses of education or training: 1981 Act, s 8(7);

- maintenance to meet expenses attributable to a child's disability: 1981 Act, s 8(8);

- orders against the 'person with care' (see 11.11 below): s 8(10);

- orders concerning lump sums and property adjustment, and residence and contact orders on the divorce of parents.

The general objective of s 8 CSA 1981 is to prevent the courts and the Child Support Agency, which administers the 1981 Act (see 11.14 below), having concurrent jurisdiction. Parents will be expected to use the Agency even though a court is considering other aspects of their family relationship.

In its report and proposals concerning the maintenance of children, *Children Come First* (1990), the Government proposed major changes in the approach to problems of child maintenance. Statistics had revealed the extent of the problem: only 30% of lone mothers received regular maintenance payments, and the contribution of maintenance payments to the income of lone-parent families was too low. Government proposals were aimed at establishing a system of child	11.9 The Child Support Act 1991

maintenance which would be available equally to all persons seeking maintenance for the benefit of a child. The proposed system would ensure 'that parents honour their legal and moral responsibility to maintain their own children whenever they can afford to do so'. It would take into account that where a liable parent has formed a second family and has further natural children, he should be liable to maintain *all* his own children. Maintenance payments would be realistically related to the costs of caring for a child and would be reviewed regularly. It would be recognised that both parties have a legal responsibility to maintain their children.

11.10 Objectives of the CSA 1991

CSA 1991, which has been in force since 5 April 1993, was intended 'to make provision for the assessment, collection and enforcement of periodical maintenance payable by certain parents with respect to children of theirs who are not in their care; and for the collection and enforcement of certain other kinds of maintenance; and for connected purposes'. It should be noted that the Act is concerned with assessing parents' liability for support of a child, with parent-child obligations, and with income payments, not payments of capital.

11.11 Definitions

The following definitions of key words in CSA 1991 should be noted.

- *Child.* For the purposes of the 1991 Act, a person is a 'child' if he is under 16, or under 19 and receiving full time education (which is not advanced education) by attendance at a recognised educational establishment, or elsewhere if the education is recognised by the Secretary of State, or he does not fall within these provisions, but is under 18 and prescribed conditions are satisfied with respect to him: s 55(1). A person is *not* a child for the purposes of this Act if he is or has been married: s 55(2).

- *Qualifying child.* A child is a qualifying child if one of his parents is, in relation to him, an absent parent, or both his parents are absent parents: s 3(1).

- *Person with care.* A person is a 'person with care', in relation to any child, if he is a person with whom the child has his home, who usually provides day to day care for the child (whether exclusively or in conjunction with another person), and who does not fall within a prescribed category of persons: s 3(3).

- *Parent.* A 'parent' is, in relation to any child, a person who is in law the mother or father of the child: s 54. (This definition includes, therefore, a natural and adoptive parent, and a person treated as a parent under ss 28, 29 Human Fertilisation and Embryology Act 1988: see 12.7.)

- *Absent parent.* The parent of a child is an 'absent parent' in relation to a child, if that parent is not living in the same household with the child, and the child has his home with a person who is, in relation to him, a 'person with care': s 3(2).
- *Child support maintenance.* 'Child support maintenance' comprises periodical payments which are required to be paid in accordance with a maintenance assessment: s 3(6).

It should be noted that for the purposes of the 1991 Act there may be more than one 'person with care' in relation to the same qualifying child: s 3(5).

11.12 The duty to maintain

A basic principle of the 1991 Act, 'the duty to maintain', is set out in s 1.

'(1) For the purposes of this Act, each parent of a qualifying child is responsible for maintaining him.'

'(2) For the purposes of this Act, an absent parent shall be taken to have met his responsibility to maintain any qualifying child of his by making periodical payments of maintenance with respect to the child of such amount, and at such intervals, as may be determined in accordance with the provisions of this Act.'

'(3) Where a maintenance assessment made under this Act requires the making of periodical payments, it shall be the duty of the absent parent with respect to whom the assessment was made to make those payments.'

Section 1 establishes that a child's parents are responsible for his financial support when he is not being cared for by both of them, that the obligation to maintain is met when payments under the Act are made, and that the duty to make child support payments arises under the Act *only* when an assessment has been made.

11.13 The 'welfare principle'

'Where, in any case which falls to be dealt with under this Act, the Secretary of State or any child support officer is considering the exercise of any discretionary power conferred by this Act, he shall have regard to the welfare of any child likely to be affected by his decision': s 2.

Welfare of the child is *not*, therefore, under the 1991 Act, a 'paramount consideration'.

11.14 The Child Support Agency

The 1991 Act is administered by the Child Support Agency (which is not mentioned in the Act). Under s 13, the Secretary of State appoints 'child support officers' and a Chief Child Support Officer who keeps the operation of the Act under review and makes a written report annually to the Secretary of State. The Agency, which has centres in various parts of the country, has powers to obtain information required by the Secretary of State: s 14. The unauthorised disclosure of information by child support officers is an offence under s 50: see *Re C* (1994).

11.15 A 'parent' under CSA 1991

No maintenance assessment may be made under the 1991 Act against a person who denies parentage *except* where a finding of parentage has been made under s 26.

Under s 26, where a person who is alleged to be a parent of the child concerning whom an application for a maintenance assessment has been made, denies that he is a parent, a child support officer must ensure that the case is within one of the following categories:

Case A Alleged parent has adopted the child.

Case B Alleged parent has a parental order under s 30 HFEA 1990: see SI 1991/1247, as amended.

Case C Declaration that alleged parent is a parent of the child in question (or a declaration which has that effect) is in force under s 56 Family Law Act 1986 (declarations of parentage).

Case D Declaration that alleged parent is one of the parents of the child in question has been made under s 27 CSA 1991 and the child has not been subsequently adopted.

Case E Child is habitually resident in Scotland, the child support officer is satisfied that one or other of the presumptions set out in the Law Reform (Parent and Child) (Scotland) Act 1986 applies, and the child has not been subsequently adopted.

Case F Alleged parent has been found or adjudged to be the father of the child in question in proceedings before any court in England and Wales which are relevant proceedings for the purposes of s 12 Civil Evidence Act 1968, or in affiliation proceedings before any court in the UK (whether or not he offered any defence to the allegation of paternity), and that finding or adjudication still subsists, and the child has not been subsequently adopted.

When the alleged parent falls outside these categories the Secretary of State may apply to the court for a declaration of parentage: s 27. A declaration of this nature has effect only for the purposes of CSA 1991.

An absent parent is required to make payments if – and only if – a maintenance assessment has been made. The assessment is calculated in accordance with a precise formula: see Sch 1. (Examples of application of the formula are available in *Notes for Advisers*, published by the Child Support Agency.)

11.16 Aspects of the assessment of maintenance

Where an absent parent fails to return the maintenance enquiry form, or fails to provide adequate information, a child support officer will give 14 days' notice of the making of an interim assessment. This is calculated by multiplying the maintenance requirement for the child (ie, income support rate for the child plus income support rate for the parent with care, plus any one-parent premium, minus child benefit) by 1.5.

See SI 1992/1815. The 'maintenance requirement' is calculated on the basis of the amount which would be paid by way of income support (see 8.10) to a parent in respect of each child. There will be added to that amount, where there is at least one child aged under 16, the following amounts: the personal allowance which is payable to a parent 'who has care', the amount of the income support family premium, and (where the child is living with a parent who has no partner) the lone-parent premium. There is a deduction of the child benefit sum payable in respect of the family. The resulting figure is *the weekly basic maintenance requirement for the family*.

11.16.1 The 'maintenance requirement'

The 'assessable income' is calculated by deducting a parent's exempt income (ie, housing costs, including rent less any housing benefits, income support personal allowance) from net income (ie, wage/salary less tax, national insurance and one half of pension contributions). The concept of a 'protected income level' is used so as to prevent the absent parent falling below the level of income support. Reference is made also to a maximum level of maintenance payments, based upon a statutory formula. In the case of an absent parent with a very high income, an application may be made under s 8 for a 'top-up' order.

11.16.2 The 'assessable income'

The assessable incomes of the 'absent' and 'caring' parents are added, and the total multiplied by 0.5. If the resulting figure is *greater* than the maintenance requirement, a further 25% of income is payable (but this is subject to a maximum limit). If the resulting figure is *equal to or less* than the maintenance requirement, the amount of maintenance to be paid by the absent parent will be *one half* of the assessable income.

11.16.3 The 'maintenance assessment'

A person who has care of children is not generally obliged to seek a maintenance assessment. But where the parent of a

11.17 Application for assessment

qualifying child receives Income Support or Family Credit (see 8.13), she must, if she is a person with care of the child, and if she is requested to do so by the Secretary of State, authorise him to take action to recover child support maintenance from the absent parent: s 6(1). Where this is not done, benefit support will be reduced: see SI 1992/1813. Note that nothing in the 1991 Act prevents persons from entering into a maintenance agreement: s 9(2). A maintenance agreement is defined in s 9(1) as 'any agreement for the making, or for securing the making, of periodical payments by way of maintenance ... to or for the benefit of any child'. Such an agreement which contains a provision purporting to restrict the right to apply for a maintenance assessment is void: s 9(4).

11.18 Jurisdiction

Under s 44(1), a child support officer has jurisdiction to make a maintenance assessment with respect to a person who is a person with care, an absent parent, or a qualifying child, only if they are habitually resident in the UK. 'Habitual residence' appears to imply a regular physical presence which endures for some time: see *Cruse v Chittum* (1974); *V v B* (1991).

11.19 Collection and enforcement

The framework of collection and enforcement under the CSA 1991 is set out in ss 29-40 and SI 1992/1989 (Child Support (Collection and Enforcement) Regulations). The wide powers of collection and enforcement include the requirement that regulations shall be made, concerning the payment of child support maintenance, empowering the Secretary of State to enforce such payments (in accordance with the assessment) by standing order or the opening of an account from which payments will be made: s 29.

11.19.1 The liability order

Where a person (the 'liable person') is liable to make payments of child support maintenance, the Secretary of State may make a 'deduction from earnings order' against that person so as to secure the payment of any amount due under the maintenance assessment. The order is directed at the employer who employs the 'liable person': it instructs him to make deductions from the earnings of the 'liable person' and pay them to the Secretary of State. The employer is liable for non-compliance after the end of seven days beginning with the date on which the order was served on him: see s 31.

11.19.2 Distress procedure

Under s 35, where a liability order has been made against the 'liable person', his goods (except tools, clothing, etc) and money may be seized.

Where the Secretary of State has sought to levy an amount by distress or to recover an amount in the county courts (after the making of a liability order), and any portion of the amount remains unpaid, he may apply, under s 40, to the magistrates' court for the issue of a warrant committing the 'liable person' to prison. The maximum period of imprisonment is six weeks: s 40(7). The warrant will be issued only where the court is of the opinion that there has been 'wilful refusal or culpable neglect' on the part of the 'liable person': s 40(3).

11.19.3 Committal to prison

The 1991 Act allows for periodical reviews of assessments, for reviews on changes of circumstances, and for reviews of decisions which have been made by child support officers.

11.20 Review and appeal

Under s 16(1), (3), the Secretary of State may make arrangements for a review by a child support officer of the original assessment, which will be conducted as if a fresh application for a maintenance assessment has been made by the person in whose favour the original assessment was made.

11.20.1 Periodical reviews

Under s 17(1), (2), where a maintenance assessment is in force, the absent parent or person with care with respect to whom it was made may apply to the Secretary of State for the original assessment to be reviewed. An application under s 17 may be made only on the ground that, by reason of a change in circumstance since the original assessment was made, the amount of child support maintenance payable by the absent parent would be significantly different if it were to be fixed by a maintenance assessment made by reference to the circumstances of the case as at the date of the application.

11.20.2 Reviews on change of circumstances

Where an application for a maintenance assessment is refused, or an application under s 17 for a review is refused, the person who made the application may apply to the Secretary of State for a review of the refusal: s 18(1). Where a maintenance assessment is in force, the absent parent or person with care with respect to whom it was made may apply for the assessment to be reviewed: s 18(2). Reviews under s 18 will be carried out by a child support officer who played no part in taking the decision which is to be reviewed: s 18(7).

11.20.3 Reviews of decisions of child support officers

Where a child support officer is not conducting a review under ss 16, 17, 18, but is satisfied nevertheless that a maintenance assessment which is in force is defective by reason of having been made in ignorance of a material fact, or having been based on a mistake as to a material fact, or being wrong in law, he may make a fresh maintenance assessment on the assumption that the person in whose favour the original

11.20.4 Reviews at instigation of child support officers

assessment was made has made a fresh application for a maintenance assessment: s 19(1).

11.20.5 Appeals

Any person who is aggrieved by the decision of a child support officer on a review under s 18, or a refusal of an application for such a review, may appeal to a child support appeal tribunal: s 20(1).

A child support appeal tribunal consists of a chairman and two others if reasonably practicable members of both sexes should be included: see Sch 3.

11.20.6 Child Support Commissioners

The Chief Child Support Commissioner and other Child Support Commissioners are appointed from among persons who have a 10-year general qualification: s 22(1). Any person who is aggrieved by a decision of a child support appeal tribunal, and any child support officer, may appeal to a Child Support Commissioner on a question of law: s 24(1). Where, on an appeal under this section, a Child Support Commissioner holds that the decision appealed against was wrong in law, he shall set it aside: s 24(2). An appeal on a question of law shall lie to the appropriate court from any decision of a Child Support Commissioner: s 25(1). Such an appeal may be brought only with leave from a Commissioner or the appropriate court: s 25(2).

11.21 Criticisms of the CSA 1991

Criticisms of the 1991 Act – its basic principles, its procedures and their outcomes – have been unremitting. In evidence presented in 1993 to the House of Commons Social Security Committee, the Law Society raised objections to the rigid approach adopted by the Child Support Agency to parents. *All the circumstances of a family breakdown ought to be considered*, argued the Law Society, and an inflexible, mechanistic formula in relation to assessment was unhelpful. The Agency, it was suggested, was, in effect, undermining an approach to family breakdown which should aim at amicable, responsible arrangements between parties.

Some commentators have noted, however, that slow, expensive, pre-1991 applications for maintenance have been replaced by assessment on the basis of a precise formula which does not leave assessment to the vagaries of chance. Variation of assessment, it is argued, is possible and the system of appeals envisaged by the legislation is extensive.

In 1994, representations were made to the Government by significant numbers of 'liable persons' who suggested that a principle which may demand sudden and unexpectedly large amounts of child maintenance is essentially unfair in operation, and is the cause of much hardship; in particular, difficulties occur where inadequate allowance is made for the outgoings of the 'absent parent' who cannot set against his assessable income the expenditure resulting from travel and from expenses relating to his second family.

The House of Commons Social Security Committee, reporting in October 1994, made the following suggestions concerning changes to the working of the 1991 Act: maintenance awards should allow for previous 'clean break' property or capital settlements; a lower tariff ought to be considered for all cases where parents separated or where children were born before April 1993; standard housing costs should be used in the maintenance formula; absent parents' travel-to-work costs ought to be allowed for in the maintenance formula.

11.22 The Government White Paper

In January 1995, the Secretary of State for Social Security presented to Parliament a White Paper, *Improving Child Support* (Cm 2745), setting out proposals for changes to the child support maintenance scheme, which were intended to 'secure that many more children are supported by their own parents whenever they can afford to maintain them, and that absent parents are not able wilfully to avoid their responsibilities'. The Government stressed its belief that the principles underlying the child support system 'are right', but that changes to the system are needed 'to ensure that it is more widely acceptable to absent parents and that more maintenance is actually paid to parents with care' (see 11.11 above).

Proposals for change include the following:

- Following primary legislation in 1996/1997, *discretion will be introduced* allowing departures from the maintenance formula assessment (see 11.16 above) in cases where an absent parent (see 11.11 above) would otherwise face hardship or where certain types of property or capital transfers took place before April 1993. Either parent will be able to apply for a departure; both will be entitled to make representations. The discretion is to be exercised initially by the Child Support Agency; a parent who is unhappy with the decision to allow or refuse a departure, or with the extent of departure granted, may ask for a fresh consideration by an independent Child Support Appeal Tribunal which may substitute its decision for that of the Agency.

- As from April 1995, *changes to the maintenance formula* would be introduced. No absent parent (see 11.11 above) is to be assessed to pay more than 30% in a combination of current maintenance and start-up arrears. A 'broad brush adjustment' will be provided in the maintenance formula in order to take account of property and capital settlements; there will be no need for lengthy and detailed investigation of cases in this area. An allowance will be made towards high travel-to-work costs. Housing costs will be allowed for a new partner or step children. The maximum level of maintenance payable under the formula will be reduced.

- As from April 1997, parents with care who are in receipt of Income Support or Jobseeker's Allowance (payable, if Parliament agrees, from April 1996 to people seeking work) will be able to build up a 'maintenance credit', which will be paid to them as a lump sum when a recipient commences in employment for at least 16 hours per week.

- Recipients of Family Credit and Disability Working Allowance will be given some *compensation for loss of maintenance* where changes in the maintenance formula result in a reduction on their assessment during an award for benefit.

- *Fees charged by the Agency for assessment and collection services will be suspended* for a period of two years until April 1997. Interest payments will also be suspended and will be replaced with penalties for late payment.

- The *administration of the scheme will be changed*. There will be a deferment of the take-on by the Agency in 1996/1997 of cases not in receipt of Income Support, Family Credit or Disability Working Allowance where there was a court order or written maintenance agreement before April 1993. (These cases will continue to be heard by the courts.) Where the agency causes delay in setting maintenance, consideration will be given to not enforcing more than six months' arrears where the absent parent gives a commitment to meet the on-going liability. Change of circumstances reports will be simplified, and periodic reviews will be made every two years. Liability will be deferred by eight weeks if an absent parent provides relevant information within four weeks of the date on which a maintenance enquiry form (see 11.16 above) was issued to him. Maintenance assessment rules will be altered so as to introduce a protected income provision when deductions from earning orders have been applied in an interim maintenance assessment.

It should be noted that none of the proposed changes envisaged by the White Paper will apply retrospectively. Absent parents will be required to pay maintenance at the rate currently assessed; they will pay arrears due at current rates. Changes in assessments will have application only from those dates specified in the appropriate legislation.

Summary of Chapter 11

Financial Provision Concerning Children, and the Child Support Act 1991

Section 15 and Sch 1 ChA 1989 allow for the making of orders for financial relief on application of a parent (including divorced and adoptive parents), guardians, persons in whose favour a residence order is in force with respect to a child, a person who has reached the age of 18, and is receiving instruction. The court may make an order of its own motion.

Orders under s 15 ChA 1989

Orders may be made against either or both parents of the child. The term 'parents' includes unmarried fathers and step parents, but not guardians.

The court will take into account the income, earning capacity of the parties, financial needs, obligations.

Orders may be made as follows: for periodical payments; for payment of a lump sum; for the transfer and settlement of property. The court may allow variation of orders and may make interim orders.

After the end of the transition period in April 1997, the court will have jurisdiction only in the following circumstances: the making of maintenance orders for step children who are children of the family and for children who are married, or formerly-married, or over 16; where the order is intended to meet expenses of education, disability, education or training; orders against a person 'with care' and orders involving lump sums, property adjustment, residence and contact orders.

Effect of the Child Support Act 1991 on the jurisdiction of the courts

The 1991 Act is intended to provide for the assessment, collection and enforcement of periodical maintenance payable by certain parents with respect to children of theirs who are not in their care. 'Child' refers to persons under 16, or under 19 if receiving full-time education. A child is a 'qualifying child' if one of his parents is, in relation to him, an absent parent, or both his parents are absent parents: s 55(1). 'Parent', as used in the Act, is a person who is *in law* the child's mother or father. (Natural and adoptive parents are, therefore, included.) 'Absent parent' is one who is not living in the same household as the child: see s 3(2). A 'person with care' is one with whom the child has his home.

The Child Support Act 1991

Each parent of a qualifying child is responsible for maintaining him: s 1(1). An absent parent is taken to have met his responsibility by making appropriate periodical payments.

Where a maintenance assessment made under the Act requires the making of periodical payments, they must be made. The duty to make child support payments arises *only* when an assessment has been made.

The Act is administered by the Child Support Agency, a Chief Child Support Officer and a staff of child support officers.

Assessment of maintenance is made in accordance with a formula from which are determined a 'maintenance requirement' and 'assessable income'.

Where a person is liable to make payments of child support maintenance, a 'deduction from earnings order' may be made against him; his employer may be liable for non-compliance. The goods and money of the person against whom a liability order has been made may be seized: s 35. Committal to prison is possible under s 40.

Periodical reviews based on changes in circumstances may be made: s 16. Appeals against decisions of child support officers on a review may be made under s 18.

Chapter 12

Parentage; Legitimacy; Parental Responsibility

The content of this chapter reflects recent social changes in doctrines and attitudes concerning concepts which were formerly held to be immutable – the relationships of parent and child, the very basis of parentage, the so-called 'legitimacy' of the child. We consider, in the light of recent legislation and judicial decision, questions such as the following: Who, in law, may be classified as 'the father' of a child? Does the concept of 'legitimacy' continue to play an important role in family law? Are there circumstances in which parental rights must yield to the child's rights?

12.1 Changing concepts within English family law

Early general definitions of 'parent' (eg 'one who has begotten or borne offspring') are no longer precisely adequate in an era in which human assisted reproduction (HAR) is practised and widely accepted. How is the earlier view of parentage to be modified when artificial insemination by an unknown donor (AID) is now an accepted technique for the production of a child? What are the legal implications? Statutes such as the Human Fertilisation and Embryology Act 1990, the Children Act 1989 and the Child Support Act 1991 have sought to take into account changing attitudes concerning the idea of parentage and, specifically, matters involving parental responsibility.

12.2 The concept of 'parentage'

The following recent statutory definitions are of significance:

- '"Parent" includes any party to a marriage (whether or not subsisting) in relation to whom the child concerned is a child of the family': Sch 1, para 16(2) ChA 1989: see *J v J (A Minor: Property Transfer)* (1993), at 11.3.
- '"Parent", in relation to any child, means any person who is in law the mother or father of the child': s 54 CSA 1991. This will include the natural parent, an adoptive parent (see 22.4) and a person who is to be treated as a child's parent under HFEA 1990 (see 12.7 below).

It should be noted that there may be differences between the 'biological', 'legal' and 'social' parent, which are taken into account in recent legislation.

12.3 Who is 'a parent'?

The *Warnock Committee of Inquiry into Human Fertilisation and Embryology* set out in its *Report* (1984) details of the main

12.4 Aspects of HAR

techniques currently employed in human assisted reproduction. A concise explanation of the technical vocabulary is given in the introductory note to the HFEA 1990 in *Current Law Statutes Annotated* (1990, Vol III, Sweet & Maxwell).

12.4.1 *In vitro* fertilisation

The essential feature of IVF (*'in vitro'* is used to indicate processes taking place within a laboratory) is the extraction of a ripe human egg from the ovary before it would have been released naturally. It is then mixed with the semen of the husband or other partner in order that fertilisation might occur. When the fertilised egg has begun to divide it is transferred back to the mother's uterus.

12.4.2 Egg donation

A mature egg is recovered from a fertile female donor and is fertilised *in vitro* using the semen of the husband of the infertile woman. The resulting embryo is transferred to the patient's uterus; if it implants, the patient may carry it to term.

12.4.3 Embryo donation and transfer

A donated egg is fertilised in vitro with donated semen; the resulting embryo is transferred to a woman whose husband is infertile and who cannot produce an egg herself.

12.5 Surrogacy

Surrogacy (which means 'substitute') should not be confused with HAR and its associated techniques. The Surrogacy Arrangements Act 1985 applies not only to *total surrogacy arrangements,* (ie where the ovum of an infertile woman is fertilised with her partner's sperm and is then transferred to the womb of the surrogate mother), but also to *partial surrogacy arrangements* (ie where the surrogate mother is genetically the mother) as where a person 'rents' her womb to a commissioning father and mother. The 1985 Act is concerned with surrogacy arrangements *on a commercial basis*.

12.5.1 Statutory definitions

Under the 1985 Act, s 1(2), 'surrogate mother' means 'a woman who carries a child in pursuance of an arrangement – (a) made before she began to carry the child, and (b) made with a view to any child carried in pursuance of it being handed over to, and the parental rights being exercised (so far as practicable) by, another person or other persons.'

An arrangement is a surrogacy arrangement 'if, were a woman to whom the arrangement relates to carry a child in pursuance of it, she would be a surrogate mother': s 1(3).

12.5.2 Surrogacy on a commercial basis

Under s 2(1), no person may, on a commercial basis, do any of the following acts in the UK: initiate or take part in any negotiations with a view to the making of a surrogacy arrangement, offer or agree to negotiate the making of a surrogacy arrangement, or compile any information with a view to its use in making, or negotiating the making of, surrogacy arrangements, and no person in the UK may knowingly cause another to do any of those acts on a commercial basis.

A person who contravenes s 2(1) is guilty of an offence, but it is not a contravention of that subsection for a woman, with a view to becoming a surrogate mother herself, to do any act mentioned in s 2(1) or to cause such an act to be done, or for any person, with a view to a surrogate mother carrying a child for him, to do such an act or cause such an act to be done: s 2(2).

A person does an act 'on a commercial basis' if any payment is at any time received by himself or another in respect of it, or he does it with a view to any payment being received by himself or another in respect of making, or negotiating or facilitating the making of, any surrogacy arrangement: s 2(3).

Under s 1A, as inserted by s 36 HFEA 1990, no surrogacy arrangement is enforceable by or against any of the persons making it.

12.5.3 Surrogacy advertisements

Section 3 applies to any advertisement containing an indication – however it is expressed – that any person is or may be willing to enter into a surrogacy arrangement or to negotiate or facilitate the making of a surrogacy arrangement, or that any person is looking for a woman willing to become a surrogate mother or for persons wanting a woman to carry a child as a surrogate mother: s 3(1).

Where a newspaper or periodical containing an advertisement to which this section applies is published in the UK, the proprietor, editor or publisher is guilty of an offence: s 3(2). A person is guilty of an offence if the advertisement is conveyed by means of a telecommunication system so as to be seen or heard (or both) in the UK: s 3(3).

12.5.4 Offences under the 1985 Act

Offences under the 1985 Act carry fines or imprisonment as penalties: s 4. Under s 4(3), criminal liability may be created for officers of a corporate surrogacy agency.

12.6 The 'legal mother'

Note the statement of Lord Simon in *The Ampthill Peerage* (1977): 'Motherhood, although also a legal relationship, is based on a fact, being proved demonstrably by parturition.' But the increasing use of IVF techniques has presented the law with a variety of problems: see, eg, *Re W (Minors: Surrogacy)* (1991). Section 27(1) HFEA 1990 states in precise terms: 'The woman who is carrying or has carried a child as a result of the placing in her of an embryo or of sperm and eggs, and no other woman, is to be treated as the mother of the child.' Essentially, therefore, *the woman giving birth* is to be treated as the 'legal mother'.

- For the purposes of HFEA 1990, a woman is not to be treated as carrying a child until the embryo has become implanted: s 2(3).

- Section 27(1) (see 12.6 above) applies whether the woman was in the UK or elsewhere at the time of the placing in her of the embryo or sperm and eggs. (There is no domicile requirement.)

12.7 The 'legal father'

Decisions in law as to who is the 'legal father' are much more complex than those relating to the determination of the 'legal mother'. It is necessary to consider the circumstances of the 'genetic' and 'non-genetic' fathers.

12.7.1 The genetic father

The genetic father is the man who has fertilised the egg. In general, he is considered as the legal father. Two *exceptions* to this general rule are recognised.

- Under s 28(6) HFEA 1990, where a person is a donor whose sperm has been used for activities for which a licence is required under Sch 2 (eg bringing about the creation of embryos *in vitro*) and who has given the appropriate consent under Sch 3, para 5, he is not to be treated as the father of the child.

- Under s 28(6) HFEA 1990, where a person's sperm, or any embryo, the creation of which was brought about with his sperm, was used after his death, he is *not* to be treated as the father of the child.

12.7.2 The non-genetic father

Section 28 HFEA 1990 makes provision for the case of a child born following the placing of an embryo or of sperm and eggs in a woman, or her artificial insemination. The following matters are of relevance to the question of who is 'the father'.

- If the woman is married, then under s 28(2), her husband will be considered as the father *unless it is shown* that he did not consent to the treatment.

- Where donated sperm is used for a woman during licensed treatment which is provided for her and a man together, then that man is to be considered as the father of the child if s 28(2) has no application (as where the woman is unmarried): s 28(3).

- Where a person is considered as the father of the child by virtue of subsections (2) or (3) above, no other person is to be treated as the father of the child: s 28(4).

12.8 Orders under s 30 HFEA 1990

Under s 30 HFEA 1990, the court may make an order providing for a child to be treated in law as the child of the parties to the marriage (referred to below as 'husband' and 'wife') if the child has been carried by a woman other than the wife as the result of the placing in her of an embryo or sperm and eggs or her artificial insemination, the gametes of the husband or the wife, or both, were used to bring about the creation of the embryo, and the conditions in s 30(2)–(7) are satisfied. (Note: 'gametes' are unfertilised male sperm or female egg cells which contain genetic material from only one of the potential parents.) See s 30(1).

- The husband or wife must apply for the order within six months of the birth of the child or, in the case of a child born before the coming into force of the 1990 Act, within six months of that date: s 30(2).
- At the time of the application and of the making of the order, the child's home must be with the husband or wife; the husband or wife, or both, must be domiciled in the UK or Channel Islands or Isle of Man: s 30(3).
- Both husband and wife must have attained the age of 18 at the time of the making of the order: s 30(4).
- The court must be satisfied that no money has been given or received by the husband or wife in consideration of the making of the order: s 30(7).

12.9 Proving parentage

Proof as to who is the *mother* of a child is relatively simple; problems may arise, however, in the case of 'acceptable proof' as to who is the *father*.

Where the mother is *married*, there is a rebuttable presumption that her husband is the father of the child. The burden of rebuttal falls on the person who denies the essence of the presumption: see *R v Luffe* (1907). In *Knowles v Knowles* (1962), it was held that the presumption of legitimacy applied in the case of a child born after the grant of a decree of divorce. Note that an adjudication of paternity made in the course of proceedings constitutes *prima facie* evidence of paternity in later proceedings: s 12 Civil Evidence Act 1968, as amended by s 12 FLRA 1987.

There is no presumption concerning the father where a child is born to an *unmarried* mother. Entry of a person's name in the register of births as the father is *prima facie evidence* of paternity. See 12.12 below.

The standard of proof concerning the rebuttal of the presumption of paternity is on *the balance of probabilities*: see s 26 FLRA 1969: see *W v K (Proof of Paternity)* (1988).

12.10 Blood tests

Blood tests in relation to the establishing of paternity, involve a comparison of the blood of the child, the mother and the alleged father. The tests may be directed by the court; a party may not be ordered to undergo such a test without his consent: ss 20(1), 21(1) FLRA 1969. Adverse inferences may be drawn by the court from a refusal to undergo a test: see *McVeigh v Beattie* (1988); *Re A (A Minor) (Paternity: Refusal of Blood Test)* (1994). When the test has been made, a report must be submitted to the court indicating whether the party is, as a result, excluded from paternity of the child in question; if he is not excluded, the value of the test must be stated: s 20(2) FLRA 1969.

Note *Re F (A Minor) (Blood Tests: Parental Rights)* (1993). The Court of Appeal held that the judge was correct in refusing to order a blood test under s 20(1) FLRA 1969 to determine the natural father of a child where the mother had established a new family unit into which the child had settled and the application was made by a putative father who had no relationship with the child, since the disturbance of that relationship or the stability of the family unit would be likely to prove detrimental to the welfare of the child, and the court would not order a blood test against the will of the parent who, since birth, had sole parental responsibility for the child.

12.11 DNA profiling

Blood, semen, hair roots, and other bodily tissues can be subjected to the process of DNA profiling. Positive proof of paternity is established by identifying a child's maternally-inherited DNA bands (a pattern which appears in laboratory tests) by comparison of the child's and mother's DNA. Those bands in the child's DNA pattern which do not match with those of the mother must be inherited necessarily from the biological father. The alleged father's DNA patterns will show whether he has bands which match the child's paternal bands; if he has, he is the child's real father: see *Re T (A Minor)(Blood Tests)* (1993).

12.12 Register of births

Prima facie evidence of paternity may be derived from the fact that a person's name appears as a father of a child in the register of births: see s 2 of the Births and Deaths Registration Act 1953. The name of an unmarried father may be entered at the joint request of the mother and father, or at the request of mother or father upon production of a declaration as to who is the father: see s 24 FLRA 1987; Sch 12, para 6 ChA 1989.

12.13 Information concerning parentage kept under HFEA 1990

The *Human Fertilisation and Embryology Authority* (see s 5 of the 1990 Act) is obliged to keep a register concerning the provision of treatment services for any identifiable individual and the keeping or use of the gametes of any identifiable individual or of an embryo taken from an identifiable woman, and information showing that any identifiable individual was, or may have been, born in consequence of treatment services: s 31(2). A person who has attained the age of 18 may apply to the Authority for information in the register: s 31(1). A person under the age of 18 may request information on the register which shows that he was, or may have been, born in consequence of treatment services. He may also request notice from the Authority stating whether or not information in the register shows that he and his intended spouse might be related: s 31(7).

12.14 Illegitimacy: changing attitudes

At common law a child was considered legitimate if his parents were married at the time of his conception or birth. The bastard – *filius nullius* ('son of no man') – suffered a large number of disabilities: he could not inherit, had no right to be supported by his father and was often 'cast on the parish' for his maintenance. In our time, however, more enlightened attitudes have prevailed, culminating in the provisions of FLRA 1987 which effectively remove most distinctions in law between a legitimate and illegitimate child. Reflecting prevailing social attitudes towards marriage and the phenomenon of the unmarried parent, the law has been concerned with the eradication of the effect of rules, provisions and precedents which, to modern eyes, appear to 'punish' a child for events which were not of his making.

12.15 FLRA 1987: the general principle

The general principle of FLRA 1987 is set out in s 1.

After the coming into force of this Act, references, however expressed, to any relationship between two persons shall, unless the contrary intention appears, be construed without regard to whether or not the father and mother of either of them, or the father and mother of any person through whom the relationship is deduced, have or had been married to each other at any time: s 1(1). In this Act, and enactments passed after this section has come into force, unless the contrary intention appears, references to a person whose father and mother were married to each other at the time of his birth include; and references to a person whose father and mother were not married to each other at the time of his birth do not include, references to any person to whom subsection (3) applies, and cognate references are to be construed accordingly: s 1(2).

Subsection (3) applies to any person who: is treated as legitimate under s 1 Legitimacy Act 1976; is a legitimated person within s 10 1976 Act; is an adopted child within the Adoption Act 1976; is otherwise treated in law as legitimate. For purposes of construing references falling within s 1(2) of the 1987 Act, the time of a person's birth is taken to include any time during the period beginning with the insemination resulting in his birth, or where there was no insemination, his conception, and, in either case, ending with his birth: s 1(4).

The general effect of s 1 is that *a new rule of construction* is introduced: parent-child relationships are to be generally construed without any regard as to whether or not the child's parents were married. In almost all respects, therefore, legal distinctions between those described as 'legitimate' or 'illegitimate' children disappear, in the absence of a declared contrary intention.

12.16 Abolition of affiliation proceedings

Under s 17 of FLRA 1987, the Affiliation Proceedings Act 1957 ceased to have effect. Proceedings under the 1957 Act were redolent of the old Poor Law; maintenance for an illegitimate child could be obtained only in circumstances which underlined the discrimination exercised against such a child.

12.17 Children of void marriages

The children of void marriages are to be treated as *legitimate* if the father was domiciled in England or Wales at the date of the child's birth, or, if he had died before, then was so domiciled immediately before the date of his death, and both or either of the parents at the time of the insemination which resulted in the birth, or where there was no insemination, the child's conception (or the time of the celebration of marriage if later) both or either of the parties reasonably believed that the marriage was valid: s 1(1) Legitimacy Act 1976.

- A belief in the validity of the marriage may be 'reasonable' notwithstanding a mistake of law: s 1(3).

- Where children were born after 4 April 1988, there is a presumption that, in the absence of evidence to the contrary, one of the parents reasonably believed the marriage to be valid at the relevant date: s 1(4).

- In *Re Spence* (1990), the Court of Appeal held that a person who was born *before* his parents entered into a void marriage was not to be treated as legitimate under s 1(1) 1976 Act.

12.18 Children of voidable marriages

Note s 16 MCA 1973, which states that a voidable marriage is to be considered as if it had existed up to the date of the granting of the decree absolute; as a result, the legitimacy of a person conceived or born between the date of the marriage and the date of the granting of the decree is presumed.

12.19 Legitimation

Legitimation effectively places the illegitimate child in almost the same legal position as a legitimate child. 'A legitimated person shall have the same rights and shall be under the same obligation in respect of the maintenance and support of himself or any other person as if he had been born legitimate': s 8 Legitimacy Act 1976.

An illegitimate child is legitimated by the subsequent marriage of his parents provided the father was domiciled in England or Wales at the date of the marriage: s 2 1976 Act. In the case of a father domiciled abroad, the legitimation must be recognised by the law of his domicile: s 3. It should be noted that legitimation does *not* have retrospective effect.

12.20 The effect of adoption

Under the Adoption Act 1976, s 39(1)(a), an adopted child is to be treated as if he were the legitimate child of the *adoptive parents*. Where he is adopted by a *single person*, he is to be treated as if he had been born to the adopter in wedlock (but not as a child of any actual marriage of the adopter): s 39 (1)(a).

12.21 Declarations

Section 56 of the Family Law Act 1986, as amended by FLRA 1987, allows 'declarations' to be sought (where the applicant is domiciled or has been habitually resident in England and Wales for one year at the date of the application) from the county court or High Court provided that:

- the person stated in the application is the father/mother, or that particular applicants are parents of the applicant;
- the applicant is the legitimate child of his parents;
- the applicant has, or has not, become a legitimated person.

12.22 Remaining discrimination against the illegitimate person

Some jurists, social workers and commentators maintain that discrimination against the illegitimate person continues to exist. It is suggested, for example, that the very terms 'legitimate' and 'illegitimate', which are inescapably discriminatory, be replaced by 'marital' and 'non-marital'. Other aspects of the alleged, continuing discrimination are noted below.

12.22.1	Section 50 British Nationality Act 1981	Under s 50(9) of the British Nationality Act 1981, for the purposes of the Act the relationship of father and child is taken to exist only between a man and any *legitimate child* born to him.
12.22.2	Section 2(2) ChA 1989	In the case of an unmarried couple, the father has no 'parental responsibility' for the child unless acquired in accordance with the provisions of s 2(2) ChA 1989.
12.23	**Parental responsibility: rights and duties**	For many years it was held that a parent's duty to his child could not be exercised fully unless the parent was invested with specific rights, eg, the right to promote the child's flourishing by controlling his education, maintaining him financially and otherwise protecting him, exercising a reasonable degree of discipline. The child, too was considered to possess some rights – few and widely-defined; but the right to act autonomously rarely appeared in an enumeration of 'children's rights'. Many of the most liberal campaigners for the rights of children stopped short at bringing together the child's right to receive the care of his parents and his right to act, when the situation so demands, against their declared wishes. But in recent years there has been a perceptible change in the concept of 'rights for children': parental rights, it is argued, should no longer overrule children's rights automatically. In particular, the rights of the 'competent, understanding child' ought no longer to be ignored by parents, legislators and judges – so it is argued: see 12.26 below.

In the ChA 1989, 'parental responsibility' means 'all the rights, duties, powers, responsibilities and authority which by law a parent of the child has in relation to the child and his property': s 3(1). Two observations noted in the Department of Health's *Introduction to the Children Act 1989* (1989) are of particular relevance.

- 'The Act uses the phrase "parental responsibility" to sum up the collection of duties, rights and authority which a parent has in respect of his child. That choice of words emphasises that the duty to care for the child and to raise him to moral, physical and emotional health is the fundamental task of parenthood and the only justification for the authority it confers.'

- 'The importance of parental responsibility is emphasised in the Act by the fact that not only is it unaffected by the separation of parents but even when courts make orders in private proceedings such as divorce, that responsibility continues and is limited only to the extent that any order settles certain concrete issues between the parties. That arrangement aims to emphasise that interventions by the courts where there is a family breakdown should not be regarded as lessening the duty on both parents to continue to play a full part in the child's upbringing.'

12.24 Who possesses parental responsibility?

Where a child's father and mother were married to each other at the time of his birth, they each have parental responsibility for the child: s 2(1) ChA 1989. But where they were not married to each other at the time of his birth, the *mother* has parental responsibility for the child; the *father* has not, unless he acquires it in accordance with the Act: s 2(2). Acquisition of parental responsibility by the father may result from him: subsequently marrying the child's mother; becoming the child's formal guardian; making a parental responsibility agreement with the mother; obtaining a parental responsibility order; obtaining a residence order (see 13.15) which involves the making of a parental responsibility order: see *Re H (A Minor) (Parental Responsibility)* (1993).

- Note *Re C (Minors)* (1992), in which Mustill LJ referred to 'the basic test' in deciding whether to make a responsibility order, as contained in the question ' Was the association between the parties sufficiently enduring; and has the father by his conduct during and since the application shown sufficient commitment to the children, to justify giving the father a legal status equivalent to that which he would have enjoyed if the parties had married?'

- Note *Re A (Minors) (Parental Responsibility)* (1993), in which X had lived with Y for three months. X's name was on Z's birth certificate and he had been present at the birth. X left Y and did not see Z for a year. Y opposed X's application for contact and parental responsibility. The order for contact was refused, but X was granted an order for parental responsibility. He was considered to have shown much commitment to the child, Z.

- An agreement for parental responsibility is to be made in the prescribed form (see the Parental Responsibility Agreement Regulations 1991) and must be filed at the Principal Registry of the Family Division.

12.25	**Other matters concerning parental responsibility**	Other matters concerning parental responsibility are set out in ss 2, 3 Ch A 1989.

- The rule of law that a father is the natural guardian of his child is abolished: s 2(3).
- More than one person may have parental responsibility for the same child at the same time: s 2(4).
- A person who has parental responsibility for a child at any time shall not cease to have that responsibility solely because some other person subsequently acquires parental responsibility for the child: s 2(6).
- Where more than one person has parental responsibility for a child, each of them may act alone in meeting that responsibility, but this does not affect the operation of any enactment which requires the consent of more than one person in a matter affecting the child: s 2(7). Examples: removal from the jurisdiction (Child Abduction Act 1984); applications by non-parents for residence and contact orders (s 10(5) ChA 1989).
- A person with parental responsibility for a child may not surrender or transfer any part of it, but he may arrange for some or all of it to be met by one or more persons acting on his behalf: s 2(9).
- A person who does not have parental responsibility for a particular child, but has care of the child may do 'what is reasonable in all the circumstances of the case for the purpose of safeguarding or promoting the child's welfare': s 3(5).

12.26	**A new look at children's rights and parental responsibilities: the *Gillick* case**	In *Gillick v West Norfolk and Wisbech Area Health Authority* (1986), the plaintiff, a Roman Catholic mother of five daughters under the age of 16, asked for a declaration that guidance given to family doctors by the DHSS, which stated that in exceptional circumstances a doctor might give advice and treatment relating to contraception to a girl under 16 *without her mother's consent*, was unlawful.
12.26.1	At first instance	Mrs Gillick's application for a declaration *failed* at first instance. Interference with parental rights could make a doctor's acts unlawful *only* if his conduct amounted to a trespass. The patient's age (under 16) did not mean in itself that she could not give consent to medical treatment: to be a true consent she must be capable of making a reasonable assessment of the advantages and disadvantages of the proposed treatment.

12.26.2 Court of Appeal

Mrs Gillick's appeal was *allowed* by the Court of Appeal. Parker LJ did not find anything in the civil law which supported the argument that at least up to the age of discretion, the child or any other person could interfere with those parental rights based upon custody. No one but the court could interfere; the question was, what was that age. Under the common law it seemed to be the age of majority. A girl under 16 was not able to give a valid consent to anything in the area which was being considered. Except in an emergency, the doctor ought to seek parental consent or apply to the court.

12.26.3 House of Lords

The House of Lords *reversed* the decision of the Court of Appeal. Lord Fraser, in his speech, stated that the appeal raised three strands of argument.

- *The legal capacity of a girl under 16 to consent to contraceptive advice, examination and treatment*. 'It seems to me verging on the absurd to suggest that a boy or girl aged 15 could not effectively consent, for example, to have a medical examination of some trivial injury to his body or even to have a broken arm set. Of course the consent of the parents should normally be asked, but they may not be immediately available. Provided the patient, whether a boy or girl, is capable of understanding what is proposed, and of expressing his or her own wishes, I see no good reason for holding that he or she lacks the capacity to express them validly and effectively and to authorise the medical man to make the examination or give the treatment which he advises ... Accordingly, I am not disposed to hold now, for the first time, that a girl aged less than 16 lacks the power to give valid consent to contraceptive advice or treatment, merely on account of her age.'

- *The parents' rights and duties in respect of medical treatment of their child*. 'Once the rule of parents' absolute authority over minor children is abandoned, the solution to the problem in this appeal can no longer be found by referring to rigid parental requirements at any particular age. The solution depends on a judgment of what is best for the welfare of the particular child ... Mrs Gillick has to go further if she is to obtain the first declaration that she seeks. She has to justify the absolute right of veto in a parent. But there may be circumstances in which a doctor is a better judge of the medical advice and treatment which will conduce to a girl's welfare than her parents. The only practicable course is, in my opinion, to entrust the doctor with a discretion to act in accordance with his view of what is best in the interests of the girl who is his patient ...'.

- *Whether a doctor who gives contraceptive advice or treatment to a girl under 16 without parental consent would incur criminal liability.* Lord Fraser stated that in his view such liability would depend on the doctor's intentions. The appeal concerned doctors who genuinely intended to act in the best interests of the girl; it was unlikely therefore that such doctors would commit any offence under s 28 of the Sexual Offences Act 1956.

12.26.4 Lord Scarman's speech in *Gillick*

In his speech, which has been described as the *fons et origo* of a new attitude of the law to parents' rights and capabilities, Lord Scarman made the following points.

'Parental rights clearly do exist, and they do not wholly disappear until the age of majority. Parental rights relate to both the person and the property of the child. But the common law has never treated such rights as sovereign or beyond review and control. Nor has our law ever treated the child as other than a person with capacities and rights recognised by law. The principle of law ... is that parental rights are derived from parental duty and exist only so long as they are needed for the protection of the person and property of the child. The principle has been subjected to certain age limits set by statute for certain purposes; and in some cases the courts have declared an age of discretion at which a child acquires before the age of majority the right to make his (or her) own decision. But these limitations in no way undermine the principle of the law, and should not be allowed to obscure it ...'

'... The underlying principle of the law was exposed by Blackstone and can be seen to have been acknowledged in the case law. It is that parental right yields to the child's right to make his own decisions when he reaches a sufficient understanding and intelligence to be capable of making up his own mind on the matter requiring decision ...'

'... I would hold that as a matter of law the parental right to determine whether or not their minor child below the age of 16 will have medical treatment terminates if and when the child achieves a sufficient understanding and intelligence to enable him or her to understand fully what is proposed. It will be a question of fact whether a child seeking advice has sufficient understanding of what is involved to give a consent valid in law. Until the child achieves the capacity to consent, the parental right to make the decision continues save only in exceptional circumstances. Emergency, parental neglect, abandonment of the child or inability to find the parent are examples of exceptional situations justifying the doctor proceeding to treat the child without parental knowledge and consent;

but there will arise, no doubt, other exceptional situations in which it will be reasonable for the doctor to proceed without the parent's consent.'

The following cases, decided after *Gillick*, are of particular interest in the context of parental responsibility.

In *Re R(A Minor) (Wardship: Medical Treatment)* (1992), X, aged 13, had a record of mental instability and was placed in a psychiatric unit where the staff wished to administer anti-psychotic drugs, It was difficult to obtain X's consent: sometimes she was rational, but at other times was incapable of understanding the matter being discussed with her. The Court of Appeal held that the concept of *Gillick* competence was of a developmental nature, necessitating long-term assessment. X could not be considered *Gillick* competent. Lord Donaldson MR suggested, however, that a *Gillick* competent child had no right to refuse treatment if the parents consent, but that the child's consent could override the parents' refusal of consent.

In *Re W (A Minor) (Medical Treatment)* (1992), the Court of Appeal held that the High Court could order a 16 year old girl who was suffering from *anorexia nervosa*, to be transferred to a unit specialising in eating disorders, contrary to her expressed wishes. The court, under its inherent jurisdiction, had power to override a refusal by a minor in relation to medical treatment. The girl's refusal to be treated was an important matter to be taken into account by the court. Further, where a minor is *Gillick* competent, those with parental responsibility could *not* override the girl's wishes: *but the court could*.

In *Re K, W and H (Minors) (Medical Treatment)* (1993), the court held that a doctor was *not* risking criminal or civil proceedings where treatment was given with the consent of a *Gillick* competent child *or* of a person with parental responsibility.

It is clear that the problems which culminated in the *Gillick* case have not been solved for all time; perhaps it is best to view *Gillick* as an important, bold step along the road leading to a fundamental re-consideration of parental and children's rights.

12.27 Some post-*Gillick* cases

Summary of Chapter 12

Parentage; Legitimacy; Parental Responsibility

A 'parent' may be any person who is *in law* the mother or father of the child in question: see s 54 CSA 1991; this includes natural, adoptive parents and persons who are treated as parents under HFEA 1990. Problems of establishing parentage have been compounded as the result of advances in HAR.

The concept of 'parentage'

A 'surrogate mother' (see the Surrogacy Arrangements Act 1985) is one who carries a child in pursuance of an agreement made before she began to carry it. It is an offence to be involved in surrogacy on a commercial basis; thus, advertising the making of surrogacy arrangements is an offence: s 3.

Surrogacy

The woman giving birth to a child is to be treated as its legal mother.

The 'legal mother'

HFEA 1990 differentiates the genetic father (who has fertilised the egg) and the non-genetic father. The genetic father is generally considered as the legal father.

The 'legal father'

Orders may be made providing for a child to be treated in law as the child of parties to the marriage if, eg, the child has been carried by a woman other than the wife. Application for the order must be made within six months of the birth of the child: s 39 (2). The court must be satisfied that no money has been given or received by the husband or wife in consideration of the making of the order: s 30(7).

Orders under s 30 HFEA 1990

Where the mother is married there is a rebuttable presumption that her husband is the father of her child; there is no presumption in the case of an unmarried mothers. Blood tests, DNA profiling may be used to establish paternity. Information concerning parentage may be kept under s 5 HFEA 1990.

Proof of parentage

Under s 1 FLRA 1987, parent-child relationships are to be generally construed without any regard as to whether or not the child's parents were married. Most legal distinctions between the 'legitimate' and 'illegitimate' child have disappeared.

Legitimacy

In general, children of void marriages are treated as legitimate. Children of voidable marriages conceived or born between the date of the marriage and the granting of the decree absolute are presumed to be legitimate.

Legitimation (by subsequent marriage of parents) places the illegitimate child in almost the same position as the legitimate child.

Parental responsibility

Under s 3(1) ChA 1989, parental responsibility means all the rights, duties, powers, responsibilities and authority which by law a parent of the child has in relation to the child and his property. Where a child's father and mother are married to each other at the time of his birth, each has parental responsibility; where they are not married, the mother has parental responsibility, the father has not, unless acquired in accordance with the Act: s 2(2). The father is no longer considered as the natural guardian of his child.

In *Gillick v West Norfolk and Wisbech Area Health Authority* (1986), the House of Lords declared that parental right yields to the child's right to make his own decisions when he reaches a sufficient understanding and intelligence to be capable of making up his own mind on the matter requiring decision.

Chapter 13

The Child's Welfare: Section 8 Orders under the Children Act 1989

13.1 General background to the Children Act 1989

The process of reviewing and revising the law as it affected children in particular received fresh impetus in 1987 from a White Paper, *The Law on Child Care and Family Services* (Cm 62). In 1988 the Law Commission issued a Report on *Guardianship and Custody* (Law Com 172) together with a draft Bill which suggested a systematic arrangement of court orders relating to children. The Bill became the centre of government plans which were introduced later into ChA 1989.

Other matters which may have affected the move towards reform were the *Report of the Enquiry into Child Abuse in Cleveland 1987* (Cm 412), the House of Lords' decision in *Gillick* (see 12.26), and the *European Convention on Human Rights*, signed in Rome in 1950 and ratified by the UK in 1951, which, together with the First Protocol, 1952, impinged directly on the law relating to family life and the rights of parents and children.

ChA 1989, which came into force on 14 October 1991, embodies principles which cover public and private law, and establishes a uniform set of powers for the courts in dealing with children.

13.2 The 'welfare principle'

A key principle of the 1989 legislation appears in s 1(1): 'When a court determines any question with respect to – (a) the upbringing of a child; or (b) the administration of a child's property or the application of any income arising from it, the child's welfare shall be the court's paramount consideration.'

It will be noted that the section does not use the phrase 'first and paramount consideration' or 'sole consideration'.

13.2.1 The meaning of 'welfare'

'Welfare' is not defined specifically in the 1989 Act. It is described subjectively, however, in a number of cases, eg, *R v Gyngall* (1893); *Re Thain* (1926); *Goldsmith v Sands* (1907), cited in *Re Alford* (1941): 'Welfare does not mean merely financial or social or religious welfare, but includes as an important element the happiness of the child'.

It would seem that the courts tend to have in mind in construing the phrase 'the welfare of the child', the general circumstances within which the child's flourishing may continue unimpeded, so far that is practically possible.

13.2.2 'Paramount'

In its everyday sense, 'paramount' means 'supreme; requiring first consideration'. A paramount consideration is the 'dominant consideration'. *Per* Lord MacDermott in *J v C* (1970): 'When all the relevant facts, relationships, claims and wishes of the parents, risks, choices and other circumstances are taken into account and weighed, the course to be followed will be that which is most in the interests of the child's welfare as that term has now to be understood. That is the first consideration because it is of the first importance and the paramount consideration because it rules upon or determines the course to be followed'.

Use of the term 'paramount' should *not* be taken as indicating that there is only one matter to be taken into account by the court. In the words of the Lord Chancellor, the term indicates that 'the welfare of the child should come before and above any other consideration in deciding whether to make an order'. Note *F v Leeds CC* (1994), in which a child was the subject of an application for a care order and the mother herself was a minor. The Court of Appeal held that the court's 'paramount consideration' was to be the welfare of the child who was the subject of the application, and not the mother: see also *Re S (A minor) (Medical Treatment)* (1993) in which the court considered the refusal of parents to consent to a blood transfusion for a child, and held, granting leave for the transfusion, that in cases of this nature, the welfare of the child remained 'the paramount consideration'.

13.2.3 Restrictions on the application of the welfare principle

It will be noted (see s 1(1)) that the principle of the paramountcy of the child's welfare applies under the 1989 Act *only* where the child's upbringing is in question or where property matters, etc, are under consideration. It has no application in matters concerning adoption (see 22.7): the court will, in cases in this area, give first, but not paramount, consideration to the promotion of the child's welfare. Nor has the principle any application to ouster orders – see *Richards v Richards* (1984), in which the court held that the children were merely one, and not the paramount, consideration in the court's decision as to whether an ouster order should be issued. Note also *Gibson v Austin* (1993). In an application for leave to apply for a s 8 order (see 13.9 below), the paramount welfare principle has no application: see *Re A and W (Minors) (Residence Order)* (1992).

13.3 The 'no-delay principle'

Section 1(2) emphasises the possibility of delay harming a child. 'In any proceedings in which any question with respect to the upbringing of a child arises, the court shall have regard to the general principle that any delay in determining the question is likely to prejudice the welfare of the child.'

Parliament may have had in mind, in this part of the Act, the delays typified in *J v C* (1970), in which a five-year delay occurred before the House of Lords was able to make a final adjudication. Under s 11(1), the court is directed, in applications for s 8 and Part IV orders, to 'draw up a timetable with a view to determining the question without delay'.

Note the comment of the Law Commission: 'Prolonged litigation about their future is deeply damaging to children, not only because of the uncertainty it brings for them, but also because of the harm it does to the relationship between the parents and their capacity to co-operate with one another in the future.'

13.4 The 'non-intervention (or 'no order') principle'

Section 1(5) introduces a significant new principle into the hearing of disputes affecting children. 'Where a court is considering whether or not to make one or more orders under this Act with respect to a child, it shall not make the order or any of the orders unless it considers that *doing so would be better for the child than making no order at all.*'

13.4.1 View of the Law Commission (1988)

'Where a child has a good relationship with both parents the law should seek to disturb this as little as possible. There is always a risk that orders allocating custody and access (or even deciding upon residence and contact) will have the effect of polarising the parents' roles and perhaps alienating the child from one or other of them ... We therefore recommend that the court should only make an order where this is the most effective way of safeguarding or promoting the child's welfare.'

13.4.2 Essence of the 'non-intervention principle'

Essentially, the onus is on the court to show that it is better, and in the interests of the child, that an order be made rather than refused. Note the Department of Health *Guidance Notes* on the 1989 Act. 'There are several situations where the court is likely to consider it better for the child to make an order than not. If the court has had to resolve a dispute between the parents, it is likely to be better for the child to make an order about it. Even if there is no dispute, the child's need for stability and security may be better served by making an order. There may also be specific legal advantages in doing so. One example is where abduction is a possibility ...'.

See *B v B (Grandparent: Residence Order)* (1992).

13.5 The 'welfare checklist'

Because of the vagueness and general imprecision of the 'welfare concept' in relation to the child, s 1(3) ChA 1989 introduces a checklist of matters to which the court is to have particular regard. The checklist is to be taken into account (see s 1(4)):

- where the court is considering whether to make, vary or discharge an order under s 8, and the making, variation or discharge is opposed by a party to the proceedings;
- where the court is considering whether to make, vary or discharge an order under Part IV of the Act.

The Law Commission believed that the existence of a checklist would assist in providing greater consistency, clarity, and a more systematic approach to decisions of the courts. The contents of the checklist are noted below.

13.5.1 Wishes and feelings of the child: s 1(3)(a)

The court should have regard to 'the ascertainable wishes and feelings of the child concerned (considered in the light of his age and understanding).' Note the likely influence of the *Gillick* decision (see 12.26). See *Adams v Adams* (1984).

The Department of Health *Guidelines* (1989) state that the objective of the 1989 Act is 'to strike a balance between the need to recognise the child as an independent person and to ensure that his views are taken fully into account, and the risk of casting on him the burden of resolving problems caused by his parents or requiring him to choose between them'.

13.5.2 Needs of the child: s 1(3)(b)

Regard has to be paid to the child's 'physical, educational and emotional needs'. This phrase may include, eg, adequate housing, food: see *Re W (A Minor: Custody)* (1982); *Re S (A Minor: Custody)* (1991). *Per* Purchas LJ in *C v C (Minors: Custody)* (1988): 'It is really beyond argument that unless there are strong features indicating a contrary arrangement ... brothers and sisters should wherever possible, be brought up together, so that they are an emotional support to each other in the stormy waters of the destruction of their family'.

13.5.3 Changed circumstances: s 1(3)(c)

Regard should be paid to the likely effect on the child of 'any change in his circumstances'. This may be of particular relevance where parents have separated: see *Re A (A Minor: Custody)* (1991). Note Ormrod LJ in *S v W* (1980): 'The more satisfactory the *status quo*, the stronger the argument for not interfering. The less satisfactory the *status quo*, the less one requires before deciding to change'.

13.5.4 Relevant characteristics: s 1(3)(d)

Regard is to be paid to the child's age, sex, background and any other characteristics of his which the court considers relevant: see, eg, *Re W (A Minor)* (1983), *per* Cumming-Bruce LJ: 'If all factors are nicely balanced, then probably it is right for a child of tender years to be brought up by his or her natural mother.'

	13.5.5	Harm: s 1(1)(e)

Regard is to be paid to any harm which the child 'has suffered or is at risk of suffering'. In s 105(1), 'harm' is taken to mean 'ill-treatment or the impairment of health or development'. In determining whether the harm suffered is 'significant', the child's health is to be compared with that which could reasonably be expected of a similar child: s 31(10).

	13.5.6	Capability of parents and others: s 1(3)(f)

The court should consider, with reference to the child, how capable each of his parents, and any other person in relation to whom the court considers the question to be relevant, is of meeting his needs: see, eg, *Re C (A Minor) (Custody of Child)* (1980)

	13.5.7	Powers available to the court: s 1(3)(g)

The court shall consider the range of powers available to it under the Act in the proceedings in question. It should take into account whether one order is more appropriate than another in promoting the welfare of the child.

13.6 Welfare reports

In considering in relation to the 1989 Act any question involving a child, the court may, under s 7(1), ask a probation officer, or ask a local authority to arrange for an officer of the authority or other person considered appropriate, to report to the court on such matters concerning the welfare of the child as are required to be dealt with in the report. The report may be made in writing or orally as the court requires: s 7(3). Regardless of any enactment or rule of law which would otherwise prevent it from doing so, the court may take account of any statement in the report and any evidence given in respect of the contents of the report: see *Re C (Minor) (Access: Attendance of Court Welfare Officer)* (1994).

13.7 The essence of s 8 orders

Under Sch 15 ChA 1989 former statutory powers of the courts to make 'care and control', 'custody', 'access orders', have ended. Under s 8, a variety of new orders appears: these are discussed below.

The s 8 orders are concerned essentially with *practical matters*, eg, where should a child reside and with whom. The Act enumerates the types of person who may seek a s 8 order (see s 10) and includes (see s 11(7)) powers for the making of directions as to how the orders will be carried out.

The orders referred to in s 8 are: contact orders; prohibited steps orders; residence orders; specific issue orders.

13.8 Family proceedings

Under the 1989 Act, all courts dealing with 'family proceedings' can make any s 8 order. For the purposes of the Act, 'family proceedings' means any proceedings under the inherent jurisdiction of the High Court in relation to children (eg wardship: see 2.1.3), and under the enactments mentioned in s 8(4): s 8(3).

The enactments referred to are as follows.

- ChA 1989, Part I: proceedings for parental responsibility orders s 4); guardianship proceedings (ss 5, 6).

- ChA 1989, Part II; free standing applications for orders (s 10(1), (2)); applications for leave (s 10(2)(b)); by the court on its own motion (s 10(1)(b)); applications for financial relief under Sch 1.

- ChA 1989, Part IV: care proceedings (s 31); proceedings concerning contact with children in care (s 34); proceedings concerning education supervision orders (s 36).

- MCA 1973: divorce, nullity, judicial separation proceedings; applications for financial relief following divorce, etc.

- DVMPA 1976: applications for non-molestation orders and (where parties are unmarried) exclusion orders.

- Adoption Act 1976: proceedings concerning adoption, freeing orders.

- DPMCA 1978: proceedings for financial relief; proceedings for injunctions concerning domestic violence.

- Mental Health Act 1983: proceedings involving ss 1, 9, concerning exclusion orders.

- MFPA 1984: proceedings under Part III for financial relief after divorce overseas.

13.9 Who may apply for a s 8 order

Under s 10 of the 1989 Act, certain persons are entitled to apply without leave for s 8 orders. Others may apply only with leave. Note that the court may make an order at its own motion: s 10.

13.9.1 Persons entitled to apply without leave

Any parent or guardian of the child, and persons with a residence order may apply for any order under s 8: s 10(4). The following may apply for a residence order or contact order without leave: any party to a marriage (whether or not subsisting) in relation to whom the child is a child of the family; any person with whom the child has lived for at least three years; any person who has the consent of each of the persons in whose favour a residence order has been made, or of the local authority, where the child is subject to a care order, or, in any other case, each of those persons who have parental responsibility for the child: s 10(5).

Persons not included in these categories may apply for discharge or variation of a s 8 order if such order was made on their application or, where a contact order has been made, they are named in the order. Under s 10, any person who falls within the category of persons prescribed by rules of court may apply.

13.9.2 Persons entitled to apply with leave

Any person or organisation who is not entitled otherwise to apply under the Act may seek leave to apply for a s 8 order: see s 10(1). There is an exception in the case of a person who is or was 'during the last six months' a local authority foster parent (see 19.2): s 9(3). Where the person applying for leave to make an application is the child concerned, the court will grant leave *only* if satisfied that he has sufficient understanding to make the application: s 10(8). Note the Family Proceedings (Amendment) Rules 1992, r 9.2.A, allowing a minor to begin and defend proceedings without a guardian *ad litem* or next friend where the court gives leave or a solicitor considers the minor to be able to give instructions: see *Re S* (1993). The welfare of the child is not to be considered a paramount factor in deciding on an application for leave to apply: see *Re A and W (Minors) (Residence Order: Leave to Apply)* (1992).

Note s 91(14): 'On disposing of any application for an order under this Act, the court may (whether or not it makes any other order in response to the application) order that no application for an order under this Act of any specified kind may be made with respect to the child concerned by any person named in the order *without leave of the court.*' See *F v Kent CC* (1993); *Cheshire CC v M* (1993); *Re F (Minors) (Contact Restraint Order)* (1995), in which the Court of Appeal stated that the exercise of the power given by s 91(14) was 'a draconian measure of last resort' which would normally be appropriate to use only to prevent a threatened abuse by vexatious or oppressive parties of the right of access to the courts afforded by the 1989 Act.

13.9.3 Criteria in relation to granting leave

Where the person applying for leave to make application for a s 8 order is not the child concerned, the court will have particular regard to:

- the nature of the proposed application;
- the connection of the applicant with the child concerned;
- any risk that the application might disrupt the child's life and cause him harm;
- where the child is being looked after by a local authority, the authority's plans for the child's future *and* the wishes and feelings of the child's parents: s 10(9).

13.10 Limitations upon the making of s 8 orders

Certain restrictions apply to the court's ability to issue s 8 orders. *First:* the court cannot make a s 8 order which is to have effect for a period which will end after the child has reached the age of 16 unless satisfied that 'the circumstances of the case are exceptional': s 9(6). *Secondly:* the court cannot make a s 8 order, other than one varying or discharging such an order, concerning a child who has reached the age of 16, unless satisfied that 'the circumstances of the case are exceptional': s 9(7). *Thirdly:* the court cannot make a s 8 order, other than a residence order, in relation to a child who is already in the care of a local authority: s 9(1). *Fourthly:* the court cannot make an order in favour of a local authority seeking a residence or contact order: s 9(2).

13.11 Timetables and other provisions

In proceedings in which the making of a s 8 order is under consideration, the court should draw up a timetable so as to determine the question without delay, and should give directions for the purpose of ensuring that the timetable is adhered to: s 11(1).

Under s 11(7), a s 8 order may contain directions as to how it is to be carried into effect; it may impose conditions which must be complied with, may be made to have effect for a specified period, and may make 'such incidental, supplemental or consequential provision as the court thinks fit': s 11(7).

13.12 The contact order

A contact order (which replaces the former 'access order') is 'an order requiring the person with whom a child lives, or is to live, to allow the child to visit or stay with a person named in the order, or for that person and the child otherwise to have contact with each other': s 8(1). Note: 'Contact with a parent is a fundamental right of a child, save in wholly exceptional circumstances': *per* Sir Stephen Brown P, in *Re W* (1994). See the Department of Health *Guidance and Regulations.* 'A contact order is a *positive order* in the sense that it requires contact to be allowed between an individual and child and cannot be used to deny contact'. The order can be made by the court subject to conditions and directions under s 11(7). Other aspects of the contact order should be noted:

- A local authority cannot obtain a contact order, nor can it apply for one: s 9(2).
- A range of contacts may include, eg, visits, contact by telephone.
- Contact orders may be made in relation to children over 16 only in exceptional circumstances: s 9(7).

- Contact orders continue in force after a child reaches the age of 16, in exceptional circumstances: s 9(6).
- The making of a care order will discharge a contact order: s 91(2).
- A contact order which requires the parent with whom a child lives to allow the child to visit, or otherwise have contact with, his other parent shall cease to have effect if the parents live together for a continuous period of more than six months: s 11(6).

For dismissal of an appeal for a contact order, see *Re F (Minors) (Contact)* (1993); *D v D* (1994); *Re A (A Minor) (Contact Application: Grandparent)* (1995).

In *Re D (A Minor) (Contact: Interim Order)* (1995), Wall J stated that justices should be cautious about making *interim contact orders* where the principle of contact was in dispute and substantial issues of fact concerning the child remained unresolved. The question which justices should ask themselves was not simply whether contact was in the child's best interests, but whether it was in his interests to make an interim order. Where the principle of contact was in issue, the test remained the welfare test under s 1, but the fact that the principle of contact was in issue itself became a factor which required consideration in the welfare equation.

13.13 Prohibited steps order

A 'prohibited steps order' is 'an order that no step which could be taken by a parent in meeting his parental responsibility for a child, and which is of a kind specified in the order, shall be taken by any person without the consent of the court': s 8(1). The order has the effect of an injunction and could be used, eg, to restrain a parent from removing the child from the jurisdiction. A court may not exercise its powers to make a prohibited steps order with a view to achieving a result which could be achieved by making a residence or contact order, or in any way which is denied to the High Court (see s 100(2)) in the exercise of its inherent jurisdiction with respect to children: s 9(5).

In *Re H (Minors: Prohibited Steps Order)* (1995), the Court of Appeal held that a prohibited steps order under s 8 could be made against a person who was not a party to the proceedings and was not present in court if it was needed to protect the children and no other means of achieving the same object existed.

13.14 Specific issue order

A 'specific issue order' is 'an order giving directions for the purpose of determining a specific question which has arisen, or which may arise, in connection with any aspect of parental responsibility for a child': s 8(1). The order is empowered to give directions; but the restrictions of s 9 which apply to prohibited steps orders apply also to specific issue orders. See *Pearson v Franklin* (1994) – an ouster order may not be made under the guise of a specific issue order.

13.15 Residence order

A 'residence order' is 'an order settling the arrangements to be made as to the person with whom a child is to live': s 8(1). It may be made in favour of more than one person (s 11(4)) and, where these persons are not living together, it may specify the periods to be spent in each household. For the award of *ex parte* residence orders (made in favour of non-parents to give some respite from urgent problems), see *Re Y* (1994). Such an order is usually necessary only to protect children from physical harm or moral danger.

Note other aspects of the residence order:

- During the subsistence of a residence order, no person may cause the child to be known by a new surname or remove him from the UK without either the written consent of every parent who has parental responsibility for the child, or the leave of the court: s 13(1).

- A residence order may be enforced by fine or imprisonment: s 14.

- Where a residence order is made so that the child lives, or is to live, with one of two parents who each have parental responsibility for him, the order ceases to have effect if the parents live together for a continuous period of more than six months: s 11(5).

- Where a residence order is made in favour of a child's father, the court shall, if the father would not otherwise have parental responsibility for the child, also make an order under s 4 giving him that responsibility: s 12(1).

13.16 Other orders under ChA 1989

Orders other than those deriving from s 8 exist: they include, eg, orders for financial relief, under s 15, which were noted at 11.7; parental responsibility orders under s 4. See *Re S (A Minor) (Parental Responsibility)* (1995)); guardianship orders under s 5 (see 20.4); assessment orders (s 43); care and supervision orders, under s 31 (see 16.4); education supervision orders, under s 36 (see 16.4); emergency protection orders, under s 44 (see 17.4).

13.16.1 Family assistance orders

Under s 16, family assistance orders (which replaced supervision orders in custody proceedings) may be made in exceptional circumstances and where the court has obtained the consent of every person to be named in the order other than the child. The order will last for a maximum of six months from the day on which it was made: s 16(5); it cannot be renewed. Where both a family order and a s 8 order are in force with respect to a child, reference may be made to the court by a local authority for variation or discharge of the s 8 order: s 16(6).

> 'A supervision order is designed for the more serious cases, in which there is an element of child protection involved. By contrast, a family assistance order aims simply to provide short-term help to a family to overcome the problems and conflicts associated with their separation or divorce. Help may well be focused more on the adult than the child': Department of Health *Guidelines*.

13.16.2 Effect of the family assistance order

The terms of the order require either a probation officer or an officer of the local authority to advise, assist and (where appropriate) befriend any person named in the order: s 16(1). Those who may be named in the order include the child himself, his parent or guardian, or any person with whom the child is living or in whose favour a contact order (see 13.12 above) is in force with respect to the child: s 16(2). The checklist which applies to s 8 orders (see 13.5 above) does *not* apply to the family assistance order.

Summary of Chapter 13

The Child's Welfare: Section 8 Orders under the Children Act 1989

When a court determines a question concerning a child's upbringing or the administration of his property or the application of income arising from it, the child's welfare shall *be the court's paramount consideration*: s 1(1) ChA 1989. 'Welfare' is not defined in the 1989 Act. 'Paramount' seems to have the meaning of 'dominant (but not sole) consideration'.

The 'welfare principle'

Section 1(2) ChA 1898 stresses the importance of 'no-delay', because a child might be harmed where an order is delayed. The 'no-order' principle (or principle of 'non-intervention') set out in s 1(5) states that the court ought not to make any of the orders available unless it considers that so doing would be better for the child than making no order at all.

Other principles to be taken into account

The court is expected to take into account a checklist (see s 1(4)) when considering matters related to the making of orders under s 8. The checklist comprises the following: wishes and feelings of the child; his needs; likely effect of changes in his circumstances; his relevant characteristics; any harm which the child has suffered or is at risk of suffering; parents' capabilities. The court should consider also the full range of power available to it under the Act.

Welfare checklist

Orders under s 8 are concerned with practical matters, such as where a child should reside or with whom. These include: contact orders; prohibited steps orders; residence orders; specific issue orders. Any parent or guardian or person with a residence order may apply for a s 8 order. The child concerned may apply for an order if granted leave by the court; the court has to be convinced that he has sufficient understanding to make the application.

Section 8 orders

A contact order requires the person with whom a child is living, or is to live, to allow the child to visit or stay with a person named in the order or for that person and child otherwise to have contact with each other: s 8(1). A local authority cannot apply for a contact order. The making of a care order discharges a contact order.

The contact order

Prohibited steps order   A prohibited steps order is an order that no step which could be taken by a parent in meeting his parental responsibility for a child, and which is of a kind specified in the order, shall be taken by any person without the consent of the court: s 8(1). The order is effectively an injunction and could be used to prevent removal of the child from the jurisdiction.

Specific issue order   A specific issue order is an order giving directions for the purpose of determining a specific question which has arisen or may arise in connection with any aspect of parental responsibility for a child: s 8(1).

Residence order   A residence order settles the arrangements to be made as to the person with whom a child is to live: s 8(1). It may be made in favour of more than one person and, where these persons are not living together, may specify the periods to be spent in each household.

Chapter 14

Local Authority Services for Children and Families (1)

14.1 Background

Part III of ChA 1989 (ss 17-30) is concerned with services which a local authority must or may provide in certain circumstances for children and families. Part III replaces, in particular, Part III of the National Assistance Act 1948 and the National Health Service Act 1977; there is now one code only which covers the voluntary services provided by local authorities. The Department of Health *Review of Child Care Law* (1985) and the White Paper, *Law on Child Care and Family Services* (Cm 62, 1987), summed up government thinking on the need for a rationalisation and unification of legislation relating to the law of children and welfare.

Public and private law affecting the local authority relationship with children were reflected in the provisions of Part III of the ChA 1989. The basic principles of this part of the Act were derived largely from the 'non-intervention' standpoint enunciated by Lord Mackay LC in 1989: 'Unless there is evidence that a child is being or is likely to be positively harmed because of a failure in the family, the State, whether in the guise of a local authority or a court, should not interfere'; and from the view that every effort should be made to preserve and strengthen the child's ties to his family; and from the concept of a local authority-parents-child partnership (see, eg, the Department of Health's *Guidance:* 'The development of a successful working partnership between the responsible authorities and the parents and the child, where he is of sufficient understanding should enable placement to proceed positively so that the child's welfare is safeguarded and promoted').

14.2 Definitions

The following statutory definitions are of significance for Part III of the 1989 Act.

- *Local authority*. Means 'in relation to England and Wales, the council of a county, a metropolitan district, a London Borough or the Common Council of the City of London ...': s 105(1).

- *Child*. Means, subject to Sch 1, para 16, 'a person under the age of 18': s 105(1).

- *Family*. Includes any person who has parental responsibility for the child and any other person with whom he has been living: s 17(10).

- *Health.* Means physical or mental health: s 17(11).
- *Development.* Means physical, intellectual, emotional, social or behavioural development: s 17(11).
- *Disabled child.* Means a child who is blind, deaf or dumb or suffers from mental disorder of any kind or is substantially and permanently handicapped by illness, injury or congenital deformity or such disability as may be prescribed: s 17(11).
- *Child in need.* A child is taken to be in need if he is unlikely to achieve or maintain, or have the opportunity of achieving or maintaining, a reasonable standard of health without the provision for him of services by a local authority under Part III of the 1989 Act, or his health or development is likely to be significantly impaired, without the provision for him of such services, or he is disabled, and 'family' in relation to such a child includes any person who has parental responsibility for the child and any other person with whom he has been living: s 17(10).

14.3 Providing services for children and their families

Under s 17(1), the local authority has the general duty to safeguard and promote the welfare of children in its area who are in need, and, so far as is consistent with that duty, to promote the upbringing of such children by their families, by providing a range and level of services appropriate to those needs. The section was viewed as providing a more positive approach to the problem than that set out in the earlier Child Care Act 1980, which had referred in s 1 to 'the duty of diminishing the need to receive children into or keep them in care...' (The word 'general' in s 17(1) in reference to the duties of local authorities should be noted: it would seem that the section was designed to avoid the effect of *A-G v London Borough of Wandsworth* (1981) in which it was held that the authority's welfare duty applied to *individual* children.) The local authority has specific duties and powers set out in Sch 2, Part I, and any service provided by an authority in the exercise of functions under s 17 may be provided for the family of a *particular* child in need or for any member of his family, if it has been provided in order to safeguard the welfare of the child: s 17(2), (3).

14.3.1 The identification of children in need

Under Sch 2, Part I, para 1, every local authority must take reasonable steps to identify the extent to which there are children in need within their area. They are required to publish information about the services they provide and to take steps to ensure that those who might benefit from the services receive appropriate information. Additionally, under para (2), a register of disabled children within their area should be kept by the authority.

Where it appears to a local authority that a child within their area is in need, the authority may assess his needs for the purpose of the 1989 Act at the same time as any assessment of his needs is made under, eg, the Chronically Sick and Disabled Persons Act 1970 para 3.

14.3.2 Assessment of children's needs

Where a local authority believes that a child who is at any time within their area is likely to suffer harm but lives or proposes to live in the area of another local authority, they shall inform that other authority. A local authority is required to take reasonable steps through the provision of services to prevent children within their area suffering ill-treatment or neglect: para 4.

14.3.3 Prevention of neglect and abuse

Under para 5, where it appears to a local authority that a child who is living on particular premises is suffering, or is likely to suffer, ill treatment at the hands of another person who is living on those premises, and that other person proposes to move from the premises, the authority may assist that other person to obtain alternative accommodation.

14.3.4 Provision of accommodation in order to protect a child

A local authority is obliged to provide services designed to minimise the effect on disabled children within their area of their disabilities, and to give such children the opportunity to lead lives which are as normal as possible: para 6.

14.3.5 Provision for disabled children

A local authority must take reasonable steps designed to reduce the need to bring proceedings for care or supervision orders with respect to children in their area, criminal proceedings against such children, any family proceedings which might lead to children being placed in the authority's care, to encourage children not to commit criminal offences and to avoid the need for children to be placed in secure accommodation: para 7.

14.3.6 Provision to reduce need for care proceedings, etc

Appropriate provision should be made by a local authority for children living with their families for counselling, recreational activities, home help, travelling facilities, etc: para 8.

14.3.7 Provision for children living with their families.

A local authority should provide such family centres as it considers appropriate; such centres may be attended by a child, his parents, any person who is not a parent but has parental responsibility for the child, any other person who is looking after him: para 9.

14.3.8 Family centres

14.3.9	Maintenance of the family home	Every local authority shall take such steps as are reasonably practicable where any child in their area who is in need and whom they are not looking after is living apart from his family, to enable him to live with his family or to promote contact between him and his family if they are of the opinion that it is necessary to do so in order to safeguard or promote his welfare: para 10.
14.3.10	Duty to consider racial groups	Every local authority shall, in making any arrangements for the provision of day care within their area, or designed to encourage persons to act as local authority foster parents, have regard to the different racial groups to which children within their area who are in need belong: para 11. See *Re P* (1989).
14.4	**Assistance in kind or cash**	The services provided by a local authority in the exercise of functions under s 17 may include the giving of assistance in kind or, in exceptional circumstances, in cash: s 17(6). Such assistance may be without, or subject to, conditions as to repayment: s 17(7). The means of the child and each of its parents will be considered by the local authority before assistance or repayment conditions are given or imposed: s 17(8). No person in receipt of income support or family credit (see 8.10; 8.13) will be liable to make repayment: s 17(9).
14.5	**The provision of day care for pre-school and other children**	Local authorities are obliged under s 18 to provide 'day care' (which means, under s 18(4)), 'any form of care or supervised activity provided for children during the day, whether or not provided on a regular basis') for under-fives in certain circumstances.
14.5.1	The duty	Every local authority shall provide such day care for children in need within their area who are aged 5 or under and not yet attending schools, as is appropriate: s 18(1). The authority *may* provide day care even though the children are not in need: s 18(2). Facilities (including training, advice, guidance and counselling) for those caring for children in day care, or who accompany such children while in day care, may be provided: s 18(3).
14.5.2	Outside school hours	A local authority shall provide for children in need within their area who are attending *any school*, appropriate care or supervised activities outside school hours or during school holidays: s 18(5). The authority *may* provide care and supervised activities for children who are not attending any school even though they are not in need: s 18(6). 'Supervised activities' are those supervised by a 'responsible person' – a term not defined in the section: s 18(7).

Under s 19(1), a local authority is under a duty to review the provision it makes under s 18 and is expected to conduct a review with the appropriate local education authority at least once in every review period. The review is to be published as soon as is reasonably practicable: 19(6). Attention is to be given to the provision made for children under eight who are in 'relevant establishments', eg, hospitals and schools. The 'review period' is the year beginning with the commencement of the section and each subsequent three-year period beginning with an anniversary of that commencement: s 19(5). The review must take into account representations from any relevant health authority, and other representations considered relevant: s 19(7).

Every local authority is obliged under s 20(1) to provide accommodation for any child in their area who needs accommodation (see 14.6.1 below). Section 20 of the 1989 Act was intended as a replacement of those sections of the Child Care Act 1980 which created the basis of the former 'voluntary care system'. The concept of 'reception into care' has been replaced by 'provision of accommodation'.

Proposals that the 1989 Act should recognise a distinction between 'short-term respite care' and 'longer-term shared care' were rejected as unhelpful. The Government's view was set out in the White Paper, *Law on Child Care and Family Services*: 'A service by the local authority to enable a child who is not under a care order to be cared for away from home should be seen in a wider context and as part of the range of services a local authority can offer to parents and families in need of help with the care of their children ... An essential characteristic of this service should be its voluntary character, that is, it should be based clearly on continual parental agreement and operate as far as possible on a basis of partnership and co-operation between the local authority and parent.'

Every local authority shall provide accommodation for any child in need within their area who appears to them to require accommodation as a result of there being no person who has parental responsibility for him, his being lost or having been abandoned, or the person who has been caring for him being prevented (whether or not permanently, and for whatever reason) from providing him with suitable accommodation or care: s 20(1). Note the phrase 'for whatever reason': accommodation is to be provided because of the disability of the child, as well as of the parent.

14.5.3	Review of provision for day care, etc
14.6	**Duty to provide accommodation for children**
14.6.1	The duty of local authorities

Where a local authority provides accommodation under (1) above for a child who is ordinarily resident in the area of another local authority, that other authority may take over the provision of accommodation for the child within three months of being notified in writing, or such longer period as may be prescribed: s 20(2).

Every local authority is obliged to provide accommodation for any child in need within their area who has reached the age of 16 and whose welfare the authority considers is likely to be seriously prejudiced if they do not provide him with accommodation: s 20(3).

A local authority may provide accommodation for a person who has reached the age of 16 but is under 21 in any community home which takes children who have reached 16, if they consider that to do so would safeguard or promote his welfare: s 20(5).

14.6.2 The child's wishes

Before providing accommodation under s 20, a local authority shall, so far as is reasonably practicable and consistent with the child's welfare, ascertain the child's wishes concerning accommodation, and give due consideration (having regard to his age and understanding) to such wishes of the child as they have been able to ascertain: s 20(6).

14.6.3 Restriction on the provision of accommodation

A local authority may not provide accommodation under s 20 for a child if there is an objection from any person who has parental responsibility for the child and is able and willing to provide accommodation for him: s 20(7).

14.6.4 Removal of the child from accommodation

A person who has parental responsibility for a child may remove him from accommodation provided by the local authority under s 20: s 20(8). (This is in sharp contrast to the requirement under the Child Care Act 1980, s 13(2) that a parent had to give notice of intention to remove the child from accommodation.) Under s 20(9), subsections (7) and (8) do not apply while any person in whose favour a residence order is in force with respect to the child, or who has care of the child by virtue of an order made in the exercise of the High Court's inherent jurisdiction with respect to children, agrees to the child being looked after in local authority accommodation. Further, subsections (7) and (8) have no application where a child who has reached the age of 16 agrees to the provision of accommodation under s 20.

14.7 Providing accommodation for children in protection, etc

There is a duty on local authorities to make provision for the reception and accommodation of children who are removed or kept away from home under Part V of the 1989 Act: s 21(1).

| | 14.7.1 | Duty under s 21(2) |

Every local authority shall make provision for the reception and accommodation of children in police protection whom they are requested to receive under s 46(3)(f) (removal of children in case of emergency) or whom they are requested to receive under the Police and Criminal Evidence Act 1984, s 38(6), or who are on remand. (Note that the Police and Criminal Evidence Act 1984, s 38(6) refers to the authorisation by a custody officer for an arrested juvenile to be kept in detention. 'Arrested juvenile' is a person arrested with or without a warrant who appears to be under 17: s 37(15) 1984 Act. See s 24 CJPOA 1994.)

| | 14.7.2 | Financial matters |

Where a child has been removed under Part V of this Act or detained under s 38 Police and Criminal Evidence Act 1984, and he is not being provided with local authority accommodation, expenses of accommodating him are recoverable from the local authority in whose area he is ordinarily resident: s 21(3).

14.8 Duties of local authority in relation to children looked after by them

A general duty is owed by local authorities to children who are looked after by them, ie, children who are subject to care orders or provided with accommodation under ss 20, 21. 'Accommodation' refers to accommodation provided for a continuous period of more than 24 hours. Specifically, the local authority has the following tasks:

- to safeguard and promote the child's welfare and to make use of services available for children catered for by their own parents: s 22(3);
- to ascertain the wishes and feelings of the child and his parents or non-parents who have parental responsibility for him, regarding the matter to be decided: s 22(4);
- to give due consideration to 'the child's religious persuasion, racial origin and cultural and linguistic background' in making appropriate decisions: s 22(6).

See also s 24(1) at 15.2; *Cleveland CC v DPP* (1994).

14.9 Possibility of serious injury to the public

Where a local authority considers that it is necessary, for the purpose of protecting members of the public from serious injury, to exercise its powers with respect to a child it is looking after in a manner which may not be consistent with its duties under this section, it may do so: s 22(6). This may necessitate an order under s 25 (see 15.6) to place the child in secure accommodation: see the Children (Secure Accommodation) Regulations 1991. Should the Secretary of State consider it necessary, for the purpose of protecting members of the public from serious injury, to give directions to a local authority with respect to the exercise of its powers with respect to a child whom it is looking after, he may give such directions to the authority: s 22(6). The authority must comply with directions given to it under the section even though doing so is inconsistent with other duties under the section: s 22(8).

14.10 Accommodation etc for children who are being looked after

The general duty of the local authority under s 23(1) is set out thus: 'It shall be the duty of any local authority looking after a child when he is in their care, to provide accommodation for him, and to maintain him in other respects apart from providing accommodation for him'.

14.11 Local authority foster parents

A person with whom a child is placed under subsection (2)(a) is to be known as a 'local authority foster parent' unless he is the child's parent, one who is not the child's parent but has parental responsibility for him, or, where the child is in care and there was a residence order with respect to him immediately before the care order was made, a person in whose favour the residence order was made: s 23(3), (4).

14.12 Regulations concerning placement with local authority foster parents

Under Sch 2, para 12, regulations under s 23(2)(a) may make provision, eg, as to the records to be kept by local authority foster parents, for securing that where possible the local foster parent with whom a child is to be placed is of the same religious persuasion as the child, or gives an undertaking that the child will be brought up in that religious persuasion.

14.13 Other matters concerning provision of accommodation

Under s 23(7), (8), a local authority is obliged to find accommodation for a child whom it is looking after, near his home and, if the child is disabled, the accommodation must be suitable to his particular needs.

14.14 Child allowed to live with parents

Schedule 2, para 14, imposes requirements on a local authority to allow a child to live with a parent and to remove a child in such circumstances as may be prescribed from the care of the parent with whom he has been allowed to live.

14.15 Contact between the child and his family

Schedule 2, para 15, is concerned with the promotion and maintenance of contacts between the child and his family. This is an important principle underlying Part III of the Act.

14.15.1 Promotion of contact

Where a child is being looked after by a local authority, the authority shall, unless it is not reasonably practicable or consistent with his welfare, endeavour to promote contact between the child and his parents, or any non-parent who has parental responsibility for him, or any relative, friend or other person connected with him: para 15(1). The parents should be informed of where the child is being accommodated, but not where this might prejudice the child's welfare: Sch 2, para 15(3), (4).

The authority may make payments to a child's parents or any other person connected with him in respect of travelling expenses incurred in visiting the child: para 16(2).

14.15.2 Visits to or by children

The local authority can appoint a visitor with the duty of visiting, advising and befriending the child: para 17(1). The appointment shall not be made if the child objects to it and the authority is satisfied that he has sufficient understanding to make an informed decision: para 17(5).

14.15.3 Appointment of visitors

A local authority may arrange for, or assist in arranging for, any child in their care to live outside England and Wales with the approval of the court: para 19(1). See *Re G (Minors) (Care: Leave to Place Outside Jurisdiction)* (1994).

14.15.4 Arrangements to assist children to live abroad

Summary of Chapter 14

Local Authority Services for Children and Families (1)

Part III of ChA 1989 is concerned with services which must be provided in certain circumstances for children and families by a local authority. 'Local authority' means the council of a county, a metropolitan district, a London borough or Common Council of the City of London: s 105(1). The basic policy underlying Part III seems to be one of 'non-intervention' save where there is evidence that a child is being or is likely to be harmed because of a failure in the family.

ChA 1989, Part III

Under s 17(1) the local authority has the general duty to 'safeguard and promote the welfare of children in their area who are in need' and to promote their upbringing by providing a range and level of services appropriate to their needs. The local authority must take reasonable steps to identify children in need and must publish information about the services they provide. There must be provision for disabled children. Family centres should be provided where considered appropriate.

Services for children and families

Services provided by the local authority may include the giving of assistance in kind or cash: s 17(6). Such assistance will not necessarily involve repayment: s 17(7).

Assistance in kind or cash

The local authority for an area must provide appropriate care for children aged five or under not yet attending school. Care or supervised activities must be provided by the local authority outside school hours or during school holidays: s 18(5).

Provision of day care for pre-school and other children

Provision of accommodation by the local authority has replaced the former concept of 'reception into care'. The local authority must provide accommodation for any child within their area who needs it as a result of there being no parent who has parental responsibility for him, or his being lost or having been abandoned. A parent who has parental responsibility for a child may remove him at any time from accommodation provided by the local authority: s 20(8).

Duty to provide accommodation for children

Accommodation must be provided also for children who are removed or kept away from home under ChA 1989, Part V.

Other duties of the local authority in relation to children looked after by them

Where the local authority is looking after a child, it has the tasks of safeguarding and promoting his welfare, of ascertaining the wishes and feelings of the child and his parents, and of giving due consideration to the child's religious persuasion and racial, cultural and linguistic background: s 22.

Local authority foster parents may look after the child: see s 23. Schedule 3, para 12, allows for regulations to be made concerning records to be kept by local authority foster parents.

The local authority has the duty to promote contact between the child who is being looked after and his parents or any non-parent who has parental responsibility for him. Visitors can be appointed with the duty of visiting, advising and befriending the child.

Chapter 15

Local Authority Services for Children and Families (2)

This chapter outlines the duties of local authorities to advise and assist children who are being 'looked after'. The problems of those children who are kept in 'secure accommodation' are noted, and the highly important procedures of handling complaints and representations concerning the discharge of functions by local authorities are set out. Co-operation among local authorities and consultation with local education authorities are examined and the principles involved in the recoupment of the cost of providing services for children are stated.

15.1 **Further matters covered by ChA 1989, Part III**

Section 24 ChA 1989 replaces ss 27-29 and 69 of the Child Care Act 1980, and strengthens the functions of local authorities concerning assistance to be given to children, with their long-term future being kept in mind. 'Where a child is being looked after by a local authority, it shall be the duty of the authority to advise, assist and befriend him with a view to promoting his welfare when he ceases to be looked after by them': s 24(1). The duty has application in the case of *all* children who are looked after by the authority – those who are provided with accommodation (ie that which is provided for a continuous period of more than 24 hours: see s 22(2)) and those who are in care, following a care order (see 16.4).

15.2 **Advice and assistance for certain children**

In this part of the 1989 Act, the phrase 'a person qualifying for advice and assistance' means a person within the local authority's area who is under 21 and who was, at any time after reaching the age of 16 but while still a child, looked after by a local authority, accommodated by or on behalf of a voluntary organisation, in a registered children's home (see 18.8), accommodated by a health authority or local education authority, or in any residential care home, nursing home or mental nursing home, for a consecutive period of at least three months, or privately fostered, but who is no longer so looked after, accommodated or fostered: s 24(2).

15.2.1 Persons qualifying for care and assistance

Where a local authority knows that within their area there is a person qualifying for advice and assistance, that the conditions in s 24(5) are satisfied, and that person has asked them for help of a kind which they can give under this section, they shall, if he was being looked after by the authority or was

15.2.2 Conditions for the giving of advice

accommodated by a voluntary organisation, and may (in other cases) 'advise and befriend' him: s 24(4). The 'appropriate conditions' are that:

- it appears to the local authority that the person concerned is in need of advice and being befriended;
- where that person was not being looked after by the authority, they are satisfied that the person by whom he was being looked after does not have the necessary facilities for advising or befriending him: s 24(5).

15.3 Financial matters involved in providing advice and assistance

Where, as a result of s 24, a local authority is under a duty, or is empowered, to advise and befriend a person, they may also give him assistance: s 24(6). This assistance may take the form of cash or kind; assistance given under subsections (1)-(6) may be in cash, but only in 'exceptional circumstances' (the phrase is not defined under the Act, so that it is not easy to tell whether it may have reference to circumstances which are exceptional for the recipient or for the community in general): s 24(7).

15.3.1 Payment of expenses, making of grants

A local authority may give assistance to any person who is under 21 and was at any time after reaching 16 looked after by the authority, by contributing to expenses incurred by him in living near the place where he is, or will be, employed or seeking employment or receiving education or training, or by making a grant to enable him to meet expenses involved in his education or training: s 24(8).

15.3.2 Continuation of assistance

Where a person is being assisted under s 24(8), the authority may continue that assistance after he reaches 21 before completing the course: s 24(9).

15.4 Duties related to contact with other local authorities

There is a duty on a local authority to inform another local authority in whose area a person who has been receiving advice, etc, under s 24, proposes to live, or is living: s 24(11).

15.5 Complaints concerning advice and assistance

Under s 24 ChA 1989 (advice and assistance), the following subsection (14) is added by the Courts and Legal Services Act 1990, Sch 16, para 13: 'Every local authority shall establish a procedure for considering any representations (including any complaint) made to them by a person qualifying for advice and assistance about the discharge of their functions under this Part in relation to him.'

15.6 The provision of secure accommodation

Section 25 of the 1989 Act concerns the use of accommodation by the local authority for the purpose of 'restricting liberty'. The section re-enacts, with some modifications, s 21A Child Care Act 1980.

> 'A child who is being looked after by a local authority may not be placed, and, if placed, may not be kept, in accommodation provided for the purpose of restricting liberty ('secure accommodation') unless it appears – (a) that he has a history of absconding and is likely to abscond from any other description of accommodation, and if he absconds, he is likely to suffer significant harm; or (b) that if he is kept in any other description of accommodation he is likely to injure himself or other persons': s 25(1).

It should be noted that s 21A(1) Child Care Act 1980 referred to the child's 'physical, mental or moral welfare' being at risk. The phrase 'significant harm' which appears in s 25(1)(a) of the 1989 Act suggests perhaps a higher degree of harm than that contemplated in the use of the phrase 'at risk'. See *Secure Accommodation Orders* by C Trimmer [1944] Fam Law 388.

Where the court is satisfied of the existence of the criteria set out in s 25(1), it should consider the principles of s 1 (delay, no order: see 13.3). In relation to the welfare checklist, note the comments of Connell J in *Hereford and Worcester CC v S* (1993): 'In my judgment the provisions of s 1(3) colloquially described as the welfare checklist are not of particular relevance when an application under s 25 is before the court, but that does not mean that they are irrelevant': see *Re M (A Minor) (Secure Accommodation Order)* (1994).

15.6.1 Regulations under s 25

The Secretary of State may make appropriate regulations concerning secure accommodation.

- He may specify a maximum period beyond which a child may not be kept in secure accommodation without the authority of the court: s 25(2)(a).

- He may empower the court from time to time to authorise a child to be kept in secure accommodation for such further period as the regulations may specify: s 25(2)(b).

No court shall exercise the powers conferred by s 25 in respect of a child who is not legally represented in that court unless, having been informed of his right to apply for legal aid and having had the opportunity to do so, he refused or failed to apply: s 25(6).

15.6.2 The making of an order

The court hearing an application under s 25 has the duty of determining whether any relevant criteria for keeping a child in secure accommodation are satisfied in his case: s 25(3).

Where the criteria are satisfied, the court will make an order authorising the child to be kept in secure accommodation and specifying the maximum period for which he may be so kept: s 25(4).

Note *Re B* (1994), in which the Court of Appeal held that an order made under s 25, authorising a period of detention in secure accommodation ran from the date of the order, *not* from the date on which the child was actually placed in secure accommodation.

15.6.3 Interim order

On any adjournment of the hearing of an application under s 25, the court may make an interim order permitting the child to be kept in secure accommodation for the period of the adjournment: s 25(5).

Note *C v Humberside CC* (1994): where justices made a secure accommodation order, the maximum of three months was to be reduced by any period for which the child had already been detained under an interim secure accommodation order. See Children (Secure Accommodation) Regulations 1991 (SI 1991/1505, reg 11).

15.6.4 Directions by the court

A court order issued under s 25 is an authorisation that the child be kept in secure accommodation; but s 25(8) states that such an authorisation shall not prejudice the power of the court 'to give directions relating to the child to whom the authorisation relates'.

15.7 Removal of the child from secure accommodation

Section 25(9) states that s 25 is subject to s 20(8) (see 14.6.4). This means that a person who has parental responsibility for a child can remove him from secure accommodation. A child over 16 who is not in care may also be able to leave the secure accommodation: see s 20(11).

15.8 Restricting the liberty of children: a reminder

Guidance and Regulations (HMSO 1991), published by the Department of Health, recapitulates the significant matters to be taken into account in making secure placements for children.

> 'Restricting the liberty of children is a serious step which must be taken only when there is no genuine alternative which would be appropriate. It must be a 'last resort' in the sense that all else must first have been comprehensively considered and rejected – never because no other placement was available at the relevant time, because of inadequacies in staffing, because the child is simply being a nuisance or runs away from his accommodation and is not likely to suffer significant harm in doing so, and never as a form of punishment. It is

important ... that there is a clear view of the aims and objectives of such a placement and that those providing the accommodation can fully meet those aims and objectives. Secure placements, once made, should be for only so long as is necessary and unavoidable.'

Section 26 provides for reviews of the progress of children who are being looked after by local authorities. Local authorities are expected, further, to institute systems for the handling of complaints and representations concerning the discharge of their functions.	**15.9**	**Review of progress of children**
The Secretary of State may make regulations requiring the case of each child who is being looked after by a local authority to be reviewed in accordance with regulations: s 26(1).	15.9.1	Review of cases
The regulations may make provision as to the manner of review, the considerations to which the local authority are to have regard in the review. Provision may be made for seeking the views of the child, his parents, any non-parent who has parental responsibility for him and any other person whose views are considered relevant.	15.9.2	Regulations
Local authorities are obliged to establish appropriate procedures for considering representations, including complaints. *Guidance and Regulations*, issued by the Department of Health, suggests that the procedures should be related to complaints about, eg, day care, services to support children within their family homes, accommodation of children.	**15.10**	**Inquiries into representations**
Under s 26(3), complaints can be made by the following persons: any child who is being looked after by the authority or who is not being looked after by them but is in need; a parent of the child or a non-parent who has parental responsibility for him; any local authority foster-parent; any person considered by the authority as having an appropriate interest in the child's welfare. Any of these persons may make representations concerning the discharge by the authority of any of their functions under this Part of the 1989 Act in relation to the child.	15.10.1	Persons who can complain
The procedure must be so designed as to ensure that at least one person who is not a member or officer of the authority takes part in the consideration and discussions concerning the action to be taken in relation to the child in the light of the consideration: s 26(4). See the Representations Procedure (Children) Regulations, 1991.	15.10.2	Procedure concerning complaints

Where a representation has been considered under the authority's procedure, the authority is expected to have due regard to the findings of those considering the representations and to take appropriate steps to notify the person making the representation, the child, and other persons likely to be affected, of the authority's decision and any action taken or proposed: s 26 (7).

A record of each complaint received by the local authority together with a statement of the outcome must be kept: reg 10 (1991 Regulations).

15.11 Other procedures for dealing with complaints

In addition to the complaints procedure under s 26, remedies are available under the 1989 Act, s 84, the procedure concerning the Ombudsman, complaints to the European Court of Human Rights, applications for judicial review, and applications for private orders. These are noted below.

15.11.1 Secretary of State: default powers

Under s 84 ChA 1989, where the Secretary of State is satisfied that a local authority has failed, without reasonable excuse, to comply with any of the duties imposed on them by or under the 1989 Act, he may make an order declaring the authority to be in default with respect to that duty: s 84(1). The Secretary of State may enforce directions by mandamus: s 84(4). (Orders of mandamus lie to compel performance of a public duty: see ss 29, 31 Supreme Court Act 1981. Application to the High Court for mandamus is made in accordance with rules of court.)

15.11.2 Complaints to the Ombudsman

The Ombudsman (Commissioner for Local Administration) may hear any complaints concerning *maladministration* ('insufficient, weak or dishonest administration'). Complaints may be made to the Commissioner directly, specifying the conduct complained of, or the action giving rise to complaint. Reports on cases investigated are sent to the complainant and the local authority: see Local Government Act 1978.

15.11.3 Hearing by European Court of Human Rights

The European Court of Human Rights may hear complaints alleging a breach of the provisions of the European Convention of Human Rights, relating to, eg, a breach by a local authority of Article 8 (respect for family life). Complainants must have been affected in a personal capacity by the alleged violation, and domestic remedies must have been exhausted (see the *Convention*, Articles 26, 27(3)). Where a violation is proved, compensation may be awarded (Art 50); but the Court must rely on the willingness of the complainant's government to act in accordance with a judgment: see, eg, *Gaskin v UK* (1990) refusal to allow access to case records concerning a child in care was held to breach Article 8: *McMichael v UK* (1995) (sight of documents in legal proceedings refused, held to be a breach of Article 8).

15.11.4	Judicial review

Judicial review is a method of control exercised by the courts over the procedures of statutory authorities and other subordinate bodies which can result in the grant of prerogative orders (eg, mandamus), or declarations of a person's rights. Judicial review of a local authority's activities will be concerned not with the decision of which review is being sought but with a review of the manner of the decision-making process. 'No application for review shall be made unless leave of the court has been obtained... The court shall not grant leave unless it considers that the applicant has sufficient interest in the matter to which the application relates': Order 53, r 3(1), (5). Application should be made promptly, and in any event within three months from the date when grounds arose, unless the court considers that a good reason exists for extending that period: Order 58, r 4(1). Grounds for judicial review of an administrative action by a local authority have been held to be 'illegality, irrationality and procedural impropriety'.

15.11.5	Application for private orders

A complainant against a local authority may make application for an order under s 8 (see 13.9). But where a child is in care (see 16.9), there are restrictions on the ability of the court to make private orders.

15.12	**Co-operation between authorities**

Section 27 of the 1989 Act is concerned with co-operation between local authorities and other bodies with the object of improving the exercise of powers under Part III.

> 'Where it appears to a local authority that any authority mentioned in subsection (3) could, by taking any specified action, help in the exercise of any of their functions under this Part, they may request the help of that other authority, specifying the action in question: s 27(1)) as amended. The authorities are: any local authority, education authority, local housing authority, health authority or National Health Service Trust, or any other person authorised by the Secretary of State': s 27(3).

15.13	**Consultation by local authorities with local education authorities**

Where a child is being looked after by a local authority and the authority proposes to provide accommodation for him in an establishment at which education is provided for children who are accommodated there, it shall, so far as is reasonably practicable, consult the appropriate local education authority before doing so: s 28(1).

15.14	**Recoupment of cost of services, etc**

Section 29(1) of the 1989 Act allows local authorities to make reasonable charges for services provided under ss 17, 18 (with the exceptions of advice, guidance or counselling). Where the local authorities are satisfied that a person's means are insufficient for him to pay, he must not be required to pay more than can reasonably be expected: s 29(2). No person shall be liable to pay any charge under subsection (1) if he is in receipt of income support or family relief: s 29 (3). Any charge under s 29(1) may be recovered summarily as a civil debt: s 29(5).

15.15 Contributions towards maintenance of children looked after by local authorities

Under Sch 2, Part III, para 21, where a local authority is looking after a child, the recovery of contributions towards his maintenance may be considered. Contributions may be recovered from any person liable to contribute only if this is considered reasonable. Those liable to contribute are each parent of a child under 16, and the child himself where he has reached the age of 16: para 21 (3).

15.15.1 Agreed contributions

Contributions to a child's maintenance may be recovered only if the local authority has served a notice ('contribution notice') on the contributor (ie, the person liable to contribute), specifying the weekly sum to be contributed and arrangements for payment. An authority may at any time withdraw a contribution notice (without prejudice to its power to serve another): para 22(5).

15.15.2 Contribution orders

Where a contributor has been served with a contribution notice and has failed to reach agreement with the local authority within a period of one month following the serving of the order, the authority may apply for a court order: para 23(1). A contribution order made by a magistrates' court is enforceable as a magistrates' court maintenance order (within the meaning of s 150(1) Magistrates' Courts Act 1980): para 24(1).

Summary of Chapter 15

Local Authority Services for Children and Families (2)

Advice and assistance for certain children

Where a child is being looked after by a local authority, the authority has the duty of advising, assisting and befriending him with the object of promoting his welfare when it ceases to look after by him: s 24(1). The duty applies in the case of all children looked after by the authority.

Complaints

A local authority must establish a procedure for considering representations, including complaints, made to them by a person who qualifies for advice and assistance, concerning the discharge of their functions in this area: s 24.

The provision of secure accommodation

A child who is being looked after by a local authority may be placed in secure accommodation where it appears that he has a history of absconding and, if he absconds, is likely to suffer significant harm, or that if he is kept in any other description of accommodation he is likely to injure himself or other persons: s 25. See *Hereford and Worcester CC v S* (1993).

The Secretary of State may make regulations specifying a maximum period beyond which a child may not be kept in secure accommodation without the court's authority. Additionally, he may empower the court to authorise that a child be kept in secure accommodation for such further period as regulations may specify: s 25(2).

A person who has parental responsibility for a child can remove him from secure accommodation: see s 25(9).

Review of progress of children

Under s 26, regulations may be made requiring the case of each child who is being looked after by a local authority to be reviewed: s 26(1). Complaints may be made by a parent of the child or a non-parent having parental responsibility for him, or by any person considered by the local authority as having an appropriate interest in his welfare. Records of complaints must be kept.

The Secretary of State may make an order declaring an authority to be in default with respect to their duties relating to children. He may enforce directions by mandamus.

Complaints may be made to the Ombudsman. Further, the European Court of Human Rights may hear a complaint alleging a breach by a local authority of Article 8 of the European Convention of Human Rights (relating to respect for family life).

Judicial review

Judicial review of the manner of a local authority's decision-making, in relation to the provision of services for children, may be requested. An application requires leave of the court: see Order 53.

Contribution towards maintenance of children

Where a local authority is looking after a child, contributions towards his maintenance may be recovered from each parent of a child under 16, and the child himself if he has reached the age of 16: Sch 2, para 21 ChA 1989. A notice should be served on the person liable to contribute, specifying a weekly sum to be collected and arrangements for payment.

Chapter 16

Care and Supervision Orders

16.1 Essence of ChA 1989, Part IV

Consider the following 'family problems'. What action might be expected from the courts by X and Y in the following circumstances? X, recently widowed, complains that her 11-year old son is completely out of control and is becoming a danger to her and himself. She wishes the court to assist her. Y, an inspector who works for the NSPCC, observes that the 14-year old daughter of parents who are known alcoholics is often absent from school and is associating with drug dealers. He believes that the court should intervene.

Part IV of the 1989 Act (ss 31-42) is concerned with public law orders which the court can make in relation to problems (such as those mentioned above) which might necessitate the care and supervision of children. The recommendations of the *Review of Child Care Law* (1985) were largely followed in the ChA 1989.

16.2 Definitions

Definitions of the following concepts are of particular relevance for Part IV of the 1989 Act:

- *harm*: see 13.5.5 above;
- *development*: see 14.2 above;
- *health*: see 14.2 above;
- *ill treatment*: this 'includes sexual abuse and forms of ill-treatment which are not physical': s 31(9). The Lord Chancellor stated (*Hansard HL*, Vol 503, col 342): 'Ill treatment is not a precise term and would include, for example, instances of verbal abuse or unfairness falling a long way short of significant harm'.
- *authorised person*: this means, in the context of Part IV, the National Society for the Prevention of Cruelty to Children and any of its officers, and any person authorised by the Secretary of State to bring proceedings under s 31 and any officer of a body which is so authorised: s 31(9)(a).

16.3 Basis of Part IV

Fundamental to Part IV is s 31(1): 'On the application of any local authority or authorised person, the court may make an order – (a) placing the child with respect to whom the application was made in the care of a designated local authority, or (b) putting him under the supervision of a designated local authority or of a probation officer'.

'Care order' and 'supervision order' include orders made under s 31(1)(a) and interim orders under s 38 (see l6.18).

Care proceedings will generally be heard by the Family Proceedings Court, consisting of magistrates from the 'family panel'. See s 92, and Sch 11. Proceedings involving s 37 may be commenced in the High Court or a county court. County courts which can hear care proceedings are known as care centres; the case will be heard by judges who have experience in proceedings of this nature.

16.4 Features of s 31

It should be noted that an application under s 31 may be made on its own or in any other family proceedings: s 31(4). Further, on an application for a care order, the court may make a supervision order (and vice versa): s 31(5).

16.4.1 Restrictions

No care order or supervision order may be made with respect to a child who has reached the age of 17 (or 16, in the case of a child who is married): s 31(3). No application made by an authorised person (see 16.2 above) shall be entertained by the court if, at the time when it is made, the child concerned is (a) the subject of an earlier application for a care order, or supervision order, which has not been disposed of, or subject to an order under s 7(7)(b) C&YPA 1969: s 31(7).

16.4.2 Consultation with local authority

Where an authorised person proposes to make an application under s 31 he shall, if it is reasonably practicable to do so, and before making the application, consult the local authority appearing to him to be the authority in whose area the child concerned is ordinarily resident: s 31(6).

16.4.3 Residence of child

The local authority designated in a care order must be the local authority within whose area the child is ordinarily resident, or where the child does not reside in the area of a local authority, the authority within whose area any circumstances arose in consequence of which the order is being made: s 31(8).

16.4.4 Nature of proceedings

Care proceedings under the 1989 Act are *not adversarial*. Thus, in *Oxfordshire CC v M* (1994), the Court of Appeal held that the court is empowered to override legal professional privilege so that all relevant information is made available in order that a properly informed decision might be made in the overriding interests of the child.

16.5 Principles which the court will keep in mind

Even though the 'threshold criteria' set out in s 31(2) (see 16.6 below) are satisfied, other basic principles enunciated in s 1(3) must also be kept in mind: see s 1(4)(b).

- The child's welfare is to be the court's paramount consideration: s 1(1). See *Re B (Minors) (Termination of Contact: Paramount Consideration)* (1993), in which the Court of Appeal held that it is the welfare of the child which is the paramount consideration under s 34 (contact with children in care) and, therefore, the court has the power to review a local authority's long-term plan involving a care order.
- There should be a minimum of delay in determining the question(s) arising: s 1(2).
- The checklist at s 1(3) (see 13.5) should be considered.
- An order should not be made unless to do so would be better for the child than not to make any order: s 1(5).
- All the orders available to the court should be considered, not merely care and supervision orders. See s 1(3)(g); *Humberside CC v B* (1993).

16.6 The threshold criteria

Section 31(2) sets out certain minimum circumstances 'which the government considers should always be found to exist before it can ever be justified for a court even to begin to contemplate whether the State should be enabled to intervene compulsorily in family life': *per* Lord Mackay LC. Essentially, therefore, if the criteria in s 31 are not satisfied, the court will not make a care or supervision order.

> 'A court may only make a care order or supervision order if it is satisfied – (a) that the child concerned is suffering, or is likely to suffer, significant harm; and (b) that the harm or likelihood of harm is attributable to (i) the care given to the child, or likely to be given to him if the order were not made, not being what it would be reasonable to expect a parent to give to him; or (ii) the child's being beyond parental control.'

16.7 Aspects of the criteria

Some important words in the statement of statutory criteria, eg, 'significant', 'care', 'likelihood', are not defined specifically in the section; as a result, problems of interpretation have arisen, some of which are considered below.

16.7.1 'Is suffering ... or is likely to suffer ...'

It would seem that this phrase relates to present and future harm; past harm suffered by the child may not *in itself* be appropriate to satisfy the statement of criteria.

In *Newham LBC v A-G* (1993), the Court of Appeal held that, in the context of s 31, the phrase 'likely to suffer' did not involve a standard of proof as high as the civil standard of 'on a balance of probabilities'. It would suffice were the court to find 'a real, significant likelihood of harm'. The phrase was to be interpreted with reference to *evaluating* the future likelihood of significant harm.

In *Re M (A Minor) (Care Order: Threshold Conditions)* (1994), the House of Lords considered whether the court can be satisfied in relation to the threshold criteria where there is an application by a third party which would remove the child from harm, although harm did exist at the time of intervention by the local authority. *Per* Lord Mackay LC: 'I would conclude that the natural construction of the conditions in s 31(2) is that where, at the time the application is to be disposed of, there are in place arrangements for the protection of the child by the local authority on an interim basis, which protection has been continuously in place for some time, the relevant date with respect to which the court must be satisfied is the date at which the local authority initiated the procedure for protection under the Act from which these arrangements follow. If, after a local authority had initiated protective arrangements, the need for these had terminated because the child's welfare had been satisfactorily provided for otherwise, in any subsequent proceedings it would not be possible to found jurisdiction on the situation at the time of initiation of these arrangements.' Lord Mackay cited, in support of his construction, *Re D* (1987). See A Brinham, *The Temporal Dimension of Care* [1994] CLJ 458.

16.7.2 'Significant harm'

The court will consider the 'significance of the harm' involved and will be guided by s 31(10). 'Where the question of whether the harm suffered by a child is significant turns on the child's health or development; his health or development shall be compared with that which could reasonably be expected of a similar child.' It is not easy to understand precisely what is meant by 'similar child'. The Department of Health *Guidance* suggests that the term has reference to 'environmental, social and cultural characteristics' of the particular child.

In *Re O (A Minor) (Care Order: Education: Procedure)* (1992), the court ruled that continued absence from school was likely to cause 'harm' (in the statutory sense) which was, likely, in the long run, to be of a significant nature.

In *Humberside CC v B* (1993), Booth J accepted a suggestion made by counsel that 'significant harm' meant 'harm that the court should consider was either considerable or noteworthy or important', ie, harm which the court should take into account in considering a child's future.

16.7.3 'Attributable to'

The phrase involves, in this context, a link, but not necessarily causation of a direct nature. 'Harm' appears to be linked to the (undefined) 'care' given by the child's parent(s). The type of 'harm' envisaged in the section might result, for example, from a failure by the parent to ensure that his child was prevented from having regular contact with a person who was known to be a drugs dealer.

'Reasonable to expect' will involve the court in considering what a reasonable parent would provide *for the child in question*, and not necessarily for any 'hypothetical, average child'. This will necessarily involve consideration of an objective standard.

16.7.4 'Reasonable to expect a parent to give to him'

This phrase, which is a relic of the former law concerning children (see s 3 C&YPA 1963) is now considered to be linked with harm to the child (which was not the case in the 1963 legislation). The Department of Health *Guidance* notes that the phrase provides for cases where, whatever the standard of care made available for the child, he is not deriving benefit from it because parental control is lacking 'It is immaterial whether this is the fault of the parents or the child.'

16.7.5 'Beyond parental control'

The court is expected, under s 32(1), to draw up a timetable with a view to disposing of the application for an order under Part IV *without delay*, and to give appropriate directions so as to ensure that the timetable is adhered to. This section is to be read with s 1(2) (see 13.3) which is designed to keep before the court the dangers of delay in bringing proceedings to a conclusion.

16.8 Timetables

Section 33 sets out the powers and responsibilities of the parties to a care order. The duty of the local authority is made clear: 'Where a care order is made with respect to a child it shall be the duty of the local authority designated by the order to receive the child into their care and to keep him in their care while the order remains in force': s 33(1).

16.9 Essential features of the care order

Additionally, where a care order has been made with respect to a child on the application of an authorised person, but the local authority designated by the order was not informed that the person proposed to make the application, the child may be kept in the care of that person until received into the authority's care: s 33(2).

'While a care order is in force with respect to a child, the local authority designated by the order shall – (a) have parental responsibility for the child; and (b) have the power (subject to the following provisions of this section) to determine the extent to which a parent or guardian of the child may meet his parental responsibility for him': s 33(3).

16.9.1 Parental responsibility

It should be noted that the power in s 33(3)(b) is subject to any right, duty, power, responsibility or authority which a parent or guardian of the child has in relation to the child and his property by virtue of any other enactment: s 33(9). The power in s 33(3)(b) must not be exercised by the authority unless they are satisfied that it is necessary to do so in order to safeguard or promote the child's welfare: s 33(4). But nothing in s 33(3)(b) will prevent a parent or guardian of the child who has care of him from doing what is reasonable in all the circumstances of the case for the purpose of safeguarding or promoting his welfare: s 33(5).

16.9.2 Restrictions concerning religious upbringing

A local authority may not, for the duration of a care order, cause the child to be brought up in a religion other than that in which he would have been brought up if the order had not been made: s 33(6)(a).

16.9.3 Restrictions concerning change of name, removal from the UK

While a care order is in force with respect to a child, no person may cause the child to be known by a new surname; or remove him from the UK without either the written consent of every person who has parental responsibility for the child, or the leave of the court: s 33(7).

(Note Practice Direction 42 and Order 63, r 10, in relation to change by deed poll of a child's surname: see *The Times* 17 February 1995. Where a person has by order of the High Court, County Court or Family Proceedings Court been given parental responsibility for a child and applies for the enrolment of a deed poll to change the family name of the child who is under 18 (unless in the case of a female who is married and below that age), the application must be supported by the written consent of every other person having parental responsibility. In the absence of such consent, the application will be adjourned unless and until the leave is given to change the child's surname in the proceedings in which the order was made and such leave is produced to the Central Office. Where an application is made by a person who has *not* been given parental responsibility, leave of the Court will be granted where the written consent of every person having parental responsibility is produced or if the person(s) having parental responsibility is/are dead or cannot be found.)

Per Booth J, in *Re J (A Minor) (Change of Name)* (1993): 'It is only in exceptional circumstances and when the welfare of the child demands it, that an application of this nature for a change of the child's surname to enable him or her to use another surname should be made *ex parte* and without notice to his or her parents I think it is right that in such a case the application should be transferred from magistrates for consideration by a higher court.'

The local authority has a duty under s 34(1) to allow a child in its care reasonable contact with: his parents; any guardian of his; where there was a residence order in force with respect to the child immediately before the care order was made, the person in whose favour the order was made; and, where immediately before the care order was made, a person had care of the child by virtue of an order made in the exercise of the High Court's inherent jurisdiction with respect to children, that person.

16.10 Contact between children in care and their families

16.10.1 Orders concerning contact

Following an application made by the local authority or the child, the court may make an appropriate order concerning the contact to be allowed *between the child and a named person*: s 34(2). See *Kent CC v C* (1992). On application made by any person mentioned in s 34(1) or any person who has obtained the leave of the court to make the application, the court may make an appropriate order concerning the contact to be allowed *between the child and that parent*: s 34(3).

16.10.2 Orders refusing to allow contact

On an application made by the authority or the child, the court may make an order authorising the authority to *refuse* to allow contact between the child and any person mentioned in s 34(1) and named in the order: s 34(4).

It was held in *W Glamorgan CC v P (No 1)* (1992), that contact could be refused under s 34(4) for as long as was considered to be in the interests of the child; s 34(4) gives the court complete discretion, exercisable within the general principles of the Act. In *Birmingham CC v H* (1994), the House of Lords held that where an application was made under s 34(4) for an order authorising the local authority to refuse contact between a child and its parent, the question to be determined by the court should relate to the child's upbringing: it was his welfare that was to be the court's paramount consideration, even where the parent in question was also a child in care.

16.10.3 Where no application has been made

When making a care order with respect to a child, or in any family proceedings in connection with a child who is in the care of a local authority, the court may make an order under s 31, even though no application for such an order has been made with respect to the child, if it considers that the order should be made: s 34(5).

16.10.4 Other matters

The court may vary or discharge any order made under s 31 on the application of the authority, the child concerned or the person named in the order: s 31(9). An order under s 31 may be made either at the same time as the care order itself or later: s 31(10).

Before the court makes a care order with respect to any child, it must consider the arrangements which the authority have made, or propose to make, for affording any person contact with a child to whom s 31 applies, and invite the parties to the proceedings to comment on the arrangements: s 31(11).

See *Re T (A Minor) (Care Order: Conditions)* (1994) for statement of the Court of Appeal that the court had no power to impose *conditions* on a care order under s 31.

16.11 Essence of the supervision order

A supervision order is made by the court on the application of any local authority or authorised parent, placing the child under the supervision of a designated local authority or of a probation officer: s 31(1)(b). As in the case of a care order, a supervision order will not be made unless the court is satisfied that the principles of s 1 and the criteria in s 31 are satisfied.

16.12 Duties of the supervisor

While a supervision order is in force, the supervisor has certain duties under s 35(1): to advise, assist and befriend the supervised child, to take such steps as are reasonably necessary to give effect to the order, and to consider applying to the court for variation or discharge of the order where it is not wholly complied with or where he considers that the order may no longer be necessary.

16.13 Duration of the order

Supervision orders last for one year; they may be extended by the court for a specified period, but not so as to run beyond the end of the period of three years beginning with the date on which it was made: Sch 3, para 6. See *Re A (A Minor) (Supervision Order: Extension)* (1994).

16.14 Features of the supervision order

Details relating to the supervision order are set out in Sch 3, Parts I and II. In the Schedule, 'the responsible person, in relation to a supervised child, means any person who has parental responsibility for the child, and any other person with whom he is living': para 1. For failure to comply with order, see *Re R and G* (1994).

16.14.1 Selection of the supervisor

A supervision order shall not designate a local authority as the supervisor unless the authority agree, or the supervised child lives or will live within their area: Sch 3, para 9(1). A court shall not place a child under the supervision of a probation officer unless the appropriate authority so request: para 9(2).

16.14.2 Supervisor's directions

A supervision order may require the supervised child to comply with the supervisor's directions requiring him, eg, to live at a specified place for a specified time, to participate in specified activities: para 2. With the consent of any 'responsible person', a supervision order may include a requirement that he shall take all reasonable steps to ensure that the supervised child complies with directions under para 2: para 3(1).

16.14.3 Psychiatric and medical examinations

Where the court is satisfied that the mental condition of the supervised child is such as requires, and may be susceptible to, medical treatment, the court may include in the order a requirement that he submit to specified treatment: para 5(1). No court shall include such a requirement unless it is satisfied, where the child has sufficient understanding to make an informed decision, that he consents to it, and that satisfactory arrangements have been made for the treatment: para 5(5).

16.14.4 Appeals

An appeal lies to the High Court against the making by a magistrates' court of any order under the 1989 Act or any refusal by a magistrates' court to make such an order: s 94(1), as amended by Sch 16, para 23 Courts and Legal Services Act 1990: see *P v P (Periodical Payments: Appeals)* (1994).

16.15 The education supervision order

On the application of a local education authority, the court may make an order putting a child under the supervision of a designated local education authority: s 36(1). Such an order will be made by the court only if the child is of compulsory school age and is not being properly educated: s 36(3). For purposes of the section, a child is being properly educated 'only if he is receiving efficient full-time education suitable to his age, ability and aptitude and any special educational needs he may have': s 36(4). It will be assumed (see s 36(5)) that a child is not being properly educated where he is the subject of a school attendance order which has not been complied with. An education supervision order will not be made with respect to a child who is in the care of a local authority: s 36(6).

16.15.1 Designated local authority

The local education authority designated in an education supervision order must be the authority in whose area the child is living or will live, or, where the child is a registered pupil at a school and the authority within whose area the school is situated agree, the latter authority: s 36(7).

16.15.2 Appropriate local authority

Where a local education committee proposes to apply for an education supervision order they must consult the social services committee of the appropriate local authority, ie, in the case of a child who is being provided with accommodation by, or on behalf of, a local authority, that authority, and in any other case, the local authority within whose area the child concerned lives, or will live: s 36(8), (9).

16.16 Further matters concerning education supervision orders

Sch 3, Part III, covers matters such as the effect, duration of orders and offences arising from failure to comply.

16.16.1 Effect of education supervision orders

Where an education supervision order is in force with respect to a child, it is the supervisor's duty to advise, assist, befriend, and give directions to the supervised child and his parents so as to secure that he is properly educated: para 12(1). The wishes and feelings of the child and his parents should be ascertained: para 12(2).

16.16.2 Duration and discharge of orders

An education supervision order has effect for one year beginning with the date on which it is made: para 15(1). It may be extended by the court, but no one extension may be for a period of more than three years: para 15(2), (4). The order ceases to have effect when the child ceases to be of compulsory school age, or on the making of a care order with respect to the child: para 15(6).

The order may be discharged on the application of the child, a parent, or the local education authority. The court may order an investigation into the circumstances of the child: para 17.

16.16.3 Offences

If the parent of a child with respect to whom an education supervision order has been made persistently fails to comply with any direction given under the order, he is guilty of an offence: para 18(1). It is a defence for the person charged to show that he took all reasonable steps to ensure that the direction was complied with or that the direction was unreasonable: para 18(2).

16.16.4 Failure of child to comply

Where the child persistently fails to comply with directions given under the order, the local authority concerned will notify the appropriate local authority. An investigation of the child's circumstances will follow: para 19.

16.17 Investigation of a child's circumstances

Where in any family proceedings in which a question concerning a child's welfare emerges, and it seems to the court that a care or supervision order might be appropriate, an investigation of the child's circumstances may be directed: s 37(1). 'Child's circumstances' should be widely construed to include any situation which might result in a child suffering significant harm in the future: *Re H (A Minor) (Section 37 Direction)* (1993). The local authority concerned in the investigation must decide whether to apply for a care order or supervision order or to take any other action with respect to the child: s 37(2). Where at the conclusion of an investigation the authority decides not to apply for a care or supervision order, they must consider whether it would be appropriate to review the case at a later date: s 37(6).

16.18 Interim orders

The court may make an interim care or supervision order where proceedings on a care or supervision order applications are adjourned, or the court gives advice under s 37(1). But no interim order will be made unless the court is satisfied that there are reasonable grounds for believing that the circumstances with respect to the child are as indicated in s 31(2) (see 16.6): s 38(2). (See *Re G* (1993), in which the Court of Appeal held that making an interim care order under s 38 was not to be used as a tactical weapon but was an impartial step to maintain the status quo pending the final hearing.) See *Re P (Minors) (Interim Order)* (1993); *Re S (Children: Interim Care Order)* (1993).

16.18.1 Examination of child

Where the court makes an interim care order, or interim supervision order, it may give directions concerning a medical or psychiatric examination or other assessment of the child; but if the child is of sufficient understanding to make an informed decision he may refuse to submit to the examination or other assessment: s 38(6).

In *South Glamorgan CC v B* (1993), a child, aged 15, was beyond parental control and care proceedings were commenced. The judge gave instructions under s 38(6) that the child be assessed at a family and adolescent unit. The child refused, and it was argued that she was of sufficient understanding and had a right to refuse assessment. It was held that the High Court *could* override the wishes of a child and give consent for medical assessment, such power not having been abrogated by ChA 1989. The child's welfare was the paramount consideration and the overwhelming professional view was that she must be admitted for her own good. The local authority was given leave to remove the child forcibly to the unit.

16.18.2 Duration

Interim care or supervision orders may be made for such periods as the court orders. They may not last longer than a period of eight weeks (in the case of an initial order) or four weeks, or eight weeks from the date of the first order (if that is longer) in the case of a second or any subsequent order: s 38(4), (5). See *Gateshead MBC v N* (1993).

On the question of renewals of interim orders, note the comments of Waite LJ in *Re G* (1993): 'Parliament intended the regime of an interim care order to operate as a tightly run procedure closely monitored by the court and affording to all parties an opportunity of frequent review as events unfolded during the currency of the order. That purpose would be frustrated if a practice were to be allowed to grow up under which renewals of interim care orders were sought routinely by local authorities without any attempt to keep the court up to date with progress, or granted by the court perfunctorily without any of the enquiries necessary to eliminate the risk of essential disclosure being lost through administrative lethargy'.

16.19 Discharge and variation of care and supervision orders

Care and supervision orders may be varied or discharged by the court on the application of a person with parental responsibility for the child, the child himself, the local authority designated by the order, or the supervisor: s 39(1), (2).

On the application of a person who is not entitled to apply for the order to be discharged, but who is a person with whom the child is living, a supervision order may be varied by the court in so far as it imposes a requirement which affects that person: s 39(3). Where a care order is in force with respect to a child, the court may, on the application of any person entitled to apply for the order to be discharged, substitute a supervision order for the care order: s 39(4).

16.20 Orders pending appeals

Where a court dismisses an application for a care order and at that time the child is the subject of an interim care order, the court may make a care order to have effect subject to the directions included in the order: s 40(1). An order made under s 40 has effect only for such period, not exceeding the appeal period, as may be specified in the order: s 40(4).

16.21 Guardians *ad litem*

A guardian *ad litem* (*ad litem* = for the suit) is one appointed by the court to represent the interests of a child: see Order 80, r 2. For the purpose of any specified proceedings, the court will appoint a guardian *ad litem* for the child concerned unless satisfied that it is not necessary to do so in order to safeguard his interests: s 41(1). He is selected from a list of persons drawn up in accordance with SI 1991/2051. For removal of a guardian *ad litem*, see *Re H* (1993).

16.21.1 Appointment of solicitor

Where the child is not represented by a solicitor and any of the conditions mentioned in subsection (4) is satisfied, the court may appoint a solicitor to represent him: s 41(3). The conditions are that: no guardian *ad litem* has been appointed; the child has sufficient understanding to instruct a solicitor and wishes to do so: and it appears to the court that it would be in the child's best interests for him to be represented by a solicitor: s 41(4).

See *Re S (A Minor)* (1993), in which the Court of Appeal held that although a child's wishes are not to be discounted or dismissed simply because he is a child, the court would not permit a boy aged 11 to participate as a party without the Official Solicitor acting as his guardian *ad litem* in 'emotionally complex and highly fraught proceedings' between his parents as to his residence and contact, because in the view of the court, he will lack sufficient understanding, and the proceedings will require the application of an objective, experienced judgment such as the Official Solicitor and those whom he consults are able to supply. See also *L v L* (1994).

Rules of court may make provision as to the assistance which a guardian *ad litem* may be required to give to the court, consideration to be given by him to the question as to whether to apply for variation or discharge of an order, and participation in reviews conducted by the court: s 41(10).	16.21.2 Rules of court
A guardian *ad litem* has to be present at consideration of an oral request to withdraw care proceedings: *Re F* (1993).	16.21.3 Withdrawal of proceedings
Guardians *ad litem* must be – and must be seen to be – independent. In *R v Cornwall CC* (1992), the court quashed a decision by the director of social services of a county council which sought to restrict the time spent by guardians *ad litem* on children's cases. It was held that the director had exceeded his authority, had committed an abuse of his powers, and had interfered with the independence of guardians *ad litem*.	16.21.4 Independence of guardians *ad litem*
In *Re C (Children Act 1989: Expert Evidence)* (1994), the court suggested that guardians *ad litem* would be suitable co-ordinators to collate reports of expert witnesses in cases under ChA 1989 and to prepare schedules of the areas of agreement and disagreement. Guardians *ad litem* should consent to being appointed for a task of this nature.	16.21.5 Guardian *ad litem* as co-ordinator of expert evidence

Summary of Chapter 16

Care and Supervision Orders

Fundamental to Part IV is s 31(1), under which on application of any local authority or authorised person, the court may make an order placing a child in the care of a local authority or putting him under the *supervision* of a local authority or probation officer. An application under s 31 may be made on its own or in other family proceedings: s 31(4).

ChA 1989, Part IV

The child's welfare will be the court's paramount consideration. An order would be made with a minimum of delay.

The court must be satisfied, under s 31(2), that the child concerned is suffering or likely to suffer significant harm, and that the harm or likelihood of harm is attributable to the care given to the child, or that he is beyond parental control.

Threshold criteria

Where a care order is made it is the duty of the local authority to receive and keep the child in their care for its duration: s 33(1). During that period the local authority will have parental responsibility for the child. The local authority must allow a child in its care reasonable contact with his parents/guardian. The court may make an order refusing to allow contact between the child and a person mentioned in the order: s 34(2).

The care order

A supervision order may last for one year, but can be extended by the court so as to run beyond the end of a period of three years. The supervised child may be directed to live at a specified place for a specified time and participate in specified activities. The supervision order may include a requirement that the child be examined medically and/or psychologically.

The supervision order

Appeal lies to the High Court against the making of, or refusal to make, a supervision or care order: s 94(1).

On application of a local education authority an order may be made by the court placing the child under the supervision of an education authority: s 36(1). The order is issued only if the child is of compulsory school age and is not being properly educated.

The education supervision order

Interim care or supervision orders may be made for periods such as the court orders. Their renewal is not automatic: see *Re G* (1993).

Interim orders

Discharge and variation of care and supervision orders

Discharge and variation of care and supervision orders may be effected by the court on application of a person with parental responsibility for the child, the child himself, or a supervisor or local authority.

Guardians *ad litem*

A guardian *ad litem* is appointed by the court to represent the child's interests: see Order 80, r 2. Where the child is not represented by a solicitor, the court may appoint a solicitor to represent him: s 41(3). Guardians *ad litem* must be – and must be seen to be – independent: see *R v Cornwall CC* (1992).

Chapter 17

Short-Term Protection of Children at Risk

17.1 Essence of ChA 1989, Part V

Part V of the ChA 1989 is concerned with the need to protect *in the short term* children who may be at risk. The measures set out in Part V (ss 43–52) are, according to the Department of Health *Guidance*, 'short-term and time-limited, and may or may not lead to further action'.

Protective measures enunciated in Part V include: the Child Assessment Order (CAO); the Emergency Protection Order (EPO); revised powers of the police, including searches for children in specified premises; a duty of the local authority to investigate cases of suspected harm to children; powers of recovery of abducted children; and the provision of refuges for children at risk.

The legislative principles of this part of ChA 1989 were influenced by highly-publicised incidents relating to children at risk. *The Report of the Inquiry into Child Abuse in Cleveland*, 1987 (1988, Cmnd 412) and *A Child in Mind: Report of an Inquiry into the Death of Kimberley Carlile* (1987) drew attention to the need for an intensification of measures of protection for children. The procedures of the Child Assessment Order and the Emergency Protection Order were intended to provide assistance in the area of child protection.

17.2 The Child Assessment Order

The CAO, first proposed in the *Kimberley Carlile Report*, was considered by its advocates as satisfying the need for a 'half-way house' in cases of children who were thought to be at risk: the child considered to be at risk would be assessed without the need for his removal from the family. The aim of the procedure is *an assessment of the child, not his family*, as a step to his protection; it is not suitable for an emergency situation (for which case the EPO – see 17.4 below – is designed). The CAO can be made in relation to any child *under 18*.

17.2.1 Making a CAO

On the application of a local authority or authorised person (currently, the NSPCC), the court may make an order under s 43, if, but only if, it is satisfied that

- the applicant has reasonable cause to suspect that the child is suffering, or is likely to suffer, significant harm: s 43(1)(a);

- an assessment of the state of the child's health or development, or of the way in which he has been treated, is required to enable the applicant to determine whether or not the child is suffering, or is likely to suffer, significant harm: s 43(1)(b); *and*

- it is unlikely that such an assessment will be made, or be satisfactory, in the absence of an order under this section: s 43(1)(c).

17.2.2 The assessment

The term 'assessment' is not defined specifically in the Act. Given the general aim of s 43, it will necessarily involve an examination of the child's physical and/or mental state by qualified persons (eg, the family doctor, a local authority medical officer) and the evaluation of resulting data in accordance with appropriate professional skills and standards. Directions may be given by the court on any matter relating to the assessment: s 43(6).

17.2.3 Threshold principles

The minimum threshold criteria in s 43(1) must be satisfied (ie, the court must be satisfied of the 'reasonableness' of the applicant's case for suspecting that a child is suffering, or is likely to suffer, harm, etc) Then, consideration must be given to the general principles of s 1(1) – see 13.2 – ie, the welfare principle and the concept that making an order will be better for the child than making no order at all.

It will not be necessary to apply the statutory checklist of s 1(3) – see 13.5 – because proceedings under Part V are not included in the proceedings specified in s 1(4). Note, too, that an order under s 8 cannot be issued by the court in lieu of a CAO, since Part V proceedings are not within the definition of 'family proceedings'.

17.2.4 Giving notice of application

A person who makes an application for a CAO must take 'such steps as are reasonably practicable' to ensure that notice of the application is given, before the hearing of the application, to the following persons: the child's parents, any person who is not a parent of the child but has parental responsibility for him; any other person caring for the child; any person in whose favour a contact order is in force with respect to the child; any person who is allowed to have contact with the child under a s 34 order; the child: s 43(11).

17.2.5 Duration of the order

A CAO will specify the date by which the assessment is to begin, and shall have effect for such period, not exceeding seven days, beginning with that date, as may be specified in the order: s 43(5). There are no provisions for an extension of the period. (Whether a period of this length gives sufficient time for an appropriate diagnosis and assessment of the child's state has been questioned: see, eg, *Investigation under the Children Act 1989* by J Eekelaar [1990] Fam Law 486.) Note s 91(15), under which a further application for a CAO cannot be made within six months of the disposal of the previous application without leave of the court.

17.2.6 CAO and EPO

The court may treat an application under s 43 as an application for an EPO: s 43(3). Further, the court will not make a CAO if it is satisfied that there are grounds for making an EPO with respect to the child *and* that it should make an EPO rather than a CAO: s 43(4).

17.2.7 Effect of the order

The CAO has two specific effects. *First*, it imposes a duty on any person who is in a position to produce the child to produce him to such person as may be named in the order, and to comply with such directions relating to the assessment of the child as the court specifies in the order: s 43(6). *Secondly*, it authorises any person carrying out the assessment to do so in accordance with the terms of the order: s 43(7).

17.2.8 Right of the child to refuse assessment

Where the child is 'of sufficient understanding to make an informed decision', he may refuse to submit to a medical or psychiatric examination or other assessment: s 43(8). The Department of Health *Guidance* proposes that a child's guardian *ad litem* (see 16.21) may advise the court concerning the child's general level of understanding, provided that no pressure is put on the child so as to coerce him into agreeing to the making of an assessment.

17.2.9 Keeping the child away from home

It is not the purpose of a CAO (unlike an EPO) to remove the child from his home. The child may be kept away from home only in accordance with directions specified in the order, if it is necessary for purposes of the assessment, and for such period(s) as may be specified in the order: s 43(9). Where the child is to be kept away from home, the order will contain such directions as the court thinks fit concerning the contact that he must be allowed to have with other persons while away from home: s 43(10).

17.3 Purpose of the CAO: a summary

The Department of Health *Guidance* summarises the purpose of the CAO thus: 'The child assessment order, established by s 43, had no parallel in previous legislation. It deals with the single issue of enabling an assessment of the child to be made where significant harm is suspected but the child is not thought to be at immediate risk (requiring his removal, or keeping him in hospital), the local authority or authorised person considers that an assessment is required, and the parents or other persons responsible for him have refused to co-operate. Its purpose is to allow the local authority or authorised person to ascertain enough about the state of the child's health or development or the way in which he has been treated to decide what further action, if any, is required. It is less interventionist than the emergency protection order, interim care order and interim supervision order and should not be used where the circumstances of the case suggest that one of these orders would be more appropriate.'

17.4 The Emergency Protection Order

The Department of Health *Guidance* sets out the purpose of the EPO as enabling the child 'in a genuine emergency to be removed from where he is, or be kept where he is, if and only if this is what is necessary to provide immediate short-term protection'. The EPO (see ss 44–45) provides authorisation for a child's *immediate removal* from surroundings which are a danger, actual or potential, to him, or for his *detention in a safe place* in an emergency.

The provisions of s 44 follow the basis of the recommendations of the *Review of Child Care Law* (1985). The former 'place of safety orders' (see s 28 C&YPA 1969) had been heavily criticised because they were often granted without sufficient investigation. Section 44 seeks to link applications for an EPO with genuine emergencies only.

The Department of Health *Guidance* summarises the essence of the EPO: 'Emergency protection orders replace the much-criticised place of safety orders which could be obtained under a number of provisions in previous legislation. The purpose of the new order, as its name suggests, is to enable the child in a genuine emergency to be removed from where he is or be kept where he is, if and only if this is what is necessary to provide immediate short-term protection. Nearly every aspect of the new provisions, including the grounds for the order, its effect, opportunities for challenging it and duration, are different'.

17.5 No automatic making of an EPO

Even where the statutory grounds apply, the court will not automatically issue an EPO. The general welfare principle and the presumption of 'no-order' (see 13.4) must be considered by the court before the EPO is made.

17.6 Application by 'any person'

Where any person applies to the court for an EPO to be made under this section with respect to a child, the court may make the order if, but only if, it is satisfied that '(a) there is reasonable cause to believe that the child is likely to suffer significant harm if (i) he is not removed to accommodation provided by or on behalf of the applicant; or (ii) he does not remain in the place in which he is then being accommodated': s 44(1).

The *court* must be satisfied that the appropriate criteria have been met. It is the *futurity* of the significant harm which is relevant, ie, there must be a likelihood of the occurrence or recurrence of such harm.

17.6.1 Significant (future) harm

'Likely' is not defined in s 44. It would seem that where there is the slightest of chances that the child might be exposed to danger, the court would act so as not to allow the risk to be run.

17.6.2 'Likely'

In the case of an application made by *a local authority*, the court must be satisfied that enquiries are being made with respect to the child under s 47(1)(b), *and* those enquiries are being frustrated by access to the child being unreasonably refused to a person authorised to seek access and that the applicant has reasonable cause to believe that access to the child is required as a matter of urgency: s 44(1)(b)(ii).

17.7 **Application by a local authority**

Note that 'a person authorised to seek access' means, in the case of an application by a local authority, an officer of the local authority or a person authorised by the authority to act on their behalf in connection with the enquiries; or, in the case of an application by an authorised person (see 17.8 below), that person: s 44(2)(b).

An 'authorised person' means one who is authorised for the purposes of s 31 (see 16.4): s 44(2)(a). The court must be satisfied, where the application is made by 'an authorised person', that the applicant has reasonable cause to suspect that a child is suffering, or is likely to suffer, significant harm; that the applicant is making enquiries with respect to the child's welfare; and those enquiries are being frustrated by access to the child being unreasonably refused to a person authorised to seek access and the applicant has reasonable cause to believe that access to the child is required as a matter of urgency: s 44 (1)(c).

17.8 **Application by an 'authorised person'**

Application for an EPO will be heard in a magistrates' family proceedings court; it will not be transferred to a higher court: see Children (Allocation of Proceedings) Order 1991. Orders may be made by a single magistrate: Family Proceedings Court (Children Act 1989) Rules 1991, r 2(5)(a).

17.9 **General procedure**

17.9.1	*Ex parte* applications	Application may be made *ex parte* in an emergency. Leave of the clerk to the justices is required: r 4(4). Where an order is made *ex parte* it must be served on respondents within 48 hours of its having been made: r 21(8).
17.9.2	Identification of parents	Any person seeking access to a child in relation to enquiries (see s 44(1)), and any person who purports to be authorised to do so, shall, on being asked to do so, produce some duly authorised document as evidence that he is such a person: s 44(3). Further, where an EPO does not name the child, it must describe him as clearly as possible: s 44(3).
17.10	**Orders taken over by a local authority**	Where an application for an EPO is made by someone other than the local authority, that authority may decide to have the order transferred to them: s 52(3)(c). See the Emergency Protection Order (Transfer of Responsibilities) Regulations 1991 (SI 1991/1414); reg 4 states that the local authority must have regard to the wishes and needs of the child and the likely effect of a change of circumstances on him.
17.11	**Effects of the EPO**	The general effects of the EPO are stated in s 44(4), (5). The order is concerned, essentially, with the removal of the child to accommodation or the prevention of his removal from accommodation provided on behalf of, or by, the applicant.
17.11.1	Authorisation, etc	An EPO operates as a direction to comply with a request to produce the child to the applicant. It authorises removal of the child, or prevents his removal, and gives parental responsibility for the child to the applicant: s 44(4).
17.11.2	Applicant's duties	Where an EPO is in force, the applicant shall take, and shall only take, such action in meeting his parental responsibility for the child as is reasonably required to safeguard or promote the child's welfare (having regard in particular to the duration of the order): s 44(5).
17.11.3	Offences	A person who intentionally obstructs any person exercising his powers under s 44 to remove, or prevent the removal of a child, is guilty of an offence: s 44(16).
17.12	**Directions**	Where the court makes an EPO it may give appropriate directions concerning contact (or no contact) between the child and any named person, and the examination or other assessment of the child: s 44 (6).
17.12.1	Refusal by child	Where any direction is given under s 44(6) (concerning examination or assessment), the child may, if he is of sufficient understanding to make an informed decision, refuse to submit to the examination or assessment: s 44(7).

A direction under subsection (6) may be given when the EPO is made or at any time while it is in force; and varied at any time on the application of any person falling within any class of person prescribed by rules of court: s 44(9).

17.12.2 Directions under subsection (6)

Where an EPO has been made, the applicant shall, subject to directions under subsection (6), allow the child reasonable contact with: his parents, a non-parent who has parental responsibility for him; any person with whom he was living immediately before the order was made; any person in whose favour a contact order is in force with respect to him; any person allowed to have contact with the child by virtue of s 34 (see 16.10); and any person acting on behalf of any of those persons: s 44(13).

17.12.3 Contact of child with parents, etc

Where an EPO is in force and it appears to the applicant that it is safe for the child to be returned, or to be allowed to be removed from a specified place, he shall return the child (or allow him to be removed): s 44(10).

17.13 Return of child

An EPO is effective for such a period, not exceeding eight days, as may be specified: s 45(1). But where the last day is a public holiday it can be extended to the next day which is not a holiday: s 45(2). An EPO can be extended once only: s 45(6). Any person who has parental responsibility for a child as the result of an EPO, and is entitled to apply for a care order with respect to the child, may apply for an extension: s 44(4).

17.14 Duration of EPO

Any of the following may apply to the court for the discharge of an EPO: the child; a parent of his; a non-parent who has parental responsibility for him; any person with whom he was living immediately before the making of the order: s 45(8). No application for discharge will be heard by the court before the expiry of a period of 72 hours beginning with the making of the order: s 45(9).

17.15 Discharge of EPO

No appeal may be made against the making or refusal to make an EPO, the extension of, or refusal to extend, the period during which such an order is to have effect, the discharge of, or refusal to discharge, such an order, or the giving of, or refusal to give, any direction in connection with such an order: s 45(10), substituted by Sch 16, para 19 of the Courts and Legal Services Act 1990. See *Essex CC v F* (1993) (no appeal against the grant or refusal of an EPO or against a direction made in connection with the order).

17.16 Police protection

Section 46 of the 1989 Act empowers the police to act *immediately*, and without a court order, where a child is in need of protection. (The section is a replacement for s 28(2) C&YPA 1969.) Under s 46(1), where a constable has reasonable cause to believe that a child would otherwise be likely to suffer significant harm, he may remove the child to suitable accommodation and keep him there; or take such steps as are reasonable to ensure that the child's removal from any hospital, or other place, in which he is then being accommodated is prevented: s 46(1). A child with respect to whom a constable has exercised his powers under this section is referred to as 'having been taken into police protection': s 46(2).

17.16.1 Duties of the police under s 46(3)

After a child has been taken into police protection, the police officer concerned will, as soon as is reasonably practicable: inform the local authority within whose area the child was found of the steps taken with respect to the child; inform the child of the steps which have been, and may be, taken; take steps to discover the child's feelings and wishes: s 46(3). He must inform the child's parents, non-parents with parental responsibility for him, and any other person with whom the child was living, of the steps being taken under this section: s 46(4).

17.16.2 Application for EPO

While a child is being kept in police protection, a designated officer may apply for an EPO in respect of the child: s 46(7). While the child is being kept in police protection, the designated officer shall do what is reasonable for the purpose of safeguarding the child's welfare: s 46(9).

17.16.3 Release of child

On completing enquiries concerning the child, the officer conducting them shall release the child from police protection unless he considers that there is still reasonable cause for believing that the child would be likely to suffer significant harm if released: s 46(5). No child may be kept in police protection for more than 72 hours: s 46(6).

17.17 Investigation by local authority

Under s 47, local authorities have duties to make investigations of certain types of case involving suspected harm to children. These duties are additional to those under s 37.

Where a local authority are informed that a child who lives, or is found in the area, is the subject of an emergency protection order, or in police protection, or they have reasonable cause to suspect that a child who lives, or is found, in their area is suffering, or is likely to suffer, significant harm, the authority shall make enquiries to enable them to decide whether to take action to promote the child's welfare: s 47(1).

Where enquiries are made and it appears to the authority that access to the child is being refused, the authority may apply for an EPO, CAO, a care or supervision order with respect to the child: s 47(6).

17.18 Powers to assist in discovery of children

Where it appears to the court making an EPO that adequate information concerning the child's whereabouts is not available to the applicant for the order, but is available to another person, the order may include a provision requiring that other person to disclose any information he may have as to the child's whereabouts: s 48(1). No person will be excused from complying with such a requirement on the ground that complying might incriminate him (or his spouse) of an offence: s 48(2). An EPO may authorise entry into and search of premises: s 48(3). It is an offence to intentionally obstruct such a search of premises: s 48(7).

17.19 Abducting children in care

A person is guilty of an offence if, knowingly and without lawful authority or reasonable excuse, he takes a child to whom this section applies away from the responsible person, keeps such a child away from him, or induces, assists or incites such a child to run away or stay away from the responsible person: s 49(1). This section applies to a child in care, or who is the subject of an EPO, or in police protection: s 49(2). 'Responsible person' means, in this context, one who for the time being has care of a child by virtue of the care order or EPO: s 49(2). For abduction generally, see 23.14.

17.19.1 Recovery of abducted children

The court may make a 'recovery order' where it appears that there is reason to believe that a child to whom this section applies (see s 49) has been unlawfully taken away or is being unlawfully kept away from the responsible person; has run away or is staying away from the responsible person, or is missing: s 50(1).

17.19.2 Who may apply for a recovery order

The court will make a recovery order only on the application of any person who has parental responsibility for the child by virtue of a care order or EPO; or where the child is in police protection, the designated officer: s 50(4).

17.19.3 Features of the recovery order

A recovery order operates as a direction to produce the child on request to an authorised person and authorises the removal of the child by an authorised person. Additionally, it authorises a constable to enter and search premises, using reasonable force if necessary: s 50(3). It is an offence to intentionally obstruct an authorised person exercising a power to remove a child from premises: s 50(9).

17.20	**Refuges for children at risk**	Section 51(1) empowers the Secretary of State to issue certificates to voluntary homes or registered children's homes so that they are excepted from offences relating to the 'harbouring of children' for whom they are providing a refuge.
17.21	**A note on self-incrimination in relation to proceedings under Part V**	In any proceedings in which a court is hearing an application for an order under Part IV or V, no person is to be excused from giving evidence on any matter or answering any question put to him in the course of his giving evidence, on the ground that doing so might incriminate him or his spouse of an offence: s 98(1). See *Re K (Minors) (Care Proceedings: Disclosure)* (1994).

Summary of Chapter 17

Short-Term Protection of Children at Risk

Part V of ChA 1989 is concerned with the importance of protecting in the short term children who may be at risk. Protective measures in Part V include Child Assessment Order, Emergency Protection Order, revised police powers, duty of local authorities to investigate suspected harm to children, powers of recovery of abducted children, provision of refuges for children at risk.

ChA 1989, Part V

The order aims to make an assessment of a child (not his family) as a step to his protection. The child in question must be under 18; the order may be applied for by a local authority or authorised person, under s 43. The court must be satisfied that the child is suffering or is likely to suffer significant harm; an assessment will be made of his health, development or of the way he has been treated. The court must be satisfied with the 'reasonableness' of the applicant's case; the 'welfare principle' will be considered and the 'non-intervention principle' taken into account. An order has effect for seven days.

The effect of the order is to impose a duty on persons to produce the child and to comply with directions related to assessment. A child of sufficient understanding may refuse to submit to assessment: s 43(8).

Child Assessment Order

The order will be issued where the court is satisfied that there is reasonable cause to believe that the child is likely to suffer 'significant harm' if not removed to other accommodation, or if he does not remain in the place in which he is then being accommodated: s 44(1). Application may be made by a local authority or 'authorised person' (NSPCC). An order may be taken over by a local authority: s 52(3)(c). The order will authorise removal of a child or prevent his removal; parental responsibility will be given to the applicant: s 44(4).

The order is effective for a period not exceeding eight days. It may be discharged on application to the court by the child, a parent, non-parent with parental responsibility.

Emergency Protection Order

Section 46 of ChA 1989 empowers the police to act immediately, without a court order, where a child is in need of protection. A constable may remove the child to suitable accommodation.

Police protection

Discovery of children

An emergency protection order may include a provision requiring that information be disclosed as to a child's whereabouts: s 48(1). The emergency protection order may authorise entry into and search of premises: s 48(3).

Recovery of abducted children

It is an offence to take away a child, or to induce him to run away or stay away: s 49(2). This section applies to a child in care or to one who is the subject of an emergency protection order or in police protection: s 49(2).

A recovery order may be made in relation to an abducted child: s 50(1).

Local authority duties

Local authorities have the duty to investigate where they have reason to believe that a child is suffering or is likely to suffer significant harm: s 47(1). Refuges for children at risk may be provided: see s 51(1).

Chapter 18

Community, Voluntary and Registered Homes for Children

Parts VI, VII and VIII of ChA 1989 are concerned with the legal regulation of institutions which look after children who are living away from their homes. Part VI (ss 53-58) deals with *community homes*; Part VII (ss 59-62) regulates *voluntary homes*, ie, those under the management of voluntary organisations; Part VIII (ss 63-65) seeks to regulate *registered children's homes* (homes of this nature, which are private homes, were largely unregulated before the 1989 legislation). The fundamental policy behind these sections of the 1989 Act rests on acceptance of the importance of protecting children in residential care by ensuring, as far as is possible, *appropriate standards of treatment* of children and *careful control* of the personnel and conditions of residential homes.

18.1 Residential care of children

Local authorities are expected, under s 53(1), to make appropriate arrangements for ensuring that community homes are available for the care and accommodation of children looked after by the authorities and for purposes connected with the welfare of children (whether or not looked after by them). Local authorities in making these arrangements must have regard to the need for accommodation of different descriptions and the requirements of different types of child: s 53(2).

18.2 Community homes provided by local authorities

A community home may be a home provided, managed, equipped and maintained by a local authority; or provided by a voluntary organisation but in respect of which a local authority *and* the organisation propose that, in accordance with an instrument of management, the management, equipment and maintenance of the home shall be the responsibility of the local authority; or so propose that the management, equipment and maintenance of the home shall be the responsibility of the voluntary organisation: s 53(3).

18.2.1 Nature of the community home

Where a local authority is to be responsible for the management of a community home provided by a voluntary organisation, the authority is required to designate the home as a 'controlled community home': s 53(4). Where a voluntary organisation is to be responsible for the management of a community home provided by the organisation, the local authority will designate the home as an 'assisted community home': s 53(5).

18.2.2 Homes provided by voluntary organisations

18.3 Management and conduct of community homes

The Secretary of State is empowered, under Sch 4, para 1(1), to make by order an instrument of management providing for the constitution of a body of managers for any home which is designated as a controlled or assisted community home (as amended by Sch 20 Courts and Legal Services Act 1990). Where an instrument of management is in force in relation to a home, the home is to be known as 'a controlled community home' or 'an assisted community home', according to its designation: para 1(8).

An instrument of management may contain provisions specifying the nature and purpose of the home to which it applies, and it may require a specified number or proportion of places within the home to be made available to local authorities and to any other body specified in the instrument: para 2(3).

18.3.1 Controlled and assisted community homes

The local authority has responsibility, as specified in the instrument of management, for the management, equipment and maintenance of a controlled community home: para 3(1). The functions of a home's responsible body are to be exercised only through the management: para 3(4). Proper accounts must be kept by the managers with respect to the home: para 3(15).

18.3.2 Regulations concerning community homes

The Secretary of State may make regulations concerning the placing of children in community homes, the conduct of those homes, and for securing the welfare of children in such homes: para 4(1). The regulations may: prescribe standards to which the premises must conform; impose requirements concerning accommodation, staff, equipment, provide for control and discipline of the children in the homes; impose requirements concerning records, facilities for religious instruction: para 4(2).

18.3.3 Directions concerning use of premises

A very important power is given to the Secretary of State under s 54(1). Where it appears to the Secretary of State that any premises used for the purposes of a community home are unsuitable for those purposes, or the conduct of a community home is not in accordance with regulations, or is otherwise unsatisfactory, he may give directions preventing use of the premises for the purposes of a community home: s 54(1).

18.3.4 Disputes concerning controlled and assisted community homes

Disputes may arise between local authorities and other organisations concerning children within the homes; in such cases the Secretary of State may intervene: s 55(1). The Secretary of State, in determining the dispute, may give appropriate directions to parties to the dispute: s 55(3).

The voluntary organisation by which a controlled or assisted community home is provided may not cease providing the home except after giving the Secretary of State at least *two years' written notice*: s 56(1). Where the notice is given and *not* withdrawn before the date specified in it, the instrument of management pertaining to the home ceases to have effect on that date and the home will then cease to be a controlled or assisted community home: s 56(3).

18.3.5 Discontinuance of voluntary organisation of homes

A local authority specified in the instrument of management for a controlled or assisted community home may give the Secretary of State not less than two years' written notice of intention to withdraw their designation of a home as a controlled or assisted community home: s 57(1). The home will cease to be a community home where appropriate notice has been given and not withdrawn: s 57(5).

18.3.6 Closure of community home by a local authority

The 1989 Act defines a 'voluntary home' as meaning any home or other institution providing care and accommodation for children which is carried on by a voluntary organisation, but does not include a nursing, mental nursing or residential care home, a school, hospital, community home, institution or home provided, equipped and maintained by the Secretary of State: s 60(3). A 'voluntary organisation' means a body (other than a public or local authority) whose activities are not carried on for profit: s 105(1).

18.4 **Voluntary homes and voluntary organisations**

Where a voluntary organisation provides accommodation for a child, they shall do so by placing him with a family, a relative or any other suitable person; maintaining him in a voluntary or community home, or a registered children's home, or in a home provided by the Secretary of State, or by making their own appropriate arrangements: s 59(1).

18.4.1 Provision of accommodation by voluntary organisations

The Secretary of State may make regulations concerning the placing of children with foster parents by voluntary organisations: s 59(2).

18.4.2 Foster parents

The general rule is that a voluntary home is not to be carried on *unless registered with the Secretary of State*: s 60(1). (See also s 2(6) of the Registered Homes (Amendment) Act 1991.)

18.5 **The registration and regulation of voluntary homes**

Schedule 5, Part I, of the 1989 Act sets out in precise terms the rules concerning the registration of voluntary homes. Application is to be made for registration by persons intending to carry on the home to which the application relates. It is to be made in the manner prescribed by the Secretary of State: Sch 5, para 1(1). Registration will be cancelled if the Secretary of State

18.5.1 Rules of registration

is of the opinion that the conduct of the home is not in accordance with regulations or is otherwise unsatisfactory: para 1(4). It is an offence to carry on a voluntary home in contravention of s 60 or of a condition to which the registration of the home is for the time being subject: para 1(5). See also s 19 CJPOA 1994.

18.5.2 Registration procedure

Where the Secretary of State intends to grant an application for registration, he will give notice of the conditions of the grant: para 2(1). Notice of intention to refuse a grant will be given: s 2(3).

18.5.3 Representations

Fourteen days will be allowed to applicants during which they may make representations to the Secretary of State: para 3(1). The representations may be made, at the option of the person making them, in writing or orally: para 3(4).

18.5.4 Regulations

Schedule 5, Part II, sets out the rules relating to the regulations intended to cover the conduct of voluntary homes. The regulations involve standards of the premises, requirements concerning accommodation, staff and equipment, discipline and control, records, and a prohibition on the use of accommodation 'for the purpose of restricting the liberty of children in such homes': para 7(2). The regulations may provide that a contravention of, or failure to comply with, any specified provision of the regulations without reasonable excuse shall be an offence against the regulations: para 7(3).

18.6 Duties of voluntary organisations

Section 61 imposes upon voluntary organisations the type of duty imposed upon local authorities involved with the problems of children.

Where a child is accommodated by or on behalf of a voluntary organisation, it shall be the duty of the organisation to safeguard and promote his welfare; to make such use of the services and facilities available for children cared for by their own parents as appears to the organisation reasonable in his case; and to advise, befriend and assist him with a view to promoting his welfare when he ceases to be so accommodated: s 61(1). Before making decisions concerning such a child, the organisation shall ascertain the wishes and feelings of the child, his parents, non-parents who have parental responsibility for him, and any other person whose wishes and feelings are considered relevant by the organisation: s 61(2).

When arriving at a decision, the organisation is expected to give due consideration, having regard to the child's age and understanding, his ascertained wishes and feelings, his religious persuasion, racial origin, cultural and linguistic background: s 61(3).

Under s 62(1), a local authority must be satisfied that a voluntary organisation providing accommodation within the authority's area for a child, are 'satisfactorily safeguarding and promoting the welfare of children so provided with accommodation'. The Secretary of State will make appropriate regulations concerning visits to be made to children by officers of an authority: s 62(3). Any person authorised by a local authority may enter children's accommodation for the purpose of inspecting the premises: s 62(6).

18.7 Duties of local authorities

A registered children's home means, in the 1989 Act, a children's home which is registered under Part VIII of the Act: s 63(8). The term 'children's home' is defined precisely: it means 'a home which provides (or usually provides or is intended to provide) care and accommodation wholly or mainly for more than three children at any one time'; but it does *not* include a home exempted by regulations or by virtue of exemptions in s 63: s 63(3).

18.8 Registered children's homes

A home is *not* a 'children's home' for purposes of Part VIII, however, if it is a community, voluntary, or residential home, a home provided by the Secretary of State, or a school (but see below).

Where children are accommodated at an independent school, it is classified as a children's home if, in each of the two previous years before the relevant date, accommodation (at the school or under the proprietor's arrangements) was provided for more than three children for 295 days in the year, or it is intended that such accommodation be provided for three or more children for 295 days of the year: s 63(6) substituted by s 292 of the Education Act 1993.

No child shall be cared for and provided with accommodation in a children's home *unless the home is registered under Part VIII*: s 63(1). Where any child is at any time cared for and accommodated in a children's home which is *not* a registered children's home, the person carrying on the home shall be guilty of an offence: s 63(10).

18.8.1 General rules

Persons who are disqualified (under s 68) from fostering children privately may not carry on, or be otherwise concerned in the management of, or have any financial interest in a children's home unless the disqualification has been disclosed to the responsible authority and those persons have their consent: s 65(1). No person shall employ a disqualified person in a children's home unless disclosure has been made to the responsible authority and they have given their consent: s 65(2). It is an offence to contravene subsections (1) or (2): s 65(4).

18.8.2 Persons disqualified from carrying on or being employed in children's homes

18.9 Registration of children's homes

Applications for the registration of a children's home must be made by a person carrying on, or intending to carry on, the home; and to the local authority for the area in which the home is, or will be, situated: Sch 6, para 1(1). The application will be refused if the authority are not satisfied that the applicant has complied with the appropriate requirements: para 8.

18.9.1 Conditions imposed on registration

Local authorities may impose conditions on an application for registration: para 2(2). Where conditions imposed (or varied) are not complied with by the person carrying on the home he shall be guilty of an offence in the absence of a reasonable excuse: para 2(3). Registrations are reviewed annually: para 3(2).

18.9.2 Cancellation of registration

Application for cancellation of registration may be made at any time by the person carrying on a registered children's home: para 4(1). Further, the responsible authority may determine that registration be cancelled where the person carrying on the home has been convicted of an offence under this Part of the Schedule, or where any other person has been convicted of such an offence in relation to the home: para 4(4).

Appeals against a decision of the local authority under Part VIII lie to a Registered Homes Tribunal. On appeal, the Tribunal may confirm the decision of the local authority or direct that it shall not have effect: para 8.

18.10 Regulations concerning children's homes

Sch 6, para 10, states that the Secretary of State may make regulations as to the placing of children in registered children's homes, as to the conduct of those homes, and for securing the welfare of the children in such homes. The regulations may cover, eg, standards of accommodation, staffing, discipline, provision of information, etc.

It is the duty of the person carrying on a children's home to safeguard and promote the children's welfare, to make available appropriate services and facilities and to advise, assist and befriend children with a view to promoting their welfare after they cease to be accommodated in the home: s 64(1).

18.11 Inspection of children's homes

Part XI of the 1989 Act (ss 80-84) is a re-enactment of the Child Care Act 1980, ss 74, 75. It empowers the Secretary of State to inspect certain types of premises in which there are children who are being cared for. These premises include: children's homes; premises in which a child who is being looked after by or on behalf of a local education authority or voluntary organisation is living; premises in which a child who is being accommodated by or on behalf of a health authority or NHS trust is living; premises on which any person is acting as a child minder (see 19.2.2): s 80(1).

The Secretary of State may require information concerning the premises and children living there, and may call for appropriate records: s 80(4). Additionally, he may arrange for the inspection of children living on the premises: s 80(6).

It is an offence for any person intentionally to obstruct an official exercising his powers of inspection under the section: s 80(10).

18.12 Inquiries

The Secretary of State may hold an inquiry (in private, if he so directs) related to any matter concerning a registered children's home or voluntary home: s 81(1).

18.13 Default power of Secretary of State

Section 84(1) provides a new power enabling the Secretary of State to issue a direction, which is enforceable by mandamus, where he is satisfied that a local authority is in default of its duties under the 1989 Act. The Secretary of State will give his reasons for making the order, which will contain appropriate directions for the purpose of ensuring that the duty is complied with: s 84(2), (3).

18.14 A note on the welfare of children accommodated in independent schools

It is the duty of the proprietor of any independent school (see 18.8 above) which provides accommodation for any child; and any person who is not the proprietor of such a school but who is responsible for conducting it, to safeguard and promote the child's welfare: s 87(1). Subsection (1) does *not* apply in relation to a school which is a children's home or a residential care home (other than a small home – see Registered Homes (Amendment) Act 1991, s 1).

The local authority has the duty, where accommodation is provided for a child by an independent school within their area, to take steps to enable them to determine whether the child's welfare is adequately safeguarded and promoted while he is accommodated by the school: s 87(4).

For inspection of independent schools in relation to the welfare of children, see s 87A, inserted by s 38 of the Deregulation and Contracting Out Act 1994.

Summary of Chapter 18

Community, Voluntary and Registered Homes for Children

Parts VI, VII and VIII are concerned with the legal regulation of institutions which look after children who are living away from their homes. As far as possible, appropriate standards of treatment of children should be ensured, and personnel and conditions of residential homes controlled.

ChA 1989, Parts VI, VII and VIII

Local authorities should make appropriate arrangements for ensuring that community homes are available for the care and accommodation of children looked after by them: s 53(1).

Community homes provided by local authorities

Where a voluntary organisation is responsible for the management of a community home, it will be designated as a 'controlled community home': s 53(4).

The Secretary of State may make an instrument of management providing for the constitution of a managing body for a community home. The nature and purpose of the home will be specified, details of management, equipment and maintenance will be specified and a stated number of places may be made available to local authorities.

Management and conduct of community homes

The Secretary of State may prevent the use of premises for a community home where he considers that premises are unsuitable or conduct of the home is unsatisfactory: s 54(1). A local authority may withdraw their designation of a home as a controlled or assisted community home: s 57(1).

A 'voluntary home' means a home or institution providing care and accommodation for children carried on by a voluntary organisation; it does not include a nursing, residential care home, community home. Voluntary organisations may provide accommodation for a child by placing him with a family, relative or other suitable person, or by making their own arrangements: s 59(1).

Voluntary homes and voluntary organisations

Voluntary homes must be registered with the Secretary of State: s 60(1).

Where a child is accommodated by or on behalf of a voluntary organisation, there is a duty imposed on the organisation to safeguard and promote his welfare and to advise, befriend and assist him: s 61(1). Visits may be made to the child by officers of a local authority: s 62(3).

Duties of voluntary organisations

Registered children's homes

The term 'children's home' is one which provides care and accommodation wholly or mainly for more than three children at any one time: s 63(3). Registration must be effected under Part VIII of the 1989 Act. Certain persons are disqualified from carrying on or being employed in children's homes. See s 65(1).

Conditions may be imposed on registration; it is an offence to fail to comply with such conditions: Sch 6, para 2 (3).

The Secretary of State may hold an inquiry (in private, if he so directs) related to matters arising from the conduct of a registered children's home: s 81(1).

Chapter 19

Fostering Children; Child Minding and Day Care

19.1 Background

This chapter outlines the main provisions of ChA 1989, Parts IX and X. Part IX (ss 66-70) is concerned with local authority overall control of private arrangements for fostering children under 16 (or, in some cases, under 18: see 19.3 below). Part X and Sch 9 regulate child-minding and day care for young children, replacing the generally unsatisfactory Nurseries and Child Minders Regulation Act 1948.

19.2 Local authority foster placements

In contrast to the arrangements for the private fostering of children is the system of *local authority foster parents* which is covered by s 23 of the 1989 Act. Briefly, public or local foster-parents are persons with whom a child has been placed under s 23(2)(a), including a family, a relative of the child, or any other suitable person, 'on such terms as to payment by the authority and otherwise as the authority may determine'. Persons falling within s 23(4) include a parent of the child, a non-parent who has parental responsibility for the child, or, where the child is in care and there was a residence order in force with respect to him immediately before the care order was made, a person in whose favour the residence order was made. See the Foster Placement (Children) Regulations 1991 (SI 1991/910); 14.11, 14.12.

Note that under s 9(3), a person who is, or was at any time within the last six months, a local authority foster parent of a child, may not apply for leave to apply for a s 8 order with respect to that child, unless he has the consent of the authority, or is a relative of the child, or the child has lived with him for at least three years preceding the application.

19.3 Private foster parents

Private foster parents are defined by implication in s 66(1): 'In this Part – (a) a 'privately fostered child' means a child who is under the age of sixteen and who is cared for, and provided with accommodation by, someone other than (i) a parent of his; (ii) a person who is not a parent of his but who has parental responsibility for him; or (iii) a relative of his; and (b) "to foster a child privately" means to look after the child in circumstances in which he is a privately fostered child as defined by this section'.

Note that in the case of a disabled child, subsection 1(a) has effect as if for *16*, there were substituted *18:* s 66(4).

19.3.1 Relatives

The term 'relative', for purposes of this part of the Act, means specifically a grandparent, brother, sister, uncle or aunt (full, or half blood or by affinity) or step-parent: s 105(1).

19.3.2 Exclusions from the category of 'fostered child'

Under s 66(2), a child is *not* a 'privately fostered child' if the person caring for and accommodating him has done so for a period of less than 28 days, and does not intend to do so for any longer period. Under Sch 8, para 1, a child is *not* a privately fostered child while being looked after by a local authority. Nor is he to be considered as a privately fostered child while he is in the care of any person in premises in which a parent of his, a non-parent who has parental control, or a relative who has assumed responsibility for his care, is for the time being living: para 2(1). He is not a privately fostered child while he is placed in the care of a person who proposes to adopt him or while he is a 'protected child' (see AA 1976, s 32).

19.4 Power of local authority to impose requirements

Under Sch 8, para 6, where a person is fostering any child privately or proposes to foster any child privately, the local authority may impose requirements (which may be limited to a particular child or class of child) concerning

- number, age, sex of children who may be privately fostered by him;
- standards of accommodation, equipment to be provided;
- arrangements concerning health and safety;
- arrangements concerning care.

19.5 Welfare of privately fostered children

Under s 67(1), it is the duty of every local authority to satisfy themselves that the welfare of privately fostered children within their area is being satisfactorily safeguarded and promoted and to secure that such advice is given to those caring for them as appears to the authority to be needed. The Secretary of State may make regulations concerning visits by local authority officers to the children: s 67(2). Premises and children residing there may be inspected by the local authority officer at any reasonable time: s 67(3).

Where a local authority is not satisfied that the welfare of a privately fostered child within their area is being 'satisfactorily safeguarded or promoted', they shall, unless they consider that it would not be in the child's best interests, take steps to ensure that care and accommodation of the child is undertaken by his parent, a non-parent with parental responsibility for him, or a relative: s 67(5).

The Secretary of State issues regulations concerning the circumstances, manner and form of notification of fostering: Sch 8, para 7(1). Persons who propose to be involved directly or indirectly with a private fostering must notify the appropriate authority. Any person who is fostering a child privately or is proposing to do so, must notify the appropriate authority of any offence of which he has been convicted: para 7(2)(e). Changes of address must also be notified.

19.6 Notification of fostering

Persons who are aggrieved by any requirements imposed by the local authority in relation to private fostering or prohibitions under ss 68, 69, may make an appeal within 14 days of being informed of any requirement, refusal, prohibition, etc: para 8(1), (2). An appeal may result in a cancellation of a requirement or prohibition, or a variation: para 8(4).

19.7 Appeals

No advertisement indicating that a person will undertake, or will arrange for, a child to be privately fostered may be published unless it states that person's name and address: para 10.

19.8 Prohibition of advertisements

Under s 68(1), unless he has disclosed the fact to the appropriate local authority and obtained their written consent, a person shall not foster a child privately if he is disqualified from doing so by regulations made under this section by the Secretary of State. A person will be disqualified where an order specified in the regulations has been made with respect to him, or, eg, where he has been convicted of a specified offence or placed on probation or discharged absolutely or conditionally for such an offence, or his rights and powers with respect to a child have been vested in an authority under a specified enactment: s 68(2).

19.9 Disqualifications

Unless he has disclosed the fact to the appropriate local authority and obtained their written consent, a person shall not foster a child privately if he lives in the same household as a person who is himself prevented from fostering a child by s 68(1), or he lives in a household at which such a person is employed: s 68(3).

Where the authority refuses to give consent under s 68, they must give written reasons for the refusal and inform the applicant of his right to appeal under Sch 8 and the time within which he may do so: s 68(4).

Where a local authority is of the opinion that an individual is not a suitable person to foster a child, or the premises in which

19.10 Power to prohibit private fostering

the child will be, or is being, accommodated are not suitable, or it would be prejudicial to the child's welfare for him to continue to be accommodated by that person on those premises, the authority may impose a prohibition on him under subsection (3): s 69(2).

A prohibition imposed on any person under this subsection may prohibit him from fostering privately any child in any premises within the area of the local authority, any child in premises specified in the prohibition, or a child identified in the prohibition, in premises specified in the prohibition: s 69(3).

The prohibition may be cancelled by the local authority of their own motion, or on an application by the person prohibited, if they are satisfied that the prohibition is no longer justified: s 69(4).

19.11 Offences

The following offences are among those noted under s 70: where a person fails to give specified information, or provides false or misleading information; where he refuses to allow a privately fostered child to be visited by a duly authorised officer of a local authority; where he intentionally obstructs another in the exercise of powers under s 67(3); where he accommodates a privately fostered child in premises in contravention of a prohibition.

19.12 Child minding and day care

The 1989 Act seeks to regulate activities under the general headings of 'child minding' and 'day care'. All child minders and day carers are now recorded on a unified register; the maximum age of children to whom the registration requirement relates is now fixed at eight; appropriate standards must be complied with, and local authorities must act where child minding and day care are below those standards.

19.12.1 The register

Every local authority shall keep a register of persons who act as child minders on domestic premises within the authority's area; and persons who provide day care for children under the age of eight on premises (other than domestic premises) within that area: s 71(1). The register, which may be computerised, must be open to inspection by the public at all reasonable times: s 71(15).

19.12.2 'Child minder', 'day care' defined

A person acts as a 'child minder' if he looks after one or more children under the age of eight, for reward, and the period, or the total of the periods, which he spends so looking after children in any day exceeds two hours; and a person does not provide 'day care' for children unless the period, or the total of the periods, during which children are looked after exceeds two hours in any day: s 71(2).

The term 'child minder' is not to be applied to a person looking after a child where that person is the child's parent or relative, or one who has parental responsibility for the child, or is the child's foster parent: s 71(4).

For the purposes of this part of the Act, a person acts as a 'nanny' for a child if she is employed to look after the child by the child's parent, a non-parent with parental responsibility for him, or a relative who has assumed responsibility for his care: s 71(13). Where a person is employed as a 'nanny' for a child, she does not act as a child minder when looking after that child wholly or mainly in her employers' home: s 71(5).

There may be circumstances in which a local authority will *refuse to register* a person who has applied for registration under s 71(1).

19.12.3 Refusal of registration

Registration will be refused where the local authority are satisfied that the applicant or any person looking after, or likely to be looking after, any children on premises on which the applicant is, or is likely to be, child minding, is not fit to look after children under the age of eight: s 71(7).

Registration may be refused where the local authority are satisfied that any person living, or likely to be living, at any premises on which the applicant is, or is likely to be, child minding; or any person employed, or likely to be employed, on those premises, is not fit to be in the proximity of children under eight: s 71(8).

Registration is likely to be refused where the premises involved are 'not fit to be used for looking after children under the age of eight': s 71(11).

Under Sch 9, para 2, no person may be registered under s 71 where he is disqualified under regulations made by the Secretary of State. Such regulations provide for disqualification under the following circumstances, for example:

19.12.4 Disqualification from registration

- an order of a prescribed kind has been made with respect to him;
- he has at any time been refused registration under Part X or any other prescribed enactment or had his registration cancelled;
- he has been convicted of a prescribed offence;
- his rights and powers concerning a child have been vested in some prescribed body.

No person who is disqualified may provide day care unless he has disclosed this fact to the local authority and obtained their written consent: para 2(4).

19.13 Requirements imposed on child minders

Under s 72(1), registration of a child minder may be accompanied by requirements imposed by a local authority.

The authority may specify the maximum number of children, or the maximum number of children within specified age groups, that may be looked after when acting as a child minder: s 72(2)(a). He may be required to ensure that premises and equipment are maintained and kept safe: s 72(2)(b). He may be required to keep records of children on the premises, assistants and 'any person living, or likely at any time to be living, at those premises': s 72(2)(c).

19.14 Cancellation of registration

A local authority may at any time cancel the registration of a person who acts as a child minder if it appears to them that the circumstances of the case are such that they would be justified in refusing registration and the person is seriously inadequate (or the premises are inadequate), or that there has been a contravention of a requirement imposed under ss 72, 73.

Under s 75(1) ('Protection of children in an emergency'), if a local authority apply to the court for an order cancelling a registered person's registration or varying a requirement or imposing an additional requirement, and it appears to the court that a child who is being, or may be, looked after by that person or (as the case may be) in accordance with the provision for day care made by that person, is suffering, or is likely to suffer *significant harm*, the court may make the order. An application under subsection (1) may be made *ex parte* and must be supported by a written statement of the authority's reasons for making it: s 75(3).

19.15 Inspection of premises

Domestic premises within a local authority's area on which child minding is carried on at any time, or premises on which day care for children under eight is provided may be entered and inspected by a person authorised by the authority: s 76(1). Intentional obstruction of a person exercising his powers under the section is an offence: s 76(7).

19.16 Enforcement notices

Where it appears to a local authority that a person has contravened s 78(3) (which forbids an unregistered person to act as a child minder on domestic premises), an enforcement notice which has effect for a period of one year may be served on him: s 78(4), (5). If a person with respect to whom an enforcement notice is in force contravenes subsection (3) without reasonable excuse, he is guilty of an offence: s 78(6).

Summary of Chapter 19

Fostering Children; Child Minding and Day Care

Local authority foster parents are persons with whom a child has been placed under s 23(2)(a) on such terms as to payment by the authority and otherwise as the authority may determine.

Local authority foster placements

A privately fostered child is one who is cared for and accommodated by someone other than his parent, or someone who has parental responsibility for him. The child must be under 16 or, in the case of a disabled child, under 18. A child is not a privately fostered child if the person caring for and accommodating him has done so for a period of less than 28 days and does not intend to do so for any longer period: s 66(2).

Private foster parents

The local authority may impose requirements, eg, as to number, age, sex of children fostered. Under s 67(1) it is the duty of a local authority to satisfy themselves as to the welfare of privately fostered children.

Persons may be disqualified under regulations made by the Secretary of State.

The local authority may impose a prohibition on an individual who is not considered to be a suitable person to foster a child, or, in the case of premises, considered unsuitable: s 69(2).

The 1989 Act seeks to regulate activities involving child minding and day care. Every local authority must keep a register of persons who act as child minders and persons who provide day care for children under the age of eight. The register is open to public inspection.

Child minding and day care

A person is a child minder if he looks after one or more children under the age of eight for reward, and he spends a daily period of two hours or more in that activity: s 71(2). The child's parents or relatives are excluded from this definition: s 71(4).

A local authority may refuse to register a person, as where they are dissatisfied with the fitness of the person, or the premises involved are unsatisfactory.

Registration may be accompanied by requirements imposed by the local authority concerning, eg, maximum number of children, maintenance and safety of equipment.

Registration may be cancelled. Premises must be inspected by persons appointed by the local authority. Intentional obstruction of a person who is exercising his powers is an offence: see s 76(1), (7).

Enforcement notices Where a local authority is of the opinion that a person who is unregistered is acting as a child minder on domestic premises, an enforcement notice (which is effective for one year) may be served on him under s 78. Should that person contravene the enforcement notice without reasonable excuse, he will be guilty of an offence: s 78(6).

Chapter 20

Guardianship

20.1 The concept of guardianship

Essentially, a 'guardian' is a person who is entrusted under the law with the supervision of another (often a child) who lacks the capacity, legal or otherwise, to order his own affairs. In England, systematised practices of guardianship existed in the 13th century. They were associated with incidents of feudal tenure, eg, knight's service, which allowed a lord to possess the lands of a deceased tenant whose heir was a minor, and, in some cases, to have the wardship of the heir's person. There were various types of guardianship, eg, guardianship by common law, statute, custom, election (where the minor himself chose a guardian). Guardianship evolved on the basis of the protection of one individual (his person and property) by another.

20.2 Guardianship prior to the ChA 1989

Statute law concerning the guardianship of minors was consolidated in the Guardianship of Minors Act 1971, later amended by the Guardianship Act 1975 and the Children Act 1975. Parental and non-parental guardianship were recognised. The father was the sole guardian of his legitimate children, and on his death the mother was considered a guardian, together with other persons appointed by the father. The courts could appoint guardians; specifically, the High Court appeared to have an inherent power of appointment: see *Re McGrath* (1893) (but see now 20.3 below). There were guardians of the person, of the estate, and those appointed for single purposes only: see *Guardianship* (Law Commission Working Paper, No 91, 1985).

20.3 Changes introduced by the ChA 1989

Law Commission Working Paper No 91 drew attention to the confusion of the ideas of parenthood and guardianship within existing legislation. The two concepts, it was urged, should be distinguished and the law changed so as to abolish the principle of 'parental guardianship'.

The ChA 1989 (see, in particular, ss 5, 6) simplified the law relating to guardianship. It is now almost entirely statutory.

- The significance of parental guardianship has been minimised by the importance attached to the status of parenthood.

- The legal position of guardians and parents is assimilated.

- Persons appointed as guardians under s 5 have parental responsibility for the child concerned: s 5(6).
- All courts have the same powers to appoint guardians.
- Subject to any provisions made by rules of court, no court shall exercise the High Court's inherent jurisdiction to appoint a guardian of the estate of any child: s 5(11). Further where rules of court are made under subsection (11), they may prescribe the circumstances in which, and conditions subject to which, an appointment of such a guardian may be made: s 5(12).

20.4 Appointment of guardians by the court

A guardian of a child can only be appointed by the court in family proceedings, with or without a formal application: s 5(1), (2), (13). The court's powers derive from s 5(1), (2).

20.4.1 Appointment of an individual

Where an application with respect to a child is made to the court by 'an individual', the court (magistrates' court, county court, High Court) may appoint that individual by order to be the child's guardian if '(a) the child has no parent with parental responsibility for him; or (b) a residence order has been made with respect to the child in favour of a parent or guardian of his who has died while the order was in force': s 5(1).

20.4.2 Exercise of the court's powers

Under s 5(2), the court's powers may be exercised where 'the court considers that the order should be made even though no application has been made for it': s 5(2).

20.4.3 Appointment of more than one person

Section 6(c) of the Interpretation Act 1978 states that in the absence of a contrary intention in a statute, the singular includes the plural. Hence the court is able to appoint more than one person to the position of guardian. Additionally, because s 5(1) of the 1989 Act refers to the appointment of 'an individual', the court may *not* appoint a local authority to act in the capacity of a guardian.

20.4.4 'The court may appoint'

The court's decision concerning an appointment must be made in the best interests of the child. The checklist in s 1(3) (see 13.5) has no application in consideration of an appointment of this nature.

20.4.5 Who may apply

The 1989 Act does not enumerate individuals or classes who may apply to become guardians. It would seem, therefore, that any person, but *not* a body of persons, may apply without obtaining leave of the court. Presumably, the child himself may apply for the appointment of a guardian. Note s 5(2) (see 20.4.2 above) empowering the court to appoint of its own motion.

Application may be made to the court concerning 'a child', ie, a person under the age of 18: see s 105(1). Whether this has application in the case of a *married person* under the age of 18 appears to be an open question.

The court is able to make, upon the application of some person or upon its own motion, an order under s 8 (see 13.7) instead of, or in addition to exercising its power of appointing a guardian: see s 10(1).

20.4.6 Persons in respect of whom application may be made

20.4.7 Section 8 orders

20.5 Appointment of guardians privately

Under s 5(3), a parent who has parental responsibility for his child (but not, therefore, an unmarried father who lacks parental responsibility) may appoint another individual to be the child's guardian in the event of the parent's death. Similarly, a guardian of a child may appoint another person to take his place as the child's guardian in the event of his death: s 5(4).

20.6 Appointment in writing

Before the 1989 Act, a private appointment of a guardian had to be made in the form of a deed or by a will. Section 5(5), while not excluding appointments made by deed or will, makes it sufficient for an appointment to be written, dated and signed.

> 'An appointment under subsection (3) or (4) shall not have effect unless it is made in writing, is dated and signed by the person making the appointment or (a) in the case of an appointment made by a will which is not signed by the testator, is signed at the direction of the testator in accordance with the requirements of s 9 of the Wills Act 1837; or (b) in any other case, is signed at the direction of the person making the appointment, in his presence and in the presence of two witnesses who each attest the signature': s 5(5).

20.7 Disclaimer

'To disclaim' is to repudiate or renounce, usually in a formal manner, claims or powers and rights, offered to a person. Thus, a person, X, appointed by a parent or guardian, without X's consent, may fear the burdens of guardianship or may not wish, for other reasons, to be involved in the affairs of the child in question. Under s 6(5), X has a formal right to disclaim. 'A person who is appointed as a guardian under s 5(3) or (4) may disclaim his appointment by an instrument in writing signed by him and made within a reasonable time of his first knowing that the appointment has taken effect.'

Where the Lord Chancellor makes regulations prescribing the manner in which a disclaimer is to be recorded, no disclaimer will be effective unless it is recorded in the prescribed manner: s 5(6).

20.8 Revocation

'To revoke' is to recall or withdraw some power, right, authority, appointment etc as guardian under the rules in s 6, set out below.

20.8.1 Basic principle

Under s 6(1), an appointment under s 5(3),(4) revokes an earlier such appointment (including one made in an unrevoked will or codicil) made by the same person in respect of the same child, unless it is clear (whether as a result of an express provision in the later appointment or by any necessary implication) that the purpose of the later appointment is to appoint an additional guardian.

20.8.2 Revocation by written instrument

Under s 6(2), an appointment under s 5(3) or (4) (including one made in an unrevoked will or codicil) is revoked if the person who made the appointment revokes it by a written and dated instrument which is signed by him, or at his direction, in his presence and in the presence of two witnesses who each attest the signature.

20.8.3 Revocation by destruction of instrument

Under s 6(3), an appointment under s 5(3) or (4) (other than one made in a will or codicil) is revoked if, with the intention of revoking the appointment, the person who made it – (a) destroys the instrument by which it was made; or (b) has some other person destroy that instrument in his presence.

'For the avoidance of doubt, an appointment under s 5(3) or (4) made in a will or codicil is revoked if the will or codicil is revoked': s 6(4).

20.9 Time at which appointment becomes effective

Prior to the 1989 Act, an appointment as guardian would take effect at the death of the parent who had made the appointment. Under s 5(7) of the 1989 Act, an appointment takes effect immediately on the appointor's death only in the following circumstances: (a) where on the death of any person making an appointment under subsection (3) or (4), the child concerned has no parent with parental responsibility for him; or (b) immediately before the death of any person making such an appointment, a residence order in his favour was in force with respect to the child.

Subsection (7) has no application if the residence order referred to was also made in favour of a surviving parent of the child: s 5(9).

Where, on the death of any person making an appointment under subsection (3) or (4): (a) the child concerned has a parent with parental responsibility for him; and (b) subsection (7)(b) does not apply, the appointment will become effective when the child no longer has a parent who has parental responsibility for him: s 5(8).

20.10 General legal effect of appointment as a guardian

Every person appointed as a guardian (save the Official Solicitor, appointed as a guardian of the estate) by the court or by private appointment *has parental responsibility* for the child: s 5(6). A guardian is therefore, effectively in the same legal position as the parents of a child who have parental responsibility. But no financial order may be made against a guardian as such; he is not classified as a 'liable relative' under s 26 of the Social Security Act 1986 (see also s 2(1), (3) FLRA 1987.) Note that the Law Commission (Law Com No 172) stated that placing a burden of financial liability on a guardian could deter the making or accepting of appointments.

It should be noted that a guardian has the right to give or withhold consent in a case of freeing a child for adoption (see 22.12). Further, the guardian has no right of succession on the death of the child. Note, too, that where A is B's guardian, B may not derive British citizenship from A.

20.11 Ending guardianship

Guardianship may be terminated automatically or by order of the magistrates' court, county court or the High Court.

20.11.1 Death of the guardian

Guardianship is terminated automatically when the death of a sole guardian occurs. Under s 5(4) he may have appointed another person to be the child's guardian in the event of his death. Where one guardian dies but others are in office, they will continue to act as guardians.

20.11.2 Majority or death of child

The guardian's duties terminate automatically when the child reaches the age of 18: s 91(7), (8). The duties cease on the death of the child.

20.11.3 Removal of guardian by the court

The appointment of any guardian made under s 5 may be brought to an end by the court: s 6(7). An order terminating the appointment may be made by the court at any time,

- on the application of any person who has parental responsibility for the child: s 6(7)(a);
- on the application of the child himself, with leave of the court: s 6(7)(b);
- in any family proceedings if the court considers that it should be brought to an end, even though there has been no application: s 6(7)(c).

The court will take into account, in considering the removal of a guardian, the implications of the welfare principle in s 1(1). Additionally, a welfare report may be ordered under the provisions of s 7 (see 13.6). The court can appoint another person to replace the former guardian, and, in proceedings concerning removal of a guardian, an order under s 8 may be made if considered appropriate in the circumstances.

20.12 A note on 'the guardian's allowance'

Under s 77 of the SSCBA 1992, a 'guardian's allowance' is payable, but it should be noted carefully that the benefit is payable to those who are looking after *orphaned children*, although in some cases only one parent is dead. The claimant does *not* have to be the formal guardian of the child, appointed under the terms of ChA 1989; he must be entitled to Child Benefit and must satisfy other conditions as set out in s 77(2) SSCBA 1992.

Summary of Chapter 20

Guardianship

A guardian is one who is entrusted under the law with the supervision of some other person, eg, a child, who does not possess the appropriate capacity to look after his own affairs. The ChA 1989 simplified the law concerning guardianship which rests now almost entirely on statute.	**The concept of guardianship**
A guardian of a child is appointed by the court in family proceedings: see s 5. The court's decision must be in the child's best interests. Application may be made by any person; the court may appoint of its own motion: s 5(2). Application may be made concerning any person under 18.	**Appointment of guardian by the court**
Under s 5(3) a parent with parental responsibility for a child may appoint a person to be the child's guardian in the event of the parent's death. A guardian may appoint a person to replace him in the event of his death: see s 5(3), (4).	**Appointment of guardians privately**
A person appointed as guardian may disclaim by written instrument. An appointment as guardian may be revoked by written instrument or by destruction of the instrument by which the appointment was made.	**Appointments of this nature should be in writing.**
A person appointed as guardian by the court or as the result of a private appointment has parental responsibility for the child: s 5(6). The guardian is, effectively, in the same position as a parent with parental responsibility. He has no right of succession on the death of the child.	**Legal effect of appointment as a guardian**
Guardianship may be terminated automatically as where, eg, the child dies. Automatic termination occurs also where the guardian dies. Where a guardian dies but others are in office, they continue to act as the child's guardians. Automatic termination also occurs where the child attains his majority. A guardian may be removed by the court under s 6(7). Order of termination may be made on application of any person having parental responsibility for the child involved, and on application of the child himself (with leave of the court). In any family proceedings the court may bring guardianship to an end where it considers such a step to be	**Ending guardianship**

appropriate even if there has been no application by any person: s 6(7)(c).

In considering the removal of a guardian, the court should take into account the essential implications of the welfare principle set out in s 1(1). The court can appoint a replacement and can make an order under s 8 if this is considered appropriate in the particular circumstances.

Chapter 21

Wardship

21.1 The essential feature of wardship

'Wardship' results from the creation of the legal status of a 'ward'. It refers to a minor who has been made a 'ward of court' by order, made on application, and over whose person and property the court will exercise, in his interests, a special jurisdiction and control. 'The golden thread running through the court's jurisdiction is the child's welfare, considered first, last and all the time': *Re D* (1977).

21.2 Background

Wardship probably originated in England in feudal times: the feudal lord possessed a right of wardship which could be exerted over heirs who were minors. He took the income from the lands which constituted the fief until the heir was able to fulfil the demands of his military service under the feudal contract; in return the lord supported and educated the minor children of the deceased vassal. Wardships were classified as chattels real and could be sold; Magna Carta 1215, cap 4, sought to prevent the destruction or wasting of land held on account of wardship. The Court of Wards was founded in 1540 so as to enforce royal rights in relation to lands held on behalf of wards. These rights and the court itself disappeared in 1660; the wardship jurisdiction passed to the Court of Chancery. In 1971, the jurisdiction passed to the Family Division of the High Court (see s 1(2), and Sch 1 of the Administration of Justice Act 1970) and until 1986 wardship was within the jurisdiction of the High Court: see s 38(2)(b) MFPA 1984.

One of the objectives of ChA 1989 is *to make wardship less necessary*: this is to be accomplished by utilising the positive features within the general code created by the Act.

21.3 Wardship jurisdiction and the inherent jurisdiction of the High Court

The concept of wardship is derived from the monarch's general duty as *parens patriae* to protect the person and property of those of his subjects (usually minors) who are unable to look after themselves. This wide jurisdiction is not based upon any statutes; it has developed largely on the basis of decisions of the courts. It should be differentiated from the inherent jurisdiction of the High Court which may be exercised whether the minor has or has not been made a ward of court: see *Re M and N (Wards) (Publication of Information)* (1990).

Note the comments of Lord Mackay LC (1989) 139 NLJ 505: 'In the Government's view wardship is only one use of the High Court's inherent *parens patriae* jurisdiction. We believe, therefore, that it is open to the High Court to make orders under its inherent jurisdiction in respect of children other than through wardship.'

In practice, where the court exercises its *wardship jurisdiction*, it has virtual custody of the minor, ie, it possesses a kind of parental responsibility for the child. This is not so, however, where the court exercises its *inherent jurisdiction* involving minors who may not be wards of court.

21.4 Some features of the wardship jurisdiction

In its exercise of the wardship jurisdiction, the court takes over 'ultimate responsibility' for the child: *per* Lord Scarman in *Re E* (1984). The powers of the court to protect the child in these circumstances are unlimited (see *Re K* (1988)) and flexible, allowing it to utilise detailed enquiries: *Re E* (1991).

21.4.1 Control during wardship

The child, his person and property, and those persons with parental responsibility, or others responsible for his care, are subject to control by the court. The control fundamental to wardship begins at the time when the child is made a ward; it ends only when wardship comes to an end.

21.4.2 Control over ward's 'important steps'

No important steps in the life of the ward should be taken without the consent of the court: *per* Cross J in *Re S* (1967). Steps of this nature, which involve the court's granting (or refusing) consent are exemplified by: a ban on information concerning wardship proceedings (see s 12 of the Administration of Justice Act 1960); applying on behalf of a ward for compensation from the Criminal Injuries Compensation Board (*Re G* (1990)); permission for major medical treatment, except in cases of emergency (*Re G* (1984)); change of whereabouts of ward other than a mere change of residence (see Family Proceedings Rules 1991, r 5.1 (9)); change in ward's status (eg, freeing him for adoption): see Family Proceedings Rules 1991, r 5.4(1)(b).

21.4.3 Wide nature of court's powers

The court is able to grant injunctions *in personam* and *in rem* (see *Re AB* (1985), injunction prohibiting publication). It can make any of the s 8 orders (see 13.7) because wardship proceedings are considered to be 'family proceedings'. See *Re R* (1991): the powers of a judge in proceedings concerning wardship are not limited merely to those considered appropriate for a parent in relation to his child. Note *Re B* (1990) for an example of an unusually flexible order considered to be in the best interests of a child, involving supervision of a child *after* he had returned to his parents.

Additionally, the court is empowered to make orders for financial provision in relation to the ward, to issue orders restraining the marriage of the ward, non-molestation orders, and orders restraining named persons from communicating or associating with the ward.

21.4.4 Detailed enquiries

Procedures employed by the wardship court often necessitate detailed enquiries: see, eg, *Re E* (1991). This is particularly so where the matter of the child's upbringing is in question, and in such a case the court will look upon the welfare of the child as a paramount consideration: see 1989 Act, s 1(1), at 13.2. The court will demand in cases of this nature reports relating to the background and present circumstances of the child.

21.5 Jurisdiction to make a child a ward

The High Court alone has jurisdiction to make a child a ward of court (see Supreme Court Act 1981, at 21.6 below). Note, however, s 38 MFPA 1984, by which wardship proceedings *except* applications for an order that a minor be made, or cease to be, a ward of court, may be *transferred* from the High Court to a county court. A transfer of this kind may be either on the application of a party to the proceedings or on the court's own motion.

Note the observation by Cross J in *Re B* (1965) that the jurisdiction of the court exercised in wardship proceedings (in large measure of a non-statutory nature and, therefore, capable of considerable adaptation) does not resemble 'ordinary civil proceedings'. Lord Scarman, in *Re E* (1984), reminded the court exercising its wardship jurisdiction, that 'it is exercising a wardship, not an adversarial, jurisdiction'; its duty is not limited to the parties' dispute, rather has it the duty to act in whatever way is best suited, according to its judgment, 'to serve the true interest and welfare of the ward'.

21.6 Section 41 of the Supreme Court Act 1981

Section 41(1) of the Supreme Court Act 1981 states:

'Subject to the provisions of this section, no minor shall be made a ward of court except by virtue of an order to that effect made by the High Court.'

By subsection (2):

'Where an application is made for such an order in respect of a minor, the minor shall become a ward of court on the making of the application, but shall cease to be a ward of court at the end of such period as may be prescribed unless within that period an order has been made in accordance with the application.'

By subsection (3):

'The High Court may, either upon an application in that behalf or without such an application, order that any minor who is for the time being a ward of court shall cease to be a ward of court.'

21.7 Exercise of the court's discretion

The court has the power to decide whether or not to exercise its jurisdiction in a particular case relating to wardship. Thus, it is unlikely to interfere, for example, in the affairs of a minor who is subject to the military law: see *Re JS* (1990), in which a minor had joined the British Army as a boy soldier and had later absented himself from military duties without leave and returned home, suffering from medical and psychological problems. His mother made him a ward of court and applied for care and control. The court struck out the summons: where a ward is under military control it is not appropriate to continue the wardship. In *Re K* (1987) a prosecution had been initiated against the parents of a minor; he was made a ward of court and was required to give evidence. The court, in hearing an application in wardship proceedings intended to determine whether the prosecution required the court's consent before calling K as a witness, held that it would be improper for a wardship court to intervene in a matter of this nature, and, therefore, the jurisdiction of the court would not be exercised. Note also, the Family Law Act 1986, Chapter II (Jurisdiction of Courts in England and Wales), which deals with the court's discretion in relation to proceedings outside the UK.

21.8 The enforcing of court orders

In wardship proceedings, the court may use an officer, known as 'the tipstaff' (originally appointed for the Court of King's Bench), who is charged with tasks including the taking of wards into custody and delivering them to named persons. The tipstaff has authority to arrest and bring before the court persons who obstruct him in the execution of a court order. Thus, where he is carrying out a 'search and find order' and the defendant who has been located refuses to disclose where a child is residing, he may arrest the defendant and bring him before the court. (The police may be instructed to assist him.)

Any actions which tend to hamper the court in carrying out its duties in relation to wardship proceedings constitute a contempt (see *Re B* (1965)) and will be dealt with accordingly.

21.9 Persons who may or may not be made wards of court

A person who is not a minor cannot be made a ward of court. Further, the court has no jurisdiction to make an unborn child a ward of court: see *Re F (In Utero)* (1988) in which a mentally disturbed woman with a history of drug abuse became pregnant and the local authority applied to have the foetus made a ward of court. The court held that the foetus had no right of action and could not be a party to the proposed action.

Per May LJ:

'I have considerable sympathy with the local authority in their position on the facts of the instant case, but I am driven to the conclusion that the judge was right and that *the court has no jurisdiction to ward an unborn child*. If the courts are to have this jurisdiction in a sensitive situation such as the present, I think that this is a matter for Parliament and not for the courts themselves. I do not think that even if the courts were minded to extend the jurisdiction in this type of case, they could in law or in practice limit this, as counsel suggested, to children having a gestation period of not less than 28 weeks.'

A minor who owes allegiance to the Crown, ie, who is a British subject, may be made a ward of court, irrespective of his country of birth, domicile, habitual residence: see *Harben v Harben* (1957).	21.9.1 British subjects
Children who are *not* British nationals are considered as owing temporary allegiance to the Crown while they are within the jurisdiction. They can be made wards during their physical presence in England and Wales (see *Hope v Hope* (1854)), or when 'ordinarily resident', though not physically present within the jurisdiction: see *Re P* (1965).	21.9.2 Non-British subjects

In *Re B-M (A Minor) (Wardship: Jurisdiction)* (1993), F, the British father, and M, the German mother of a girl, C, never married. After their separation F applied for parental responsibility and contact; M took C to Germany and F issued an originating summons in wardship; the court made a 'seek and search' order which was served on M. She did not return to England and F issued a summons under the Hague Convention on the Civil Aspects of International Child Abduction, Article 3, asking for a declaration that C's retention in Germany was wrong. It was held that the English court had jurisdiction in wardship if the child was either physically present in England or M and C were 'habitually resident' at the date of the order. There was evidence that M had not changed her habitual residence in England by the date of the wardship order. As the custody of C was vested in the court from the date of the wardship order, M was guilty of wrongful retention after service of the order. A party could seek a declaration concerning a third party's rights of custody even if they did not have rights of custody.

21.9.3 Restrictions

There are some few but important restrictions on the availability to the court of the power to make orders in wardship proceedings. Thus, ss 1(1)(d), 2, 3 of the Family Law Act 1986 impose statutory limitations on the powers of the court to make orders in wardship proceedings concerning the care of a child, or orders relating to his education, where the child is *not* habitually resident in England or Wales or is neither habitually resident in Scotland or Northern Ireland nor physically present in England or Wales or where his parents are involved in divorce proceedings in Scotland or Northern Ireland. Note also that a child who is subject to a care order *cannot* be made a ward of court: s 100(2)(c) ChA 1989. Further, the court may not make a wardship order when application has been made in a court in the UK for the return of a child under the Hague Convention concerning child abduction (1980): see the Child Abduction and Custody Act 1985.

21.10 Persons who may apply to make a child a ward of court

The general rule is that *any person* may issue a summons concerning making a child a ward of court: see, eg, *Re D (A Minor) (Wardship: Sterilisation)* (1976), in which an educational psychologist who was on the staff of a local authority applied for X, a mentally retarded child with Sotos Syndrome, to be made a ward of court and sought an order that wardship be continued so as to prevent or delay a proposed sterilisation operation. The order was granted: X could not give an informed consent and, therefore, the court should exercise its protective powers. The court held that the proposed operation involved the deprivation of a basic human right, and where its performance on a minor was proposed, the court should consider the exercise of its wardship jurisdiction. Note, too, that the child himself may initiate proceedings (see Family Proceedings Rules 1991, r 92).

An applicant for a wardship order is required to state his relationship to, or interest in the affairs of, the minor; where the court considers that the application is a mere abuse of process it will be refused.

21.11 The child's welfare and the public interest

There are circumstances in which the public interest and the rights of third persons may override the demands of the welfare of the child. Thus, in *Re X (A Minor) (Wardship: Jurisdiction)* (1975) the Court of Appeal held that the wardship jurisdiction of the court ought *not* to be extended to stopping the publication of a book, the contents of which might have adversely affected the ward psychologically. The book referred to the alleged depravity of the ward's deceased father, and the welfare of the child had to be balanced against the important public right to freedom of information. In *Re M and N* (1990), the Court of Appeal held that the court should impose by injunction no wider restraint on publication of matter relating to a ward than is necessary to protect him: see *R v Central TV* (1994).

The following statistics concerning originating summonses for wardship suggest a dramatic change in the demand for the procedure:

1988 – 3704	1991 – 4961
1989 – 4327	1992 – 492
1990 – 4721	1993 – 141 (January-July)

It should be noted that the use of wardship proceedings by local authorities has virtually ended: see s 100 ChA 1989. The making of a care order with respect to a child who is a ward of court will bring that wardship to an end: s 91(4). While a child is in care it is *not* possible to make him a ward of court: see s 100(2)(c) ChA 1989; s 41(2)(A) Supreme Court Act 1981 (added under Sch 13, para 45(2) ChA 1989).

21.12 Effects of ChA 1989 on wardship

The High Court possesses an inherent jurisdiction to protect children. Under that jurisdiction it can grant, for example, an *ex parte* injunction immediately to protect a child from molestation or to prevent a child from being removed from the jurisdiction. Application to invoke the jurisdiction generally involves an originating summons and the filing of an affidavit. For the case of local authorities wishing to invoke the inherent jurisdiction (which will require the leave of the court) see s 100(3) at 21.14.2 below.

21.13 The inherent jurisdiction of the High Court

As a result of s 100(1) ChA 1989, s 7 FLRA 1969 (which empowers the High Court to place a ward of court in the care, or under the supervision, of a local authority) ceases to have effect.

21.14 Local authorities and the use of wardship jurisdiction

Under s 100(2), no court shall exercise the High Court's inherent jurisdiction with respect to children:

21.14.1 Local authorities and the inherent jurisdiction

(a) so as to require a child to be placed in the care, or put under the supervision, of a local authority;

(b) so as to require a child to be accommodated by or on behalf of a local authority;

(c) so as to make a child who is the subject of a care order a ward of court;

(d) for the purpose of conferring on any local authority power to determine any question which has arisen, or which may arise, in connection with any aspect of parental responsibility for a child.

21.14.2 Leave of the court

Under s 100(3), no application for any exercise of the court's inherent jurisdiction with respect to children may be made by a local authority *unless* leave of the court has been obtained.

Under s 100(4), the court will grant leave *only* if satisfied that:

(a) the result which the authority wish to achieve could not be achieved through the making of any order of a kind to which subsection 5 (below) applies; and

(b) there is reasonable cause to believe that if the Court's inherent jurisdiction is not exercised with respect to the child he is likely to suffer significant harm.

Subsection (5), which is referred to in s 100(4), states that it applies to any order made otherwise than in the exercise of the court's inherent jurisdiction, and which the local authority is entitled to apply for (assuming, in the case of any application which may only be made with leave, that leave is granted).

For an example of an order made recently under the inherent jurisdiction, see *Re O (A Minor) (Medical Treatment)* (1993). In this case, a premature baby suffered from respiratory distress syndrome and her doctor thought that a blood transfusion might be necessary, but the parents, because of religious beliefs, would not consent. The court made an emergency protection order. Two questions arose: whether the court should override the wishes of the parents, and what was the appropriate legal framework for making the necessary decisions, It was held that the duty of the court was to give directions so as to ensure that the child would receive the blood transfusion in accordance with medical advice, and that the order which would authorise the medical treatment was to be made *under the inherent jurisdiction of the court* rather than under ChA 1989 (compare *Camden LBC v R (A Minor) (Blood Transfusion)* (1993)).

Summary of Chapter 21

Wardship

A 'ward of court' is generally a minor over whose person and property the court will exercise a measure of control. The objective of wardship is the child's welfare: see *Re D* (1977).

The court takes over ultimate responsibility for the child; its powers of protection are very wide indeed. The control exercised by the court ends only when wardship comes to an end.

The concept of wardship

No important step in the ward's life may be taken without consent of the court: this may involve, eg, granting permission for major medical treatment, change of whereabouts. Injunctions *in personam* and *in rem*, and s 8 orders are available.

Control over 'important steps'

The High Court alone has jurisdiction to make a child a ward of court. Wardship proceedings may be transferred to a county court in some circumstances. Essentially the court is concerned with serving the true interest and welfare of the ward: see s 41 Supreme Court Act 1981.

The court will exercise its discretion in cases relating to wardship: see *Re JS* (1990). An action which hampers the court in carrying out its duties in relation to wardship proceedings is a contempt: see *Re B* (1965).

Making the child a ward

Only minors may be made wards of court. The court has no jurisdiction to make an unborn child a ward: see *Re F (In Utero)* (1988). Any person may issue a summons concerning the making of a child a ward of court. An applicant for a wardship order is required to state his relationship to, or interest in the affairs of, the minor.

Persons who can be made wards of court

The High Court possesses an inherent jurisdiction in relation to the protection of children. It can grant, for example, an *ex parte* injunction to protect a child from being removed from the jurisdiction.

The inherent jurisdiction of the High Court

Under s 100(2) no court can exercise the High Court's inherent jurisdiction so as to require a child to be placed in the care of a local authority, or to require a child to be accommodated by or on behalf of a local authority, or so as to make a child who is the subject of a care order a ward of court.

Local authorities and the inherent jurisdiction

Under s 100(3), no application for any exercise of the court's inherent jurisdiction concerning children may be made by a local authority unless they have obtained leave of the court. Leave will be granted (see s 100(4)) only if the court is satisfied that the result which the authority wishes to achieve could not be achieved in some other way and there is reasonable cause to believe that significant harm might be suffered by the child unless the jurisdiction is exercised: see, eg, *Re O (A Minor) (Medical Treatment)* (1993).

Chapter 22

Adoption

22.1 Background

Adoption (*optare* = to choose) involves the termination of a child's legal rights and duties toward his *natural* parents and the substitution of similar rights and duties toward his adoptive parents. It necessitates *a move*, sanctioned by the law, and in accordance with statute, *from one family to another*. Legal historians and anthropologists claim that adoption is an institution of a worldwide nature with foundations in antiquity. (See, eg, references in the early part of Sir James Frazer's *The Golden Bough* (1890) to the ceremonies of imitative magic surrounding adoption as practised in very early and primitive cultures.) Roman law recognised the process of *adoptio*, whereby a person under the paternal power of the head of his family came under the power of another; the adopted person had the same rights (eg of succession) and the same duties (eg, *sacra*, involving attention to family rites) as a natural son.

In English law, adoption was recognised fully in the Adoption of Children Act 1926 (resulting, in part, from the problems of children orphaned in the First World War and based upon The Hopkinson Report). Criticisms of the procedural aspects of the Adoption Act 1926 and a questioning of its basic principles resulted in the *Report of the Houghton Committee* (1972); many of the Committee's recommendations were used in the Children Act 1975. The AA 1976 consolidated the law; together with the amendments of ChA 1989 (see below), the 1976 Act constitutes the statutory basis of adoption.

ChA 1989 harmonises adoption law so that adoption agencies (see 22.3 below) can work closely together; it replaces the concepts of 'parental rights' and 'custody' which appeared in the earlier legislation, and it introduces reforms concerning the age limits of parent applicants, the 'freeing' of a child for adoption, registration, and notification of intention to adopt.

22.2 Current trends

Statistical data indicate a *fall* in the number of adoptions; in 1993 there were some 8,000 adoptions in the UK as compared with 27,000 in 1968 (the peak year). The proportion of children adopted under the age of one fell from 21% in 1975 to 12% in 1993; the proportion aged 10 or over increased from 19% to almost 25%. It has been suggested that the increased acceptability of contraception and abortion, the disappearance of the stigma attached to illegitimacy, the growth of a wide scheme of state benefits, have contributed to a decline in the numbers of babies available for adoption. Nevertheless the procedure remains of some importance: a growth in the popularity of inter-country adoption has created problems of control, an increase in transracial adoption, together with its opportunities and challenges, has involved an important re-examination of the concept of children's welfare within the context of adoption: see eg, *Re JK* (1991). There remain some 750,000 adoptees in the UK and moves in the direction of reform of this section of family law continue (see 22.16 below).

22.3 Adoption agencies

The functioning of the adoption process demands a systematised and integrated adoption service. Adoption agencies now operate within a statutory framework; control of the agencies is effected by the Adoption Agencies Regulations 1983.

22.3.1 The Adoption Service

Under s 1(1) AA 1976, it is the duty of every local authority to establish and maintain within their area a service designed to meet the needs, in relation to adoption, of children who have been or may be adopted, parents and guardians of such children, and persons who have adopted or may adopt a child, and for that purpose to provide the requisite facilities, or secure that they are provided by approved adoption societies. The facilities to be provided include arrangements for assessing children and prospective adopters, and counselling. Services maintained by local authorities are referred to as 'the Adoption Service', and a local authority or approved adoption society are referred to as an 'adoption agency': s 1(2), (4).

22.3.2 Voluntary societies

Non-profit making, incorporated voluntary adoption societies may act as adoption agencies subject to the approval of the Secretary of State: s 3(1). Approval may last for a period of three years, and can be renewed: s 3(4).

22.3.3 Adoption panels

Agencies are obliged (see Adoption Agencies Regulations 1983) under reg 5 to set up adoption panels so as to consider adoption applications and recommend whether someone who wishes to adopt is or is not a suitable person. The agency collects information concerning the child also, and will make a recommendation as to whether or not adoption is 'in the best interests of the child'. The panel should include a medical adviser, a social worker and at least two independent members; its advice is tendered to the agency which has the task of making and recording a decision.

22.4 Who may apply for an adoption order

Under the AA 1958, there was a lower age limit of 25 for applicants, save where an applicant was a parent or relative of the child. Sch 10, para 4 ChA 1989 allows in some cases adoption where one of the adopting spouses is at least 18. There appears to be no official maximum age for an adopter.

Single and joint applications are permissible, but in the case of a joint application, it must be made by a married couple: s 14(1) AA 1976. Hence, applications by unmarried cohabitants or adult siblings will be rejected. (It is of interest to note that the *Review of Adoption Law* (1992) recommended that this restriction ought to continue, in the interests of the 'security and stability' of the children.)

22.4.1 Married couple

Where the applicants are parent and step parent, the parent should be at least 18; the spouse must be 21 or over: see s 14(1B) AA 1976; Sch 10 ChA 1989. At least one of the applicants should be domiciled in a part of the UK or Isle of Man or the Channel Islands (unless the application is for a Convention order: see 22.4.5 below).

22.4.2 Unmarried person aged 21 or over

A single person aged 21 or over may adopt if the requirements concerning domicile are satisfied: see s 15(1) AA 1976.

22.4.3 Married person aged 21 or over

A married person aged 21 or over may adopt if the requirements concerning domicile are satisfied, and the court is satisfied that:

- his/her spouse cannot be found; or
- the spouses are separated and are living apart and the separation is likely to be permanent; or
- his/her spouse is by reason of ill-health (physical or mental) incapable of making an application for an adoption order: see s 15(1).

22.4.4 Application by mother or father of the child alone

An adoption order will not be made on the application of the mother or father of the child alone unless the court is satisfied (see s 15(3)) that:

- the other natural parent is dead or cannot be found, or, by virtue of the HFEA 1990, that there is no other parent (see Sch 4, para 4 HFEA 1990), or
- there is some other reason justifying the exclusion of the other natural parent.

Where the court makes such an order, the reason justifying the exclusion of the other natural parent must be recorded.

22.4.5	Convention adoption orders	Section 17 AA 1976 deals with the (few) 'Convention countries' designated by the Secretary of State in relation to the Hague Convention on the Adoption of Children (1965). The High Court only may make this type of order. Adoption orders may be made relating to unmarried persons under 18 who are nationals of the UK or a Convention country and who habitually reside in British territory or a Convention country. A sole applicant must habitually reside in the UK and be a national of a Convention country, or habitually reside in a British territory or a Convention country and be a UK national. Joint application may be made by a husband and wife who satisfy one of the residence conditions.
22.4.6	Suitability of applicants	The Adoption Agencies Regulations 1983, reg 8(2), require a report on the health of prospective adopters and their family history: see *R v Secretary of State for Health ex p Luff* (1992), in which the court held that it was not unreasonable for the Health Secretary to advise the Home Secretary that a prospective adoptive parent was not suitable for the purpose of adopting a child because his life expectancy was thought to be about ten years. (Note, too, the seemingly general preference of adoption agencies for a maximum age for adopters of 30-40 years.)
22.5	**The question of adoption by relatives and step-parents**	Section 37(1) of the Children Act 1975 made it necessary for the court, given certain conditions, to consider an application to adopt made by relatives as an application under s 33 for a custodianship order; this appeared to be in line with a general policy of discouraging adoptions by relatives of the child. Custodianship is now *abolished* by ChA 1989; s 8 allows relatives to apply for residence orders (see 13.15) and, because adoption proceedings are classified as 'family proceedings', the court may make of its own volition a s 8 order on an application for adoption. It may be that this will be preferred by relatives.

Step-parent adoptions have not been encouraged in the past, but ChA 1989, Sch 15 repeals the restrictive provisions of s 14(3) AA 1976. Schedule 10, para 4 ChA 1989, which added s 14(1B) to AA 1976, clearly recognises the step-parent adoption application. |
| **22.6** | **Who may be adopted** | Children under 18 who are not and have not been married can be adopted: see ss 12(5), 72(1) AA 1976. An adoption order may be made notwithstanding that the child is already an adopted child: s 12(7). |

Where the applicant, or one of the applicants, is a parent, step-parent or relative of the child, or the child was placed with the applicants by an adoption agency or in pursuance of a High Court order, an adoption order shall not be made unless the child is at least 19 weeks old and at all times during the preceding 13 weeks had his home with the applicants or one of them: s 13(1) See *Re K T (A Minor) (Adoption)* (1993).	22.6.1	Child to live with adopters before order is made

Where subsection (1) does not apply, an adoption order shall not be made unless the child is at least 12 months old, and at all times during the preceding 12 months had his home with the applicants or one of them: s 13(2).

An adoption order will not be made unless the court is satisfied that sufficient opportunities to see the child with the applicant, or, in the case of an application by a married couple, both applicants together in the home environment have been afforded where the child was placed with the applicant by an adoption agency, to that agency, or in any other case, to the local authority within whose area the home is: s 13(3) AA 1976.	22.6.2	Seeing the child in the home environment
The welfare of the child to be adopted is *the first consideration* of the court and adoption agency: it is *not* the paramount consideration. *Per* Gibson LJ, in *Re Adoption Application (Surrogacy)* (1987): 'In adoption proceedings the welfare of the child is the first consideration and may be the weightiest. But it is not exclusive, and must be weighed against other matters, and must outweigh them if it is reasonable that it should do so. The test of reasonableness is objective and it is to be made at the date of the hearing. The burden of proving that the withholding of consent is unreasonable is upon the applicants. Being mistaken or wrong is not the same as being unreasonable.'	22.7	**The welfare principle**

See also *Re K (A Minor) (Adoption Order: Nationality)* (1994); the Court of Appeal held that was not legitimate for a judge, in considering an adoption application, to take into account the fact that the child, who was eight days short of her eighteenth birthday at the hearing of the application, would obtain British Nationality (see British Nationality Act 1981, s 1(6)). The criterion for adoption is the wider test of the child's *general welfare*. In this case the adoption would have no effect on the child's general welfare in the eight days remaining.

Note also *Re C (A Minor) (Adoption Notice: Local Authority)* (1994).

In reaching a decision concerning a child's adoption, a court or adoption agency shall have regard to all the circumstances, first consideration being given to the need to safeguard and	22.7.1	Duty to promote welfare of child

promote the welfare of the child throughout his childhood; and shall, so far as practicable, ascertain the child's wishes and feelings regarding the decision and give due consideration to them, having regard to his age and understanding: s 6.

Compare the *United Nations Convention on the Rights of the Child* (see 23.4.5) which calls upon Member States to recognise and permit the system of adoption to ensure that the best interests of the child 'shall be the paramount consideration'.

22.7.2 The child's religious upbringing

Note s 7 AA 1976, which requires that an adoption agency shall, in placing a child for adoption, have regard, so far as is practicable, to any wishes of the child's parents and guardians 'as to the religious upbringing of the child'.

22.8 Private placements

By 'placement' is meant the act of transferring the child; it does *not* refer to the continuing process of caring for the child. The general rule is that it is an offence (punishable by imprisonment or fine) for a person other than an adoption agency to make arrangements for the adoption of a child *unless* the proposed adopter is a relative of the child or the person who is making the arrangement is acting in pursuance of a High Court order: see s 11(1) AA 1976.

22.8.1 'Relative of the child'

The term 'relative' in relation to a child means a grandparent, brother, sister, uncle or aunt, whether of the full or half-blood or by affinity and includes, where the child is illegitimate, the father of the child and any person who would be a relative within the meaning of this definition if the child were the legitimate child of his mother and father: s 72(1) AA 1976.

22.8.2 Prohibition on payments

It is unlawful, under s 57(1) to make or give to any person any payment or reward for or in consideration of the adoption by that person of a child, the grant by that person of any agreement or consent required in connection with the adoption of a child, the handing over of a child by that person with a view to the adoption of the child, or the making by that person of any arrangements for the adoption of a child. See also Sch 10, para 24(1) ChA 1989.

Note that the Secretary of State may make regulations for the purpose of enabling adoption agencies to pay allowances to persons who have adopted, or intend to adopt, children in pursuance of arrangements made by the agencies: s 57A of AA 1976, inserted by Sch 10, para 25 ChA 1989.

For the question of the retrospective authorisation by the court of an illegal transaction under s 57, see *Re C (A Minor) (Adoption Application)* (1993), in which it was held that the High Court should authorise an illegal placement, involving payments, with circumspection and *only* if the placement and adoption were in the child's best interests.

A private person may act so as to arrange a foster placement, allowing the foster parent to adopt at a later stage, always provided that the applicant has given appropriate notice within the two years preceding the application: see s 22(1A) AA 1976, added by Sch 10, para 10(1) ChA 1989. When notice is given, the child is classified as a 'protected child'; the local authority will arrange for the child to be visited periodically so as to secure his well-being: see ss 32, 33. A child will cease to be 'protected' where no adoption application is made within a period of two years from the giving of notice to make an application, or when he becomes 18, or marries, or when a guardian is appointed: see s 32 AA 1976; Sch 10, para 18(4) ChA 1989.

22.8.3 Foster placements

Where application is made to adopt a child placed independently, the local authority must prepare an appropriate report for the court: see Adoption Rules 1984, r 22(2).

22.8.4 Application to adopt a child placed independently

The majority of placements today are *arranged* by adoption agencies; placements of this nature are *effected* by adoption agencies or local authorities. Proposals for placement are referred to an adoption panel (see Adoption Agencies Regulations 1983, reg 9), the members of which meet to consider a report prepared by the agency. The panel's recommendation concerns the advisability of adoption in the child's best interests, and the suitability of the prospective adopter. A recommendation on the making of a 'freeing order' (see 22.12) may be made.

22.9 Agency placements

When the panel's recommendation is made, the agency must then decide its course of action. If adoption is accepted as being in the child's best interests, and the child should be freed for adoption, and the proposed adopter is acceptable, the child's parents and the adopter should be informed: reg 11. The child will be visited soon after placement; if no application or adoption follows within three months of placement, that placement will be reviewed: reg 12.

An adoption order will not be made by the court unless the child is 'free for adoption' under s 18 (see 22.12 below) or, in the case of each parent or guardian, the court is satisfied that he freely, and with full understanding of what is involved, agrees unconditionally to the making of an adoption order (whether or not he knows the identity of the applicants), or his

22.10 Consent to the adoption order

agreement to the making of the adoption order should be dispensed with on a ground set out in subsection (2) (see below): s 16(1).

Agreement may be given before or at the hearing. A mother may not give her agreement until the child is six weeks old: s 16(4) AA 1976. Agreement may be withdrawn at any time before the order is made: see *Re K* (1953). Once agreement is given, the child must not be removed against the will of the person with whom he resides except with leave of the court: s 27(1) AA 1976.

22.11 Dispensing with consent

The grounds mentioned in s 16(1) are set out and discussed below. There are six grounds set out in s 16(2)(a)-(f), as modified by Sch 10 ChA 1989, allowing the court to dispense with the agreement of parent or guardian.

22.11.1 The parent or guardian cannot be found or is incapable of giving assent.

Under s 16(2)(a) the court will dispense with agreement, if, in spite of all reasonable steps having been taken, the parent or guardian cannot be found, or is incapable. 'Incapable' refers to mental incapacity *and* to circumstances such as those in *Re R* (1966) where the parents lived under a political dictatorship and there was no way of communicating with them.

22.11.2 Agreement is withheld unreasonably

Agreement will be dispensed with where a parent or guardian withholds consent unreasonably: s 16(2)(b). See *Re EH and MH (Step Parent Adoption)* (1993).

Note *Re C (An Infant)* (1964), *per* Pearson LJ: 'We are not concerned in cases of this kind, where the question is simply whether the mother's consent is being unreasonably withheld, with, in itself, the question as to which course would be in the best interests of the child. It is not enough to show – indeed, it is not strictly a relevant consideration by itself – that, in the interests of the child, it would be better that the child should remain with the foster-parents or that the child should be taken by the mother. What is relevant is the mother's attitude to questions concerning the welfare of the child. Counsel for the applicants has pointed out that there are two aspects in this case. The judge in the first instance has decided primarily that the mother unreasonably withheld her consent, having regard to the medical evidence, which she had the opportunity of seeing and considering, and, indeed, did see and consider. The second aspect raises the question whether the mother's attitude of withholding consent was reasonable in relation to the arrangements – or lack of arrangements – which had been made for the child's future in the event of the child's being returned to her.'

Per Lord Hailsham, LC, in *Re W (An Infant)* (1971):

'... The test is reasonableness and nothing else. It is not culpability. It is not indifference. It is not failure to discharge parental duties. It is reasonableness, and reasonableness in the context of the totality of the circumstances. But, although welfare *per se* is not the test, the fact that a reasonable parent does pay regard to the welfare of his child must enter into the question of reasonableness as a relevant factor. It is relevant in all cases if and to the extent that a reasonable parent would take it into account. It is decisive in those cases where a reasonable parent must so regard it ... Two reasonable parents can perfectly reasonably come to opposite conclusions on the same set of facts without forfeiting their title to be regarded as reasonable. The question in any given case is whether a parental veto comes within the band of possible reasonable decisions and not whether it is right or mistaken. Not every reasonable exercise of judgment is right, and not every mistaken exercise of judgment is unreasonable. There is a band of decisions within which no court should seek to replace the individual's judgment with his own.'

Per Ormrod LJ in *Re H (Infants) (Adoption: Parental Consent)* (1977): 'The relative importance of the welfare of the children is increasing rather than diminishing in relation to dispensing with agreement. That being so, it ought to be recognised by all concerned with adoption cases that once the formal agreement has been given or perhaps once the child has been placed with the adopters, time begins to run against the mother and, as time goes on, it gets progressively more and more difficult for her to show that [the withdrawal of her agreement] is reasonable.'

Agreement may be dispensed with where the parent or guardian is shown to have failed persistently without reasonable cause to discharge his parental responsibility for the child: s 16(2)(c), amended by Sch 10 para 5(2) ChA 1989. The failure must be of a culpable nature; 'persistent' refers to failure over a long period.	22.11.3 Persistent failure to discharge parental responsibility
Agreement may be dispensed with if the parent or guardian has abandoned or neglected the child: s 16(2)(d). See also s 1 C&YPA 1933; *Watson v Nickolaisen* (1955).	22.11.4 Abandonment or neglect of child
Agreement may be dispensed with under s 16(2)(e) if the parent or guardian has persistently ill-treated the child. This involves repeated assaults over a period of time.	22.11.5 Persistent ill-treatment of the child

22.11.6	Serious ill-treatment of the child, and his rehabilitation is unlikely	Agreement may be dispensed with under s 16(2)(f) where the parent or guardian has ill-treated the child severely (one act will suffice) so that the rehabilitation of the child within the parent's or guardian's household is unlikely: see s 16(5).
22.12	**Freeing for adoption and its effect**	The 'freeing for adoption' procedure, which applies only in agency cases, involves the court in making an order which *declares a child free to be adopted* where the court is satisfied that the parent or guardian freely and with full understanding of what is involved, agrees generally and unconditionally to the making of an adoption order, or his agreement to the making of an adoption order should be dispensed with under s 16(2): s 18(1). An agency may apply for a freeing order if the child is in the care of a local authority under a care order: s 18(2), (2A), amended by Sch 10 para 6 ChA 1989: see *Re U (A Minor)* (1993).
22.12.1	Father lacking parental responsibility	Under s 18(7) AA 1976, inserted by Sch 10, para 6(3) ChA 1989, the court must satisfy itself before making an order in the case of a child whose father does not have parental responsibility for him, that such a person has no intention of applying for a residence order (see 13.15) or a parental responsibility order or that if he did make any such application it would be likely to be refused.
22.12.2	Effects of freeing order	On the making of an order under s 18, parental responsibility for the child is given to the adoption agency: s 18(5), as amended by Sch 10, para 6(2) ChA 1989: see *Re A* (1993); *Re E* (1994); *Re P* (1994). The order extinguishes other orders issued under ChA 1989. If, 12 months after the making of a freeing order, no adoption order has been made and the child is not living with the person with whom he was placed for purposes of adoption, a parent or guardian may apply for the *revocation* of the freeing order. A revocation will bring to an end the parental responsibility given to the adoption agency and effectively return it to the parent(s) or guardian: s 20(3) AA 1976, substituted by Sch 10 para 8(2) ChA 1989.
22.12.3	Abolition recommended	The *Review Report* (1992) recommended the abolition of 'freeing for adoption'. It suggested in its place a 'pre-placement hearing' allowing an agency wishing to place a child to apply for a 'placement order' within the context of a specifically proposed placement.
22.13	**General procedures for adoption**	General procedures relating to an adoption order are governed in the High Court and the county courts by the Adoption

Rules 1984, and in the magistrates' courts by the Magistrates' Courts (Adoption) Rules 1984.

22.13.1 Application

The person(s) wishing to adopt will apply to the High Court, county court or magistrates' court. The child's parents or guardian (where the child has *not* been freed for adoption) will be made a respondent to the prospective adopters' application, with the local authority, agency or other person added by the court: see Adoption Rules 1984, rr 4, 15. Where the applicant intends to ask the court to dispense with parental consent, an appropriate statement must accompany the application.

22.13.2 Appointment of a reporting officer or guardian *ad litem*

A reporting officer will be appointed by the court to check that requirements concerning parental consent (eg its voluntary nature) have been complied with: see Adoption Rules 1984, r 17. A guardian *ad litem* (see 16.21) is appointed, eg, where parental consent has *not* been given: see r 18. (Both the reporting officer and the guardian *ad litem* are independent of the local authority or agency.) The guardian *ad litem* must submit a confidential report; for judicial discretion to disclose the report to a parent, see *Re D (Minors) (Adoption Reports: Confidentiality)* (1994).

22.13.3 Making the order

The court hearing takes place in private and the court may order any person to attend: Adoption Rules 1984, r 23. The child, applicants, respondent may attend the hearing. The court must be satisfied that all formal requirements are complied with, that consents are given, that an adoption order is appropriate and relevant given the general requirements of the 1976 Act as amended. The order is then made.

Note the following points carefully:

- The court, if it considers adoption to be inappropriate in the particular case, may make an interim order (see s 25 AA 1976) which vests parental responsibility in the applicants for a probationary period of two years.
- The court may refuse an order and, in such a case, a child placed with applicants by an adoption agency must be returned to the agency within seven days (see s 30(3) AA 1976, amended by Sch 10, para 17 ChA 1989).
- The court may make a residence order or some other s 8 order.
- Where an applicant is refused an order, no further application is possible unless it appears to the court that there has been a change in circumstances making it proper to proceed with the application: s 24(1)(b).

22.13.4 Order with conditions

The adoption order may contain such terms and conditions as the court thinks fit (s 12(6)), eg, concerning contact with relatives or natural parents: see *Re C* (1988) (access condition concerning brother of adopted child); *Re S* (1994) (refusal to attach conditions relating to the speculative circumstances of a possible blood transfusion).

22.14 Some legal effects of the order

An adoption order vests parental rights and duties relating to a particular child in his adopters: s 12(1). It extinguishes any parental responsibility which any person possessed before the order was made.

22.14.1 The child's status

An adopted child shall be treated in law where the adopters are a married couple, as if he had been born as a child of the marriage (whether or not he was in fact born after the marriage was solemnised); in any other case, as if he had been born to the adopter in wedlock (but not as a child of any actual marriage of the adopter): s 39(1). An adopted child shall, subject to subsection (3), be treated in law as if he were not the child of any person other than the adopter(s): s 39(2).

In the case of a child adopted by one of its natural parents as sole adoptive parent, subsection (2) has no effect as respects entitlement to property depending on relationship to that parent, or as respects anything else depending on that relationship: s 39(3).

Note s 39(4) which declares that the section prevents an adopted child from being illegitimate.

22.14.2 Rights of succession

Subject to a contrary indication, the rules of construction contained in this section apply to any instrument other than an existing instrument, so far as it contains a disposition of property: s 42(1). In applying s 39(1) (see 22.14 above) to a disposition which depends on the date of birth of a child or children of the adoptive parent(s), the disposition will be construed as if the adopted child had been born on the date of the adoption, or two or more children adopted on the same date had been born on that date in the order of their actual births, but this does not affect any reference to the age of a child: s 42(2).

22.14.3 Nationality rights

A child who is not a British citizen acquires British citizenship on adoption *if his adoptive parent is a British citizen*: see s 1(5) of the British Nationality Act 1981.

Where there are joint adopters, the adopted child acquires British citizenship if one of the adopters possesses such citizenship. Should the adoption order become ineffective, the child retains British citizenship: s 1(6) of the 1981 Act.

Note the question of prohibited degrees: see Sch 1 of the Marriage Act 1949. An adopted child and his adoptive parents are considered to be within the 'prohibited degrees' (of consanguinity); they may not intermarry. But an adopted child may marry his/her adoptive brother or sister, or other adoptive relatives: see s 47(1) AA 1976.	22.14.4 The problem of prohibited degrees
An adoption order may be revoked if an illegitimate child, adopted by his father or mother alone becomes legitimated by the marriage of his parents: s 52(1) AA 1976. For a recent attempt to have an adoption order set aside, see *Re B* (1994).	22.14.5 Revocation
The Registrar General maintains the *Adopted Children Register*: s 50(1). It may be searched with the leave of the court; but a person over 18 who has been adopted can request a copy of a record of birth: s 51(1). An adopted person under 18 intending to marry in England or Wales may obtain information as to whether the applicant and the person he intends to marry are within the prohibited degrees of relationship: s 51(2). Under s 51A, inserted by Sch 10, para 21 ChA 1989, the Registrar General keeps an *Adoption Contact Register*, allowing adopted persons to make contact with relatives. Part I of the Register contains names and addresses of adopted persons over 18 who wish to contact relatives, having obtained a record of birth under s 51. Part II contains names and addresses of relatives who wish to contact adopted persons. Note *R v Registrar General ex p Smith* (1991), in which the Court of Appeal upheld the denial of right of access to his birth certificate by a patient in Broadmoor who had a violent hatred of his adoptive parents: see Re X (1994), in which the Court of Appeal held that where the welfare of an adopted child required protection from a parent who would try to breach the confidentiality of the register, the High Court, in the exercise of its inherent jurisdiction, could attach to an adoption order an order that the Registrar General should not reveal the recorded details of that adoption without leave of the court.	22.15 **Registration**
The White Paper, *Adoption: The Future* (Cm 2288), was introduced in the House of Commons in November 1993. It suggested, among other reforms, that: all adoptions should continue to be authorised by the courts; children over 12 should have the right to participate in their own adoption and should give their consent before an adoption order can be made; where both parents oppose adoption, the courts should be positively satisfied that adoption does offer significantly better prospects for the child than less permanent alternatives; step-parents should continue to adopt, but it should be made	22.16 **Reform proposals**

possible to make and register joint parental responsibility for the child without severing the child's relationship with his other natural parent; a new type of guardianship order would give long-term carers legal recognition of their role without going as far as adoption.

The Family Rights Group (see [1994] Fam Law 326) has suggested a scheme for the reform of steps *preceding* adoption. The Group proposes that in all cases where a local authority decide that a child who is being looked after in care or accommodation needs placement in a permanent substitute family, the following steps should apply: the local authority should convene a *family group conference* of all members of the immediate and wider family to plan the child's future care; the local authority would then consider the family proposals and, if unable to agree, would apply to the court for a long-term placement order; the court would check that the requirement to call a conference had been complied with, and would apply the welfare principle and check list in s 1 ChA 1989; if a placement order were granted, the adoption agency would recruit foster carers or prospective adopters able to meet the child's identifiable needs. After the placement had been tried and tested for a given period of time, the foster parents or prospective adopters would apply to the court for an appropriate order; in the absence of parental consent the court would have power to dispense with it.

Summary of Chapter 22

Adoption

Essence of the adoption process

Adoption involves the termination of a child's legal rights and duties toward his natural parents and the substitution of similar rights and duties towards his adoptive parents. The child moves from one family to another.

The governing statute is the Adoption Act 1976, as amended by ChA 1989.

Adoption services

Every local authority has the duty to set up an adoption service (known also as an adoption agency): s 1 AA 1976. Non-profit making adoption societies may act as adoption agencies, subject to approval which is given for three years: s 3(4).

Who may apply for an adoption order

The lower age limit for persons wishing to adopt is 18; there appears to be no official maximum age. Where applicants are parent and step-parent, the parent should be at least 18. A single person aged 21 or over may adopt. A married person aged 21 or over may adopt if requirements concerning domicile are satisfied and the court is satisfied that his/her spouse cannot be found, the spouses are living apart, or a spouse is incapable of making an application for an order: see s 15(1).

An adoption order will not be made on the application of the mother or father of the child alone unless the court is satisfied that the other parent cannot be found or is dead.

A report on the health and family history of prospective adopters may be called for.

Who may be adopted

In general, children under 18 who are not and have not been married may be adopted.

The child's welfare

The welfare of the child to be adopted is the first consideration of the court and adoption agency; it is not the paramount consideration.

Private placements

It is an offence to make arrangements for an adoption unless the proposed adopter is a relative of the child or the person who is making the arrangement is acting in pursuance of a High Court Order: s 11(1).

Agency placements

Most placements for adoption are made by adoption agencies. Proposals for placement are referred to adoption panels which make recommendations to the agencies.

Consent to an adoption order

An adoption order is made where the child is declared 'free for adoption' (see s 18): this necessitates the court being satisfied that the parent or guardian of the child has freely consented to the making of an order, *or* consent has been dispensed with.

Consent may be dispensed with where the parent or guardian cannot be found or is incapable of giving assent, where agreement is withheld unreasonably, where there has been a persistent failure to discharge parental responsibility, where the child has been abandoned or neglected, or otherwise persistently ill-treated.

Legal effects of the adoption order

An adoption order vests parental rights and duties relating to a particular child in his adopters: s 12(1). It extinguishes parental responsibility possessed by any other person before the order was made. The adopted child is to be treated generally in law as if he were not the child of any person other than the adopter(s). A child who is not a British citizen acquires British citizenship if his adoptive parent is a British citizen: s 1(5) of the British Nationality Act 1981.

The Registers

The Registrar General maintains the Adopted Children Register which may be searched with leave, and the Adoption Contact Register, allowing adopted persons to make contact with relatives who may wish to make contact.

Chapter 23

Children's Rights and Their Significance (1)

23.1 The question of children's rights

In this chapter and the next we consider those interests of children which have been given expression by the common law and statute in the form of 'rights'. We note some jurists' definitions of 'rights' and set out some aspects of the rights of children under the law with particular reference to crime, contract and torts. What are rights specifically in relation to children? Questions of this nature have become particularly significant in recent years with the appearance of international Conventions concerning rights of the family and children, and with moves in the direction of a Bill of Rights for the UK which, presumably, might enshrine some children's rights now taken for granted, eg, the right of the child to life, welfare, education.

23.2 The basic concept of rights

Some examples of jurists' definitions of rights follow. It is suggested that the reader consider their relevance and validity in relation to the following family law rights which have been noted in previous chapters: the rights of the child to have his wishes taken into account by the court in the determination of certain questions concerning his future; the right of the child to commence proceedings under s 8 ChA 1989; the right of an adopted child, under 18, who intends to marry, to gain access to records concerning his birth.

Ginsberg (*On Justice in Society* (1965)) states that a person's rights are constituted by those *claims* he may make on his fellows in relation to the conditions of his well-being. Hohfeld (*Fundamental Legal Conceptions as applied to Judicial Reasoning* (1923)) defines a right as 'an enforceable claim to performance (action or forbearance) by another'. Holland (*Elements of Jurisprudence* (1880)) considered a right as 'the capacity residing in one person of controlling, with the assent and assistance of the State, the actions of others'. Holmes (*The Common Law* (1881)) referred to a right as 'nothing but permission to exercise certain natural powers and upon certain conditions obtain protection, restitution or compensation by the aid of public force'. Raz ('Legal Rights', in 4 Oxford Journal of Legal Studies 1 (1984)) considers law as creating a right 'if it is based upon and expresses the concept that a person has an interest which is sufficient ground for holding another person to be subject to a duty'.

These and many similar definitions seem to express the concept of 'a right' as a legally enforceable *claim* of one person against another that the other person shall do or shall not do a given act. It is in that wide sense that the essence of children's rights is perceived in this chapter and the next. The child is viewed as possessing claims on other persons which, within the context of the legal system are acknowledged, protected and met.

23.3 The problem of the correlative

Some jurists emphasise the correlative nature of rights and duties in maxims such as: 'No rights, no duties; no duties, no rights'. Others (see, eg, Radin, *A Restatement of Hohfeld*, Harvard Law Review, vol 51 (1938)) argue that rights and duties are absolutely equivalent statements of the same thing. Thus, the duty of parents to care for their child does not follow from the right of the child to protection and care, nor is the duty 'caused' by the right. The parents' duty *is* the child's right. Right and duty are one and the same thing to which different terms apply. The 'correlative thesis' has been expanded so as to suggest that there are no children's rights, since rights may be bestowed only upon persons who are capable of carrying out reciprocal duties, and children lack this capacity. This argument becomes less than attractive when its implications for neonates, two-year old children, the physically and mentally disadvantaged, for example, are considered.

(Note the statement of Lord Donaldson MR in *Re R (A Minor) (Wardship: Criminal Proceedings)* (1991): 'Children ... are citizens owing duties to society as a whole ... which are appropriate to their years and understanding.')

The generally pragmatic approach of English law to children's rights, in the areas of family law, criminal law, contract, etc, has not been affected by the 'correlative problem' and its implications for the child. Respect for persons generally and the desirability of promoting human flourishing have given rise to the necessity of protecting and nurturing the child, and have brought into existence clusters of *connected rights* often characterised by their non-derogability, such as the child's right to life and to freedom from violence. Rights of this nature have received recognition in the international Conventions and Declarations concerning the 'universal' rights of the child.

23.4 The international recognition of children's rights

Since the decade following the end of the First World War, the international community has expressed recognition of the importance of children's rights and their translation into effective legislation. The more important attempts to articulate and uphold these rights are noted below.

23.4.1 The Geneva Declaration 1924

The Fifth Assembly of the League of Nations published the First Declaration of the Rights of the Child in 1924. It made reference to basic requirements such as shelter, food and protection against exploitation, and set out general principles concerning child welfare.

23.4.2 The Universal Declaration of Human Rights 1948

The United Nations adopted a Declaration of Human Rights in 1948. It recognised the right of children to education and provided that motherhood and childhood were 'entitled to special care and assistance'. All children, legitimate or illegitimate, should enjoy the same social protection.

23.4.3 The European Convention on Human Rights 1950

The European Convention on Human Rights was promulgated by the Council of Europe in 1949, signed in Rome in 1950 and ratified by the UK in 1951. (It should not be confused with the laws of the European Community.) The Convention is not a part of English domestic law, but its influence is important: the declarations of the European Court of Human Rights are of significance in that where the UK is found to be in breach of the Convention, it is obliged to take appropriate action so as to secure compliance with it. Thus, the adverse finding of ECHR in *Campbell v UK* (1982) relating to corporal punishment in schools resulted in amendments to the law.

Among the provisions of the Convention is Article 8 which proclaims that everyone has the right to respect for his private and family life and his home. Article 12 sets out the right of persons of marriageable age to marry and found a family. Article 2 of the First Protocol states: 'No person shall be denied the right to education. In the exercise of its functions in relation to education and teaching, the State shall respect the right of parents to ensure such education and teaching in conformity with their own religious and philosophical convictions'. (The UK expressed its acceptance of Article 2 only so far as it is compatible with the provision of efficient instruction and training.)

23.4.4 Declaration of the Rights of the Child 1959

The Declaration of the Rights of the Child 1959 expanded the 1924 Geneva Declaration and applied general principles to the claims of children in relation to housing, education, recreation, social security, etc.

23.4.5 The United Nations Convention on the Rights of the Child 1989

The United Nations Convention on the Rights of the Child was ratified by the UK in December 1991. The 'rights' of which it speaks are, in some cases, not recognised by English courts, but the UK Government is obliged to give *general* recognition to them.

The UN Convention applies 'to every human being below the age of 18, unless, under the law applicable to the child, a majority is attained earlier': Article 1. Parties to the Convention must respect and ensure that the rights in the Convention are extended to all children within their jurisdiction without any discrimination: Article 2. In all actions concerning children, 'the best interests' of the child shall be a primary consideration: Article 3(1).

Under Article 6, States must recognise that every child possesses an inherent right to life; States must ensure, as far as possible, the child's survival and development. Article 7 requires that a child shall have the right to a name, to acquire a nationality, and, as far as possible, 'the right to know and be cared for by his parents'. The right not to be separated from one's parents against their will is recognised in Art 9. Children have the right to express their views freely: Art 12. Articles 14-17 give recognition to the child's right to freedom of thought, conscience and religion, freedom of association and peaceful assembly, privacy and access to information. Both parents are recognised as having common responsibilities for the upbringing and development of the child: Art 18(1). Article 21 requires that States shall ensure that the best interests of the child shall be the paramount consideration in adoption. Articles 32-35 express the right of the child to protection from certain forms of exploitation. Article 37 concerns protection of the child against cruel, inhuman or degrading treatment or punishment.

In January 1995, a UN committee, monitoring the progress of the UN Convention on the Rights of the Child, produced a report, in the form of an 'audit' of children's rights in the UK. The report welcomed the Children Act 1989, praised government initiatives to deal with the bullying of children and sexual abuse, and commended plans for the introduction of new legislation relating to adoption and domestic violence. But there was criticism of what was perceived as repeated violation of the Convention by the UK.

- Attention was drawn by the committee to the high number of children estimated to be living in poverty in the UK and to the high rates of divorce and teenage pregnancies.

- The committee noted the effects of benefit allowances which it considered to be inadequate.

- The committee recommended: that policy on the treatment of child refugees in the UK be reviewed; that a legal ban on the chastisement of children at home and on corporal punishment in private schools be introduced; that there be a review of plans to set up detention centres for offenders aged 12-24; that the age of criminal responsibility be raised.

- The committee called for the appointment of a children's Ombudsman and urged that children be taught about their rights.

23.5 The criminal law and the life of the child

Some of the ways in which the law seeks to protect the life of the child and to punish offenders are noted below.

Under the Infant Life (Preservation) Act 1929, 'any person who, with intent to destroy the life of a child capable of being born alive, by any wilful act causes a child to die before it has an existence independent of its mother, shall be guilty of an offence ... of child destruction ... Provided that no person shall be found guilty of an offence under this section unless it is proved that the act which caused the death of the child was not done in good faith for the purpose only of preserving the life of the mother': s 1(1).

The offence cannot be committed during the first stages of pregnancy. It can be charged against any person, not merely the mother: see *Rance v Mid-Downs Health Authority* (1991). No offence under this Act is committed by a registered medical practitioner who terminates a pregnancy in accordance with the provisions of s 5(1) of the Abortion Act 1967, substituted by s 37 HFEA 1990.

Under the Infanticide Act 1938, it is an offence for a mother to cause the death of her child, under the age of 12 months, where the balance of her mind was disturbed by her not having recovered fully from the birth or the effect of lactation.

The crime does not apply in the case of unborn children, and has application only in the case of a killing by the child's mother. See *R v Scott* (1973).

23.6 Manslaughter

Manslaughter may be described, in general terms, as unlawful homicide which cannot be classified as murder. Thus, X may be guilty of manslaughter where, for example, as a result of grossly negligent conduct, he kills a child, C; or, suffering from diminished responsibility or acting under provocation, he kills C; or, by an unlawful act, likely to cause bodily harm, of a non-grievous nature, he kills C.

23.7 Child cruelty

Under s 1(1) C&YPA 1933, 'if any person who has attained the age of sixteen years and has responsibility for any child or young person under that age, wilfully assaults, ill-treats, neglects, abandons, or exposes him, or causes or procures him to be assaulted, ill treated, neglected, abandoned, or exposed, in a manner likely to cause him unnecessary suffering or injury to health (including injury to or loss of sight, or hearing, or limb, or organ of the body, and any mental derangement, that person shall be guilty of an offence.'

Note *R v Young* (1993): to establish defendant's guilt of child cruelty it is enough that the jury are unanimous that cruelty in the sense alleged by the prosecution has been established. There is no need to agree on specific evidence.

23.8 Neglect

Under s 1(2) C&YPA 1933, a parent or other person legally liable to maintain a child or young person or the legal guardian of a child or young person shall be deemed to have neglected him in a manner likely to cause injury to his health if he has failed to provide adequate food, clothing, medical aid or lodging for him, or if, having been unable otherwise to provide such food (etc), he has failed to take steps to procure it to be provided under the enactments applicable in that behalf. See, eg, *R v Harvey* (1987); *R v Pelling* (1988).

23.9 The question of corporal punishment and the child

In general, chastisement of a child by his parent(s) involving corporal punishment, appears to be outside the criminal law, provided that in the particular circumstances it is *moderate and reasonable*. Note that under the Children's Homes Regulations 1991, reg 8(2)(a), corporal punishment is abolished in local authority children's homes. Under the European Convention for Human Rights, Art 3, concerning inhuman and degrading punishment, corporal punishment which exceeds a minimum level of severity may infringe that article: see *Costello-Roberts v UK* (1993). Note also the UN Convention, Art 19, which requires States to take all appropriate measures to protect the child from all forms of physical or mental violence while in the care of parents, legal guardians or any other person who has care of the child. See *Y v UK* (1994).

Under the Education (No 2) Act 1968 corporal punishment is prohibited in State-funded schools and in relation to any State-funded pupils in independent schools: see s 47. It remains generally lawful in the independent school sector. Punishment of a degrading or inhuman character cannot be justified: see s 293 of the Education Act 1993. In determining whether punishment is inhuman or degrading, all the circumstances of the case must be considered including the reason for its administration, nature, manner, mental and physical effects.

Note *London Borough of Sutton v Davis* (1994) (a non-school case) in which the court held that justices were entitled to conclude that a child minder (see 19.12.2) was not unfit to look after children despite her refusal to agree to the local authority's policy and to undertake not to smack them. See *Guidance, Childminding and Smacking* by C Barton [1994] Fam Law 284.

Assault, battery, wounding were noted at 5.11. They are often at the basis of cases of child abuse (see 23.12 below).	23.10	**Assault, battery, wounding**
Most categories of sexual offence cover adult and child alike; some few relate specifically to young girls. It should be remembered that the law on sexual offences has changed as public attitudes to deviations from social norms have changed. 'What is striking in one age is normal in another; the perversions of yesterday may be the routine or the fashion of tomorrow': *per* Lord Wilberforce in *DPP v Boardman* (1975).	23.11	**Sexual offences involving children**
A man commits rape if (a) he has sexual intercourse with a person (whether vaginal or anal) who at the time of the intercourse does not consent to it; and (b) at the time he knows that the person does not consent to the intercourse or is reckless as to whether that person consents to it: s 1 Sexual Offences Act 1956, substituted by s 142 Criminal Justice and Public Order Act 1994. Intercourse is deemed complete upon proof of penetration only: s 44 Sexual Offences Act 1956. Note that the presumption that a boy under 14 was incapable of committing rape was abolished under the Sexual Offences Act 1993, s 1.	23.11.1	Rape
It is an offence for a man to have sexual intercourse with a woman whom he knows to be his granddaughter, daughter, sister or mother: s 10(1) 1956 Act. Consent of the female is no defence. If the female is aged 16 or over and consents in full knowledge of the relationship, she, too, is guilty of the offence.	23.11.2	Incest
It is an offence for a man to have unlawful sexual intercourse with a girl under 13: s 5 of the 1956 Act. Belief, even though reasonable, that the girl is not under 13 is no defence: see *R v Oakley* (1990).	23.11.3	Intercourse with girls under 13
It is an offence subject to certain exceptions for a man to have unlawful intercourse with a girl under 16: s 6(1) 1956 Act. The exceptions relate to intercourse during an invalid marriage where the husband believes the girl to be his wife and has reasonable cause for that belief: s 6(2); and where the husband is under 24, has not been charged with a like offence and believed (with reason) that she was over the age of 16: s 6(3).	23.11.4	Intercourse with girls between 13-16

23.11.5	Indecent assault	It is an offence for any person male or female to make an indecent assault upon a male or female: ss 14, 15 of the 1956 Act. There is no statutory definition of 'indecent assault'. It was stated in *R v Kowalski* (1988) that the offence is concerned with contravention of standards of decent behaviour in regard to sexual modesty or privacy. In *R v Thomas* (1985), the Court of Appeal held that there are two requirements for an indecent assault on a child under 16: the act complained of must be indecent, and it must be an act which, without the victim's consent, would be in the nature of an assault.
23.11.6	Indecency with Children Act 1960	Under the Indecency with Children Act 1960, it is an offence for any person to commit an act of gross indecency with or towards a child under the age of 14 or to incite such a child to do such an act with him or with any other person: see *R v Francis* (1989).
23.11.7	Abduction of females	Under the Sexual Offences Act 1956, it is an offence to abduct an unmarried girl under 18 from her parent or guardian, if she is taken with the intention that she shall have unlawful sexual intercourse with men or a particular man: s 19(1). It is an offence to take an unmarried girl under the age of 16 out of the possession of her parent or guardian against his will: s 20(1). 'Guardian' means any person having parental responsibility for or care of the girl: see Sch 10 ChA 1989.
23.11.8	Protection of Children Act 1978	It is an offence under the Protection of Children Act 1978 for a person to take, or permit to be taken, any indecent photograph of a person under 16, to distribute or show it, to advertise that he distributes, shows or intends to show such a photograph. The offence is extended, under s 84 CJPOA 1984, to 'pseudo-photographs', ie, images made by computer graphics which appear to be photographs.
23.12	**Child abuse**	The widely-used term 'child abuse' does not refer to any one particular offence: it tends to be used generally to cover a variety of recognised crimes which cause significant harm to a child, such as rape, indecent assault, cruelty, incest, wounding. It was described in a generic sense in *Working Together Under The Children Act* 1989 (HMSO, 1991) as 'actual or likely sexual exploitation of a child or an adolescent'. (Note the important problem of 'emotional abuse' of a child: see *F v Suffolk CC* (1981) – in proceedings related to C&YPA 1969, s 1(2), it was held that in considering the question of whether a child's proper development is being prevented or neglected, the court should have regard to the child's mental and emotional development.)

Note *Re H (Minors) (Wardship: Sexual Abuse)* (1991) in which the court considered the question of removal of an abused child from his home and parents. The Court of Appeal held that when assessing an allegation of sexual abuse of a child, the judge should initially make an evaluation of the evidence of fact and expert opinion in order to establish whether there was any evidence of sexual abuse. Then he should establish whether there was any evidence identifying the abuser. In keeping the question of the child's welfare paramount, the judge should have regard to the danger that in attempting to prevent the child from sexual abuse, society might cause greater harm to the child by removing him from his home and parents, no matter how inadequate, to whom he was attached.

For a case in which the Court of Appeal held that access should *not* be allowed to continue after sexual abuse had been found, see *Re R (A Minor) (Child Abuse: Access)* (1988).

23.12.1 Standard of proof

In *Re W (Minors) (Sexual Abuse: Standard of Proof)* (1994), the Court of Appeal considered the standard of proof in relation to sexual abuse (in civil proceedings). *Per* Balcombe LJ, with reference to 'the appropriate standard': '(1) The burden of proof lies upon the party who asserts that abuse has occurred ... (2) The standard is *the balance of probabilities* ... (3) The more serious the allegation, the more convincing is the evidence needed to tip the balance in respect of it.' See also *KVS v GGS* (1992); Children (Admissibility of Hearsay Evidence) Order 1991 (SI 1991/1115); *Sexual Abuse: Standard of Proof* by V Smith [1994] Fam Law 626; *Re B (A Minor) (Sexual Abuse: Standard of Proof)* (1994).

23.12.2 Interviews, investigation

In *Re M (Minors) (Sexual Abuse: Evidence)* (1993), involving the dismissal of allegations of so-called 'satanic abuse' and emotional abuse of children, the Court of Appeal stated that it was important that interviews with young children should be conducted as soon as possible after allegations have been made and should have investigation as their primary purpose. But interviews by experts conducted later in an appropriate manner could provide valuable evidence as to the occurrence of abuse. (Note [1994] Fam Law 406, in which there is reference to a three-year expert enquiry into 'satanic abuse', defined as 'sexual and physical abuse of children as part of rites directed to a magical or religious objective'. The enquiry concluded that 'satanic abuse' is a myth: no evidence was found to substantiate 84 cases in which it was alleged to have taken place.)

See, for an overall survey of this topic, *Re-focus on Child Abuse – Medical, Legal and Social Work Perspectives*, ed A Levy (1994).

23.13 Kidnapping

The essential feature of kidnapping under common law is 'the stealing and carrying away, or secreting of some person' (East, cited and approved in *R v Reid* (1973)). The offence may be committed in relation to a person of any age who is stolen and carried away against his will, or, if that person is a minor, against the will of his lawful guardian or friends. The use of fraud or force is an essential element of the offence: see *R v Hale* (1974). It suffices that the victim be carried away even for a relatively short distance and time: see *R v Wellard* (1978). In *R v D* (1984), the House of Lords stated explicitly that a father could not plead his so-called 'rights as a father' in order to carry off his child.

23.14 Child abduction

Section 1 of the Child Abduction Act 1984 created the offence of 'child abduction' which is committed by a person connected with a child under the age of 16, who takes or sends that child out of the UK without the appropriate consent. Persons 'connected with a child' include its parents or guardians or one who has custody of the child or who has a residence order in his favour in force. 'Appropriate consent' means the consent of each of the following: the child's mother, the child's father (if he has parental responsibility for him), any guardian of the child, any person in whose favour a residence order is in force with respect to the child, any person having custody of the child. The court may grant leave by virtue of any provision of ChA 1989, Part II. See *R v Sherry* (1993).

23.14.1 Defences

A person does not commit an offence under the 1984 Act, s 1, if he is a person in whose favour there is a residence order with respect to the child and he takes or sends him out of the UK for a period of less than one year: s 1(4). But subsection (4) does not apply where the person taking or sending the child out of the UK does so in breach of an order under ChA 1989, Part II: s 1(4A). Nor is an offence committed by a person doing anything without the consent of another person whose consent is required if he does it in the belief that the other has consented, or would consent if he was aware of the circumstances, or he has taken all reasonable steps to make communication with the other person but has been unable to communicate with him or the other person has unreasonably refused consent: s 1(5). The defence that the other person has unreasonably refused consent has no application where that person is one in whose favour there is a residence order in force with respect to the child, or he has custody of the child, or the person taking or sending the child out of the UK is acting in breach of an order made by a court in the UK: s 1(5A).

23.14.2 The Hague Convention

The Child Abduction and Custody Act 1985, Part I, introduced into English law the *Hague Convention on the Civil Aspects of International Child Abduction* signed in October 1980. The objects of the Convention are to secure the prompt return of children wrongfully removed to or retained in any Contracting State, and to ensure that rights of custody and of access under the law of one Contracting State are effectively respected in the other Contracting States. The 1985 Act implemented, additionally, the *European Convention 1980 on the Recognition and Enforcement of Decisions Concerning Custody of Children*. See *Child Abduction and the Hague Convention,* by N Lowe and M Nicholls [1994] Fam Law 191; *Re B (A Minor) (Abduction)* (1994).

The Hague Convention applies to any child under 16, habitually resident in one Contracting State, who has been removed wrongfully or retained in another Contracting State: Art 4. Where both parties have equal rights of custody, unilateral action by one parent cannot change the child's habitual residence save by agreement or acquiescence of the other parent or a court order: *Re S* (1994). A removal or retention is considered 'wrongful' if it is in breach of rights of custody vested in a court or of the rights of defendant: see *Re H* (1990).

Under Art 12 the court may order the return of the child forthwith. Litigation under the Hague Convention is neither adversarial nor inquisitorial, and the court is bound to order the abducted child's return if the criteria in the Convention are met: *Re N* (1993).

Under Art 13, a return of the child may be refused if the person, institution, body having the care of the child was not actually exercising custody rights at the time of removal or retention, or had consented to or subsequently acquiesced in that removal or retention, or there is a grave risk of the child's return exposing him to physical or psychological harm or otherwise placing the child in an intolerable situation. There *may be* a refusal to return the child if it is found that the child objects to being returned and has attained a degree of maturity and an age at which his views ought to be taken into account. For an example of children returned despite their wishes, see *Re R (Minors: Child Abduction)* (1994).

23.14.3 The European Convention

The European Convention 1980 may be invoked if the applicant has a court order in his favour and the child has been improperly removed across international boundaries in breach of custody decisions. The central authority in the child's original country of residence must register the custody order in a court of the Contracting State to which he has been removed. This latter court has the same powers of enforcement as if it had made the original order concerning the child, so that his return may be ordered.

Where an application is made under the Hague *and* European Conventions, precedence is given to the Hague Convention.

23.14.4 Abduction within the UK

Under the Family Law Act 1986, court orders concerning children under 16 made in one part of the UK are recognised in any other part of the UK. Further, the court may order disclosure of where a child is (see s 33), order the child's recovery (see s 34), place restrictions on the removal of the child from the jurisdiction (see s 35). Under s 37, the court may order the surrender of a UK passport which has been issued to, or contains particulars of, a child where there is an order restricting removal.

23.15 A note on the literature concerning children's rights

The range of literature on rights in general and children's rights in particular is unusually wide. The following examples will be of interest to students making an initial approach to these topics.

- *Rights*. J Waldron's *Theories of Rights* (1984) examines a variety of rights theories in detail. In Chapter 1 of *Civil Liberties* (1994), H Fenwick outlines the general nature of rights and liberties.

- *Children's rights*. J Eekelaar, in *The Importance of Thinking that Children have Rights* (1992) (6 IJLF 221) explores the basis of rights in relation to children. In his *Emergence of Children's Rights* (1986) (6 Oxford JLS 161) he considers the 'basic interests' of the child: it is the obligation of parents to secure these interests, but the State ought to intervene where this duty is neglected. M Freeman's *The Rights and Wrongs of Children* (1983) examines children's rights in relation to welfare and protection. A Bainham's *Children: The Modern Law* (1993) includes a review of controversies concerning children's rights.

- *The child as legal object*. In the chapter headed 'The Child as Legal Object'(1993), in *Family Law Matters*, Professor K O'Donovan provides an unusual and compelling critique of traditional concepts of children's rights. She suggests that children's legal subjectivity is denied by the existing legal system, and their judicial capacity to act is inherently weak. Her solution to the problem of developing the quality of children's rights rests on an enlarging of the concept of *the trust* (see 6.1.3) so as to embrace the person and property of the child.

Summary of Chapter 23

Children's Rights and Their Significance (1)

Rights are constituted by the *claims* a person may make on his fellows in relation to his well-being. Children's rights in the UK are concerned with the protection and well-being of the child, leading to his flourishing.

The basic concept of rights

The *Geneva Declaration* 1924 referred to basic requirements (food, shelter) in terms of child requirements. The *Universal Declaration of Human Rights 1948* recognised the right of children to education and social protection. The *European Convention on Human Rights* 1950 proclaims, eg, the right to marry and found a family, the right to education. The *Declaration of the Rights of the Child* 1959 spoke of the claims of children to housing, education, recreation, etc.

The *UN Convention on the Rights of the Child 1989* applies to all children under 18 and enunciates rights such as an inherent right to life, the right of a child to a name and nationality, the child's right to freedom of thought, etc.

International recognition of children's rights

The criminal law seeks to protect the life of the child and to ensure his freedom from violence. The Infant Life (Preservation) Act 1929, the Infanticide Act 1938, the law against unlawful homicide are examples of the law punishing those who seek to offend against the child's right to life. Cruelty to children is dealt with under s 1(1) C&YPA 1933. See *R v Young* (1933).

Neglect of the child resulting in injury to him is covered by s 1(2) C&YPA 1933. See *R v Harvey* (1987).

Corporal punishment is generally forbidden. Where it is allowed, in very restricted circumstances, it must be neither degrading nor inhuman.

The criminal law and the child

Sexual offences involving children are covered in the Criminal Justice and Public Order Act 1994 (in which rape is re-defined), and the Sexual Offences Act 1956 (incest, unlawful sexual intercourse with young girls, indecent assault, abduction).

The widely-used term 'child abuse' has been described as 'actual or likely sexual exploitation of a child or adolescent'. It generally refers to rape, indecent assault, etc.

Assault, battery and wounding are often at the basis of cases of child abuse

Kidnapping is prohibited, as is abduction of a child: see s 1 of the Child Abduction Act 1984.

The Hague Convention

The Hague Convention on the Civil Aspects of International Child Abduction 1980 operates so as to secure the prompt return of children wrongfully removed to or retained in any of the Contracting States. The Convention applies to any child under 16 habitually resident in a Contracting State who has been wrongfully removed to or retained in another Contracting State. The court may order, under the terms of the Convention, the return of any such child.

The Child Abduction and Custody Act 1985 is based on the Hague Convention and the European Convention on the Recognition and Enforcement of Decisions Concerning Custody of Children 1980.

Chapter 24

Children's Rights and Their Significance (2)

24.1 Protection of the child from harmful goods and activities

The criminal law is concerned to establish a variety of prohibitions and other controls which may protect the child from the likelihood of certain types of harm.

- Under s 169 of the Licensing Act 1964, it is an offence to knowingly sell intoxicating liquor to a person under 18: see *Howker v Robinson* (1973).

- Under the Protection of Children (Tobacco) Act 1986, it is an offence to sell any tobacco product to persons under 16. The Children and Young Persons (Protection from Tobacco) Act 1991 increased the penalties for the sale of tobacco to persons under 16 and prohibited further the sale of unpackaged cigarettes. Warning statements on vending machines and in retail premises must inform customers of the illegality of the sale of tobacco to persons under 16. See *Hereford and Worcester CC v T & S Stores* (1994).

- Under the Intoxicating Substances (Supply) Act 1985, it is an offence for a person to supply or offer to supply a substance other than a controlled drug to a person under 18 whom he knows, or has reasonable cause to believe, to be under that age, or to a person who is acting on behalf of a person under that age and whom he knows, or has reasonable cause to believe to be so acting, if he knows or has reasonable cause to believe that the substance is, or its fumes are, likely to be inhaled by the person under 18 for the purpose of causing intoxication: s 1(1).

24.2 Protecting the child from exploitation as an employee

Employment law as it relates specifically to 'children' and 'young persons' is concerned to a large extent with protecting these groups from exploitation. The relevant legislation differentiates 'children' (those below school-leaving age) and 'young persons' (those above school leaving age), and is based upon C&YPA 1933 and the Employment Act 1989.

24.2.1 General restriction upon the employment of children

Sections 18-21 C&YPA 1933, as subsequently modified by Sch 3 of the Employment Act 1989, impose restrictions on the employment of children under 13, and prohibit children working before the ending of the school day, before 7 am or after 7 pm on any day, or for more than two hours on any school day. The child is prohibited, additionally, from carrying, moving or lifting any objects so heavy as to be likely to cause injury to him. Local authorities may make byelaws allowing for the employment of children in limited circumstances: see Sch 3 Employment Act 1989.

24.2.2 Specific restrictions upon the employment of children

There are specified types of employment closed to children as a result of legislation, eg, work in factories (see s 167 Factories Act 1961), mines (Mines and Quarries Act 1954, as amended by s 9 Employment Act 1989). Employment in street trading is prohibited; but children aged 14 may be employed in a limited capacity by their parents: see Sch 3 Employment Act 1989. For the employment of children in entertainment, see C&YPA 1933, 1969. A local education authority may initiate proceedings concerning offences under C&YPA 1933: s 39. Under s 59 of the Education Act 1944, a local authority may prohibit or limit children's employment where it appears to them that a child's employment is prejudicial to his health or is rendering him unfit to benefit fully from his education.

24.3 Protecting young persons

Legislation such as the Young Persons (Employment) Acts 1938, 1964 regulated many aspects of the employment of those classified as 'young persons'. These statutes were repealed by the Employment Act 1989 which abolished many aspects of protective legislation concerning employment. The Employment Act 1989 was intended to provide a measure of deregulation of the labour market. Section 10 removed a number of restrictions on the hours of work of young persons and on the types of employment which may be performed by them. Additionally, the Secretary of State was given wide powers to amend or repeal statutory provisions concerning the employment of persons under 18. The Government's Consultative Document, *Restrictions on the Employment of Young People and the Removal of Sex Discrimination in Employment* (1987) noted that legislation concerning the employment of young people had developed in a piecemeal fashion since the beginning of the 19th century, and was now highly complex, inconsistent and in many cases out of date, either because the processes to which it referred were obsolete or because the conditions and social attitudes which inspired it no longer prevailed. Many of the restrictions were hard to justify and ought to be repealed, particularly because of the administrative burdens which result and because they may have a detrimental effect on young persons' employment opportunities. The Employment Act 1989 sought to translate these views into the form of legislation.

24.4 A note on the criminal responsibility of minors

For purposes related to responsibility under the criminal law, minors are classified as follows: those under 10; those of 10 and under 14; those over 14.

There is a conclusive presumption that a child under 10 at the date of his having allegedly committed the offence is *doli incapax*, ie, incapable of criminal intention or malice, so that he cannot be guilty of any offence. See s 16 C&YPA 1963; *Walters v Lunt* (1951).

Additionally, there is a presumption that children in the 10-under 14 age group are *doli incapax*; that presumption might be rebutted by proof that the child knew that what he was doing was seriously wrong; the burden of rebutting the presumption of *doli incapax* is on the prosecution. See, eg, *A v DPP* (1991). In *Curry v DPP* (1994), a Divisional Court held that the presumption was now out of date, no longer accorded with the changing conditions of society and is therefore to be treated as no longer good law. *Per* Mann LJ:

> 'The rule is divisive and perverse: divisive, because it tends to attach criminal consequences to the acts of children coming from what used to be called good homes more readily than to the acts of others; perverse, because it tends to absolve from criminal responsibility the very children most likely to commit criminal acts.'

(The House of Lords later overturned this decision.)

Minors above the age of 14 are held, in general, to be responsible for their actions 'entirely as if they were forty': *per* Erle J in *R v Smith* (1845).

The C&YPA 1969 sought to prohibit the prosecution of a child (aged 10-13 inclusive) for any crime except murder; the prosecution of a young person (aged 14-17 inclusive) was to be limited. The Criminal Justice Act 1991, Sch 13, effectively repealed these prohibitions. Today, where a child or young person appears before a magistrates' court charged with an indictable offence other than homicide he will be tried *summarily*; but this will not apply unless he has attained the age of 14 and the offence is one which, in the case of an adult, carries a penalty of 14 years' imprisonment or more (not being an offence for which the sentence is fixed by law) and the court considers that if he is found guilty of the offence it ought to be possible to sentence him to be detained under s 53(2) C&YPA 1933; or he is charged jointly with an adult and the court considers it necessary in the interests of justice to commit them both for trial: s 24(1) Magistrates' Courts Act 1980. A child or young person who is not accused jointly with an adult is to be tried in a youth court (formerly 'juvenile court'): s 29 Magistrates' Courts Act 1980.

For recent legislation concerning 'secure training orders' for young offenders (ordering young offenders to undergo a period of detention in a secure training centre, followed by a period of supervision), and custodial sentences for young offenders, see CJPOA 1994, ss 1, 16.

24.5 Accountability of parents

The question of whether and how far accountability for a child's criminal offence ought to be attached to the parents was answered in part by s 55 C&YPA 1933. Under s 55(1), where a child or young person is convicted and fined, the court can order that the fine be paid by the parent or guardian unless they cannot be found or the court considers that it would be unreasonable to make such an order having regard to the circumstances of the case.

In 1990, a Government White Paper, *Crime, Justice and Protecting the Public* (Cmnd 965) was published, suggesting an intensification of the measures for enforcing parental responsibility in relation to offences committed by minors.

24.5.1 Section 56 Criminal Justice Act 1991

Section 56 of the Criminal Justice Act 1991 inserted into C&YPA 1933 a new section (s 34A) which concerns the attendance at court of a parent or guardian. Where a child or young person is charged with an offence, the court may in any case, and shall, in the case of a child or young person under 16, require the parent or guardian to attend court 'during all stages of the proceedings', unless the court is satisfied that this is unreasonable in the circumstances.

24.5.2 Section 57 Criminal Justice Act 1991

Section 57 of the Criminal Justice Act 1991, adds to s 55(1) C&YPA 1933 (see 24.5 above) a new s 55(1B): 'In the case of a young person who has attained the age of 16, subsections (1) and (1A) shall have effect as if, instead of imposing a duty, they conferred a power to make such an order as is mentioned in those subsections'. Note that s 55(1A) provides that where a child or young person would otherwise be required to pay a fine because of a failure to comply with a supervision order or a community service order, the court may order the parent or guardian to pay the fine, subject to the qualifications in s 55(1).

24.5.3 Section 58 Criminal Justice Act 1991

Section 58 of the Criminal Justice Act 1991, which applies where a child has not attained the age of 16, deals with the binding over of an offender's parent or guardian. The court may order the parent or guardian to enter into a recognisance to take proper care of the offender and exercise proper control over him, and where the parent refuses unreasonably, to pay a fine.

24.6 Children as witnesses in criminal proceedings

The general competence of a child to give evidence in criminal proceedings is determined largely by the Criminal Justice Act 1988, as amended. Under s 33A, a child's evidence is to be given unsworn. A deposition of a child's unsworn evidence may be taken for purposes of criminal proceedings as if that evidence had been given on oath. ('Child' in this context refers to a person under 14.)

Reports of proceedings in which children or young persons are concerned are set out in s 49 C&YPA 1933, substituted by s 49 CJPOA 1994. Reports may not be published which reveal the name, address, or school of any child or young person concerned in proceedings or which include particulars likely to lead to the identification of the child or young person.

24.6.1 The determining of competence

In establishing a child's competence, a child aged 14 or over is treated in the same way as an adult. See *Re Z* (1990), *per* Lord Lane CJ: 'The question in each case which the court must decide is whether the child is possessed of sufficient intelligence to justify the reception of the evidence and understands the duty of speaking the truth. These criteria will inevitably vary widely from child to child, and may indeed vary according to the circumstances of the case, the nature of the case, and the nature of the evidence which the child is called upon to give ...'

Where a judge makes an inquiry as to the child's competence to give evidence, he should not merely follow the decisions of the justices who had raised the question: see *R v Surgenor* (1940). The child ought to be examined in open court in the presence of the jury and defendant: *R v Dunne* (1929).

24.6.2 The child's unsworn evidence

Under s 34(2) of the Criminal Justice Act 1988, as amended by s 32(2) CJPOA 1994, any requirement whereby at a trial on indictment it is obligatory for the court to give the jury a warning about convicting the accused on the uncorroborated evidence of a child, is abrogated.

For the use of video technology in cases involving child witnesses, see the Criminal Justice Acts 1988, s 32A, and 1991, s 54(7), and CJPOA 1994, s 50. For the use of screens while a child is giving evidence, see *R v X* (1990): see *R v Rawlings* (1994).

24.7 Children as witnesses in civil proceedings

In civil proceedings the court may make an inquiry as to the competence of a child under 14 who is to be sworn prior to giving evidence. In *R v Hayes* (1977), Bridge LJ set out a criterion based upon the importance of finding whether the child has a sufficient appreciation of 'the solemnity of the occasion' and the added responsibility of telling the truth, which is involved in taking an oath, over and above the duty to tell the truth 'which is an ordinary duty of normal social conduct'.

24.7.1 Section 96 Children Act 1989

Where a child who is called as a witness in any civil proceedings does not, in the opinion of the court, understand the nature of an oath, his evidence may be heard if, in the court's opinion, he understands that it is his duty to tell the truth, and he has sufficient understanding to justify his evidence being heard: s 96(1), (2). Under s 96(3), the Lord Chancellor may make provision by order for the admissibility of evidence which might otherwise be inadmissible under any rule of law regarding hearsay. See the Children (Admissibility of Hearsay Evidence) Order 1991 (SI 1991/1115) made under s 96(3).

24.7.2 Examination of a child in relation to proceedings

Under the Family Proceedings Rules 1991, no person may examine a child medically or psychiatrically in relation to the preparation of evidence to be used in proceedings without having obtained the leave of the court.

24.8 Minors and the law of contract

Common law and statute combined for long in an attempt to protect young persons who lacked general maturity and business acumen from those who would exploit their ignorance. The law was concerned, too, with the protection of adults who entered into business transactions which implied contractual relationships with minors. At common law contracts for 'necessaries' were fully binding on minors, while other types of contract were considered to be voidable. In the area of voidable contracts there were those by which he was bound until he avoided them during his minority or within a reasonable time after his majority had been attained; there were those by which he was not bound unless he ratified them on attaining his majority.

The Infants Relief Act 1874 declared that certain types of contract (concerning loans, non-necessaries, accounts stated) were 'absolutely void', and that any ratification by a person who had attained his majority of a contract into which he had entered during his minority was unenforceable.

24.8.1 The current situation: valid contracts

Contracts for necessaries and contracts of service bind the minor if they are beneficial to him. Where a young person has entered a contract for the supply of goods or services to him, he is generally bound by its terms. 'Necessaries' are goods suitable to the condition in life of the minor and to his actual requirements at the time of sale and delivery: see s 3(3) of the Sale of Goods Act 1979. There is an added measure of protection for young persons in that where a contract contains onerous terms it will not generally be enforced.

A contract of apprenticeship or service will bind the minor, but only where, as a whole, it is beneficial to him: see *Roberts v Gray* (1913).

24.8.2 Voidable contracts

Voidable contracts bind the minor unless they are repudiated by him during his minority or within a short time of attaining his majority. Contracts of this nature include marriage settlements, purchase of company shares, contracts involving land, and partnership agreements. Where the minor repudiates a voidable contract future liabilities under that contract end; he may not recover any money he has paid unless there has been a total failure of consideration: see, eg, *Steinberg v Scala (Leeds) Ltd* (1923).

24.8.3 Void contracts

A contract which is neither valid nor voidable cannot be enforced against a minor. The Minors' Contracts Act 1987 seeks to remove certain restrictions on the enforceability of contracts into which minors have entered. The Act repealed the Infants Relief Act 1874 (see 24.8 above) and the Betting and Loans (Infants) Act 1892, s 5, which invalidated contracts to repay loans advanced during minority.

- Under s 2 of the 1987 Act, where a guarantee is given in respect of an obligation of a party to a contract made after the commencement of this Act, and the obligation is unenforceable against him (or he repudiates the contract) because he was a minor when the contract was made, the guarantee shall not for that reason alone be unenforceable against the guarantor.

- Under s 3 of the 1987 Act, where a person ('the plaintiff') has after the commencement of the Act entered into a contract with another ('the defendant'), and the contract is unenforceable against the defendant (or he repudiates it) because he was a minor when the contract was made, the court may, if it is just and equitable to do so, require the defendant to transfer to the plaintiff any property acquired by the defendant under the contract, or any other property representing it.

24.9 Minors and the law of torts

The law of torts provides an important measure of protection for minors which may be illustrated by reference to the liability of occupiers of premises and land toward children, and the liability of parents and others who care for children toward their charges. The question of damage to the unborn child is noted together with the matter of responsibility of a child's parents for his torts.

24.9.1	Liability of occupiers under the Occupiers' Liability Act 1957	The Occupiers' Liability Act 1957 abolished the distinction under common law between 'licensees' and 'invitees' in relation to those who visit land: the occupier owes a 'common duty of care' to visitors. He must accept that children will be less careful than adults and must be prepared for this. Thus, to fail to take into account 'allurements' to a child (eg, the presence on land of poisonous fruits of tempting appearance) may lead to a breach of the occupier's duty: see *Simkiss v Rhondda BC* (1983).
24.9.2	Liability of occupiers under the Occupiers' Liability Act 1984	The Occupiers' Liability Act 1984 deals with the liability of occupiers of premises for injury suffered by persons other than their visitors. The test for liability toward non-visitors (who may include children who are trespassers) is based upon s 1(3). The occupier of premises owes a duty to one who is not a visitor if he is aware of a danger or has reasonable grounds to believe that it exists; if he knows or has reasonable grounds to believe that the other is in the vicinity of the danger (in either case whether the other has lawful authority for being in that vicinity or not); and the risk is one against which, in all the circumstances of the case he may reasonably be expected to offer the other some protection.
24.9.3	Liability of parents, foster parents	The actions of the reasonably careful, prudent parent in relation to his child constitute one touchstone of parental responsibility. Thus, the use of corporal punishment by a parent (see 23.9) might be tortious if administered in circumstances which suggested that he was acting unreasonably. In *Surtees v Kingston upon Thames BC* (1991), the Court of Appeal considered the duty of care of foster parents. X, aged two, was scalded when placing her foot in a hot bowl at a time when she had been left alone. The Court of Appeal held that the test of reasonable foreseeability of injury demanded an objective standard, but the test should be decided with reference to the person to whom it was to be applied. X's foster mother had been performing normal household duties and the injury sustained by X was not reasonably foreseeable. To hold the foster parents liable would involve the imposition of a standard which was impossible and to which few persons could measure up.
24.10	**The minor's capacity to sue**	The capacity of a minor to sue is, in general, virtually the same as that of an adult; the minor sues, however, by his 'next friend'. A question has arisen as to whether children who were born disabled because of injuries sustained *before* their birth by their parents can sue (by 'next friends'). Under the Congenital

Disabilities (Civil Liability) Act 1976, an action lies in the case of a child born alive and disabled. The liability is of a derivative nature: the child must show that the defendant would have been (actually or potentially) liable to the parent in relation to the disability, but it is not necessary to show that the parent did in fact sustain an injury. Thus, where a mother uses a drug during her pregnancy, and that drug has been produced negligently, so that her child was born disabled, that child may sue the drug manufacturer even though the mother was not injured personally in any way.

On the question of medical negligence and liability at common law, see *Burton v Islington Health Authority* (1992). Plaintiff was born with disabilities allegedly resulting from negligent treatment of his mother by doctors in hospitals managed by the defendant authority. (Plaintiff was born before the 1976 Act came into force.) The judge held that defendant could be liable at common law for injuries inflicted before birth. The Court of Appeal dismissed defendant's appeal. An unborn child is deemed to be born whenever its interests require and is therefore clothed with all the rights of action when born which it would have had if in existence at the date of the accident to its mother.

24.11 Liability of minor to be sued

A minor may be sued for his torts as if he were of full age: infancy is not, in itself, a defence: see *Gorely v Codd* (1967). But a minor may not be sued if the action in tort is, in effect, a method of enforcing a contract which would otherwise not bind him: see *Jennings v Rundall* (1799).

24.12 Responsibility of a minor's parents for his torts

A parent, and other persons with parental responsibility concerning the child, will not be generally liable for torts committed by the child. But this principle has no application where the parent has given specific authorisation for the child's acts; in such a case the parent will be held vicariously liable for those acts. Further, where the parent is held to have been negligent by failing to prevent the child from carrying out some act which has caused injury to another person, the general principle has no application: see *Newton v Edgerley* (1959).

Summary of Chapter 24

Children's Rights and Their Significance (2)

The criminal law seeks to protect the child through legislation such as the Licensing Act 1964, s 169, the Protection of Children (Tobacco) Act 1986, the Intoxicating Substances (Supply) Act 1985.

Protection of child from harmful goods and activities

Employment law places a general restriction on the employment of children. Local authorities may make appropriate byelaws concerning the employment of children in their areas: see Sch 3 Employment Act 1989.

Protection of the child from exploitation as an employee

The Employment Act 1989 was intended to assist in deregulation of the labour market; as a result a number of restrictions on the hours of work and on the types of employment pertaining to young persons have been removed.

Protection of the young person from exploitation as an employee

There is a conclusive presumption that a child under 10 at the date of an alleged offence is *doli incapax*, so that he cannot be guilty of an offence. The presumption that children aged 10-under 14 were *doli incapax*, but that the presumption might be rebutted by proof that the child knew that what he was doing was seriously wrong, has been challenged by a Divisional Court in *Curry v DPP* (1994). Minors above the age of 14 are held, in general, to be responsible for their actions.

The criminal responsibility of minors

Section 56 of the Criminal Justice Act 1991 obliges a parent or guardian to attend court proceedings involving a minor charged with an offence. Section 57 of the Criminal Justice Act 1991 obliges a parent or guardian to pay a fine imposed because of a minor's failure to comply with a supervision or community service order. Section 58 of the 1991 Act empowers the court to order a parent or guardian to enter into a recognisance to take proper care of an offender under 16.

Accountability of parents

In criminal proceedings a child's evidence is generally given unsworn. In civil proceedings the court may make an inquiry as to the competence of a child who is to be sworn prior to giving evidence.

Children as witnesses in criminal proceedings

Minors' contracts

Contracts for necessaries and contracts of service bind a minor if they are beneficial to him. Voidable contracts bind a minor unless he repudiates them during his minority or within a short time of attaining his majority. A contract which is neither valid nor voidable may not be enforced against a minor: see the Minors' Contracts Act 1987 which repealed the Infants Relief Act 1874 and s 5 of the Bettings and Loans (Infants) Act 1892 which invalidated contracts to repay loans advanced during minority.

Minors and the law of torts

A minor may be sued for his torts as if he were of full age; infancy is not in itself a defence. A minor's capacity to sue is the same as that of an adult. A parent is not generally liable for torts committed by the child, except where they have been authorised by the parent.

Recommended Reading List

Alston P (ed), *Children, Rights and the Law* (OUP)

Bainham, A, *Children: The Modern Law* (Family Law)

Black J, *A Practical Approach to Family Law* (Blackstone)

Bromley P and Lowe N, *Bromley's Family Law* (Butterworths)

Cretney S, *Elements of Family Law* (Sweet & Maxwell)

Dewar J, *Law and the Family* (Butterworths)

Freeman M, *The Rights and Wrongs of Children* (Pinter)

Gravells N (ed), *Family Law Statutes* (Sweet & Maxwell)

Harris P and Scanlon D, *The Children Act 1989: A Procedural Handbook* (Sweet & Maxwell)

Hoggett B and Pearl D, *The Family, Law and Society: Cases and Materials* (Butterworths)

King M and Piper C, *How the Law Thinks about Children* (Gower)

Morgan D, *The Family* (Routledge)

O'Donovan K, *Family Law Matters* (Pluto Press)

Index

A

Abduction	17.19, 23.11.7, 23.14, 23.14.4
Abuse of children	23.12
interviews concerning	23.12.2
proof of	23.12
Accommodation for children	14.3.4, 14.6
protection concerning	14.7
secure	15.6-15.8
Adoption	22.1-22.16
agencies	22.3, 22.9
applications	22.4
background	22.1
consent	22.10, 22.11
freeing for	22.12
legitimacy and	12.20
nationality and	22.14.3
orders	22.13.3, 22.14
panels	22.3.3
persons who may be adopted	22.6
placements	22.8-22.9
procedures	22.13
reform	22.16
register	22.15
relatives and step-parents	22.5
service	22.3.1
succession rights and	22.14.2
trends relating to	22.2
welfare principle	22.7
Adultery	4.3
definition	4.3.1
proof of	4.3.2
Affiliation proceedings	12.16
Ancillary relief	9.2-9.9
Ante- and post-nuptial settlements	9.7.3
Assault	
children and	5.11, 23.10
indecent	23.11.5, 23.11.6
Authorised person defined	16.2, 17.8

B

Banns	2.2.1, 2.2.2
Battery	5.11, 23.10
Biological paternity	12.7.1
Birth registration	12.12
Blood tests, paternity	12.10

C

Canon law	1.2.2, 3.3.2
Capacity to marry	2.3
Care orders	6.4-16.11
criteria for	16.6
essence of	16.9
parental responsibilities	16.9.1
Principles	16.5
proceedings	16.4
timetables	16.8
Child assessment orders	17.2-17.3
duration	17.2.5
effect	17.2.7
principles	17.2.3
purpose	17.3
refusal by child	17.2.8
Child benefit	8.14
Child minder	19.12
defined	19.12.2
registration	19.12.2
Children	
abuse of	23.12
advice and assistance for	15.2, 15.5
contact with family	14.15
contracts of	24.8
corporal punishment of	23.9
criminal law and	23.5
cruelty to	23.7
defined	11.11, 14.2
discovery, powers concerning	7.18
employment of	24.2.1-24.3
examination of	16.14.3
financial provision for	11.1-11.22
harm to	13.5.5, 24.1
in need	14.3.1
investigation of circumstances of	16.17
liberty, restriction of	15.8
name, change of	16.9.3
needs of	13.5.2
neglect of	23.8
qualifying	11.4
refuges for	17.20
relief, financial, orders	11.2-11.9
religious upbringing	16.9.3
residential care	18.1-18.11
responsibility, criminal	24.4
rights of	12.26, 23.1-24.12
risk, at	17.1
sexual offences involving	23.11
torts and	24.9-24.12
unborn	21.9
visits by and to	14.15.4
welfare of	13.1-13.16
wishes and feelings of	13.5.1
witnesses, as	24.6
Cohabitation	2.9-2.10, 10.5
contrasted with marriage	2.9
defined	2.9
social acceptance	2.10

statutory recognition	2.10
wills and	6.10
Common law spouse	2.1.6
Community homes	18.2-18.3
Consent orders	8.4, 10.1-10.9
essence of	10.2
fundamentals of	10.3
non-disclosure in	10.3.1
professional advice	10.4.5
Constructive desertion	8.5.5
Consummation, wilful refusal	2.6.1
Contact orders	13.12
Contracts and children	24.8
Co-ownership	6.14
Corporal punishment	23.9
County courts	1.8.2
Courts, jurisdiction of	1.8, 2.8
Criminal law and children	23.5-23.14

D

Day care of children	19.12.2
registration concerning	19.12.3, 19.12.4
Death, presumption of	3.10
Declaration of the Rights of the Child 1959	23.4.4
Defraud, dispositions intended to	10.7
Desertion	4.5, 8.3.4
animus deserendi	4.5.1
constructive	4.5.5
five years	4.7
two years	4.6
Development of the child	14.2
Disabled children	14.3.5
Divorce	3.1-4.14
background to	3.2
bars to	4.8
decrees	3.6, 3.7
definition	3.1
facts relating to	4.1, 4.2
foreign, recognition of	4.9
ground, sole, for	4.1
jurisdiction	3.4
legal history	3.3
mensa et thoro	3.1
petition	3.5
reform of	4.10-4.13
special procedure	3.8
vinculo matrimonii	3.1
DNA tests	12.11
Domestic violence	5.10
criminal law and	5.11
exclusion of spouse	5.12, 5.15
injunctions	5.16
molestation and	5.14.3

E

Education supervision order	16.15
Emergency protection orders	17.4-17.19
applications for	17.6-17.9.1
directions concerning	17.12
discharge of	17.15
duration of	17.14
effect of	17.1
police protection and	17.16
procedure	17.9
purpose of	17.4
refusal of child concerned	17.12.1
European Convention on Human Rights 1950	15.11.3, 23.4.3
European Court of Human Rights	15.11.3
Evidence, children and	24.6, 24.7

F

Family	
centres	14.3.8
child of the	2.3.5
defined	1.5, 1.9.3, 14.2
types of	1.6
Family assistance orders	13.16
Family credit	8.13
Family Division	1.8.3
Family law	
criticised	1.9.1
described	1.1
functions of	1.3
myth and	1.2.5
scope of	1.1.3
sources	1.2
Family life data	1.4
Family proceedings	13.8
courts	1.8.1
Father	
defined	12.7
guardian as	12.25
genetic	12.7.1
non-genetic	12.7.2
Financial provision	
children concerning	11.1-11.22
foreign divorces, following	9.20
marriage, relating to	8.1-8.8, 9.1-10.9
Formalities of marriage	2.2
Foster parents	14.11, 19.3
acting for local authority	19.2
advertising, concerning	19.8
disqualifications	19.9
private	19.3
prohibitions concerning	19.10
welfare of children and	19.5
Freeing for adoption	22.12

G

Geneva Declaration 1924	23.4.1
Guardians	20.1-20.12
appointments	20.4, 20.5
concepts relating to	20.1
disclaimer of	20.7
effect of	20.10
revocation of	20.8
termination of	20.11
Guardians *ad litem*	16.21
care proceedings	16.21
court proceedings	16.21.2
independence of	16.21.4

H

Hague Convention 1980	23.14.2
Harm to child	
significant	16.7.2
suspected	17.17
Health	14.2
Homelessness	5.17
Housing benefit	8.16
Human assisted reproduction	12.4
orders relating to	12.8

I

Ill treatment	16.2
Incest	23.11.2
Income support	8.10, 8.11
applicable amount	8.10.3
entitlement	8.10.1
liable relatives	8.11
severe hardship and	8.11.2
Independent schools	18.14
Inherent jurisdiction	5.16
Injunctions	5.16, 10.8, 10.9
Anton Piller	10.9
Mareva	10.8
Intercourse, unlawful	23.11.3
Intestacy	6.7-6.9
Intolerability and divorce	4.3, 4.3.3

J

Joint tenancy	6.1.5
Judicial review	15.11.4
Judicial separation	5.1-5.18
decree, grounds for	5.2
financial relief	5.7.2
jurisdiction of court	5.4
petition	5.5
reform	5.9

K

Kidnapping	23.13

L

Legitimacy and legitimation	12.14-12.22
attitudes towards	12.4
discrimination and	12.22
principles concerning	12.15
Local authorities	
accommodation for children	14.3.4, 14.6, 14.7, 14.10, 18.7
assistance in kind or cash	14.4
children looked after by	14.8
contact with other authorities	15.4
co-operation among	15.12
day care and	14.5
definition	14.2
foster parents and	14.11
provision of services	14.3
recoupments	15.14
representations to	15.10
services provided by	14.1-15.15.2
wardship and	21.14
Lump sums	9.6, 10.4.6, 11.7.2

M

Maintenance	
common law duty of	8.1
failure to provide	8.3.2
Maintenance orders	8.3, 8.7
applications for	8.3.1
pending suit	9.4
variation of	8.7.2
Manslaughter	23.6
Marriage	2.1-2.11
attitudes to	2.10, 2.11
capacity	2.3
contract, as	2.1.4
ceremonies	2.2.3
defined	2.1.1
engagement	2.1.5
financial provision relating to	8.1-8.8, 9.1-10.9
licences	2.2.2
Matrimonial home	7.1-7.16
acquisition of interests in	7.2
charges over	7.16
problems	7.1
Mediation, family	4.12, 4.13
Mental disorder	2.6.3
Monogamous union in marriage	2.3.4
Mother	
genetic relationship to children	12.6
legal status	12.6

N

Neglect of children	23.8
No-delay principle	13.3
Non-intervention criteria	13.4
Nullity	2.6, 2.7
bars to relief	2.7

O

Occupation rights to the home	7.6-7.8
bankruptcy and	7.15
registration of	7.12, 7.13
Ombudsman	15.11.2
One year bar to divorce	3.5.3
Orders	
applications for	11.3
breakdown of marriage guidelines	9.9-9.18
care and supervision	16.2-16.21
child assessment	17.2
education and supervision	16.15
financial relief	11.2, 11.7
matters relevant to	11.6
section 8, Ch A, under	13.7
Ouster orders	5.13

P

Paramountcy principle	13.2.2
Parent	
absent	11.11
accountability of	24.5
Parentage	11.15, 12.1-12.14
Blood tests	12.10
concept of	12.2
DNA tests	12.10
information concerning	12.13
proof of	12.9
Parental responsibility	12.23-12.27
agreement for	12.24
care order	16.9.1
defined	12.23
possessors of	12.24
rights and duties	12.23-12.27
torts, child's	24.1
Parental rights	12.26
Periodical payments	8.5, 9.5, 10.6.7, 11.7.1
Pregnancy *per alium*	2.6.4
Prohibited degrees	2.3.5, 22.14.4
Prohibited steps order	13.13
Property	
adjustment orders	9.7, 11.7.3
defined	6.1.1
family	7.1-7.16
interests in	6.3
rights	6.1, 6.4
Proprietary estoppel	7.3
Protection of children at risk	17.1-17.21

Q

Qualifying child, defined	11.4
Queen's Proctor	3.7

R

Rape	23.11.1
Reconciliation	3.11, 8.3.5
Registered children's homes	18.8
Residential orders	13.15
Rights, children's	
concepts of	23.2, 23.3
conventions and declarations	23.4.1-23.4.5

S

Sale of property orders	9.8
Section 8 orders	13.7-13.16
applications for	13.9
contact order	13.12
essence of	13.7
family proceedings and	13.8
leave to apply for	13.9
limitations upon issue of	13.10
prohibited steps order	13.3
residence order	13.15
specific issue order	13.14
timetables concerning	13.11
Separation agreements	8.8
Sexual offences	23.11
Specific issue orders	13.14
State benefits	8.9-8.16
child benefit	8.14
family credit	8.13
housing benefit	8.16
income support	8.10
one-parent benefit	8.15
rationale of	8.9
social fund	8.12
Succession rules	6.7-6.10
Supervision orders	16.11-16.21
discharge	16.19
duration	16.13
duties relating to	16.12
education	16.15, 16.16
essence of	16.11, 16.14
interim	16.18
supervisor	16.14
Surrogacy	12.5

Index

T
Tenancy in common 6.1.6
Tipstaff 21.8
Torts and children 24.9-24.12
Transsexuals 2.3.3
Trusts 6.1.3, 6.3.2, 6.3.5, 7.5

U
United Nations Convention on Rights of the Child 1989 23.4.5
Universal Declaration of Human Rights 1948 23.4.2

V
Variation of orders 10.4, 10.4.6, 11.7
Venereal diseases, void and voidable marriages 2.6.4
Visitors 14.15.3
Void and voidable marriages 2.4, 2.7
  features of 2.6
  legitimacy and legitimation 12.17, 12.18
Voluntary homes 18.4-18.6

W
Wardship 21.1-21.14
  applications 21.9, 21.10
  background 21.2
  court's discretion 21.8
  essential features of 21.1
  jurisdiction 21.3-21.5, 21.13
  leave of court 21.14.2
  restrictions 21.9.3
  unborn children and 21.9
  welfare of child 21.11
Welfare
  benefits 8.9-8.16
  checklist 13.5
  children 13.1-13.6
  defined 13.2.1
  principle 11.13, 13.2, 22.7
  public interest and 21.11
Wills
  cohabitants and 6.10
  divorce and 3.9
Wounding 5.11, 23.10